JUST BEFORE DAWN

JUST BEFORE DAWN

*From the Shadows of Tradition
to New Reflections in Trauma Assessment
and Treatment of Sexual Victims*

Jan Hindman

Published by:

 AlexAndria Associates
911 S.W. 3rd Street
Ontario, Oregon 97914
(503) 889-8938

Printed in the United States of America
Northwest Printing
Boise, Idaho
ISBN # 0-9611034-4-2
Library of Congress # 89-086063

Dedication

To my mom who taught me to cheer for the underdog,
and to my dad who taught me about deer.

   ... And to Suzie

who once told me,

God didn't like secret touching.

How do you know?, I asked.

It's in the DEMANDMENTS,

she said.

What does it say?

I asked.

She replied with vigor,

THOU SHALT NOT UNCOVET THY NEIGHBOR'S ASS!

All case presentations in this publication represent actual suffering of specific human beings and their families. Only identifying characteristics have been altered to protect the privacy of patients.

CONTENTS

ACKNOWLEDGEMENTS

A special thanks to the Malheur County Child Abuse Team Members for their tenacity not only in protecting children, but also in their search for ways to prevent *system* damage to children. None of this work would be possible without these *soldiers* in the trauma battle: Honorable F.J. Yraguen, Verne Flock, Irv Smith, Sherie Taggart, Toni Jones, Paula Becks, Betty Marquina, John Burke, Caroline Nysingh, Alan Preston, Jacques DeKalb, Linda Manchee, Bill Cummings, Terry Thompson, Ed Pierson, Ray Hartley, Dr. Maggie Miller, Clay Hooker, Clint Bryant, Glen Morinaga, Don Howes, Betty Kessel, Larry Murray, Randy McLay, Dennis Frances, Pat Sullivan, Sue Faw, Barbara Edwards, Sandy Shelton, Pam Seiders, Jim Mosier, Kristen Munson, Greg Munson, Jose Delgado, Carol Husfloen, and many others from Children's Services Division, District Attorney's Office, Malheur County Mental Health Center, Law Enforcement, Malheur County Juvenile Department, Oregon State Corrections Division, and Restitution Treatment and Training Program.

And to Lucy Hutchens, *Grand Poo Bah* (Director), for her undying dedication to children.

And to Jim Peters for his diligence and patience in teaching me about the law.

Most importantly, a special thanks to hundreds of victims who courageously shared their pain and made an important contribution to future victims.

And, yes, acknowledgement must be made to hundreds of sexual offenders who also provided important information, helping us to understand the trauma suffered by victims of sexual abuse.

Finally, appreciation to all those at AlexAndria Associates — including the cats, Clyde and Claude — who strained and suffered to the limit so this publication could come to fruition.

INTRODUCTION

In the past two decades, the problem of child sexual abuse in the United States has rocked an ill-prepared nation. Questions abound! How can a nation so rich in wealth and opportunity be so plagued with the demoralizing problem of *Sexual Exploitation of Our Children?* Can this same nation, with so many gifts, be the same country where child prostitution and pornography are multi-billion dollar businesses, where one-quarter of its children are sexually abused, and where the family is determined *a most dangerous* place for its most precious resource — children? This *schizophrenic* stance, with so much opportunity and so much shame, perplexes lawmakers, baffles prosecutors, and terrorizes communities. How can it be?

As we have been forced to accept the reality of sexual abuse, most of our national endeavors have been misdirected toward other issues rather than the precious child who was robbed of childhood. Treatment of the sexual offender, understanding arousal patterns, deviancy, etiology, and *perpetrator profiles* have been the favored topics for professionals in the field of sexual abuse. Numerous national seminars, workshops, and learning experiences are offered regarding the topic of sexual abuse, but rarely does specific research emerge on assessing the damage done to the victims. Instead, a complicated matrix pertaining to offender issues dominates the forefront of education in the field.

Whenever damage to victims has been contemplated, the "Big Four" — *CONSENT, VIOLENCE, PENETRATION, AND FREQUENCY* — form the cornerstone of trauma assessment in the professional community. These guidelines were *not* the result of comprehensive work relating to the trauma suffered by victims. These four issues are legal factors set by legislators pertaining to the dangerous-

1

ness of the sexual offender. Little, if any, of the Big Four matrix system was designed to reflect an empathic response to how sexual victims suffer.

Just Before Dawn is a comprehensive look at how victims have been traumatized by sexual abuse. This publication teaches an innovative method of evaluating trauma and planning for rehabilitation. This method is based on *damage*, not on a matrix designed for the sexual offender. ***Just Before Dawn*** carefully examines the nature of trauma for the purpose of solving the problem, not concentrating on why the problem exists. Certainly, understanding why sexual offenders offend or understanding the dangerousness of criminals is important, but those guidelines should not determine how we heal the wounds of sexual abuse. When professionals continue to follow a legal system, which focuses on the offender, it would seem that sexual offenders have the final exploitation of their victims through our improper responses.

Take A Sad Song

The spectrum of child sexual abuse in this country should cause all of us, regardless of ethnicity, religion, or zip code, to be concerned. Sexual abuse of children is not confined to large cities where children are pulled into alleys, screaming and yelling. On the contrary, national statistics vary, conflict, and correlate. Regardless of numerical differences and research designs, it can be generally suggested

that sexual abuse occurs at a rate of approximately one out of five females and perhaps one out of ten males. Alarmingly, however, some experts contend that perhaps males are abused even more often than females, which would suggest the statistical perspective regarding males is even worse. Whether children reside in Harlem or rural America, one-quarter of our children will be sexually exploited before their 18th birthday.

With a statistical representation of this magnitude bringing us to our knees, let us also raise questions about the kind of damage resulting from this tremendous problem. Since the numbers are staggering, so must be the devastation. What price do we pay? Do we truly understand the price tag for the exploitation of thousands of innocent children?

With further questions, we can ask, *Can we truly believe with the magnitude of this problem that all children are traumatized in the same manner?* Can we believe that each child within this pool of hundreds of thousands will be traumatized in nice, tidy packages, more similar than different? Is our damage assessment accurate, well planned, and comprehensive enough to meet the tremendous need? It is easily and readily accepted that sex offenders come in different sizes, shapes, and packages. For some offenders, the arousal toward children is the focus of difficulty. Viewing the prepubescent child, with no pubic hair or muscle tone, is a primary erotic preference. Other offenders seem to be attracted to children because of psychological problems, such as power, control, and anger mismanagement. Some offenders seem to be offending because they have no power in their lives, while other offenders seem to have an insatiable need for power. Some offenders seem to be *addicted,* with their lives out of control in a quest for securing children as sexual partners. Other offenders demonstrate long periods of control and offend children sporadically. We can agree, then, that, sex offenders are not offending children for the same reasons. Perhaps we should also agree that, or at least consider whether, children are not traumatized by sexual abuse in the same manner.

. . . And Make It Better

So can something be done about this perplexing problem not only of childhood sexual abuse, but of designing a plan to understand trauma suffered by sexual victims? Can we make this *sad song* better? And, if so, why should we? There are several motivations for taking a more profound, productive look at the trauma suffered by victims. The first of these motivations involves the vicious cycle of sexual abuse. Not only is the problem itself staggering, but the cycle of abuse drastically compounds the nature of the problem.

Cycle Races

Common theories suggest children who are sexually abused often become abusers themselves in adulthood, thus continuing the cycle of abuse. According to some statistics, 30 percent to 80 percent of offenders were sexually abused in childhood (Longo/Groth). Recent research suggests that perhaps the cycle of *abused to abuser* is not as prevalent as once believed (Hindman). As the debate rages concerning the offender cycle, it can nonetheless be recognized that one residual effect of child sexual abuse is that some abused children become abusers in adulthood.

A perhaps more compelling aspect of the cyclical nature of sexual abuse, however, is that sexual victims who do not become offenders often set lifelong patterns of *abusability* . It is not uncommon for sexual victims to continue self-abusive cycles into adulthood. Substance abuse, domestic violence, criminal behaviors, and psychiatric problems are all examples of the abusive cycle of *victim-to-victimization.*

And so what? Does it really matter if sexual victims continue to be self-abusive in adulthood? Does it matter to those members of society who are not sexual victims that the cycle of sexual abuse continues from *abused to abuser* or from *abused to abusable?* Except for vague humanitarian reasons, is there a need to be concerned about those sexual victims who continue suffering through a cycle of victimization, setting lifelong patterns of repetitive trauma?

The Concept of Victimization

It is the concept of victimization that provides the motivation, the foundation, or the vehicle of concern. It is through this rather complicated concept of victimization that we should learn that sexual abuse is not an isolated problem, not a problem separate from those who may not be directly impacted. The work of sexual offenders envelopes all of us in trauma.

The concept of victimization begins with the special, unique child who was robbed of the right to grow up sexually safe and secure. When a child becomes a victim of this *robbery of childhood*, that unique individual human being has certainly been traumatized. The child's sexual development is impacted and the child may be affected for a lifetime. The first level, and perhaps the most important level, of victimization, then, involves an innocent child who is robbed of something precious.

The second level of victimization, however, concerns the entire family connected to the sexual victim. Society is a strange sexual world, indeed, being extremely promiscuous and sexually active on one hand, while advocating very specific and traditional views about such issues as sexual consent and virginity, on the other hand. It is often the child's family that experiences profound effects of shame, degradation, and financial burden due to the sexual abuse of a family member. It is rare that a child is sexually abused without trauma affecting the entire family.

The crime of sexual abuse proceeds to a third level of victimization into the community where the victim resides. Because of sexual abuse, agencies within communities are overloaded, neighborhoods are no longer safe, and money originally set aside for math books may instead be appropriated for sexual abuse prevention programs. Children who are sexually abused often act out in school, disrupt classrooms, and may even sexually involve children in the school lavatory. The trauma experienced by a child in the community is not left to the child and the family to endure. Even though the problem itself may be indirect for the community, residual effects of sexual abuse affect those who reside in the same community as a victim. These issues of safety, financial demands, overburdening of agencies, and a general sense of fear are traditional ways in which an entire community is traumatized by the work of sexual offenders.

Society, in general, comprises the fourth and final level of victimization. Commonly, sexual victims remain encased in conspiracy and secrecy throughout childhood, quietly suffering various forms of trauma. Due to society's rejection of, or lack of empathy toward victims, these traumas are usually tucked away and cultivated during childhood. In adulthood, it is not uncommon for victims to require services, resources, and financial contributions as a result of the *deadly silence* since childhood.

Sexual victims need support from society in adulthood through such services as drug and alcohol centers, psychiatric units, and mental health clinics. The unconvinced, ill-prepared and ignorant society pays the debt as childhood victims require, in adulthood, services to heal not only the wounds of sexual abuse, but also the psychological damage of secrecy. In adulthood, the trauma that has been simmering for years explodes, and society becomes responsible for services to the victim, and again, responsible for the work of sexual offenders.

The four-tiered concept of victimization should cause all to take a more respectable look at the trauma suffered by victims. If sexual abuse does not touch our lives personally, we must understand that the trauma suffered by victims eventually affects us all. Society needs to question whether it is prepared to continue with sex offenders taking a toll not only on children and families, but on our community and society as well.

From the Shadows of Tradition

From the recognition that we are all traumatized directly or indirectly by sexual abuse, the natural response is to ask for change, to *Take A Sad Song and Make it Better.* As we become outraged at the damage from crimes committed by sexual offenders, a search for solutions emerges. What is the first step in ending the power offenders seem to have over our society through their selfish deeds?

The first step in eradicating the trauma suffered by the child, the family, the community, and society is to understand the trauma. No problem can be solved unless it is understood. Until now, trauma suffered by victims has been

conceived in traditional and archaic ways based upon a system designed for the offender. Treatment plans designed according to a system for offenders cannot be successful and will result in damage to all four levels of *VICTIMS.*

The trauma of sexual abuse does not begin or end with a penis inserted in a vagina and a following disclosure. The crime of sexual abuse is not like the theft of a bicycle: A bicycle can be replaced; a childhood cannot. Until we better understand the trauma, we will not be able to provide a prescription for healing. And until we understand how to heal victims, we will all continue to be damaged by the work of sexual offenders. The first step, then, is to more adequately understand trauma by rejecting archaic and traditional ideas. We must re-examine, evaluate, and understand trauma so that appropriate rehabilitation can occur.

An Ounce of Prevention

With better-planned rehabilitation methodologies, victims will hopefully heal and all four levels of victimization will be impacted successfully. But what about prevention of the problem? Is there an answer or a solution to preventing the problem of sexual abuse by better understanding how children are damaged?

Unfortunately, traditional prevention efforts are also commonly built around archaic and traditional ideas. Children are told, *Watch out for strangers,* and *Don't let anyone touch you in your nasty parts.* Too often, sexual abuse prevention programs are geared toward a specific kind of sexual encounter, warning children of dangers that have been learned from sexual offenders. And it is often assumed that children's perceptions of sexual abuse are similar to those of adults. Traditional prevention programs are designed without appreciation of children's perceptions and developmental differences from adults. With a better understanding of how children are traumatized, prevention efforts will be more appropriately molded and based on children's perceptions, not the perceptions of adults.

Children perceive sexual contact according to their stage in sexual development, not according to adult perceptions. Through better understanding of how children are damaged, a better understanding can be cultivated in preventing child sexual abuse. The perceptions of children will be the cornerstone of teaching children how to correctly respond to inappropriate behaviors on the part of adults. Until we readjust our prevention programs according to children's perceptions (as outlined in the Trauma Assessment), our prevention programs will satisfy adults, but will be ineffective in preventing sexual abuse.

Another example of prevention issues relating to trauma awareness involves those who commit sexual crimes. The ultimate in prevention of sexual abuse would prevent recidivism on the part of perpetrators. Better understanding of the unique nature of trauma may provide an important treatment modality for preventing recidivism. In order to understand this concept,

questions surface regarding those issues that divide sex offenders from the rest of society? How can some individuals feel arousal to children while others feel nauseated? What separates those who offend from those who are offended by such actions?

If given the exercise of closing our eyes and imagining ourselves sexually involved with children, most individuals experience feelings of repulsion and degradation. What is this taboo or boundary that seems so easily broken by sex offenders and seems so repulsive to those who do not offend children?

At the core of the difference between sexual offenders and those who do not offend children is an understanding of the special nature of children, of the damage that may be caused to children through sexual abuse. Non-offenders have some sense of the developmental incapacities of children. When presented with ideations of sexual involvement with children, common responses from non-offending adults include *That's my baby, That's just a child*, or *That's a horrible thing to do to a child*. Even though children may be physically capable of providing satisfaction to adults, the special nature of children and the trauma that would befall the child prevent non-offending adults from fulfilling their own needs at the expense of children.

Sexual offenders, for a variety of reasons, have developed the ability to break through taboos that cause most adults to be nauseous at the thought of engaging in cunnilingus or fellatio with a child. Perhaps this occurs because the sexual offender cannot think, or chooses not to think, about the trauma involved in sexual contact with children. Would it seem appropriate, then, to involve sex offenders in a process of more intensely understanding the damage caused through sexual abuse? If the damage to children is the major reason why most adults do not offend children, then an effective treatment component for sexual offenders would include teaching about the pending damage to the child. If the Trauma Assessment teaches about the damage, would not understanding specific issues relating to the Trauma Assessment give sex offenders themselves the best opportunity for rehabilitation and the best opportunity to avoid recidivism? Would not the Trauma Assessment give offenders the best chance at thinking like the rest of us who treasure children?

To New Reflections

Preventing sexual abuse, although important, does not alleviate pain for current victims who desperately need empathy and more appropriate understanding of their trauma. It would seem that a closer look is required. Quite clearly, if a burglar robs a poor man or a millionaire, the trauma experienced by each theft victim will not be the same. Although the burglar may be required to serve the same time in jail for either crime, the millionaire who was robbed of his television will obviously not suffer the same as the man who has spent five years depositing dollar bills in his Christmas Club in order to buy his teenage daughter her first Magnavox. The same can be true for sexual victims. Victims are not traumatized in the same manner or under the same circumstances. The legal system may need to be specific, absolute, and unbending. But if we wish to impact this problem properly, we must recognize that not all victims are damaged the same and, therefore, our responses should not assume the same consistency.

The differences in how children suffer are the key to *new reflections* in responding to the devastating problem of child sexual abuse. Yes, innovations in understanding the trauma have a major impact on stopping the cycle of sexual abuse. Yes, our prevention efforts may be improved through a better understanding. And, yes, our treatment responses to sexual offenders will also improve as we teach about the suffering. But the most important reason for *new reflections* is alleviating the pain of our precious children.

This publication is about big trauma, little trauma, insignificant trauma, and horrifying trauma. It is a book designed to help us better understand so that we can make better responses to victims. Just as we must know where the cancer lies before surgery, we must be able to understand the nature of trauma of sexual abuse before it can be eradicated and before we can be helpful to victims. This book is about *new reflections* leading us to new approaches. This book is about hope.

WHO SAYS?

Where can we look for answers about trauma? Who knows how victims suffer? Can we ask victims, offenders, our society, our system, victims' caretakers, or professionals to teach us about the unique nature of sexual victimization?

Why Not?

Why shouldn't we have sex with kids? Usually, sexual abuse occurs between a child and someone the child trusts, someone known to the child, and often someone who cares for the child. Aren't these good people to entrust with our children's sexual futures? Rarely do children bleed or show physical signs of trauma as a result of sexual involvement with adults. Children have the physiological capabilities of having orgasms from the time they are born. If we teach children all other aspects of becoming an adult, why not include sexuality in our teaching?

Because, we say, that's why! As a society, in spite of our sexual promiscuity, an importance is placed on the issue of sexual consent. This country's sociological perspective dictates that children cannot consent to sexual involvement because they are, in fact, *children*. In recognizing the developmental differences between children and adults, children's inability to consent is clear. *It ain't equal* makes consent between a child and an adult impossible.

Even though children can be coerced into cooperation, even though children voluntarily participate, may initiate the sexual contact, or may enjoy the sexual contact, consent is not possible due to the inequalities between children and adults. As Dr. Gene Abel eloquently stated, *Saying yes means nothing if NO is not one of your choices.* By virtue of being a child, *NO* is not an option, making any form of *YES* meaningless.

It is clear that this society, although states vary, has decided it is not acceptable for adults to engage in sexual encounters with children due to issues of consent. The definition of *children* varies from state to state, suggesting that children are able to consent according to county boundaries or the water they drink. Nonetheless, society generally agrees in a prohibition of sexual relationships with children. Reasons for these decisions may be based on Biblical foundations or genetic risks related to procreation through incestuous contact. There may be a variety of reasons for the foundation of these laws, but the overriding issue is one of consent, which is ultimately related to the inequality of children as compared to adults.

parents. The same is true for sexual involvement between children and adults.

Although states vary on the definition of children and, therefore, the *age of consent*, common thought indicates that since children are incapable and not equal, they cannot make sexual decisions. But the question arises, *Have we really examined this process carefully?* The improprieties in a sexual involvement between a child and an adult are clear to most adults, but is the foundation for these reasons clear?

The underlying reason for the decision to attach a *criminal label* to the sexual interactions between children and adults lies in the belief that participation without consent is harmful. In this society, sex without consent is wrong. It's a crime! Without emotional and psychological consent, sexual behavior between a child and an adult is a crime on the part of the person who is capable of consenting — the adult. But, have good decisions been made about how this happens and what kind of trauma occurs within these fine lines of technicality?

It Ain't Equal

It is obvious that children in a family could be taught to steal. Children from a family of thieves could become very adept at shoplifting for their parents. If parents were particularly coercive in their shoplifting training programs, it would be difficult to blame their children for acts of thievery. The act of the child would be a reflection of the coercion from the child's

How Equal is Equal

Can it be assumed that all victims of sexual abuse are traumatized in the same manner simply because consent is absent? The child who watches her father rape the cat and then watches the cat die from injuries may or may not be traumatized in the same way as the child who ejaculates for the first time engaging in mutually consenting masturbation with his P.E. teacher. If the child who observes her cat dying is *just fondled*, then perhaps she would be more traumatized because consent was not given regarding her fondling as compared to the child who consented to masturbate himself to orgasm in the Physical Education locker room. Can comparisons be accurately made between these two sexually abusive scenarios based only upon *how much* consent occurred? Is inequality, unequal, in equal proportion?

Obviously, the answer is no! Consent does not vary. By virtue of the fact that a child is a child, consent did not occur in either situations. But, where do the variations occur in the trauma to sexual victims? What are the degrees of trauma and why are the degrees important? Will the *just fondled* child who observed her cat dying be traumatized in the same way as the child who actively participates in the sexually abusive activities? Our system concerning the age of consent would answer, *yes*. Those who work with victims suffering from childhood sexual abuse understand the answer to be *no*. Clearly, degrees of trauma are important in order to understand the rehabilitation necessary for victims. Without knowing how children are traumatized, how can appropriate treatment plans be developed or reach fruition? Where are the answers for understanding degrees of trauma in order to find the most effective ways toward rehabilitation?

So Where Do We Look?

If the primary reason for posing the question is related to caring for sexual victims, perhaps victims themselves can provide answers to the dilemma. Should not victims be given ultimate power over their rehabilitation by asking them to diagnose their own pain? Aren't victims reliable sources of information regarding their trauma or trauma from sexual abuse in general?

Young Victim Voices

Commonly, younger children often enter into the *system* with therapists, social workers, attorneys, doctors, law enforcement officers, etc., being asked to make decisions about trauma. A four-year-old who has been anally raped by her brother may, if given the chance to decide, *consent to* wanting her brother returned to the home as soon as possible.

At day care, Frances' rectum is bleeding. Without hesitation, Frances answers questions, which result in a disclosure of her sexual abuse by her 16-year old brother. Although Frances readily accepts medical treatment, she nonetheless expresses regret about the absence of her brother from the household. Frances becomes extremely upset at being forbidden to see her brother, and eventually therapeutic decisions are made to allow the perpetrator to visit and return to the home where Frances resides. The foundation for the therapist's action is Frances' attitude toward her brother and her requests for contact with him.

At the core of why it was unacceptable for Frances' brother to engage her in sexual activities was the inequality between a 16-year-old and a four-year-old, or Frances' inability to consent. Even though later, as an adolescent, Frances would angrily describe her efforts to *hold very still* and being forced to please her brother, was she unable to make those decisions as a child because of her developmental delays? Her older brother had no problem coercing Frances into believing that she would be acceptable to him if she cooperated and that she would avoid punishment from him in his role as the caretaker if she cooperated. Even though it could be stated that Frances *consented*, as a four-year-old, clearly she was unable to consent.

Why then, did the therapist allow Frances to consent to important therapeutic decisions regarding her trauma? Was Frances a reliable source of information regarding the damage that had been caused to her? Why did the therapist allow a child, who was incapable of making sexual decisions, make profoundly important decisions regarding her trauma and her treatment? The first tragedy is Frances' abuse. The second tragedy is that therapeutic decisions were made according to Frances' requests without any appreciation for her inability to consent, not only to sexual abuse, but to her therapeutic treatment recommendations.

And what of the epilogue? In adulthood, Frances suffers chronic elimination problems and permanent phobic reactions to any sexual activity. The family has quickly forgotten, since immediate family reunification occurred. But Frances remembers, each day as she struggles through the pain of bowel movements. There is no one to hear her screams since the problem was quickly fixed, decades ago.

Interestingly, since children are children, they are rarely allowed to make decisions on their own in other areas. Children are not asked if they would like to wear wires on their teeth and be teased for at least two years in the fifth grade. Because children are children, adults recognize they are often incapable of making decisions about their future. Adults are required to make decisions for children that are important for their future. Crooked teeth in the fifth and sixth grade do not mean the same as crooked teeth in the 25th year of life when the adult is applying for a job. These decisions are made for children because they are children. Should not the same be true for sexual abuse?

Adolescent Victim Voices

And what about older children who may be more cognizant of sexual consenting decisions, but also may be just as inadequate in providing accurate information regarding what they have suffered?

As Tina indicates, *Jan, my dad is really a nice guy. See, he got hurt in the war and he has had this problem for a long time. My mom drinks and doesn't take care of herself. If you'll let my dad come home, I will wear my long coat around the house, even in the summertime. I think if he just doesn't see my body, if he can't look at my breasts,he won't think about it and he'll be okay. I don't mind wearing my coat if it keeps the family together.*

Is Tina an accurate source of information regarding her trauma? Not only does Tina want her father to come home, but Tina is willing to accept responsibility for keeping her father safe. Tina cannot consent to sexual involvement because she is 13. Should Tina be allowed to consent and direct her own treatment program?

Listen to the Footsteps

If inequality makes children unable to predict trauma, what about adults who were victimized as children? Does adulthood bring reliability to understanding trauma? When children who have been sexually abused become adults, can they provide accurate information regarding the trauma they suffered as children? Generally, this is not true. Typically, victims have difficulty understanding their pain and articulating accurate information regarding their suffering. This is not because adult victims are dishonest or manipulative. It is because they have been forced to distort reality, to develop cognitive distortions, to rearrange what happened to them in childhood in order to survive. In order for victims to cope with the sexual abuse they suffered, they were forced to recreate and rearrange reality. This *rearrangement* allows the victim to survive. Unfortunately , this rearrangement of reality is often the victim's tool for blurring and smearing reality in the future.

FOOTSTEPS or (FOOTPRINTS) created as victims walk away from the sexually abusive scene are often the coping skills or survival mechanisms of the future. Those professionals working with adults recognize the commonality of victim's statements, such as:

Well, it wasn't real sex so I am okay. (Patient has three marriages, inpatient involvement in drug and alcohol centers, and major mental health difficulties.)

I am fine. I have forgiven him. It's all right, after all, he's my father. (Patient provides information on intake to Psychiatric Unit following suicide attempt.)

The abuse by my sister didn't really affect me. If I just stay away from women, I'm fine (42-year-old male victim).

I was abused by my mother and I have survived. If she abuses my kids, too, they will survive as well.

I want my husband prosecuted. There is no doubt he abused my little girls because he split them wide open. They were hospitalized for several days. The court says they are too little to testify, but he isn't allowed to come back and live with us until he is forced into treatment. He won't go to treatment without being prosecuted. I was abused by 15 offenders when I was a child. Most of them were my mother's husbands. I only want to have one husband and I want my marriage back. God sanctioned our marriage and everything will be all right if we get our family back together.

Would these victims have survived their abuse had they recognized the reality of their damage? These statements are compelling. The unspoken thought screams to these adults. *But, don't you see?* Clearly, in order to survive, the footsteps of these victims recreated reality. Throughout that rearrangement, inadequate perceptions regarding trauma emerged for the safety of the abused child. Sadly, the adult still hears the footsteps in the future.

Generally, sexual victims are an unreliable source of information about how they were traumatized when they were children. When victims are adults and they have proceeded through years cultivating their distorted cognitions and rearranging reality, they cannot be reliable sources of information. Although sexual victims need a sense of empowerment, personal pride, and control, they nonetheless need professional assistance in evaluating their trauma. The *child within* the adult victim is often using the same footprints or coping skills needed in childhood to survive. Those coping skills are developed upon a foundation of denial, escape, and misperception. To use the victim's perceptions for evaluating trauma may prevent rehabilitation opportunities and may contribute to further victimization.

Perpetrators, Please!

Is the offender, the person who commits the crime, an accurate resource for evaluating trauma? Are those individuals who abuse children reliable sources of information on the trauma experienced by their victims? Can offenders predict or determine how badly children suffer from the offender's behavior? Common voices from offenders portraying knowledge of trauma are heard.

She loved it. I taught her to have orgasms by nine.

This didn't hurt him at all. He was always coming into my room and trying to be close to me.

This was just her sex education. She will appreciate the information at a later time.

I was kind and gentle to her and very affectionate during our times. I wasn't like the other jerks she had for step-fathers who had all abused her.

I never tied her up or held her down. She hardly ever cried.

I always bought her treats afterwards, especially the treats that I never got for any of the other kids. She wasn't about to turn down pizza when we were finished.

I tested my male students at the beginning of the year in regards to self-esteem. I only molested the boys who already had many problems in their home, especially those kids who did not have a father figure. I took them into my confidence and even though I did sexual things to them, I made them feel cared about by a male figure.

I gave these kids so many other things. I taught them to feel confident in themselves through our wrestling program. All of their parents testified as character witnesses in my sentencing. I am sure the children haven't been traumatized because everything was so cooperative.

I didn't hurt my sister at all. She was going to learn how to masturbate anyway. My brother and I just taught her the tricks.

I wanted to show my grandson what

the world was about. Women are cruel to men and my teaching was an extension of my caring for him in the struggles he faces.

The denial systems of sex offenders are an important component in sex offender treatment. Sex offenders have different stages of denial, but generally in all phases of denial, offenders blame other people, minimize their acts, or rationalize to avoid examining the reality of the crime committed. Not only would recognizing the reality of the crime be uncomfortable, but if the reality of the crime would have been realized during the sexually abusive activities, perhaps the sexual activities would have been impossible.

Most individuals who do not offend children find interruptions or distractions during sexual activities uncomfortable. A knock on the door, a television blaring, or children playing in a hallway may result in inhibiting factors for adults, making sexual capacity limited. A couple who decide to *get frisky* on Sunday morning while the children are playing outside usually is brought to the sobriety of a cold shower with one tiny turn of the screen door handle by their four-year-old. Sexual arousal which only moments previous was great fun may take hours to rekindle due to this distraction.

This is true for individuals who don't offend children, however. For sexual offenders, a different issue exists. Offenders commonly maintain erections, experience sexual pleasure, and often ejaculate while children might be screaming, crying, trying to get away, or bleeding. Certainly, a great deal of *readjustment* in the offender's mind must occur in order to continue sexual pleasure with these distractions. While most adults suffer from Sunday morning bewilderment at distraction, the offender uses readjustment, discounting, minimizing, or disbelieving. They have tremendous capability to crash through taboos in order to maintain arousal. The sex offender must practice thinking in ways that eliminate feeling the trauma experienced by their victims in order to be sexually active.

While most of us are distracted, the sexual offender maintains pleasure. How reliable then are these individuals in assessing the damage to their victims? If the trauma their victims suffer must be discounted in order to maintain pleasure, then it would certainly seem impossible for those same individuals to provide any important information regarding the trauma suffered by victims.

A Class In Social Studies

The question can be raised about our society's empathy toward trauma suffered by sexual victims. Can society determine how children have been traumatized? Does the sexual victim live in a world that clearly understands trauma, recognizes the damage that has been caused, and treats sexual victims with empathy and understanding?

Jessica McClure is the two-year-old child trapped inside a well for days. Her trauma is clear. The entire nation stands by, vigilant, as she survives this ordeal. Entire communities rallied around Jessica in her strength and courage. She stole this nation's heart. Although Jessica is not yet aware of the realities of her situation, in her future she will learn of society's attitude toward her. Our society clearly supported her, and although the experience was certainly traumatic, Jessica McClure was this nation's hero.

Does the same society rally around a child who courageously endures anal intercourse at the day care center from age two to four? Will our society applaud another little Jessica, or Janie, or Jennifer who states, *He stuck his peep in my pooper.* Will we cheer for the child who is forced to take a stool softener for the rest of his life due to the damage caused through anal intercourse by the Boy Scout Leader? Each morning as he reaches in the medicine chest for a laxative, will he be secure that he can discuss his courage and his *survivorship* at the same cocktail party he may attend with Jessica McClure? Will he or another little Jessica be greeted in our society with the same hero status? Or will the world say to the sexual victims, *Hush, hush, forget about it. Don't embarrass me, don't talk?*

Can we turn to the same society then and get an accurate description of how children are traumatized? If we are so willing to give hero status to one two-year-old, why are we not willing to give the same status to another?

Although our society clearly sets about the task of setting up laws to protect children from abuse, the protection seems to stop at the doors of the legislatures. Our society does not seem to welcome the rehabilitation of a victim but certainly welcomes other tragedies suffered by children in a different manner. Quite cruelly, our society rejects sexual victims. It is as though our society wishes to make laws indicating the unacceptability of sexual contact between children and adults, but does not take the next step to be empathic or understanding to the plight of sexual victims. The question can be asked, therefore, is society an accurate source of information regarding the trauma suffered by victims?

The System As Perpetrator

If our neighbors, PTA group, or church members are unable to be empathic toward sexual victims, how does our *system* fare in understanding trauma? Does the system designed to hear the cries of help from sexual victims respond appropriately? Our system, which is primarily composed of the prosecution, law enforcement, child protection, mental health, and juvenile court, is intended to protect children. These disciplines should be the cornerstone in the foundation of protection, and of empathy toward trauma. Does our system defend or offend victims of sexual abuse?

Sadly, the system designed to protect children often becomes the perpetrator of even more trauma. It would seem from the words of

participants in the *system* that the trauma to victims is misunderstood, misperceived, and founded on archaic views.

A Wisconsin judge, in sentencing a 24-year-old man to three years of probation on a first degree sexual assault conviction, said of a five-year-old victim, *I am satisfied that we have an unusually sexually promiscuous young lady and that this man just did not know enough to knock off her advances* (Hechler).

Additionally, a jury returning the acquittal of an offender stated, *The child was obviously making up the story because she didn't cry or show any emotion. If those things really had happened to her, she wouldn't have been able to speak.*

But another jury, when interviewed after an acquittal, indicated *the child couldn't even tell us when it happened or give us any details. She just kept crying. It seemed as though she was really sad about something, but we couldn't be sure it was abuse if she couldn't even talk about it.*

Obviously, the child loses in either situation. The system designed to protect children, on one hand, denies the status of a victim due to a lack of emotion, while, on the other hand, because of so much emotion, the child is not believed. How can the victim win? How can the victim take the first step toward rehabilitation in such a cruel system?

What seems to be ironic about the system which was designed to protect victims is again related

PROMISES, PROMISES
A child's view of incest

I asked you for help
and you told me you would
if I told you the things
my dad did to me.
It was really hard for me
to say all those things,
but you told me to trust you —
then you made me repeat them
to fourteen different strangers.

I asked you for privacy and you sent
two policemen to my school,
in front of everyone,
like I was the one being busted.

I asked you to believe me,
and you said that you did.
Then you connected me to a lie detector,
and took me to court where lawyers
put me on trial like I was a liar.

I asked you for help
and you gave me a doctor
with cold metal gadgets and cold hands
who spread my legs and stared,
just like my father.

I asked you for confidentiality
and you let the newspapers
get my story.

I asked for protection,
you gave me a social worker
who patted my head
and called me *Honey.*
She sent me to live with strangers
in another place, with a different school.

I asked you for help
and you forced my Mom
to choose between us
She chose him, of course.
She was scared and had a lot to lose.
I had a lot to lose too,
the difference was,
you never told me how much.

I asked you to put an end to the abuse
you put an end to my whole family.
You took away my nights of hell
and gave me days of hell instead.
You've exchanged my private nightmare
for a very public one.

Excerpts from a poem by Cindy
Edited and reprinted by permission from
Kee MacFarland

to the inequality of children. As previously indicated, the reason legislators have set about the task of establishing laws against offending children is because of inequality between children and adults. The issue of *consent* indicates that children are not capable of consenting due to the unequal balance between children and adults. Ironically, it is this same system that demands equality once disclosure of sexual abuse occurs.

It Ain't Equal But...

The same system which said, *It is against the law to have sex with children because they are unequal*, also demands complete equality from children in court, in investigations, in interviews, and in any other *system* proceedings. The system which set about to protect children because they are unequal, cruelly demands total equality. The system demands that children be as competent as adults. It demands that they remember dates, times, and peripheral events with the competency of an adult. The system questions thoroughly and disbelieves children who can only remember the color of their pajamas or the wall paper designs observed during their sexual abuse. The system doubts the veracity of children who cannot remember times, places, and centimeters of penetration needed for Grand Jury indictments.

Five-year-old Marcus testifies about his father's abuse. Different than in most cases, Marcus is a competent witness.

He can remember the date (his birthday). He remembers taking a nap with his father, and *he sucked on my peep!* rang out loudly through the courtroom when Marcus testified. Unfortunately, Marcus is noticed by the Defense Attorney as being unable to make eye contact with his father. On cross-examination, Marcus is simply asked to look at his father, which he refused. Finally, with careful prodding, Marcus denies his father is in the courtroom. In spite of his competency as a witness, his testimony fails because he is a child and his childhood solution was to avoid looking at his father. The jury acquits his father because Marcus failed to be as competent as adults.

As a child, Marcus is unaware of the significance of his *solution*. Walking away from the witness stand, Marcus asked, *I did good, didn't I? You know what, I knew that was my dad sitting there, but every time I looked at him, I got water in back of my eyes, so I just said it wasn't him.*

Although the system was originally designed to understand the trauma that could befall children who were sexually abused by adults, the system does not always seem to protect children and would not appear to be a reliable source of information regarding the trauma children suffer.

Caretaker Care

If not victims, if not offenders, if not society, if not the system, can we look to those close to the victim for answers regarding trauma? Would it be appropriate to ask the caretakers, the parents, the guardians, the families of victims for answers regarding the damage that has been caused to their loved ones? The coldness and cruelty of those outside the victim's support system can perhaps be understood. Surely, support, empathy and understanding regarding the trauma suffered by victims could be found from those closest to the victim???

FROM THE PARENTS OF SUSAN . . . *She doesn't need treatment. She is little. She'll outgrow it. We don't want her to remember.*

FROM THE MOTHER OF TONYA . . . *It wasn't real sex, so we didn't do anything about it when we found out. She was still a virgin, so what?*

FROM THE FATHER OF MICHAEL . . . *Kids outgrow things, all things, even their Levis. He'll outgrow this, too.*

FROM THE PARENTS OF JENNIFER . . . *She never yelled, fought, or screamed. We always see her telling her brothers NO when they want her to do something she is supposed to do. It must not have been so bad.*

AND FROM THE CHILD'S MINISTER . . . As the leader of the church, I made a decision not to overreact and why should I? Now that we know what happened, we know he never once touched the bare skin of any of the 32 boys.

FROM THE FATHER OF MICHAEL AND MATTHEW . . . *I won custody of the boys from their mother who abused them. They don't need treatment now. They will spend the rest of their lives with me and that's enough.*

FROM THE FATHER OF JOANNE . . . *She's already had sex with her boyfriend. Now we find out my brother raped her. What did she lose anyway?*

FROM THE FATHER OF ALEX . . . *I don't know what he is complaining about. The 18-year-old babysitter is a fox. He should want any sex he gets.*

The lack of empathy in some cases is due to ignorance. However, in some cases, the lack of understanding is questionable and concerning. On one end of the spectrum, some caretakers seem to have the child's interests at heart, but seem to be misinformed about such issues as childhood development. In other cases, the lack of empathy finds its root in extremely sexist ideas, cultivating archaic and outdated thoughts regarding the roles of men and women. Regardless of the motivation or the degree of insensibility, it would *not* appear that caretakers, or those closest to the victim, demonstrate empathy and understanding regarding trauma.

It is also common for caretakers or those close to victims to need to rearrange reality and formulate rationalizations. Denial systems are often developed in order to avoid experiencing the depths of trauma within the family. As an adult brother once commented in learning of his sister's childhood sexual abuse,

> *My God, I don't know why she has to bring it up now. It happened 30 years ago. Why do we have to deal with it now? Our family was doing just fine until she brought this up.*

The struggles of the victim's brother reflect his own inability to admit to the family secret. His isolated feelings toward his sister express outrage at both his challenge to accept her abuse and the reflections upon himself as an incest family member. His response, however painful to the victim, is quite common among the caretakers of victims. Although the denial of those surrounding the victim is understandable, this group of caretakers again demonstrates the futility of examining how victims are traumatized through sexual abuse.

Closed Doors, Opened Doors

In a futile attempt to find a reliable source of information regarding trauma, what doors are open to rehabilitate victims who have suffered through sexual abuse? Have we closed the door entirely on victim rehabilitation due to the doors that have been closed regarding reliable sources of understanding trauma? Of course, the answer is NO. Treatment centers for sexual victims are scattered throughout the country. National workshops and international conferences are held each year regarding victim rehabilitation. Many therapists and treatment specialists claim expertise in such efforts. Entire centers have been developed specializing in the treatment of those who suffer childhood sexual abuse.

The question remains, however. *Where have these individuals gained their knowledge in understanding the trauma to victims?* From what knowledge have the treatment plans been organized? What road maps are used? What has become the blueprint for repairing a damage that appears to be confusing or, at best, unpredictable? Where are therapists receiving information regarding the damage to victims so that effective treatment plans can be organized to respond to the damage?

The Blueprint

As hundreds of professional people were examined in informal research, four factors appeared to emerge as the foundation for understanding degrees of trauma suffered by sexual victims. Through interviews and data collection efforts of professionals (mostly those professionals involved in the rehabilitation of victims), *AGE, FREQUENCY, VIOLENCE AND PENETRATION* appear to emerge as the four most commonly held conditions or factors determining degrees of trauma. Through further research, the roots or the etiology of the *Big Four* was questioned. Most often, therapists or other professionals indicated that not only did these four factors seem to determine trauma, but these four factors seem to have inconspicuously entered into the minds of therapists without forethought, examination or question. Common responses, rating the most severely traumatizing situations were:

It was very brutal abuse. She was tied up and weapons were used.

It was so hard on him because it happened when he was very little.

It was horrifying for him. The offender was very violent.

It was a serious crime. He used a weapon.

It lasted for three years.

It involved real sex, penetration.

Those factors in the reverse order were typically viewed as less traumatic by professionals:

It only happened once.

The abuse involved just fondling and did not appear to be devastating.

He did everything else except intercourse for which she was very lucky.

He was actually her favorite person and he was very gentle.

There was no force or coercion. She always felt loved.

It only happened three times.

When professionals dedicated to victim rehabilitation were asked to rate and compare levels of trauma, the presence or lack of presence of these four factors seemed to lead away or toward trauma. If violence occurs, responses quickly indicated high probability of trauma. On the other hand, gentleness or the general opposite of violence seemed to approach the minimal rating. If penetration occurred, ratings were toward severe trauma, while the less significant the sexual act, the more likely respondents were to minimize trauma. If the victim was young, especially an infant, respondents viewed the crime more severely, while the older the victim, the more likely the responses were to suggest resilience and survivorship of the child. If abuse was ongoing or more frequent, respondents indicated more trauma than if the abuse involved a single or small number of incidents.

From where did this wisdom come? Where did these professional people learn that *only once* or with *a weapon* or *just fondled* determine varying degrees of trauma? The answer, upon further questioning, is unclear. Yet, initial responses are:

MORE IS ALWAYS WORSE.

REAL IS ALWAYS MORE THAN ALMOST.

VIOLENCE IS ALWAYS BAD.

YOUNGER IS ALWAYS MORE PRECIOUS.

The legal system seems to have provided the etiology for this thinking. It would seem likely that the professional community, in setting about the task of rehabilitating victims, adapted a system of degrees of trauma based upon an entirely different matrix designed for the offender.

In the Beginning

Etiology for this thinking begins with the legal system. From the legal system, varying degrees of crimes and criminals emerge. As an example, in the case of murder, degrees of seriousness are described. Typical degrees in murder convictions are manslaughter, self-defense, first degree, and so on. It would seem ridiculous to believe that degrees relating to the crime of homicide were set according to trauma to the victim. Obviously, a murder victim has lost a life. Rehabilitation of the murder victim is not possible and, in fact, the degrees set to examine the perpetrator in cases of murder have nothing to do with the rehabilitation of the victim. The degrees of seriousness have clearly been set about to determine the dangerousness of the criminal and, therefore, punishment. In cases of murder, the legal system had no intention of being empathic toward the damage caused to the victim. Why has this same, perhaps unempathic system been adapted by professionals attempting to rehabilitate the victim? The degrees set by the legal system were not intended to pertain to the victim, yet professionals seem to have followed this path without forethought. If it is clear, sexual contact with children is unacceptable *because it's against the law*, then perhaps examinations should be made regarding this path of legality which is followed, perhaps, blindly.

THE WRONG STUFF

by Jim Peters — Senior Attorney
National Center for Prosecution of Child Abuse

What is the foundation, or direction of the law when responding to abused children? Is trauma suffered by victims the focus of the criminal justice system?

Historical Perceptions

Sexual abuse of children is not a recent phenomenon. However, recognition that children deserve legal protection from abuse is relatively recent. In ancient times, children were not seen to have special needs or rights. Records from early Greece and Rome indicate that children were frequent objects of adult sexual expression. Historical references to pederasty, incest, and other sexual activities between adults and children are common. Religious ceremonies and initiation rites in ancient civilization sometimes involved sexual activities between adults and children.

Pedophilia and incest have been common practices in many cultures by large numbers of people. Children have been bought and sold as prostitutes throughout recorded history in Athens, China, and Europe.[1]

In Anglo-American law, the first dated knowledge that children needed special protection occurred in the early 1700s when the king assumed the royal prerogative to act as guardian to persons with legal disabilities such as *infants, idiots, and lunatics* through a doctrine known as *parens patriae.* Current laws granting states the power to protect children and intervene in the family are based on this principle.[2]

The social problem we now know as child abuse did not reach public consciousness in the United States until 1874. That year, the case of Mary Ellen Wilson, an eight-year-old child who had been subjected to beatings, bondage, and other indignities by her step-parents became a *cause celebre* in New York City. The legal system at the time provided no clear basis for intervening in cases of child abuse. However, the newspaper accounts of Mary Ellen's case attracted the attention of members of the Society for the Prevention of Cruelty to Animals, which hired a lawyer to successfully intervene on Mary Ellen's behalf. Seemingly it was more readily accepted that animals needed protection. The child's removal from the home of her abusive step-parents became the first widely known precedent for the legal protection of abused children.[3] Following Mary Ellen's case, concerned citizens formed the New York Society for the Prevention of Cruelty to Children. Late nineteenth century advocates focused on protecting children from physical cruelty inflicted by adults. By 1905, there were more than 400 organizations working to discover or prevent cruelty to children[4] and people were beginning to understand the trauma abuse causes children. Laws were eventually passed in every state giving young people protection against those who would victimize them. Today, maximum potential penalties for perpetrators who engage in sexual relations with children range from one year in jail to death.

Gender Inequities

Unfortunately, clear answers regarding protection of children were not immediately forthcoming from the legal system. Until the beginning of the twentieth century, protection against sexual abuse was typically extended only to female children and only to those under the age of ten by laws prohibiting *carnal knowledge* or *carnal abuse*. Sexual abuse was seen as a crime committed by men against girls. Boys were not considered victims. Females were not viewed as perpetrators. By the middle of the century, however, most states had raised the age of consent to as high as 18 and adopted gender neutral crimes such as *statutory rape*, *indecent liberties*, and *lewd and lascivious contact with a minor*.[5]

Vestiges of statutory gender discrimination remain a part of child abuse laws of a few states even today, confusing the issue of child protection even more. One Mississippi statute (97-3-65) makes it unlawful for a person to have carnal knowledge of a *female* under 12; another protects children under the age of 18 from *carnal knowledge* or *seduction* — but only when the child is *unmarried and of previously chaste character* (97-3-67) and (97-5-21). In South Carolina, a man can go to prison for five years for *deflowering or contracting matrimony with an abducted maid under 16* (16-15-40). In the District of Columbia, it is unlawful for a *male* teacher, superintendent, tutor, or instructor to have sexual intercourse with a *female* between 16 and 21 under his instruction (22-3002). Until recently, in New York, a *male* 21 years or older who engaged in sexual inter-course with a *female* under 17, or a male 18 or older who engaged in sexual intercourse with a female under 14, or any male who engaged in sexual intercourse with a female under 11 was guilty of rape. But, an adult who did the same with a male child could not be prosecuted for rape (130.35-30-25).

Modernization?

The seriousness with which society views criminal offenses is quantified by Congress and state legislatures which define crimes and set the maximum sentence a judge may impose on criminals. Legislative bodies have typically based the seriousness with which they view crimes against children upon four factors:

1) The age of the victim and perpetrator;

2) The type of sexual activity involved;

3) The amount of violence involved;

4) The number and frequency of crimes.

The following chart summarizes the age at which a child can consent to sexual intercourse with another person regardless of the age of the other participant. Where the state enhances the penalty for sexual behavior against younger victims, the age at which the maximum penalty is imposed is listed. This information is current through December 31, 1988.

State	Age of Consent		Increased Penalty
Alabama	16		U-12
Alaska	16		U-13
Arizona	18		U-15
Arkansas	14		n/a
California	18		U-14
Colorado	15	*	U-10
Connecticut	16	*	n/a
Delaware	16		n/a
District of Columbia	16		n/a
Florida	18		U-12
Georgia	14		n/a
Hawaii	14		n/a
Idaho	16		—
Ilinois	18		U-9
Indiana	16	*	U-12
Iowa	14	**	U-12
Kansas	16	***	—
Kentucky	16		U-12
Louisiana	17		U-12
Maine	16		U-14
Maryland	14		n/a
Massachusetts	16		n/a
Michigan	16		—
Minnesota	16	*	U-14
Mississippi	18		U-12
Montana	16	*	U-14
Nebraska	16		n/a
Nevada	17		U-14
New Hampshire	17		U-13
New Jersey	13	****	—
New Mexico	16	*	U-13
New York	17		U-11
North Carolina	16		U-13
North Dakota	18		U-15
Ohio	15		U-13
Oklahoma	15		U-13
Oregon	18		U-12
Pennsylvania	16		U-14

State	Age of Consent	Increased Penalty
Rhode Island	16	U-13
South Carolina	14 **	U-11
South Dakota	16	U-10
Tennessee	18	U-13
Texas	17	U-14
Utah	16	U-14
Vermont	16	n/a
Virginia	18	U-13
Washington	16	U-12
West Virginia	16	U-11
Wisconsin	18	U-12
Wyoming	16	U-12

* Age of consent increases to 18 if perpetrator is victim's guardian or responsible for general supervision of victim's welfare.

** When perpetrator is a relative or member of victim's household or in position of authority over victim, or is six or more years older than victim, the age of consent is 16.

*** When one participant is under 18, aggravated incest may be charged.

**** Age of consent can be 16 or 18, depending on age differences between victim and actor or presence of familial, supervisory, professional or guardianship status.

According to state legislatures children must be able to give consent according to their zip codes. What is most important, however, is not necessarily how legislatures made geographic decisions concerning the age of consent, but that each state made decisions regarding how the age of sexual consent would be viewed. It is doubtful that any legislative action took place based on the damage that might befall certain children who were engaging in sexually abusive activities. It would seem that each state made a decision based upon other factors.

Criminal laws were primarily written to punish and/or rehabilitate the people who violate them, deter those who may be considering the commission of similar crimes, and satisfy society's desire for retribution. In general, the *age of consent* laws do not necessarily bear any relationship to the amount of crime induced trauma experienced by the victim. These legislative actions were primarily a state's decision regarding responses to criminals.

Although discrepancies continue throughout the nation, some states have enacted statutory innovations which take into consideration trauma to victims. The states of Delaware and Washington, for example, have recently enacted new child sexual abuse laws. Washington is one of the many states which has a provision for victim impact statements to be presented at the criminal hearing. The victim's feelings and the impact of the crime on the victim are taken into account at sentencing insofar as the judge has discretion to grant or deny probation, impose treatment requirements on the offender, order restitution, and set the length of time the perpetrator spends in jail or prison.

Delaware enacted a new sexual abuse law in 1986 (11:772/775), and sought to incorporate the effects of the crime on the victim into the penalty structure. The maximum penalty (more than or equal to 20 years without probation, parole or supervision) is reserved for *unlawful sexual intercourse in the first degree* and occurs when an actor engages in sexual intercourse with a child under 16 without consent where serious physical, mental, or emotional harm results. Delaware considered trauma, but also stipulated the kind of sexual activity that must occur (penetration).

Although Delaware and Washington have attempted to require judges to take into consideration the trauma victims experience as they impose sentences, this is not a common practice among states. Most legislatures have created guidelines for sentencing sexual abusers based on factors unrelated to the actual trauma experienced by the crime victim. The general picture across the country suggests that the younger the child the more serious the crime.

Geographic Discrepencies

Not only does there appear to be a great deal of confusion about the age of consent in states' actions against child sexual abusers, even more confusion occurs as states set about the task of describing sexual abuse in a hierarchy of seriousness of crimes. Although *penetration* appears to be one of the most important factors, there is confusion about the definition and the seriousness of criminal's behavior.

Comparisons from state to state reveal numerous variances and inconsistencies among child sexual abuse laws. Some state statutes still use such terms as *carnal knowledge* without defining what that means. Other statutes specifically enumerate the organs considered intimate and prohibit touching of them or the clothing directly covering them.

Regional differences abound. For the same conduct, sentences can range from death or life in prison to probation, depending on the state in which the crime is committed.[6] For example, there is a point at the northeastern corner of Oregon where one could take a single step northward and be in Asotin County, Washington. Another step to the east would place an individual in Nez Perce County, Idaho, and a single southwesterly step would place an individual in Wallowa County, Oregon. Such geographical quirks occur across the United States and are seldom of practical interest to anyone other than tax collectors, map makers, and trivia enthusiasts.

However, the location in which an adult is convicted of fondling the breasts of a 15-year-old girl can mean the difference between a sentence to state prison for up to life, if the crime were committed in Idaho; a prison sentence of no more than five years (with a presumptive actual term of one to three months) if the crime occurred in Washington State; and a misdemeanor conviction with a maximum of one year in jail if the crime occurred in Oregon.[7] Does this mean the girl in Idaho is more likely to commit suicide because the crime was committed slightly to the east? Does this mean that the girl in Oregon or Washington will have a better chance to be a Rhodes Scholar because her molestation occurred in the refreshing breeze of northern Oregon or Southeast Washington?

Another extreme example of geographic discrepancy occurs in contrasting sexual abuse laws in the state of Minnesota and Washington with two Southern states. Florida's 1984 sexual battery statute (794.011) makes a death sentence possible for a person over 18 who engages in ... *oral, anal, or vaginal penetration, or union with the sexual organ of another or the anal or vaginal penetration of another by an object with a victim under the age of 12.* A maximum prison term not to exceed 30 years is enacted if the victim is 12 or older and either physically helpless or the offender coerces the victim to submit by threatening to use force likely to cause serious injury. The punishment is reduced if the victim is not seriously injured. A death sentence is also possible in Mississippi (97-3-65) for perpetrators over 18 years who commit rape or carnal knowledge of a female under the age of 12.

In contrast, as we travel north and west, both Washington and Minnesota have special sex offender sentencing alternatives setting out specific conditions when the judge may suspend or defer imposition of sentence while the offender enters a treatment program to control sexual deviancy. Offenders who have sex with children under 12 years of age in either Washington or Minnesota may receive probation and treatment, while a person committing the same offense in the state of Florida could face a possible death sentence!

Violence

This crime equals more time! If all criminal laws could be viewed on a continuum, it would be obvious that the most punitive sentences are reserved for offenses which contain actual or threatened violence. For instance, a typical maximum sentence for entering a residence with the intent to commit a crime (burglary) is ten years. But, if the perpetrator assaults the homeowner or carries a weapon into the building, the crime is more serious. Some states raise the maximum possible sentence from 10 years to life imprisonment. The legitimate legislative intent with such laws is to severely punish those who engage in violent crimes and discourage others who may be considering similar behavior.

This same principle applies to sexual offenses. Thus, a stranger who attacks a child, threatens the victim with a knife, and forces submission to sexual intercourse will, in most cases, face a much more serious consequence than a father who without physical force, entices and emotionally traps his daughter into sexual activity and mutual orgasms. The stranger who raped the child will likely go to prison, often with a lengthy term, while the father, who could receive a prison sentence, will in many cases be placed on probation.

Violence seems to be an easy and understandable method of establishing a value or matrix of seriousness of crimes. Knives and guns are much easier for legislators and judges to understand compared with orgasms, sexual enticement and sexual consent. Is it so difficult to believe that the child who is held by a stranger at knife point may, in fact, feel more victimized and have a better chance at rehabilitation than one who has learned to accommodate repeated molestation by her father? Why then do our lawmakers enact laws which tell us that the stranger's use of a weapon is so much more serious than a father's betrayal of trust? When looking at the issue of violence and sexual abuse, the focus has always been on the dangerousness of the offender. Little regard has been paid to the victim and the comparative trauma involved in violent and nonviolent sexual encounters.

Sub Frequency

If someone sexually abuses a child over a long period, the perpetrator can face many additional charges and hence a longer sentence, simply by the number of indictments or charges documented by the prosecutor through the victim (assuming the victim is able to isolate separate acts). Just as with a burglar, if 25 break-ins are proven, the calculator tells us that the accumulation of charges indicates a more serious criminal pattern. *Frequency* has been adapted by those both inside and outside the legal system as an indicator of victim trauma. However, while the number of charges against a criminal may bear an important factor in determining the dangerousness of the criminal, they may have very little relationship to the trauma experienced by the victim.

Additional Confusions And Inequalities

The reluctance of legislators and the general public to recognize that crimes within the family are as serious, or more serious, in terms of victim trauma, is reflected in states statutes regarding mandatory prison sentences. Such sentences are also affected by assumptions that a child who learns that a family member will face an automatic prison sentence will be discouraged from reporting the crime or from telling the truth throughout the investigation and court procedure. Family members and friends do, in some cases, pressure children into recanting a truthful description of the crime so that a family member does not have to suffer the consequences of prison. Many experts have, therefore, urged that any state law providing for mandatory imprisonment also contain a provision that allows the judge to impose a sentence of probation when he/she determines it is in the victim's best interest that the defendant not be sent to prison.[8] Washington and Minnesota, whose laws were previously discussed, are examples of jurisdiction which heeded this advice.

Others argue that there should be a different standard for persons who abuse children within the family unit than that used for persons who abuse other people's children. These voices argue that intra-family sexual abuse should be handled by a medical model outside the criminal justice system.[9] Perhaps no conflict has caused greater dissention among professionals working on behalf of abused children. Dr. Eli

Newberger, a prominent physician who specializes in sexual abuse, has called prosecution of child abusers *a cruel alternative to giving people help.*[10] The former director of the National Center on Child Abuse and Neglect, Douglas Besharov, has written, *Child protective agencies rarely considered criminal prosecution as an appropriate response to child maltreatment. These agencies fear that the arrest and possible prosecution of a parent will impair efforts to treat the parent and reunite the family.*[11] What do these statements say about the seriousness of the criminal offense? Is it really more serious for a stranger to rape or seduce a child than for the child's father to commit the same crime? Are the effects of an ongoing sexual involvement with a family member less harmful than involvement with someone outside the home? Is the underlying agenda or belief of these commentators that sexual abuse should not be a crime if it occurs within the family?

Scott Harshbarger, District Attorney for Middlesex County, Cambridge, Massachusetts, spoke for most prosecutors when he wrote, *There is absolutely no legal or moral justification for ignoring cases where the acts of physical or sexual abuse are committed by a family member, while strangers are treated as criminals for committing similar acts.*[12]

Protector Or Perpetrator

One of the principal arguments made for those who oppose prosecution of the intra familial abuser is that the *system* focuses on obtaining convictions and is not responsive to the needs of victims. Critics contend that the criminal justice system views children only as *players* under the authority of a *quarterback* (prosecutor) who sets the rules and doesn't listen to what subordinates, the victims, have to say.[13]

Persons who oppose prosecution for family member abusers believe that criminal investigation and litigation further victimize children. They point to evidence that children are sometimes forced to repeat their story over and over, confront the offender, and endure repeated continuances and hostile cross examinations. Physical configuration of some courtrooms, removal from the home, fear of retaliation, the presence of spectators, judge and jury, and fear of identification in the news media have also been cited as adding trauma to child victims.

The Criminal Justice System Awakens To Children

After centuries of neglect, lawmakers have placed some of the responsibility for protecting children from sexual exploitation on the criminal justice system. The system was ill-prepared to deal with the unique problems of the thousands of sexually abused children who were thrust into its care. Confusing and contradictory mandates from Congress and state legislators compound the problem of discrepencies from state to state.

The tools available to combat child abuse, however, are changing rapidly. Each legislative session, new laws are passed in virtually every corner of the nation attempting to help society cope with sexual abuse of children. Some general trends in the law can be observed:

1) Trends indicate that sexually abusing younger children is more harmful than committing the same crime against an older child.

2) Behavior that is tolerated by someone near the age of the child is prohibited to persons substantially older than the child.

3) The use of violence is typically viewed as more serious than seduction.

4) Oral genital contact or sexual penetration of a child are punished more severely than fondling.

5) Being related to the victim is often a mitigating factor in practice if not in law, resulting in the tendency to treat inappropriate sexual behavior by a family member less seriously than the same contact with someone else's daughter.

Whether wise or wrongheaded, these general legal trends not only affect the legal system, but the therapeutic community, as well. The community is left with the task of rehabilitatiing not only damage to victims in sexual abuse, but potential trauma from the system designed to protect those children.

Research is underway at the National Center for the Prosecution of Child Abuse* and affiliated universities and research groups to determine which aspects of the system are beneficial and which may be harmful to children. Hopefully, this work will determine whether the laws should remain focused on the offender's dangerousness rather than leaning toward the trauma to the victim. The legal system may continue to respond based on the perceived dangerousness of the sexual offender, and taking into account such factors as *force, frequency of crime, the sexual activities, or the age of the child.* Perhaps this general direction is appropriate for legislators.

However, it would seem that the legal profession needs to determine what the roots of the criminal justice system should be. If, in fact, the roots or the *etiology* of the system are founded in an approach to the offender, then let us examine whether that should remain the case. If so, let us have the courage to recognize that these factors may have little to do with the actual trauma experienced by the sexual victims.

---

*In 1985, the National Center for the Prosecution of Child Abuse was founded by the American Prosecutors Research Institute, a non-profit research and public education affiliate of the seven thousand member National District Attorneys Association. Through training, oportunities, publications, legal research, and collaborative work with child sexual abuse experts and key children's organizations, the Center plays a major role in improving the justice system's response to child sexual abuse.

1. Schetky, D., *Child Sexual Abuse in Mythology, Religion, and History.* In Child Sexual Abuse: A Handbook for Health Care and Legal Professionals, by D. Schetky and A. Green, New York; Brunner/Mazel, 1988, pp 19-29.

See also: Walker, C., The Physically and Sexually Abused Child: Evaluation and Treatment. New York; Pergamon Press, 1988, pp 4 and

Loken, G., *The Oldest Oppression.* In Child Pornography and Prostitution. Washington, D.C.: National Center for Missing and Exploited Children, 1987, pp 47-49.

2. Haugaard, J. and Reppucci, N., The Sexual Abuse of Children, San Francisco; Jossey-Bass, Inc., 1988, pp 1-2.

3. Walker, C., Ibid at pp 3-7.

4. Freiman, M., *Unequal and Inadequate Protection Under the Law: State Child Abuse Statutes. The George Washington Law Review,* Vol. 50, January 1982, pp 243-245.

5. Haugaard and Reppucci, Ibid at 19.

6. Haugaard and Reppucci, Ibid at 13-30.

7. Idaho Laws, 18-1508; Washington Revised Statutes 9A.44; Oregon Revised Statutes 163.415.

8. National Center for Missing and Exploited Children, *Selected State Legislation: A Guide for Effective State Laws to Protect Children,* January 1985, pp 18.

9. Chapman, J. and Smith, B., *Response of Social Service and Criminal Justice Agencies to Child Sexual Abuse Complaints. Response to the Victimization of Women and Children,* Vol. 10, Number 3, 1987, pp 7-13.

10. Newberger, E., *Prosecution: A Problematic Approach to Child Abuse, Journal of Interpersonal Violence,* 1987, pp 112, 115.

11. Besharov, *Child Abuse: Arrest and Prosecution Decision Making, American Criminal Law Review,* Vol. 24, 1987, pp 315, 317-18.

12. Harshbarger, S., *Prosecution is an Appropriate Response in Child Sexual Abuse Cases. Journal of Interpersonal Violence,* March 1987, pp 108-112.

13. Newberger, E., *Prosecution: A Problematic Approach to Child Abuse. Journal of Interpersonal Violence,* March 1987, pp 112-117.

ROOTS

If not the legal system, what system can lead toward the proper focus? And what does it require to organize and maintain a system empathic to a single purpose — victim rehabilitation?

If the *roots* of the legal system's response to sexual abuse is founded on an approach to the sexual perpetrator, the response to sexual victims hopefully could be rooted in a system designed with the victim in mind. Criticism of the legal system, whose obligation may not be rehabilitation of victims but protection of the community, may not be needed. Perhaps *roots* for the legal system enmeshed with the offender is appropriate.

In fact, those professionals who evaluate sex offenders may agree that the **Big Four** has some bearing on categorizing offenders. If an offender engages in intercourse, uses violence, has multiple offenses, and is involved with prepubescent children, *Red Flags* may be hoisted. These factors, to sex offender specialists, may indicate a perpetrator who is more dangerous. Different treatment approaches may be required for the perpetrator who has all of these characteristics. The road map or direction in designing therapeutic intervention for victims, however, should come from a course different than one charted for the offender.

The Blueprint

The blueprint, or the foundation of an innovative understanding for the trauma suffered by victims, evolved from a unique treatment program based on a philosophy of rehabilitating victims. The *roots* or etiology of this program has grown and developed with nine years of sometimes intense and sometimes accidental focus on the trauma suffered by victims. The history of this unique program laid the foundation for a comprehensive and unique examination of sexual traumatization.

The *Sexual Victim Trauma Assessment* evolved from a comprehensive study of the trauma to sexual victims not just from a therapist's view, nor from any *one* perspective. This endeavor occurred through interagency cooperation and unification in the struggle to understand. This unique aspect of understanding trauma to victims required coordination of the *system*. Without that networking, this work would not have been possible. Not only was interagency involvement a requirement in order to assist sexual victims, but *VICTIMS* became the source of motivation for interagency cooperation. This two-fold enhancement has resulted in the work designed in this publication. After nine years of intense interagency coordination and cooperation, a great deal has been learned about the trauma to victims. With victims as the focus, the program has been successful and has learned extremely important information about trauma suffered by victims of sexual abuse.

Historical (Hysterical) Perspective Of A Rural Program

Previous to 1980, Malheur County like most rural communities in Eastern Oregon had its share of sexual abuse cases. Although it was common for many children to report sexual abuse to counselors, teachers, pastors, or friends, it was typical for a *yearly* case to emerge in the Malheur County Court System. Children's Services Division, Mental Health, and the Juvenile Department were aware that the problem of sexual abuse was more serious than community members realized. The only access of information to citizens was the typical, yearly case, with a sex offender being convicted or charged with sexual abuse. From the community's perspective, Malheur County was a nice place to live because sexual abuse occurred approximately once a year, very similar to the bloom of tulips.

From the perspective of involved agencies, Children's Services Division, the Juvenile Department, and Mental Health, a very different story emerged. Victims were often returned to the home after disclosure or separated and *sentenced* to a deadly term of foster care. Frustrations abounded! Perpetrators were interviewed and required to attend therapy *in lieu* of prosecution. Social workers were required to return children to live in incestuous families and yet monitor their safety in order to *keep the family together.* Mental Health intervention required the offender to guarantee the sexual abuse *would never happen again* based on the offender's honesty and moral character. The Juvenile Department hopefully and optimistically believed that Children's Services Division and the Mental Health Clinic would balance protection and therapy to avoid another return to the Juvenile Justice System.

Professionals within each discipline in Malheur County believed and understood that the sexual abuse problem seemed to be closing in. As each year progressed, the problem seemed to become more profound. The responses, however, continued to be the same *Band-Aid* approach. Astute professionals recognized a change was needed, but the same professionals recognized that archaic and traditional views contributed to the confusion and hampered *New Thinking*.

Perfect Prosecution

Previous to program organization, typical responses in Malheur County were the same as most rural if not urban communities. The prosecution often contended that a crime had been committed, but legal proceedings would be avoided if the evidence was not overwhelming. As a humorous prosecutor once indicated, *The rule of thumb for taking cases to court is, if three clergymen witnessed four inches of penetration and they will testify!* Cases with less evidence were dropped.

Save the Child? Save the Family?

Typical responses from Children's Services Division and the Juvenile Court seemed to be manifested in removal of the child from the home or somehow pretending as though the crime would not be committed in the future if the family was reunited. Some philosophies purported that if the child was removed from the home and placed in a nice, clean foster home, where foster parents had a family room and a late model sedan, somehow success had taken place. If that situation could not occur immediately, a second alternative was to hope that the offender would promise *not to do it again* and the family could be reunited in their own home with a late model sedan in the garage.

Jack Webb, Where Are You?

Law Enforcement harbored much of the same frustration yet with different avenues of concern. Talking about *wee wees* and *pee pees* was not comfortable for most dedicated and sensitive law enforcement officers in Malheur County. Astute officers recognized that the *Jack Webb DRAGNET* approach did not work in cases that involved four-year-old children talking about *poops and peeps!* Additional frustration reigned for law enforcement officers who, after proceeding through these very difficult cases, later learned that the charges were dismissed against the perpetrator if *THE CURE* took place, across the street at the local Mental

Health Clinic. Law enforcement officers rarely saw any fruits for their labor when these very difficult cases were investigated.

Deep Dish Therapy?

Mental Health therapists traditionally learned in graduate school that all patients presenting themselves for therapy wanted to improve and were basically honest, compliant and interested in change. Very little training typically occurred regarding *mandated* clients, deviant arousal cycles, or understanding those patients who had enjoyed crimes while children were screaming and crying. Mental Health therapists viewed problems within the family as needing a *family system's* approach where all family members were required to share in responsibility for the problem. Historically, the Mental Health approach was to *cure*, to reunite, to mend, to rehabilitate, and to resolve the sickness. Consideration that one family member was a *criminal* was unimportant and immaterial.

The Burning Shed Treatment

The community in Malheur County had a quite different approach to the problem of childhood sexual abuse. Since the community did not view the problem as being serious and because the community was kept from the enormity of the problem, the community often joked about solutions to the problem. A typical response was outlined in the *Burning Shed Treatment*.

When notoriety of a sexual abuse case occurred (periodically, like the tulips), the typical community response suggested the *Burning Shed Treatment* should be implemented. This *treatment* was described as taking a sex offender into the sagebrush areas of Malheur County, forcing him into an old building, nailing him to the floor by his genitalia, and handing him a rusty knife while the building was set afire. This *solution* caused a great deal of laughter among community members and seemed to be a reasonable solution.

Sadly, the laughter and jokes regarding the Burning Shed Treatment encouraged community members to avoid thinking about the reality of the problem. The preposterousness or absurdity in this discussion prevented community members from taking any action about child abuse. Even though most citizens who joked about the Burning Shed Treatment recognized it was unrealistic, the humor allowed a plan of *NO ACTION* to occur. The joviality sounded tough, hard line and swift, yet, in reality, said *we will do nothing*. Thus, the community remained naive and uninvolved in the problem of child sexual abuse previous to 1980.

The Case

In 1980, a very typical case emerged in Malheur County. A father was arrested for rape of his daughter and criminal proceedings were taking place. A new and energetic District Attorney intended on prosecution. The child remained in a home with her mother and family, but the offender *promised* to reside elsewhere. When the child was interviewed, she explained that she felt quite lucky because when her father visited the house, her food was served to her in the basement. Clearly, the child knew she was not allowed to eat upstairs with her father because of *telling*.

The local prosecutor contacted the Mental Health Clinic for assistance in preparing the child for court.

> *Will you help prepare this child for court?*
>
> *Yes, when is the trial?*
>
> *Tomorrow!*

The victim was obviously unprepared and seemed destined for trauma since the rest of the family intended to provide total support for the father. The perpetrator's *cheering section* was clearly envisioned.

A preview of the evidence in the upcoming trial included an affidavit the child had signed indicating she had made false claims against her father. When the child was interviewed about the affidavit, she obviously did not understand the meaning of the document, innocently proclaiming, *I signed a paper saying God was proud of me for telling the truth.*

Additional evidence included nine and eleven-year-old boys who would testify against the victim in the upcoming trial. The boys' testimony would indicate that she *diddled* them in her own backyard during several summer vacations. The victim's credibility and morality was at stake and she had already indicated a lack of veracity by signing the affidavit against her own testimony. Perusal of the evidence clearly indicated the victim's character would be on trial and the success of prosecution in this case looked hopeless.

Hope Upon Hope

Mental Health therapists were hoping to *cure* the sexual offender while the prosecution was hoping to convict. Law Enforcement officers tirelessly hoped the community would be protected. Children's Services Division hoped to protect the child through separation or harmonious family reunification. The Defense Attorney, on the other hand, was hoping to *defend* and find the best possible alternative for the defendant. The community, of course, remained hopeful for the Burning Shed Treatment.

With the victim's emotional safety in mind, recommendations were made to avoid the criminal trial and offer treatment to the perpetrator. The prosecution agreed to this arrangement, but only if the defendant admitted to the charges against him, eventually allowing the prosecutor to have his hope, a conviction! The defense was guaranteed treatment through a diversion agreement, in lieu of a criminal trial, which allowed reasonable success for both the defense attorney and client. The child was allowed to remain in the home due to efforts of Children's Services Division, whose primary goal is to keep the family together. The prosecution and defense each claimed victory. Law Enforcement saw some fruits of their labor in at least a prosecution of the case. And Mental Health finally had the opportunity to lay their hands on the offender and *cure* the family.

Who Won?

This very typical case became unique in the history of the Malheur County Treatment Program. The case was unique in teaching each interagency discipline that somehow if cooperation occurred, the pie of victory could be shared. This did not suggest that any one discipline would gain the entire piece of success, however. Many years of struggling taught the agencies within Malheur County that failure was much more prevalent in sexual abuse cases than was success. In this case, however, each discipline won a piece of success — not the pie, but a piece of the pie.

In order to succeed on a continual basis, however, a philosophy in approach, a goal or a *glue* was needed. Typically, agencies and disciplines come together with entirely different focuses. Law Enforcement has the goal of investigation, the court has the goal of protecting the community, the prosecution has the job of monitoring state laws, child protection must protect children and the family, while Mental Health traditionally must rehabilitate. It is often difficult for agencies with these varying goals and objectives to come into reasonable focus. Conflict is more common. Malheur County was no exception.

There were tremendous difficulties involved in attempting to work together in order to repeat the small pieces of success demonstrated in this early case. Difficulties in interagency networking were common to this community as in other communities. Being able to work together within different disciplines seems to be a problem plaguing most communities.

Unfortunately, or perhaps fortunately, child sexual abuse involves all disciplines. When a child is sexually abused, balance is needed to investigate, prosecute, protect children, and rehabilitate. Different than other mental health issues, child sexual abuse does not belong to only the therapeutic discipline, but to all disciplines. A united force was needed to focus on the trauma suffered by victims. In order to protect and rehabilitate children, agencies need to work together. And what a difficult task it is!

The Burger King Syndrome: Why Can't We Work Together?

In order to rescue victims, agencies must work together. Why is it so difficult to coordinate and cooperate for the benefit of children? The difficulty seems to lie in a special syndrome. The Burger King Syndrome involves the professional's complaint, *I want it my way*. The fast food hamburger chain advertises that *at Burger King, you can have it your way*. However, Burger King advertisements pertain to such things as relish, mustard, and processed cheese. *Have it your way* does not relate to indictments, treatment plans or adjudication hearings. One of the most common reasons then, why professionals have a difficult time working together is that *we want it our way*.

Your Way, My Way

As indicated previously, the problem of child sexual abuse is a crime, a mental health problem, a protection problem, and a law enforcement problem. It is a judicial problem and it is a prosecution problem. If professionals involved in this hodgepodge system *want it their way*, the system will fail. *Have it your way* implies tunnel vision, never understanding anything beyond a single perspective. The first failure of the system involves that inability to appreciate other disciplines, an inability to look at the need, desires, and demands of others and to appreciate the priorities of the disciplines needed for cooperation.

As an example, a perfectly drawn penis on the Easter Bunny in a play therapy session is extremely meaningful to a therapist, especially when the child drawing the perfectly anatomically correct penis is a suspected sexual abuse victim. To the Juvenile Department Director who receives a demand to remove the child

from the home, the penis on the rather bewildered Easter Bunny is not factual information appropriate for a legal petition. Both disciplines *see it their way* and only their way.

Likewise, a five-year-old child sitting on the lap of a caseworker, munching oat meal cookies, drinking lemonade, and discussing his sexual abuse scenario may appear to the social worker as an extremely competent witness. If reports to the prosecutor are submitted without understanding the implications and involvements of a true criminal trial, the caseworker may be disappointed. If, after interviewing the child, without lemonade and cookies, the charges are dropped due to the child's incompetency, the social worker may informally evaluate the prosecutor as an *insensitive, cold, arbitrary politician who obviously does not care about children*. The inability to understand the priorities of the prosecutor's office and the legal requirements and restrictions in the courtroom arena may cause interdisciplinary chaos and conflict.

While the Juvenile Court petition needs four *facts*, the Mental Health therapist only needs an anatomically correct penis on the Easter Bunny. While the prosecutor needs the witness to pass the competency phase of the trial, the social worker needs to establish rapport and confidence with the child who has been betrayed. If none of these professionals are willing to understand the intricacies or requirements of the other agency disciplines, then conflict will result and the child will be the battle victim.

Tunnel Vision

Not only does it seem to be difficult for professionals to understand the disciplines of others, but another difficulty in agency coordination is the preconceived ideas professionals in one discipline have for other professionals. These preconceived ideas of how others operate as human beings allow decisions to be made about other individuals, thus avoiding the risk of coordination. These *assumptions* build up the deadly layer of conflict between professionals.

Although some are rather humorous, the following statements were explained by professionals when asked about their fellow professionals. Lack of understanding pervades. Some of the responses were obviously made in jest; nonetheless, preconceived, prejudicial ideas form the foundation of these humorous remarks:

Law Enforcement officers believed that prosecutors tended to be cold, arbitrary politicians always thinking about getting elected.

Prosecutors tended to think Mental Health therapists were *mushy-headed* and knew nothing about the law.

Social Workers and Mental Health workers tended to view Prosecutors as cold, insensitive people who rarely had children of their own.

Judges believed Social Workers were *magic*, because they could protect children even if the court chose to reunite an incestuous family without treatment.

Prosecutors thought Law Enforcement officers had seen too many Jack Webb movies or had been Perry Masonized, giving them very little understanding about *real* court.

Law Enforcement officers thought that Mental Health therapists were *dipbats* who knew nothing about crime and criminals.

Mental Health therapists tended to think that Social Workers had tunnel vision and could only understand protecting the child.

Probation officers felt as though Mental Health therapists had deviant problems of their own, thus providing the only reason they would work in this field.

Cops believed attorneys were born in three-piece suits and male therapists were born with beards.

When one professional discipline feels in full possession of accurate information regarding the ideas, background, philosophy, or religious persuasions of their *partner* disciplines, coordination barriers are erected and fortified, preventing the goal of working together.

Heeding Needing

Another pervading idea in the difficulty of professionals working together speaks of the dilemma involved when one professional needs another professional. Somewhere in graduate school, in Home Economics, or perhaps in the sandbox, adults tend to learn that *to need* others smacks of not being whole or complete. It seems to be a particular burden or conflict for those individuals who, as an example, have a master's or doctorate degree, to *need* other professionals with bachelor's degrees or no formal education. The vulnerability of professionals plays into concert. Does the prosecutor, as an example, weaken if a person without a degree becomes invaluable in preparing a case involving the five-year-old? In some communities, interagency cooperation has failed because professionals were not able to feel confident in needing others. To fail in court, as an example, would be more respectable than having to say *please help me.*

Debits, Credits, Pluses, Minuses, Success, Failure

Additionally, other things were learned in the sandbox (or wherever else) that prove deadly to interagency networking. Unfortunately, success is often measured by professionals in the failure of others.

My sand castle looks better than yours. . . but . . . if yours is gone, mine won't look quite so good in comparison.

Not only is it difficult to need other professionals, but it is often the *attack* of other professionals that leads to a sense of success. How often do professionals indicate:

I am the only one the child will talk to.

I have been successful with this offender and, therefore, your concerns about the victim are inappropriate. You obviously don't understand the intricacies of offender treatment.

I am the only one the child likes. No one else is able to get her to explain what happened.

This child simply doesn't like men. She did fine in the investigation and the medical exam with females. She will not talk to a prosecutor who is male.

Rather than working together and sharing success, it appears more successful if one professional can succeed in the light of failure of others. This seems to be another contribution to the Burger King Syndrome. While these statements may appear to be protective of the child, they in fact have a counter response. They are not protective of the child; they are protective of the professional's need to be successful in the light of others' failure.

The Glue

Finally, it seems to be difficult for agencies to work together unless a common goal is established. Each interdisciplinary area has goals, priorities, conflicts, and guidelines. The failure of a common goal or a *glue* would not only prohibit interagency networking, but would hamper the fruits of this publication. It was the adoption of a very simple goal that allowed the program in Malheur County to flourish and to continue the process of working together to better understand the trauma of sexual abuse.

The focus of the Malheur County Treatment Program and resulting success occurred because victim rehabilitation or *repairing the damage to the victim* became the common goal that allowed each professional discipline to find a nitch in the program.

Working with other professionals for sheer pleasure, appreciating the disciplines of other professionals, hoping for the success of other professionals sound like nice ideas, but in reality it is extremely difficult unless one simple goal is established reaching into each disciplinary *pie*. It would be helpful if professionals could overcome these difficulties and coordinate simply for the pleasure of working together. This does not appear to be the case. The reality is that each professional discipline must have a common thread, or else coordination is doomed and sexual victims will not be protected. The goal that holds all disciplines together is, in fact, children. Without this *glue*, success is not attainable.

Victim Thinking

What became predominantly clear in Malheur County was that the *focus on children* allowed every agency to be successful. Law Enforcement officers were not particularly interested in being involved in a program that worked toward repairing the self-image or self-esteem of deviant sexual offenders. Additionally, it seemed counter-productive for the prosecutor to work on a sexual abuse team to prosecute offenders and then work toward offender *help*.

Likewise, *the family* seemed to be a major concern for child protection yet it was the family unit that was often most abusive to the child in an incestuous situation. How could those interested in the issue of child protection be involved in a program that worked toward rehabilitating the person who is least protective to the family unit? With these confusions and obvious dilemmas, a philosophy was needed.

The philosophy of organizing a treatment program toward victims seemed to reach into all disciplines and all priorities. It was *for children* that the Interagency Team could unite. It was *for children* that each one of the interdisciplinary agencies could set aside professional antagonisms, agendas, and priorities. The protection of children in some capacity weaved its way into each discipline so the goal of repairing damage to victims could become the needed philosophy. It was only with this goal and this philosophy that the Child Abuse Team was able to organize. And it was only with this goal that working together laid the foundation or the roots for understanding the true trauma suffered by sexual victims.

To quote a great philosopher, Ray Hartley, Detective, Ontario Police Department, inter-agency professional coordination is not always easy. But, for the value of repairing the damage caused to children by child sexual abuse, a common ground can emerge.

> *Before we started this program, I would visit the local Mental Health Clinic and find something amazing. It was difficult for me to tell the patients from the therapists. Since we started this program in 1980, I visit the treatment center and, you know what, I still can't tell the difference between the therapists and the patients. I will tell you, however, that, for kids, I will still visit the treatment center, I will still work in the program, and I will continue to work with these individuals. It's not that I believe sex offenders should receive treatment; it's not that I believe there is even a possibility for rehabilitation. It is simply that I believe kids are the **glue** for me, working with those people who work with those people!*

Not only does this philosophy of working toward repairing the damage to children keep the team of professionals intact, but this philosophy requires attention to specific trauma of sexual victims. If the program focused on repairing the damage to victims, then those professionals involved in the program must constantly evaluate or understand the trauma to victims. If offenders were required to repair the damage to their victims, then professionals were required to understand the trauma in order to know when, in fact, offenders have succeeded or failed. The focus on victim treatment provided the *glue*, the impetus, and the success for the treatment program. It also provided the foundation for truly understanding the trauma suffered by sexual victims.

In the nine years following the beginning of the Incest Treatment Program, strange issues and ideas have evolved. The commonly held ideas of *violence, frequency, age, and sexual activity (penetration)* were the cornerstones of under-standing of trauma in the program's early years. Gradually, those ideas have eroded as more pertinent information has emerged regarding trauma to victims.

> The sexual victim who has been raped for five years appears to be bubbly, confident, and in control. She recog-nizes her status as a victim and she only faults her mother for not believing.

> The *just fondled* victim attempts suicide at the age of nine.

> A *good* case results in conviction. The program applauds. The child is devastated.

> The *worst* offender is *best* liked by the victim.

The victim of satanic rituals easily proceeds through grand jury, seemingly unaffected.

The community status of the perpetrator is so positive, the charges are handled informally. The victim *formally* takes his own life.

For nine years, commonly held ideas and concepts have unfolded and dissolved. Time frames, failures, successes, and the nine-year period provided an observation of children that eventually, in itself, provided important information needed for the task at hand — understanding trauma and repairing the damage.

Numbers Please

The statistical framework or the roots of the Sexual Victim Trauma Assessment contains victims ranging in age from nine months to age 73. A two and one-half year old victim testified in Grand Jury and an indictment was filed. The average age for the MAC (molested as children) Group was forty-two. In 1984, as an example, seven female children were involved in group therapy for children under the age of five, and five boys were involved in the same age group comparison. Previously, it was believed that only adolescent children with budding breasts would be treated. In four years, statistics indicated that very young children *were* abused and that boys were abused at an alarmingly high rate.

In the first five years following 1980 approximately 500 individuals were involved in a program designed to serve only residents from a county of approximately 25,000. The numbers were staggering. One hundred and forty offenders were processed through the program from 1980-1985. Over 350 victims, non-offending parents and family members were also treated. Those numbers have continued at the same rate up to 1989, providing valuable lessons in understanding trauma.

System Success/Failure

As children were traumatized, lessons were also learned by the treatment program regarding not only the damage, but what worked and what did not work in the effort to alleviate the trauma. As an example, the program began on a *family systems* model, keeping the family together. Offenders were allowed to stay in the home and bring their children to treatment. Offenders were placed on diversion programs rather than *criminalizing* sexual abuse for the family. With recidivism rates of approximately 33 percent (known recidivism), the lesson was indeed a hard one to learn. Children were continually abused either directly or indirectly with the offender's presence in the home. Lack of identification of the perpetrator and the victim did not occur under the family systems model. Offenders remained in contact with the stimulus material preventing them from having any opportunity to change. As the treatment program saw more children being traumatized, changes were made.

In 1989, the National District Attorneys Association's Annual Conference was held in San Francisco, California. The Malheur County Program (now officially named *Restitution Treatment and Training Program*) was described as *one of the nation's most restrictive outpatient treatment programs for sexual offenders*. From the family systems model of keeping the family together, the same program evolved to boast having the most restrictive *no contact* order and outpatient treatment programs in the nation for sexual offenders. And how was this lesson learned? It was learned from attending to the trauma suffered by children through the inappropriate responses from the system.

Another example of learned failure throughout this historical perspective was the honesty of sexual offenders. It was originally believed that sexual offenders, like other mental health patients, desired treatment, would be cooperative, and could be believed. In the early years of the treatment program, offenders came into the program with 1.13 victims and at the completion of their sexual history had 1.50. It was realized that the treatment for offenders involved only the victim for which the offender was charged. As years went by, other victims came forward with abuse that was undetected in previous therapeutic efforts. The trauma of those victims had been ignored. When children were abused by offenders who were not monitored by behavioral methods, the program had failed and again needed readjustment based on the trauma to sexual victims.

Currently, the Restitution Treatment and Training Program requires sex offenders to be polygraphed on their sexual histories. They are given immunity from prosecution for crimes committed previous to their involvement in the treatment program. The typical incest offender involved in community treatment (after completing polygraph) has between 9 to 14 victims, rather than 1.50. Under the previous methodologies, children who were abused did not receive rehabilitation and were continually traumatized by a system that believed sex offenders would be honest. Without making these drastic changes, the program which philosophically believes in repairing the damage to victims would have failed in basic philosophy and contention.

And how do these changes affect The Sexual Abuse Team members? It is particularly difficult for Law Enforcement and prosecution professionals to recognize that a sex offender who has perhaps committed 20 crimes against children will not be prosecuted for any of those offenses. In debates, in confusion, in rejection, the only saving issue regarding the immunity dilemma is that the children this offender molested will be contacted and efforts will be made to rehabilitate these children. Again, without the philosophy of alleviating trauma suffered by children, providing offenders with immunity from prosecution would not be palatable to many professionals on the Sexual Abuse Team. Once again, the focus of trauma to victims becomes the guiding force toward program organization.

Harmony has not always befallen the Child Sexual Abuse Team. Conflicts, confusion, failure, disagreements, and concerns have been as commonplace as success. With each failure, some direction has been taken to readjust and re-evaluate in an effort to be more successful in the primary goal of victimology. The concept of victimization over the nine year period has been expanded to the child, the family, the community, and society, but the concept of victimization has always been at the forefront of the decision-making process. Without this guiding force, the lessons could not be learned regarding the trauma suffered by victims. And, of course, without understanding the trauma, there is very little opportunity for the trauma to be repaired.

THE STUFF . . .
A CLOSER LOOK

*If we abandon the **Big Four**, if we embrace the effort to better evaluate trauma, what do we find? What is behind the previously closed doors to truly understanding how victims suffer? What are the secrets of trauma?*

Difficulties in Research

The difficulties in research regarding the trauma suffered by sexual victims is profound. First, statistics would suggest that one-quarter of our children will be sexually abused before age eighteen. Abuse occurs at different ages, at different times, and in different families, with different sexual behavior, and different frequency. Children cannot be damaged the same.

It is not unusual for therapists involved in this field to see four children sexually abused in the same family, in the same community, by the same offender, with the same sexual behavior. It is also not uncommon for these same four children to manifest completely different symptoms and responses to similar sexual abuse situations. It is not unusual for these four children to rehabilitate or recover at different rates even with the same therapeutic intervention.

Three sexual victims, James, Sara, and Tiffany, were all subjected to anal intercourse and fondling. The children were close in age, with a range being between age seven and eight and one-half years. The same offender committed the crimes and used the same basic level of violence. Symptoms of these three children ranged from one child making suicidal attempts by setting her bed on fire, to another child testifying in an informal juvenile hearing as a character witness for the sexual offender.

Sara said, *He was the best Latch-Key teacher we had. I liked him and he isn't mad for us telling. I told the judge he was nice after the lawyer man asked me to.*

James said, *I think I was usually asleep when this happened. I don't remember.*

Tiffany said, *I set my bed on fire because I wanted to visit God.*

How can this happen? How can Sara be supportive of a perpetrator who betrayed her trust and used her for his own pleasure? How can James try to retreat to safety by dissociating while Tiffany tries to take her own life? How can three children with so many similarities emerge so different? How can we begin to methodically undo the secrets of trauma?

Just perhaps, rather than looking at the sexually abusive scenario, the offender, or the sexual behavior, sexual victims could be categorized according to their symptomatology or their complaints. The question emerges, *If categorization or degrees of trauma could be made, would certain similarities among victims emerge to teach about trauma?* In order to understand trauma, it would seem appropriate to evaluate traumatic effects and then examine etiology of the damage.

Research Sample

The total sample for this research, compiled for over 15 years, included 543 victims involved with the author . The majority of these victims were connected through the Malheur County Incest Treatment Program as described in Chapter Three. A great deal of collateral information was obtained regarding trauma as offenders and non-abused family members attempted to describe trauma and relate important information regarding victim suffering. Often, the victim in the sample provided information, but additional supporting information was also obtained for research. Most specifically however, 282 adult or married adolescents were evaluated to provide a numerical or statistical basis for research.

In the original sample, 529 victims were categorized into age groups with the following age delineations:

Sexual Victim Trauma Assessment Data

Adults	268	Age 18 and Older
Adolescents	129	Age 13 through 18
Preteens	84	Age 7 through 12
Preschool	48	Age 6 and Under

As the publication worked toward completion, fourteen additional adults were included in the sample. Fourteen adults who were determined to be *asymptomatic* eventually were added to the sample of MINIMAL TRAUMA category. These adults were not part of the original sample of patients who were automatically *symptomatic* due to the research taking place within a mental health facility. These adults represent groups of individuals who will not traditionally be part of research on trauma since they are not presenting symptoms of trauma.

Also, part of the original intent of the research included efforts to examine children like Sara, Tiffany, and James and to attempt to understand why traumatic responses ranged from suicide to being apparently *asymptomatic*. Efforts were made to combine seven-year-olds with 70-year-olds in order to understand the trauma suffered. First attempts were mind boggling. Those adult patients often described being asymptomatic through many stages of development. In other words, it became clear that many younger children were at one time asymptomatic, yet later showed tremendous trauma as adults even though sexual abuse did not always continue. How could Sara be compared to Sara's mother in the same sample since Sara's mother, as a child, was also dedicated to her perpetrator during childhood?

Children do not have the capabilities of understanding the significance of what has happened to them through sexual abuse. Being asymptomatic at seven does not necessarily mean that the same child will be asymptomatic at seventeen or at thirty-seven. Although younger children were obviously part of the *clinical impression* for this research, they were set aside in order to develop a methodology for dividing victims into certain areas or levels of trauma. Children needed to be excluded because they

have not yet crossed through all developmental stages (or hit traumatic **POTHOLES**) which traditionally allow trauma to emerge.

Potholes In The Road To Trauma

There appear to be five generally consistent time frames which seem to signal trauma for victims. These *potholes* in the road to trauma occur in various stages of development and lifetime patterns. These stages seem to allow traumatic experiences to emerge and certainly reflect important information regarding attempts to categorize levels of trauma.

Pothole #1 First Sexual Step

It seems to be common for sexual victims to manifest the first general symptoms of trauma during early pubescence or during the sexually developing years. Puberty seems to be an uncomfortable time with hormones raging and body betrayals being commonplace. At the time when a child's body is changing from childhood to adulthood, the child is also recognizing the significance of sexually inappropriate behavior. It is not uncommon for children in this stage of development to begin to manifest the first signs of crisis or emerging trauma. Very small children who were abused during earlier developmental years often seem to come *to crisis* or react with the first symptoms of abuse during this time period.

Pothole #2 Arousal Reality

The second area of general crisis emerges when the victim attempts to become sexual. In the backseat of the Chevrolet, as a hand seductively begins to fondle the penis or another hand begins to caress a nipple, the *somewhat previously safe* victim may have emerging thoughts of deviant fantasy and repulsiveness. As the victim attempts to attach feelings of arousal with the experience of someone else's touch, the victim is often horrified and humiliated as degrading fantasies enter into the victim's arousal pattern.

For those patients who chose dissociation or amnesia as a *footprint*, this can be particularly difficult since there is no cognitive foundation for these deviant feelings and thoughts. Victims personalize the horror; they believe themselves to be the author of those thoughts. Even for those victims who remember the abuse but chose to detach themselves, the connection between deviant thought and what should be sexual pleasure causes the second crisis to emerge.

Pothole #3 Sanctioned Sex

The third pothole or stumbling in the road to trauma seems to occur as the victim attempts to **sanction sex**, or somehow resolve the mind boggling deviancy.

When I meet the right girl, I will be okay.

When I am married in the church and God blesses my marriage, things will work out.

Sex is kind of nasty and unclean now, but it will really improve when someone really loves me.

Often, the victim believes the deviant feelings and concerning thoughts will subside when somehow the sexual relationship is sanctioned. Unfortunately, it is not uncommon for victims to experience tremendous crisis six to twelve months following the sanctioned sex experience.

Before we were married, sex was great. As soon as we got married, I felt dead.

I just accepted it as being wrong with all the other girls. When I met Phylis, I knew once we were married, it wouldn't be the same. It is and I hate it.

Pothole #4 And Baby Makes Three

The fourth general area of trauma seems to occur when the victim has a child. As will be discussed in Chapter Six, the victim is often in a raging battle between the *adult* and the *neglected child*. When victims have children of their own, many feelings surface. Paranoia toward the protection of a child is one common response from adult victims who have just become a mother or father. Anger toward the child because of the attention from a spouse is another rather *four-year-old*, but common, response. Outrage toward the innocence of the child may be manifested, as well as guilty and humiliating feelings toward the victim's *child within*. Regardless of how the symptoms are manifested, it is often common for victims to stumble in the road to trauma, consistent with the birth of a child, especially the child of the same sex as the victim.

Pothole #5 Age at Onset Crisis

The fifth pothole often occurs when the victim's child turns the age of the victim when the abuse in the victim's childhood took place. Distorted cognitions often forced the child to take on responsibility or guilt regarding the abuse. Often, anger toward the naughty *child within* has been simmering for a lifetime. Conflict often occurs with the adult victim as these feelings surface toward the innocent child, reminding the victim of many uncomfortable experiences and events connected to abuse that occurred long ago. It is as though the child forces the adult victim (parent) to relive many of the affective responses to the childhood abuse.

This is not to suggest that victims become traumatized in these tidy packages of lifetime crisis events. Many other occurrences in a victim's life can cause a return to trauma or upheaval. For the purposes of designing a research model, these commonly observed times of crisis provided an important answer to the dilemma of attempting coordination of small children with adult victims in a research plan.

Quite clearly, children have not traveled through many of the common potholes in the road to trauma. Since children are often asymptomatic, they clearly do not have the developmental capability of understanding what has happened to them and, therefore, do not have the capability of indicating future trauma. Since many of these lifetime crisis points were in the far distant future for many of the victims, a decision was made to limit the research samples to adults or *married with children* adolescents. In this way, nearly all the victims have had an opportunity to proceed through many of the points of crisis commonly experienced by victims.

Research Design

Eleven characteristics or evaluators were used to examine trauma to sexual victims. These characteristics were chosen by the author from clinical experience. The purpose of this approach was to place victims in specific categories of trauma so that similarities and differences could emerge and teach about the mysteries of suffering. These eleven characteristics were used to categorize adult victims into four basic levels of damage. These four categories can be described as:

Trauma Categories

- Primary Severe Trauma
- Secondary Severe Trauma
- Moderate Trauma
- Minimal Trauma

Research design required victims to be evaluated according to severity of trauma and then placed in these four categories by a numerical rating. Once victims were categorized according to similar levels of trauma, perhaps questions could be answered.

Caution — Road Work Ahead

These eleven characteristics are subdivided into three areas. These characteristics used to evaluate sexual victims should be used with caution:

RELATIONSHIP DYSFUNCTIONS,

PSYCHOLOGICAL DYSFUNCTIONS,

LIVING SKILL DYSFUNCTIONS.

These functioning levels of victims were examined to determine how severely or minimally traumatized victims seemed to be. These characteristics report nothing about how the victim came to suffer. These characteristics only place victims in four categories to further understand the etiology of the victims' trauma.

Another area of caution needs to be exerted whenever *categorization* of human beings, especially victims, occurs. This research design attempted to have general characteristics applied in order to study differences and similarities. A counterproductive result of this categorization would occur if victims tended to rate themselves in order to deny their pain, if this structure was applied to determine valid from invalid claims, or if this research design was used to make decisions regarding the culpability of offenders. *Labeling* is always a dangerous proposition especially for those who have already experienced trauma through insensitivity from others.

A further breakdown of the eleven evaluators is indicated within the three general dysfunction categorizations.

RELATIONSHIP DYSFUNCTION CATEGORIZATION

1. INTERPERSONAL RELATIONSHIP INVOLVEMENTS
   Numerical

2. INTERPERSONAL ADJUSTMENTS IN RELATIONSHIPS
   Quality

3. CHILD INTERPERSONAL RELATIONSHIP DIFFICULTIES
   As a Parent

4. SEXUAL RELATIONSHIP DYSFUNCTION
   As A Partner

PSYCHOLOGICAL DYSFUNCTION CATEGORIZATION

5. MENTAL HEALTH INVOLVEMENT
6. MENTAL HEALTH DIAGNOSIS

LIVING SKILL DYSFUNCTION CATEGORIZATION

7. CRIMINAL BEHAVIOR
8. SUBSTANCE ABUSE
9. VOCATIONAL/ACADEMIC PROBLEMS
10. ANGER MISMANAGEMENT
11. SELF-ABUSIVE BEHAVIORS

Within each of these categories, numbers were given to victims according to their demonstrated symptoms. A rating of "3" generally indicated a PRIMARY SEVERE or the highest rating. A "2" indicated a SECONDARY SEVERE rating, while a "1" indicated a rating of MODERATE. The total number given to a patient who may be manifesting symptoms in several categories, provided information as to which category the victim would be placed. In order to be categorized in the PRIMARY group, the victim would have had to earn a rating accumulative of over 50% (or half) of the ratings within the PRIMARY SEVERE group. In other words, a score of "3" would have been given to the victim at least six times in the PRIMARY SEVERE group.

Rating Scale Breakdown

PRIMARY SEVERE   33-28

SECONDARY SEVERE   27-14

MODERATE   13-0

MINIMAL   0

Scores ranging from 33 to 28 were given to the PRIMARY SEVERE group. Although these patents were required to score only six times within the PRIMARY SEVERE (#3) rating, all other ratings were required to be in the SECONDARY SEVERE rating of (#2). Scores ranging from 27 to 14 were given to the SECONDARY SEVERE group and those patients scoring 13 or below were rated in the MODERATE group.

SECONDARY SEVERE patients were certainly struggling with trauma, but at a lower level. The purpose of this research was to identify minimums and maximums; therefore with the PRIMARY SEVERE category numerically established, as well as the *asymptomatic* group established with a zero score, the remaining scores were divided equally.

The eleven characteristics were applied to each patient under the following criteria:

RELATIONSHIP DYSFUNCTION CATEGORIZATION

Category #1

INTERPERSONAL RELATIONSHIP INVOLVEMENTS

Numerical

Primary Severe Rating #3
Four or more marriages or living as spouse (LAS) relationships or sixty partners post age 16, or reports never establishing nor ever desiring to establish a single relationship.

Secondary Severe Rating #2
Three marriages or living as spouse (LAS) relationships, or estimates 25 sexual partners post age 16, or reports attempting less than two relationships.

Moderate Rating #1
Reports dissatisfaction with the number of established relationships or has been unable to establish a relationship, but continues to put forth effort at relationships.

Explanation

Each of the 282 patients were examined within the Relationship Perspective. The numerical approach attempted to examine trauma to victims according to the number of relationships established. It was decided that those patients who either had an extremely high number of relationships would seem to be having difficulty establishing intimacy while, at the same time, a patient who had never been able to establish a single relationship was also suffering. The rating attempted to look at extremes in order to give the patient a rating of primary severe or lesser levels of trauma. It is important to note that this rating was simply a numerical observation and did not deal directly with the quality of the relationship.

*RATING CATEGORIES — Relationship Quality Indicators

A. Domestic Violence as a Victim or Partner

B. Symbiosis with Family Member of Childhood

C. Alienation or Rejection from Family of Childhood

D. Extra-Marital Relationships for Self or Partner

E. Excessive Verbal Conflict with Partner

Category #2
_____

INTERPERSONAL ADJUSTMENTS IN RELATIONSHIPS

Quality

Primary Severe Rating #3

Three or more diagnoses* of relationship quality indicators.

Secondary Severe Rating #2

Two or more diagnoses* of relationship quality indicators.

Moderate Trauma Rating #1

Reports at least one diagnoses* of relationship quality indicators.

Explanation

This categorization attempted to examine the quality of relationships for patients. The marital or LAS relationship was the focus of examination or the patient chose the *most significant* relationship. Five factors were chosen, which seem to indicate problems in relationships. The ratings between PRIMARY SEVERE, SECONDARY SEVERE, and MODERATE were simply the number of problems sighted in these relationships by the patient. Those relationship issues, such as substance abuse, problems relating to child abuse, and anger mismanagement, would be included in other categorizations and were not part of the rating list. These five issues appeared to be reasonably accurate measures of how the patient functioned in relationships with others.

Category #3

CHILD INTERPERSONAL RELATIONSHIP DIFFICULTIES

As a Parent

Primary Severe Rating #3
Involved in legal or child protection system due to abuse of children.

Secondary Severe Rating #2
Admits to behavior which, if known, would have required intervention from child protection system.

Moderate Rating #1
Admits to fears or fantasy regarding child abuse, or behavior of patient is diagnosed that patient should be involved with child protection under *protective* or *preventative* intervention.

Explanation
In examining relationship dysfunction for the patient as a parent, the issue of child abuse emerges. A deadly symptom for adult victims seems to be continuing the cycle of abuse for their own children. This rating carefully considered, however, only the patient's involvement with children and did *not* account for the abuse by others to the child. This category is designed to discuss the patient's inability to parent or care for children. In cases where someone else abused the patient's child, but the patient was unable to respond appropriately, those factors will be documented elsewhere in the research design.

Category #4

SEXUAL RELATIONSHIP DYSFUNCTION

Primary Severe Rating #3
Patient reports being completely sexually dysfunctional — desires to be asexual, refuses treatment.

Secondary Severe #2
Dissatisfied with sexual relationships and is currently dysfunctional, but remains interested in change.

Moderate Rating #1
Two or more phobic reactions to sexual encounters or reports of general dissatisfaction with sexual relationship, but reports being sexually functional.

Explanation
The sexual dysfunction rating was designed to determine those patients who were extremely dysfunctional and had no desire to continue working on the sexual issues as compared to patients who at least desired appropriate intimate relationships. Those receiving a PRIMARY SEVERE rating were currently dysfunctional and had no desire to change as compared with the other patients who may have been dysfunctional, but desired change or were only dysfunctional in certain areas of sexuality.

PSYCHOLOGICAL DYSFUNCTION CATEGORIZATION

Category #5

MENTAL HEALTH INVOLVEMENT

Primary Severe Rating #3
Has received inpatient treatment for a mental health problem.

Secondary Severe Rating #2
Has received outpatient treatment.

Moderately Traumatized Rating #1
Contemplated treatment or desired treatment, but mental health intervention did not occur.

Explanation
This rating within the psychological perspective simply attempted to categorize victims according to their mental health involvement. This rating determined those patients who had received inpatient or institutionalized care as compared to those patients who seemed to be struggling on their own or had not come to the attention of professionals for the purpose of hospitalization. This categorization examined those patients who seemed able to function well enough to avoid institutionalization

Category #6

MENTAL HEALTH DIAGNOSIS

Primary Severe Rating #3
Has been diagnosed from DSM III classification list in at least two categories.*

Secondary Severe Rating #2
Has received at least one diagnosis from the DSM III classification* or could have been diagnosed in at least two areas of categorization from classification list.

Moderating Rating #1
Has never been diagnosed within DSM III classification list*, but history suggested diagnosis would have been possible.

*DSM III Classification List

- Schizophrenia
- Delusional (Paranoid Disorders)
- Psychotic Disorders
- Mood Disorders
- Anxiety Disorders
- Somatoform Disorder
- Dissociative Disorders
- Factitious Disorders
- Impulse Control Disorders
- Adjustment Disorders
- Personality Disorders
- Eating Disorders

The DSM III was used to delineate those patients who were, or should have been, diagnosed under the broad range of categories listed. The purpose for this categorization was to use the diagnosis of psychiatrists and psychologists as an indicator of trauma, but also to recognize that the *potential* for diagnosis was also significant. Many patients needed to be diagnosed and receive treatment, yet were not diagnosed primarily due to their ability to function in some way, avoiding mental health commitments or institutionalizations. This rating delineated between the PRIMARY SEVERE and the SECONDARY SEVERE groups, on the consideration that if patients were able to escape being officially diagnosed, they more than likely were somewhat more functional than patients who could not escape. Care should be made to recognize that the DSM III classification was not available for many adult patients in the past and, therefore, reasonable compensations were made.

LIVING SKILL DYSFUNCTION CATEGORIZATION

Category #7

CRIMINAL BEHAVIOR

Primary Severe Rating #3
Have been involved with legal system through a conviction of a crime or three or more official arrests. (Traffic misdemeanors not included).

Secondary Severe Rating #2
Have been involved with legal system informally but without arrest or conviction.

Moderate #1
No convictions, arrests or direct involvement with legal system, but describes behavior that would have resulted in either a conviction or arrest.

Explanation
For categorization within the Living Skill Dysfunction area of *criminal behavior*, the PRIMARY SEVERE patient was required to demonstrate involvement in criminal activity to

the point of being charged with a crime or being chronically arrested. Varying degrees of involvement with the legal system or in the description of behavior that *would* have involved the legal system indicated lower rating. Being unable to avoid criminal involvement was viewed as an example of Living Skill Dysfunction.

Category #8

SUBSTANCE ABUSE

Primary Severe #3
Received inpatient treatment for substance abuse problems.

Secondary Severe #2
Received outpatient treatment for substance abuse problems.

Moderate #1
Reports out of control behavior with substance abuse, but has not sought treatment.

Explanation
Substance abuse problems were simply categorized according to severity through outpatient or inpatient involvement. Those patients who needed to be institutionalized for substance abuse problems would appear to be more traumatized or having more serious problems, as compared to those patients involved in an outpatient program. Some patients should have been involved in an outpatient program, but due to family issues may have avoided that involvement. Some compensation was made for this numerical rating, especially in cases where the patient received medical care

for the residual effects of alcoholism, but the issue of substance abuse was not the primary diagnosis. As an example, if the patient was hospitalized for anemia or injuries resulting from an alcohol related accident, the patient was, in fact, *institutionalized* or involved in inpatient care due to substance abuse problems.

Category #9

VOCATIONAL OR ACADEMIC DIFFICULTIES

Primary Severe Rating #3
School phobia and termination of academic pursuits previous to high school graduation, (described as due to trauma, not other factors), or received vocational disability or could have received vocational disability as an adult due to factors other than physical reasons (these patients were unable to continue attempting academic or vocational pursuits).

Secondary Severe #2
Chronic failure in either vocational or academic pursuits, but patient continues attempting these endeavors.

Moderate #1
Reports dissatisfaction with vocational or academic pursuits.

Explanation
Vocational or academic difficulties were examined in order to determine trauma in failure to fulfill goals. If the patient had not been able to continue an educational program or had

received a disability from vocational interests, they received a PRIMARY SEVERE rating. It is important to note that these patients were unable to continue *attempting* involvement in vocational academic pursuits. Quite different were those patients from the SECONDARY SEVERE category who were experiencing chronic failures, but continued making attempts at academic and vocational efforts. If patients had no interest in academic/vocational pursuits and did not appear to be dissatisfied, no ratings were noted.

Category #10

ANGER MISMANAGEMENT

Primary Severe Rating #3
Level of anger causes injury to self or others, and either mental health intervention or criminal intervention is required.

Secondary Severe Rating #2
Reports out of control rages causing losses and immobility to victim within living skill areas (absence of injury or mental health/criminal involvement as a result of anger mismanagement).

Moderate #1
Reports uncontrollable feelings of outrage with residual effects causing discomfort, but not actual immobility or losses with living skill arena.

Explanation
The Anger Mismanagement category attempted to examine those patients who seemed out of control through anger and who had caused

physical injury to self or others. In order to be given a PRIMARY SEVERE rating, the patient had to have caused injury to themselves or others due to anger, which resulted in either a mental health or criminal response. In other words, the anger was so out of control that attention of others occurred. In order to be rated in the SECONDARY SEVERE category, the patient reported out of control rages causing losses or immobility within the living skill dysfunction area, but there was a clear absence of injury or notations being made to authorities due to these behaviors. Losses to the victim included failure in relationships, losing jobs, or damage to victim's property. In other words, in the SECONDARY SEVERE rating, the victim was the recipient of the traumatic effects of anger mismanagement rather than as in the PRIMARY SEVERE category where children, partners, fellow workers, etc., were the recipients of the victim's outrage. MODERATE rating indicated patient discomfort with thoughts or tendencies causing extreme stress, but patient maintains control.

Category #11
_____

SELF-ABUSIVE BEHAVIOR

Primary Severe #3
Two or more suicidal attempts or significant self-mutilating behavior causing injury and/or mental health intervention.

Secondary Severe #2
One or more suicide attempts or self-mutilating behavior without mental health intervention.

Moderate Rating #1
Suicidal ideations or threats, but no significant attempts or mental health involvement.

Self-abusive behaviors generally encompassed such behaviors as self-mutilation and suicidal attempts. Patients were categorized according to actual attempts and actual injury to themselves with mental health intervention, delineating from those patients who had suicidal or self-mutilation ideations, but did not follow through. It should be recognized that many self-abusive behaviors occur for sexual victims beyond suicide attempts. The research design, however, accounted for other behaviors in different categories.

Again, Caution

A caution should again be raised regarding the research design. The first question should be, *What was the purpose of categorizing 282 adult victims?* The answer to the question is to develop a mechanism for organizing victims into similar levels of pain. The purpose of attempting to categorize these victims was to teach, to learn, and hopefully to find similarities and differences so that trauma can be better understood. It is very important to recognize that these categories are very *general* items described by professionals as likely to be areas of evidenced trauma.

Certainly, the categories are arbitrary as chosen by the author. Obviously, some categories would be weighted more than others for some patients. If a patient, as an example, is making suicide attempts on a regular basis, that symptom alone should be enough to place the patient in the SEVERELY TRAUMATIZED group. Diagnosis within the DSM III classification quite clearly indicates that some categories are more severe than others and causing greater risk to either the patient or those concerned about the patient.

Additionally, some factors are designed so that a single incident or activity could give the patient several ratings in the SEVERE group. As an example, if a woman caused physical injury to her child, she could be rated in the PRIMARY SEVERE category of relationship dysfunction *as a parent* and *anger mismanagement,* since she caused injury and because she was involved in the mental health system. She could also find herself in the PRIMARY SEVERE category for *criminal behavior* since she received a felony conviction for assault. Finally, if she was consuming alcohol during the commission of the crime, she may have required institutionalization or inpatient care for the same crime, giving her another severe rating. In summary, this 11 point rating system was designed simply to separate victims into categories or groups in order for further examination to take place.

A Word About Numbers

Unfortunately, responses from sexual victims are often a discounting, a minimization, or a rationalization of trauma. Much the same as offenders, victims commonly have heavily entrenched denial systems. Careful attention to the numerical rating of this system is required. Sexual victims are often enmeshed in intense dysfunction, yet hoping to cope, rationalize, or deny by viewing themselves in a better light. Different from other psychiatric patients who may be more clear in self diagnosis, the sexual victim patient seems intent on compensating, coping, and denying.

This pattern of rationalization, minimization, or denial comes from childhood coping mechanisms. It is common for five-year-old sexual victims to rearrange or re-evaluate what has happened in order to survive. In examining the sexual victim patient in this research, it became apparent that not only were victims verbally willing to discount their own problems, but the semantic categorizations became extremely important.

In the early years of this author's attempt to categorize trauma, victims who were not in the category of SEVERELY TRAUMATIZED would refuse treatment or typically discount their pain. Labeling of the categories emerged as extremely important in the rehabilitation of victims. Cognitive distortions pervade the sexual victim patient. It was not uncommon for a sexual victim to be extremely symptomatic, but still walking, breathing, and moving about. The rationalization of sexual victims concerning *proper* categorization provided delays in rehabilitation.

The Race Is On

For this reason, the MODERATELY TRAUMATIZED patients were placed between MINIMALLY TRAUMATIZED and SECONDARY SEVERELY TRAUMATIZED. Actually, it would seem entirely inappropriate to suggest that children were not traumatized by sexual abuse which may be numerically represented in the MINIMAL group. The MINIMALLY TRAUMATIZED victims had very few, if any, numerical ratings and seemed entirely asymptomatic. It would be difficult and dangerous to argue that a sexually abusive situation would be entirely insignificant. It is important to realize that most victims of sexual abuse were traumatized. Great fear from victim's interpretation of this study is experienced by those who authored the publication. It is important not to suggest that children can be sexually abused without trauma. That suggestion would ease the responsibility for offenders and could compound the problem.

Survival of the . . .?

Are there people who survive sexual abuse with minimal pain? The answer is yes. Those people will generally not be represented in research and typically will not find themselves in mental health centers. The MINIMALLY TRAUMATIZED patients in this research did not manifest symptoms any more than perhaps other adults who are asymptomatic because of a broken leg as a result of being bucked off a horse in the fifth grade. The lack of symptoms for these patients should *not* suggest offenders

do not commit serious crimes, nor should these categorization efforts encourage victims to discount or deny their pain.

The PRIMARY SEVERELY traumatized patients in this category would be nearly dysfunctional. The word SEVERE is indeed severe. Those victims in the SECONDARY SEVERE and the MODERATELY traumatized groups have many difficulties and should recognize their symptoms as being profound, yet workable. This numerical rating was designed to research and should not be a screening device to accept or reject patients for treatment.

It is also important to note that many patients involved in this study may be partially *asymptomatic* in relation to their own abuse or they may be unaware of the depths of trauma that could occur. It is not uncommon for sexual victims to disconnect themselves from trauma and then a *trigger* occurs and traumatic experiences are rekindled. The birth of a baby, the death of a perpetrator, menopause, or the onset of sexual development for a victim's child are all commonly known triggers of stress. Many victims in this study may not be experiencing *all* symptoms that have the potential to be devastating at an unpredictable time in the future.

Again, this numerical rating was not mystical or profound. It was not developed to be absolute or to describe a constant picture of trauma. This numerical rating was designed to assist those who are interested in understanding how victims are traumatized for the purposes of preventing trauma, stopping the cycle of trauma, and planning better treatment.

Numerical Breakdown

From 282 adult or married adolescents with children, the following breakdown occurred in classification:

PRIMARY SEVERE	45
SECONDARY SEVERE	143
MODERATE	69
MINIMAL	25
Male Patients	58
Female	224
Average Age of Victim	33

No Known Sex Offenders in this Sample.

It should be noted that only 24 married adolescents were considered in this study and each adolescent had at least one child. Although some of these adolescents were already manifesting symptoms, it should be recognized that the likelihood of further response to post-traumatic stress may be possible for these individuals.

THE BIG FOUR — Where Are You?

Before examining these categories of victims to search for similarities and differences, it is important to return to the legal system's matrix and to the most commonly held ideas about trauma and examine the potential for correlation. *Violence, penetration, age and frequency* have been demonstrated to be the most commonly held ideas for trauma — how did these issues correlate within the four categories of trauma?

Once victims were placed in categories relating to SEVERE, MODERATE, and MINIMAL trauma, examination occurred regarding those four characteristics that seemed to be blindly guiding therapeutic approaches to trauma. Criteria were established regarding the definitions of those powerful terms and then application was made to each category.

Violence

Before examining the correlation of violence, the definition of violence needs clarity. Violence seems to cause a great deal of concern, yet there seems to be a great deal of discrepancy regarding the actual term *violence*.

Was the child who was forced to watch her cat being raped and then die involved in a *violent* scenario? Her actual contact with the perpetrator was soft, sensuous, and *just fondling*. Was the child who was forced to be tied in contorted body positions with leather straps and dog leashes involved in a *violent* abusive scenario? Bruises, black eyes, and knives make for easy definition, but the boundary regarding violence is not always clear.

For this study, violence was defined as *the use of a weapon, excessive physical force*, or *behaviors that caused injury*. Additionally, violence was applied to the victim and to the specific sexually abusive scenario. There were many times when violence, under the research definition, was a peripheral issue but not directly part of the sexual abuse *scene*.

Kristy's father was a violent man and he ruled the household with physical force. It was not uncommon for Kristy's father to administer beatings to all five children when one child needed punishment. During Kristy's sexual abuses, her father was quiet and cold, but never forceful. The pervading flavor of violence in the family kept Kristy from being resistive, yet she denied any form of force or violence during the sexual abuse. Kristy's abuse was not categorized within the violent group.

		Violence Correlation
Category I N = 45	Primary Severe	14 (31%)
Category II N = 143	Secondary Severe	52 (36%)
Category III N = 69	Moderate	21 (30%)
Category IV N = 25	Minimal	4 (16%)

What appeared evident was that violence oc-curred in all categories, even in the minimally traumatized group which reported to be *asymptomatic*. A rape victim is included in the 25 minimally traumatized patients. The rape victim was hospitalized with injuries. It would seem that other factors allowed this rape victim to survive and it is those factors (as will be discussed later) that determined why the victim was minimally traumatized.

Lillian was sexually abused by her brothers. Her sister was also involved in these extremely violent scenarios. The two small girls were forced to disrobe and submit to penetration of their vaginas and anus by a variety of objects, including sticks, rocks, and penises. Bleeding often occurred. Lillian's screams were drowned out by the pillow forced over her head. Lillian's sister's screams were not heard except by Lillian. Lillian finds herself in the moderately traumatized group. Lillian has survived! Certain issues which will be explained later reveal that the precognitions for Lillian during the abuse allowed the violence to be an unimportant factor. In Lillian's case, however, violence is an important factor for looking at the perpetrator.

Lillian's offenders were indeed extremely dangerous and violent. The fact that they could maintain arousal during these violent scenarios is indicative of the seriousness of their crimes. These young men were building their arousal patterns around violence and quite clearly they seemed to prefer the violent scenarios with Lillian and her sister over intimate and consenting scenarios with peers. The issue of violence, however, seemed to have a counterproductive effect for Lillian. In fact, it may have been the issue of violence that allowed Lillian to see herself more clearly as a victim than other children who experienced different sexually abusive scenarios.

The screaming of my sister can still be heard in my ears. I knew this was not okay to be happening, yet she was little and I was little. As I laid there and felt the pain, I knew it would be over and I knew I would be able to help her as soon as he was finished. I hated him and I hated his friends. I only loved my sister who didn't understand. I hated everything about him. It was so clear. When it was over I would wash my sister and I felt so good. She loved me and we had each other. Afterwards were the only nice times in my childhood. Once I found out she had let the neighbor touch her and that she liked it! I was so mad. She cheated me out of helping her.

Another case of extreme violence connected with sexual abuse may have profound effects on a victim yet careful examination may cause questions to be raised about the kind of violence involved.

Ryan's father was an extremely explosive person. It was not uncommon for Ryan to be thrown to the floor and *wrestled or managed* in a violent way. Some of these episodes were in the form of play, which usually resulted in bruising and pain. Ryan's father seemed to enjoy forcing the children into physical restraints and forcing them to verbally *give in*.

Often, Ryan's father would force the children into crying, making statements of love, or into admitting they were wrong. Everything about Ryan's father's disciplinary action was violent, but the sexual activities were always under the guise of either play or wrestling. It should also be noted that Ryan's father never touched the children except during these very explosive scenarios. The only kind of human contact or physical touching from Ryan's father came in the form of the altercations.

The abusive scenes began when Ryan was young and not knowledgeable about sexual arousal. By the time Ryan was in a prepubescent stage of development, he became aware that his father's pelvic thrusts during these scenes were for the purpose of arousal. By this time, Ryan noticed his own arousal. Ryan had made a deadly combination of violence, arousal, and affection because of his abuse. Never being touched by his father except in these horribly violent, yet arousing, situations caused profound trauma to Ryan. The fusion of violence and sex has caused ongoing psychiatric problems for Ryan's entire life. It is important to remember that Ryan's bare skin was never touched.

Terror or Violence?

Finally, delineation between the term *violence* and *terror* must be made. The kind of violence that emerged in an overwhelming number of severe trauma cases involved *terror building* activity. This issue will be discussed further in Chapter Five. For understanding the lack of correlation of violence, however, it is important to briefly explain the difference between terror and violence. When there was a prolonged period of terror or degrading activity that required the child to wait for upcoming victimization, this seemed to be particularly important.

Pamela's father began sexually abusing her in the preschool period. The family-owned grocery store provided the place where Pamela spent her preschool period, being cared for by her father while Pamela's mother worked outside the home. From approximately age three to age six, Pamela lived a nightmare of sexual abuse in the grocery store. Obviously, Pamela welcomed the first grade as she was removed from the abusive situation during part of the day. Once Pamela

became involved in an academic program, her access to her father was limited. Thus began the ritual of *terror building* activities, which seemed to be the focus of Pamela's trauma for many years.

Pamela reports feeling terror with the ritualistic behavior of her mother making sure all of the children kissed their father *good-bye* in the morning before going to school. Pamela was the youngest child of four. In the busy kitchen, all four children would say good-bye to their father and kiss him as they left with their mother for school. Often, Pamela's father would announce that she needed to take the bus to the grocery store after school rather than coming home because she was needed there for her chores. *It's your work day* was the terrorizing statement made to Pamela, which signalled what she must endure later in the day.

On these days, Pamela spent the day thinking about the after-school activities of abuse. The sexual behaviors themselves were degrading and uncomfortable, but not violent. Pamela's father actually seemed to be quite interested in Pamela's physiological responses. Pamela describes, however, feeling terrorized all during the day as she attempted to participate in school. Pamela finds herself in the SEVERELY TRAUMATIZED category. She views the most devastating and damaging behaviors for her as not occurring during the sexual abuse scenario, but in waiting for the abuse to occur.

Another important aspect in considering the issue of violence seemed to be in peripheral issues or events that contained a *spirit* of violence.

Shawna is sexually abused by her mother's boyfriend. This individual is a trapper and also a very clever sex offender. Shawna's molester forced her to accompany him on his rounds, checking the trap lines. Shawna can never remember any verbal correlation being made between the animals dying in traps and what would or might happen to her if she did not cooperate with sexual abuse. Shawna is a SEVERELY TRAUMATIZED patient who made the connection on her own in regards to violence. If only the behavior of the perpetrator toward the victim is examined, this would be absolutely a nonviolent situation, as would the case with Pamela. Unfortunately, this victim's perceptions of bleeding, hysterical, shrieking animals, and her own potential for being treated the same if she resisted, formed violent cognitions in her own mind. Was that the offender's intention? It is difficult to determine whether the behavior was purposeful or not. The message to Shawna, however, was quite clear.

Penetration

It could be said that this nation is *big on penises!* With respect to male genitalia, it is sadly clear that mystical properties are often applied to penises in society's general attitude. Penetration by a penis is often a very profound issue and vaginas even seem to change magically with things going in or out of them. Does the issue of penetration correlate with trauma? The legal system said *yes*; professionals surveyed said *yes*; the data says *no*.

The issue of penetration does not appear to correlate with more severe trauma. However, sociological and psychological aspects concerning the issue of penetration seem to have a more profound effect on trauma. The world seems to be obsessed with the issue of penetration. A centimeter of penile penetration in many states is a much more serious crime than exposing a child to pornography, performing cunnilingus on the child, or engaging in a wide variety of extremely bizarre behaviors.

		Penetration Factor
Category I N-45	Primary Severe	19 (42%)
Category II N-143	Secondary Severe	61 (42%)
Category III N-69	Moderate	17 (24%)
Category IV N-25	Minimal	6 (24%)

As an example, the adolescent female who has made a decision to be sexually active may eagerly share her sexual escapades with her friends at the Friday night slumber party. Data shows that the issue of penetration is involved in the first experience of intercourse for many adolescents before high school graduation. The question can be raised about whether the girl who has had intercourse with her father speaks about her sexual escapades with the same excitement at the same slumber party. Obviously, she doesn't and why? Penetration occurred in both vaginas, yet one adolescent can't wait to tell and the other may wait in a lifetime of secrecy.

What seems to be clear is that the act of intercourse or the issue of penetration did not seem to have a factor in determining severe trauma to victims, since only 42% in both severe categories involved penetration and slightly more than half (58%) had no penetration. It appears that the perceptions of intercourse at a later time may have an effect.

A severely traumatized patient presents herself for support therapy relating to a current crisis. Linda was seen by the same therapist eight years previous, as a result of sexual abuse she had endured by her natural father between age eight and eleven.

At age 16, Linda is forced to testify in a custody hearing against her father who is attempting to gain custody of Linda's nine-year-old sister. It is at this time when Linda's previous sexual abuse is revealed. Linda testified and was encouraged to receive therapy,

which she did for a short period of time. Linda reported that she felt as though she was not traumatized by the abuse and terminated her therapeutic involvement after three months.

Eight years later Linda contacts the same therapist seeking assistance in *surviving* her wedding reception. Linda belongs to the Church of Jesus Christ of Latter-Day Saints (Mormon) and has strong religious convictions. Linda chooses to be married in the Mormon Temple and to proceed through her wedding reception in a traditional style. Linda has a suicide plan for the time period following the reception. Calmly, Linda explains that she cannot bear the thought of her fiance knowing she is not a *virgin*. Linda's father is a Bishop in the church and his power keeps Linda from reporting the abuse to her fiance. Linda is seeking therapeutic intervention simply to help her *survive* her wedding and subsequent death.

Is Linda's perception of her trauma in actuality the trauma she is suffering? How powerful is the penetrated vagina? There were years in Linda's life where she did not believe she was traumatized by what her father had done. Now, however, Linda views herself as *damaged goods* following her commitment to marry a young man. Could it be said, then, that only LDS or Mormon girls will be traumatized by intercourse? What about girls who don't attend Sunday School? Is this an anatomical, sociological, or psychological issue?

A common response for men whose partners have been raped is impotence. What are the underlying causes for a man's response to a vagina that has now been penetrated by another penis? The vagina is certainly the same in all physical aspects. The frustrated husband's penis is certainly the same, yet his psychological perceptions and response concerning the meaning of penetration seem to be particularly traumatizing. Would it be fair to say, then, that if a woman is raped and does not have a husband, she is not, traumatized?

Obviously, some of these propositions are absurd. The issue of penetration seemed to have nothing to do with the physical contact between an object and the orifice of a child. What seems to be blatantly clear is that the perceptions or the meaning of penetration either for the victim or for those who are significant to the victim has the most profound effect on trauma. Sexual behaviors during sexual abuse seem to be less important than how the victim perceives those behaviors in the future.

There does appear to be a sexual behavior that correlated significantly with trauma. For the purpose of summary, it is not behavior of the perpetrator that seems to be a significant factor, at least concerning penetration. As will be discussed in the next chapter, the sexual behavior of the perpetrator seems much less significant than the sexual behaviors of the *victim*.

Laura presents herself to the Mental Health Clinic for the problem of *blushing*. Many other psychiatric problems for Laura are discovered in the intake process during the next four sessions. Finally, Laura reports that she was sexually abused by her father from age nine to eleven. Laura's therapist unfortunately states, *Oh, that must have been awful!* A year later and following a great deal of therapy, Laura teaches the therapist her error. In fact, Laura stated, *it was not awful at all. That's the bad part. I really liked it.*

Laura describes a scene where she is lying on the couch watching television. Her father enters the room and lies next to her under a blanket. Typically, Laura's father was gruff, unaffectionate, and cold. Now, her father cuddled Laura close, with warmth and tenderness, underneath the blanket.

Soon, Laura's father's hands begin to caress her body. Not only does Laura enjoy the touching which is soft, gentle, and affectionate, but in comparison to other times, her father's tenderness is exciting and treasured. Finally, Laura describes a warm feeling reaching a crescendo and traveling all over her body. Laura also feels the intensity and pleasure from her father's touching.

When the scenario ends, Laura feels drained, but pleasured and content.

As months go by and Laura proceeds through her sexual development, this behavior is repeated occasionally. It was not until the sexual abuse had discontinued and Laura was much older that she realized she had experienced her first orgasm during her abuse. Laura spent the remainder of her sexual development being embarrassed, degraded, and shameful, not about what her father had done, but about *what I did*.

The case of Laura demonstrates that if the sexual behavior of the perpetrator (especially considering penetration) is evaluated, Laura should not necessarily be traumatized. Actually, in Laura's mind, her father seems to be *selfless* as he gave pleasure to his daughter. It is Laura's later perceptions about *her* involvement and *her* participation that have placed Laura in the SEVERELY TRAUMATIZED category. Laura's subsequent perceptions of her involvement destroyed any opportunity she had for proceeding through sexual development with appreciation of intimacy. Additionally traumatic to Laura is that her father remains the source of her fantasies. Laura's self-abusive behavior in response to her *participation* is one of the reasons Laura seems so traumatized.

Age At Onset Of Abuse

As indicated in Chapter Two, the age at which

children are abused is often viewed as a primary factor in determining trauma. It is believed, without careful consideration, that young children will be traumatized more severely than older children who are sexually abused. The *innocence* of children perhaps may be the focus or etiology for this idea. Or, perhaps this idea is related to the fact that younger children are considered to be precious and more the property of their parents. Perhaps the younger the child, the more serious the crime against the parents who *own the child*.

It seems strange that even though the younger child is viewed as more traumatized, small children are not equally represented in therapy programs. It is very common for parents, caretakers, and even professionals to view a happy four-year-old child who has engaged in intercourse at the day care center as not needing treatment. Additional frustrations occur as small children appear to be asymptomatic as far as using DSM III Diagnostic Codes. From where did we learn that it is more traumatizing to be abused as a young child, yet on the flip side, young children do not need therapy? Does the age itself cause the trauma or is it the neglect following abuse that determines trauma?

The age at which the abuse occurs is represented in a *fruit basket* numerical statistic. Clearly, a large percentage of the SEVERELY TRAUMATIZED patients were sexually abused as young children, yet victims in other categories of less trauma were also sexually abused during the preschool period. What can these numbers tell us?

AGE AT ONSET

	0-8	9-12	13-18
Category I Primary Severe N-45	31 (68%)	11 (24%)	3 (8%)
Category II Secondary Severe N-143	64 (45%)	67 (47%)	12 (8%)
Category III Moderate N-69	18 (26%)	28 (40%)	23 (34%)
Category IV Minimal N-25	9 (36%)	11 (44%)	5 (20%)

The age *at onset* presents a confusing picture. Some children who were MINIMALLY TRAU-MATIZED — in other words, had no present-ing symptoms in adulthood — were abused during the same time period as many patients who were SEVERELY TRAUMATIZED. In comparison, many of these children had the same sexual behaviors also occur. Why then did some of them escape nearly unharmed from sexual abuse that occurred with the same sexual behavior, in the same time period of their development?

The answer to this dilemma will be fully described and explained in later chapters. For the purpose of unleashing therapists from the traditional approaches of understanding trauma, it must be understood that *age at onset* may not be a contributing factor alone.

In examining the numerical representation, it seems clear that for those patients who were SEVERELY TRAUMATIZED, a significant number (68%) were abused under the age of eight. While 36% of the asymptomatic group were abused in the same age category. Was age the issue or were other factors such as develop-ment, memory, future perceptions, etc., the issues relating to trauma?

Certainly, the smallest percentages of age groups were found in the adolescent category. Since gradations of damage are charted, the older child becomes less represented. What seems most important is that the total within each category should be examined rather than the total of N=282. A comparison within each category will be represented in the next chap-ter. For the purposes of this study, age does not seem absolute. It does not automatically determine trauma, especially if specific situa-tions are examined.

Marsha is a 53-year-old woman who is categorized in the SEVERELY TRAU-MATIZED group. Her abuse occurred when she was approximately age four. Marsha was plagued with amnesia until her fiftieth year. For a *half of a century* Marsha had affective responses to her abuse. She had a gagging reflex that was uncontrollable. She had a variety of phobic reactions and suffered from clinical depression. She was institution-alized several times and had chronic relationship problems. Eventually and quite by accident, Marsha came into contact with a therapist who inquired about possible sexual abuse. Marsha's affective response was severe, yet cognitive memory failed her.

After intense therapy and *memory recapturing exercises*, Marsha recalls being orally raped by her Sunday School teacher. Although Marsha was hospitalized as a response to the memory, she nonetheless experienced tremendous relief in recapturing her sexual abuse. With trepidation, Marsha eventually inquired of her mother regarding the possibility that Marsha's memories were accurate. Not only does Marsha's mother confirm the abuse, but she informs Marsha that the assault was so severe that Marsha was hospitalized as a child. The family felt extremely humiliated by the event and eventually removed themselves from the church and relocated.

The reasons why Marsha is placed in the SEVERELY TRAUMATIZED category clearly relates to her self-abusive cycles, her depression, and her symptoms that had an unknown origin. Marsha experienced a wide variety of phobic reactions and affective responses without a clear cognitive etiology. Her life has been in shambles. Is Marsha's trauma clearly related to what took place during the abuse or could some questions be raised about the damage to Marsha proceeding through her lifetime (one-half of a century!) being vulnerable

to feelings of unknown origin? Other victims in the MINIMALLY TRAUMATIZED group (asymptomatic) had experiences similar to Marsha's. They did *not* proceed through sexual development with the same vulnerability. Questions could be raised and clinical impressions suggest that perhaps the age at which the abuse occurs is not the most important issue. Perhaps it is the age at which the victim receives assistance, rehabilitation, and rescue.

Those victims that proceeded through development without assistance, intervention, or rehabilitative efforts were SEVERELY TRAUMATIZED regardless of their age at the time of the abuse. It seems that victims who are left to drown regarding their perceptions of the abuse and society's influence of the abuse will tend to be more traumatized. The age, the sexual behavior, and the issue of violence seem to be less significant in how the child is burdened, carrying the pain through critical years of development.

Frequency Of Abuse

Frequency of sexual abuse is clearly viewed within the professional community as a major factor in determining trauma to sexual victims. *If once is bad, then five is worse.* The superficial numerical presentation of frequency does seem to lean toward the fact that ongoing abuse always seems to be found in the SEVERELY TRAUMATIZED group.

FREQUENCY OF ABUSE

(Number of Incidents)

	1	1-5	5 +
Category I Primary Severe N-45	10 (22%)	8 (18%)	27 (60%)
Category II Secondary Severe N-143	31 (22%)	42 (29%)	70 (49%)
Category III Moderate N-69	22 (32%)	13 (19%)	34 (49%)
Category IV Minimal N-25	10 (40%)	8 (32%)	7 (28%)

It can be seen, however, that approximately 1/4 (10 victims) of those patients in the SEVERELY TRAUMATIZED category had only one incident. Although the majority were ongoing cases of abuse, it seems important at least to examine those factors that allowed a one-time incident to be profoundly traumatic to a patient.

Isolated examples appeared in the research sample where victims had endured years of abuse and appeared to be relatively able to survive, although the percentages seem to be weighted toward more frequency being a traumatizing factor. However, a great deal of information can be learned about those patients who had ongoing abuse and somehow seemed to be able to survive.

Michelle is sexually abused by her father from age 3 to 16. If frequency and the kind of sexual behavior, as well as age, are calculated from traditional responses, Michelle should be in the SEVERELY TRAUMATIZED category. Contrarily, Michelle finds herself in the MODERATELY TRAUMATIZED group and nearly in the MINIMALLY TRAUMATIZED categorization.

Michelle earned a full scholarship to a prestigious college in Washington. She is an athlete and socially competent. Michelle has had positive relationships with males and from all outward appearances, at age 23, Michelle seems to be a talented and accomplished young woman.

It is important to note that in Michelle's therapy, effort was made to determine whether her competencies and accomplishments were of an *obsessive-compulsive* nature. This did not appear to be the case. Michelle seems to respond appropriately to peers, her accomplishments are mixed with accepted failures, and she seems to have realistic expectations of her abilities. How, then, did Michelle survive those abuses that would traditionally place her in the SEVERELY TRAUMATIZED group?

Specific rehabilitating factors in Michelle's case will be reflected in the next chapter. In general, however,

Michelle reports that during her entire abuse (with the exception of ages 3-5), Michelle knew her father was committing a crime and she knew she had no other choice but to cooperate. Michelle's sister was protected (from Michelle's perception) by Michelle's compliance with the abuse. Michelle's mother was chronically depressed, weak, ineffective, and not a positive resource for disclosure or help. Michelle seems to reflect on her perceptions of her abuse as one would describe an additional household chore. Michelle learned quickly that if she cooperated with her father, the household ran smoothly. Michelle was the caretaker of her sister and perhaps of the entire family. According to Michelle, her role in the family as the *caretaker* allowed her to survive as she endured her father's extremely overt and complicated sexual abuse. The identification of her father as the sexual offender was never in doubt. Her tenacity in enduring this experience is obviously reflected in her tenacity to accomplish goals for herself today.

While Marsha has only a few incidents occurring in a very short period of time, Marsha is categorized in the SEVERELY TRAUMATIZED group. Michelle, on the other hand, spent her entire childhood being sexually abused. Perhaps,

a significant difference is in the fact that Marsha proceeded through development with affective responses and no cognitive awareness. Michelle's awareness of the *offender/victim* identity was always clear. In fact, Michelle seemed to have adopted a *savior* stance in the protection of her sister and in her efforts to hold the family together. It should never be suggested that Michelle was not traumatized. In comparison between Michelle's situation and that of Marsha, questions would be raised whether frequency is the most important issue or whether years spent with distorted cognitions contribute an extremely traumatizing factor.

In summary, it becomes quite clear that many children survive abuse that occurs over a long period of time, and conversely, many children who are abused during a very short period of time have the potential for being traumatized. Perhaps, FREQUENCY as well as AGE should be re-examined on a specific basis and considered when similarities and differences between the SEVERELY TRAUMATIZED and MINIMALLY TRAUMATIZED groups are examined.

What do these numbers explain? At the core of this numerical representation is a failure of traditional methods. Is the suffering of victims important enough to abandon old ideas and close the door of tradition. The answer is *yes!* And the door is open to innovations and new understanding concerning why some victims survive and some continually bleed.

OUT WITH THE OLD, IN WITH THE NEW

What separates those devastated by sexual abuse from those who miraculously survive? What can minimums and maximums tell us about the past, the present, and the future?

If the traditional *Big Four* must be discarded or at least demoted from its absolute status, careful examination must occur regarding a replacement. A closer look is needed. Comparing the maximum trauma with minimal trauma should provide a framework for more clearly understanding the trauma or potential trauma.

For the terms of this research sample, the word majority will be represented by 79% or higher. If examination of the SEVERELY TRAUMA-TIZED group is made, did the majority of those patients experience certain things in a similar manner or the majority of the time? The answer is *yes*. Within the SEVERELY TRAUMA-TIZED group, nine factors appeared. In other words, there were nine significant factors similar to 45 patients at a rate of 79% or higher.

For review, those factors traditionally viewed as causing trauma did not correlate at the same rate. This is especially significant since the nine factors of correlation discussed in this chapter occurred at a rate of 79% or higher.

Comparisons of the *old and the new* occur as follows:

Careful Comparison

THE BIG FOUR/
CORRELATING FACTORS
Primary Severe
N-45

The Big Four

Factor	#1	Under Age Eight	68%
Factor	#2	Violence	31%
Factor	#3	Frequency	60%
Factor	#4	Penetration	42%

Correlating Factors

Factor	#1	Sexual Responsiveness	87%
Factor	#2	Terror	92%
Factor	#3	Distorted Offender I.D.	82%
Factor	#4	Distorted Victim I.D.	86%
Factor	#5	Under Age 12	92%
Factor	#6	Footprints	96%
Factor	#7	Withheld Report	79%
Factor	#8	Disasterous Response	100%
Factor	#9	Trauma Bond	85%

Obviously, there is a much stronger correlation for the *new* nine factors than with the BIG FOUR of tradition. It should also be noted that these are extremely high correlations ranging from 79 to 100%, which should point to significant understanding.

Severe Trauma Factors

Factor #1

Sexual Responsiveness

First, the majority (87%) of patients in the SEVERELY TRAUMATIZED category reported sexual responsiveness. Sexual stimulation and/or sexual responses included clitoral or penile erection, vaginal lubrication, ejaculation, or any other kind of genital stimulation pleasure. These patients seemed to be extremely pained in describing their sexual responsiveness, much the same as *Marsha* described in Chapter Four. The stimulation or pleasure received from the experience seemed overwhelming and a tremendous source of trauma.

Commonly related to this issue was the sex offender's interest, either verbal or nonverbal in the victim's sexual responses. As an example, vibrators used on children appeared to be more commonly related to severe trauma than guns or knives. Teaching children to respond orgasmically in early stages of development seemed to have a profound effect on those patients in the SEVERELY TRAUMATIZED category. If *equipment* was not used to stimulate children, the offender seemed to engage the victim in a belief of the victim's sexual responsiveness.

Jacques was forced to display his penis to the daycare worker several times a day. She would observe his penis, fondle him, and pose the question, *I don't know if you're ready or not.* By the fourth or fifth incident, Mrs. T would finally announce that *she could tell what he wanted*. She performed fellatio each day, five days a week, for two years because *Jacques wanted it*.

Maribel's father always closed the sexually abusive activities with statements regarding her desires or his duty to please her. *I wouldn't do this if I didn't know you wanted me to do it.* Can Maribel, at 45, clearly recall vaginal lubrications, clitoral erections, and tightening of the introitus at the age of five? She, like the majority of SEVERELY TRAUMATIZED patients, if without complete recall of actual sexual responsiveness, could clearly recall the offenders attention toward the victim's sexual contribution.

What also seemed perplexing for this group of SEVERELY TRAUMATIZED individuals was that their sexual responsiveness during the sexually abusive scenarios did not seem to dissolve or discontinue into adulthood. What seems to be a tragic effect of the most SEVERELY TRAUMATIZED patients is that because of their sexual responsiveness, many patients manifested signs of continued arousal toward either the perpetrator or to the kinds of activities taking place during the sexual abuse. It seems to be a deadly combination for the horrors of abuse to be remembered, but with the additional trauma of arousal to those horrors.

Sexuality is something that most adults attempt to repeat in adulthood. Unlike other kinds of abuse, sexual abuse involves repeating a pattern for the purpose of pleasure, which was once a form of terror. For those patients who are aroused to their own abusive scenarios, this provides a vehicle for constant trauma in the future.

Factor #2

Terror, Not Violence

In the majority (92%) of the SEVERELY TRAUMATIZED sexual victims, there appeared to be vivid examples of terror building activities, prolonged periods of abuse, or ritualistic activities. In general terms, there was a strong correlation in those patients who either had to wait for their abuse or who were involved in ritualistic behaviors that seemed to create painful and degrading *anticipation*.

Frankie lived on a farm where animals were routinely castrated, doctored, and butchered. From an early age, Frankie was ritualistically and sadistically abused by his uncle using a variety of equipment and apparatus typically used on animals. Frankie's uncle appeared to enjoy the anticipation, discussing the torturous behaviors that would occur with Frankie, sometimes days before the actual event. Frankie's body was probed with a variety of bizarre equipment and he was often left shackled and bound for hours at a time, awaiting his uncle's arrival. Frankie never suffered physical injury and cannot report experiencing pain.

Frankie's only method of survival was to *check out*. Frankie is a severely traumatized patient who has been diagnosed with a Dissociative Disorder.

Clinical impressions suggest that the amount of time between when the abuse was anticipated by the victim and when the abuse occurred seems to have strong correlation. In other words, when children were told on Saturday, *on Thursday, we are going bowling and Juanita will babysit*, the time period from Saturday to Thursday seemed to build a great deal of terror. Juanita's ritualistic abuse using kitchen utensils was traumatizing in and of itself, but *waiting* for Juanita, and the five sleepless nights remembering what will happen with Juanita, seemed to have a terrorizing effect.

Tony would often go weeks without being abused by her father. Suddenly, during the evening, her father would say the code word, *tomorrow morning*. Tony knew that she should walk into the alley rather than getting on her school bus. She was to wait there for her father who would eventually take her to the family butcher shop where he would have intercourse with her. In diagnosing Tony's responsiveness, two things clearly emerge.

First, the most painful time period for Tony was the night-long anticipation, sleep disturbances, and rage that occurred anticipating her father's abuse. As Tony attempted to sleep lightly, she would be plagued with reoccurring dreams, memories, and horrifying mental pictures.

Conversely, what seemed to be pleasurable for Tony was finally getting into the car with her father, and she also recalls feeling a sense of comfort moving through her grade school classes with seminal fluid in her vagina. The act of getting into the car stated to Tony, *it's almost over*, and moving around in the fourth grade class with seminal fluid in her vagina told Tony, *it is over*. The anticipation, the terror, and the prolonged wait impacted these patients perhaps even more than the sexual abuse itself.

It is very important to recognize the difference between terror and violence for the purpose of studying trauma. The terms *ritualistic or terrorizing* often seem to be connected to guns, knives, and violence. This did not appear to be the case in the SEVERELY TRAUMATIZED group. Many patients who would be described as being terrorized were involved in situations with no violence, weapons, or physical damage. Ninety-two percent of these patients, however, clearly were involved in *terrorizing or anticipatory* activities. Michelle also knew her abuse was going to take place and she endured that abuse for approximately 13 years. The differences seem to be in Michelle's attitude, in her expectations as compared to those patients who felt hopelessly trapped and terrorized.

Factor #3

Identification, Please

The majority of victims in the SEVERELY TRAUMATIZED category emerged with particular information regarding the relationship with the offender. In 82% of the cases, the offender(s) was someone whom the victim could not identify as a *sexual offender,* as guilty, as responsible. In other words, the offender held positive characteristics in the victim's mind. Confusion about the offender/victim role was extreme especially in cases where the sexual offender was important to the victim or held extremely positive attributes in the victim's eyes.

Carol is sexually abused by two brothers in the same household with very much the same behavior. Her brother Benjamin is described as being a *jerk.* He is obnoxious, hateful, and his sexually offending behavior seemed to be normal in Carol's eyes. On the other hand, her brother David was the family favorite. David combined his abuse of Carol with positive attention toward her. In a family where children were left to fend for themselves, David made sure Carol had new shoes to wear, and lunch money for the school cafeteria. Carol's abuse by Benjamin seemed easier for Carol to resolve. David, however, remained not only Carol's favorite, but other family members idolized David. David could not take on the role of the perpetrator and, therefore, that job was left to Carol.

Another specific example points out the difference between stranger molestation and sexual abuse that occurs between children and a loved one.

Josephine was abducted by her mother's boyfriends during one of her mother's alcoholic binges. She was subjected to brutal and, at times, satanic rituals while this offender *sold* her to customers. Defecation, urination, bondage, bestiality, and a variety of other bizarre behaviors were included in the repertoire of abuses committed against Josephine for a three-month period. When Josephine's plight was made known to neighbors, she was rescued and eventually returned to the custody of her natural father whom she had not seen since age five. Josephine reestablished a relationship with him and remained in his care.

Unfortunately, Josephine's natural father began sexually abusing her when she was approximately age 10. The abuse was soft, gentle, nurturing, and apparently much more traumatic than the bizarre and cruel abuse during her abduction. As an adult, Josephine clearly states, after years of rehabilitative and recovery work, *my father's abuse is much more painful than the abuse of my kidnappers.*

Secondarily, the sex offenders who had abused children in the SEVERELY TRAUMATIZED category also seemed to be able to refrain from taking on the role of the offender from those people who were significant to the sexual victim. Sex offenders who were highly respected in the community or were important to the victim's non-offending parents or siblings seemed to have their identity as a perpetrator *blurred*. Sexual offenders who generally had physical or personality characteristics that were positive seemed to cause victims to doubt the *role of perpetrator* because of accolades given to offenders by others.

It is important to recognize that it is not the therapist's or the researcher's view of the sexual offender which is important in understanding this aspect of the SEVERELY TRAUMATIZED factors. Many sex offenders who would be considered clearly responsible and *guilty* by professionals had created situations in the sexually abusive situation that caused victims to concentrate on pleasing the offender or on being accepted by the sex offender. This is not to suggest that the offender deserved accolades or support, but that the sex offender set up a situation where the victim viewed survivorship as being connected to either pleasing the offender or being closely attached to the offender.

Factor #4

Victim Who?

A fourth characteristic found in the majority (86%) of SEVERELY TRAUMATIZED patients was confusion about the victim's role as an innocent child, robbed of something precious. Not only was the identity of the perpetrator unclear, but the identity of the victim was also blurred. Obviously, if the perpetrator cannot take on the characteristics of being responsible and guilty, the victim is left to take on these characteristics. Often this occurred with direct intention of the perpetrator and, in other cases, confusion regarding the *victim status* was unintentional on the part of the offender.

Some perpetrators clearly chose children who seemed to have low self-esteem or who were already struggling with negative attitudes about themselves. Strong, assertive, competent children did not seem to be as acquiescent to sexual abuse and seemed to view themselves as being victims. Offenders typically chose children who were already struggling, creating tremendous potential for trauma.

As an example, a teacher in a grade school administered personality inventories to children during the first of the school year in order to choose those children who had low self-esteem and who would provide a dependent partnership. This brilliant pedophile knew it would be very unlikely that the boys with low self-esteem would view themselves as being supported by others. The result of this *scientific study* was that he could abuse boys who had no access to reporting. This process was successful, since the offender carefully chose children who were already feeling guilty and unacceptable.

Often the offender's behavior during the sexually abusive activities encouraged the child to feel guilty, wrong, or unacceptable. Making children feel like partners is a common way sex offenders enhance children's guilt and blame. In the majority of these cases, the child felt much more like a partner than an innocent child deserving of protection.

Clearly, the *relief period* between sexually abusive situations has a profound effect on how the victim will relate to the abuse at a later time. Sexual victims, much the same as victims of domestic violence, are commonly *hopeful* that through their change in behavior — i.e., by becoming more attractive, more compliant, a better wife, a better mother, a better daughter, etc. — the abuse will discontinue. It is very difficult for these victims to attach negative characteristics or blame the actual perpetrator because of their *hope.* If blame or guilt is within the victim, then the victim seems to believe that control or the possibility of control exists. This is a resolution process during the relief period. This coping mechanism allows the victim to discount the motive, intentions, and behaviors of the sexual offender and gives the victim *hope.* Hopefully, if the victim is guilty or responsible, control will emerge by the victim owning the abuse and being in charge. Obviously, the abuse does not stop and the victim practices being responsible and being *hopeful.* The underlying residual trauma from this attitude leaves the SEVERELY TRAUMATIZED patient guilt-ridden, unworthy, and responsible. The victim is not innocent. If the victim is guilty, the sexual offender, quite clearly, is not! And it goes on and on.

Factor #5

Younger Children

There was a prevalence of younger children abused in the SEVERELY TRAUMATIZED category. Sixty-eight percent of the group was under the age of eight, while a combined total of sixty-eight percent and twenty-four percent provides a 92% rating for *under the age of 12.* Quite clearly, there is a preponderance of children under 12, who were SEVERELY TRAUMATIZED. The issue may not necessarily be age, as previously explained, but what happened to these children's development in the years following the abuse. It seems that the majority of these children were sexually abused under the age of 12 but the most significant factor is that these children proceeded through childhood without assistance or rescue.

Factor #6

Footprints

The responses or the *situation* of the sexually abusive scenario seems to shed light on some very important factors in understanding SEVERE, as compared to MINIMAL TRAUMA. In following chapters, the issue of *footprints* or coping skills will be thoroughly discussed as an indicator of trauma. In general terms, victims appear to respond to their abuse much the same as sex offenders respond. It is common for sex offenders to deny, rationalize, minimize, and rearrange facts in a psychological process to avoid looking at the reality of the crime they are committing. Victims go through much of the same process, but for different reasons.

When children are sexually abused, they are usually forced to engage in activities that are beyond their comprehension. Especially in cases where bizarre sexual activity occurs, children lack the ability to formulate reality or to understand what is happening. Factors such as the relationship between the victim and the offender, the age of the child, and information available to the child at the time of the abuse will have a bearing on how the victim will perceive what is happening and respond. Children cope in a wide variety of ways in response to their sexually abusive situations and that *coping* assists the victim in avoiding the reality of the pain. It is often these footprints that set lifelong patterns for trauma at a later time.

Clearly encased in the SEVERELY TRAUMA-TIZED category appeared to be two specific kinds of coping mechanisms or *footprints*. The first coping skill involves memory impairment reflected by amnesia or dissociation. As Dr. Catherine Cameron states, *Amnesia is the most profound form of denial. Amnesia places the victim in an out of control situation without the ability to understand the feelings that seem to be manifested at inappropriate and unusual times in adulthood.*

I watched my little tennis shoes slowly step down out of the bunk house. Carefully, I watched my tennis shoes walk back to the house where my mother awaited my arrival. She had promised me Alphabet soup for lunch, telling me we would spell my name with the letters. I watched my little tennis shoes try to move me back toward the house. How could I fit it all together — my bleeding rectum and my lovely lunch with mother? It won't fit! It can't fit. I just won't remember.

Dissociation is another kind of *memory* footprint used by victims who cannot put the pieces together, who cannot cope with the incongruity of sexual abuse. Amnesia and dissociation make the victim vulnerable to memory *zaps* throughout the rest of their lives giving them no cognitive awareness for many of their affective responses to the memories. It is a cruel world for the 57% of victims who choose the footprint of amnesia or dissociation. There is no connection, there is no understanding, there is no peace.

Carla reports having very few memories of her early childhood before the age of nine. In the third and fourth grade, Carla becomes obsessed with perfec--tion. She is an obedient child, she gets excellent grades, and, most importantly, Carla lives in a comfortable and congenial family. Carla proceeds through grade school, junior high, and high school with near perfection. In Carla's first year of college, she attempts to become intimate with a young man for the first time.

In the enclosure of a parked car, Carla welcomes signs and feelings of her own arousal. With her eyes closed, however, Carla sees pictures of horrifying scenes. Coupled with her own arousal, Carla is horrified by her thoughts of children being tied to beds and nuns bleeding from their vaginas. Carla is horrified by her thoughts and repulsed by her behavior. Carla is beginning the process of attaching deviant sexual thoughts to her physiological responses.

It will be more than 12 years before Carla is clearly able to recall (with the offender confirmation) that these behaviors actually occurred and that many of the scenes, so grotesque and horrifying, were pornographic presentations made to her to enhance her cooperation in ritualistic and sadistic behaviors orchestrated by both Carla's mother and father. It was the physiological connection in arousal that caused these memory attacks to occur. Unfortunately, Carla's lifestyle prevented her from accepting those pictures as part of her repertoire of experiences. Carla spent the next 12 years resisting, fighting, and eventually succumbing to her memories, which had been safely tucked away in the *footprint* of amnesia.

Carla's case has a direct relation to sexual behavior and sexual abuse. Carla's coping skill or footprints were typical of SEVERELY TRAUMATIZED patients with the coping mechanism being, *This is so awful, I will forget*. There are cases, however, in the SEVERELY TRAUMATIZED group where nonsexual skin memories also bring the patient to horrifying memories, feelings, and experiences of being subjected to re-victimization. Without the clear cognitive perception of the roots or the etiology of these memories, the victim is constantly traumatized.

An emergency room contacts the local mental health clinic for intervention. A patient with multiple sclerosis is being administered a massage in response to lower back pain. In the safety of a hospital, the patient's lower back is stimulated for the purpose of relieving pain. Hysterical responses occur with the patient screaming, shrieking and eventually accusing medical technicians of rape. Although approximately fourteen people were near or about the patient, she continued to have an anxiety/panic attack to the point of needing sedation. The patient believed that the medical personnel were raping her and even when she was revived she was unclear about her experience.

Following six months of therapeutic intervention, the patient recalls being held down on a tailgate of a pick-up while her uncle, her brothers, and several other individuals raped her. The coping mechanism for this patient at age eight was to forget. Yet the life history of this patient, as memories or flashes peered into her cognitive process, forced the patient into the SEVERELY TRAUMATIZED category. The sense and feeling of being out of control or being in ownership of horrible *skin memories* can clearly explain how these patients find themselves in lifelong patterns of abusability, depression, suicide, or other psychiatric disorders.

If Not . . . Then . . .

If amnesia or dissociation was not the coping skill or *footprint*, the remainder of the patients (39%) primarily responded with self-abusive cycles. Often, the original coping mechanism with clear cognitions of the inappropriateness of the behavior forced the patient to cope by accepting responsibility or blame. It was common in the SEVERELY TRAUMATIZED category for the patients who were not plagued with amnesia to cope through manifestations of guilt and responsibility. The result was self-abusive cycles beginning in early childhood and most often continuing through adulthood.

Marge does not remember a time when abuse did not occur. Her early remembrances of the abuse are negative and her attitudes about herself were also as negative. Marge states, as a 37-year-old adult, *What was happening to me was bad, so I said, I'll be bad and then it will match!*

For Marge, the resolution occurs with compatibility of her own negative attributes coinciding with the negative situation. Although for adults this may be difficult to perceive or understand, for a child this is a kind of resolution. If consideration is made to a child's world, it is quite clear that children spend much of their grade school years *matching*. Little girls are asked to match their socks, while both little girls and boys are asked to match the birds, the animals, or those products that belong in the Seven Basic Food Groups. Matching, comparing, or fitting together, is a common tool or skill taught to children. *Matching the badness is a technique that seems to be a resolution for children.*

If the footprints were not amnesia (57% have some memory disorder through amnesia or dissociation), patients in the SEVERELY TRAUMATIZED category developed self-abusive coping mechanisms that proceeded throughout childhood and adulthood (39% for a total of 96%). By the time the patients were admitted to therapy, the coping skill with self-abusive tendencies automatically categorized the patient in the SEVERELY TRAUMATIZED group. The residual effects of this coping skill were alcohol and drug abuse, criminal behavior, domestic violence, eating disorders, suicide attempts, etc. Tremendous difficulties for the patient were observed as a result of this deadly solution.

Factor #7

Secrecy Issue

The seventh factor in the SEVERELY TRAUMATIZED category responds to the issue of secrecy. The majority of the time (79%) patients did not report the sexual abuse in childhood and spent most of their lives suffering in silence. The damage to children seemed to be building upon the sexually abusive perceptions and making deviancy the foundation of development.

Clearly, from the research, some SEVERELY TRAUMATIZED patients had only one incident (10 victims). In comparison, the same number (10) were found in the minimal trauma group, which were basically asymptomatic. What is the difference between these groups where 10 people were SEVERELY TRAUMATIZED and 10 people had no symptoms at all? The issue seems to be what happened to the child's development when secrecy pervades. 100% of the MINIMALLY TRAUMATIZED patients reported immediately or within a very short period of time. They did not spend a lifetime building upon a foundation of sexual abuse. Contrarily, the 10 SEVERELY TRAUMATIZED victims used the vehicle of sexual abuse to carry them through childhood development. The issue of secrecy seemed extremely traumatic.

Factor #8

Disclosure Disaster

Disclosure did not occur in childhood for 79% of the SEVERELY TRAUMATIZED patients. For those who did report (21%), all of the situations following disclosure, the victim experienced more trauma. In other words, even though some patients (21%) reported the abuse, the response to the disclosure seemed

to add trauma rather than assist in the healing process. The victim would have been better off to have never reported.

Karen is sexually abused by her brother for approximately three years. As Karen becomes more aware of the inappropriateness of her brother's sexual behavior, she finally reports to her mother. Karen's mother becomes extremely upset, screaming at her, and eventually sends Karen to her room. Karen's mother forbids Karen to eat dinner with the rest of the family.

Finally, Karen is brought into the living room and her father proceeds to beat Karen's brother unmercifully. Karen reports being barely able to recognize her brother when the beating concluded. Her mother sobs, does not comfort Karen in any way. Bleeding and nearly unrecognizable, Karen's brother is forced to apologize on bended knees for his transgressions. That same evening Karen lies in bed and listens to her brother crying. Suddenly, her father enters her room and quietly rapes Karen.

For patients in the SEVERELY TRAUMATIZED group who reported, the response to the report was always disastrous. This is not to suggest that disastrous responses to reports did not occur in other categories, but it was very clear that the response to these disclosures was profoundly negative. Disclosure usually resulted in more abuse, beatings, institutionalization or total family abandonment. Clearly then, factors 7 and 8 demonstrate that severe trauma can occur through a lifetime of secrecy or from horrible responses to efforts of stopping the secret.

Factor #9

Trauma Bond

A final factor of correlation in this group indicates the majority (85%) of the SEVERELY TRAUMATIZED patients had continued demands for a relationship with the perpetrator or those significant to the perpetrator. This required the patient to struggle in attempting to resolve the abuse and feelings about the perpetrator, even though in some cases physical or actual contact with the perpetrator was not a factor. Even if the perpetrator was incapacitated, incarcerated, or absent, the victim remained connected and in a *trauma bond*.

In cases when the perpetrator was deceased, a demand for some kind of relationship between the perpetrator and the victim still existed.

> Christina, at 37, dreads the holiday season. She must attend holiday festivities with people who continue to discuss her perpetrator's attributes. Although the family does not know about Christina's abuse, they are certainly aware of Christina's struggles in her adult life. Her hospitalizations, her suicide attempts, and her failed vocational efforts are very obvious to the family. The attributes of the offender, who is deceased, far outweigh negative responses Christina earns. *In death*, most individuals become heroes and Christina's offender is no exception.

The nature of TRAUMA BONDING becomes quite clear for these individuals. No cases in the SEVERELY TRAUMATIZED group were situations where the sexual offender was unknown or disconnected to the victim. In all situations, the offender remained with a traumatic hold on the victim, with lack of resolution and clarification.

Minimal Trauma — *Asymptomatic Patients*

As issues and answers emerge from those victims who are SEVERELY TRAUMATIZED, it is also important to look at the variances or pertinent indicators found in those sexually abusive situations of less trauma. Perhaps those patients who survived their sexual abuse with less severe symptoms can provide important information about the trauma of sexual abuse.

In this category, varied degrees of violence, sexual behavior, duration of sexual contact, and age at onset were observed. The actual sexual abuse scenario was extremely varied in consideration of most factors commonly used to determine trauma. With such varying degrees, it was difficult to determine what consistent issue continued to surface. Those 25 patients seemed to be asymptomatic, leaving very little consistency on which to focus. There were, however, four factors that emerged at a rate of 95-100% of the time, while traditional factors were much less consistent.

Minimal Trauma Factor Comparison

Big Four

Violence	16%
Age (8)	36%
Penetration	24%
Frequency, Less Than 5	28%

New Reflections
95 - 100%

1. Precognitions Offender/Victim I.D.
2. Immediate Report
3. Report Response
4. . . .And to the Future

Factor #1

Offender/Victim Identification

This category demonstrates issues of consistency with the first relating to the offender/victim identity. It was very clear that during the sexually abusive scenario, the victim was abused with the precognition of the *criminal* aspect of the offender's behavior. In nearly all of the MINIMALLY TRAUMATIZED and in many of the MODERATELY TRAUMATIZED victims,

the victim knew the behavior of the perpetrator was inappropriate and was able to assign inappropriateness to the offender. In other words, the identification of the victim and the offender was profoundly clear to the patient at the time of the abuse.

In comparison, those patients who were SEVERELY TRAUMATIZED not only had difficulties recognizing the offender/victim identification during the abuse, but that confusion continued throughout childhood and often pervaded into adulthood. Individuals who were MINIMALLY TRAUMATIZED knew from the inception of the abuse that the offender was the guilty party and that the victim was innocent.

Even though many of these victims were forced to endure brutal, violent, or degrading sexual activities, the fact that the identification of the victim and the offender was clear seemed to allow the patient the best opportunity to take the next step which also appeared at a factor rate of 95-100%

Factor #2

Report

Secondly, the response following the sexual abuse made an important contribution to rehabilitation. Except for one situation, 100% of the MINIMALLY TRAUMATIZED patients reported within three days. Most reported *immediately*, which can be defined as whenever the victim had the first opportunity. As an example, a single case occurred when a female child waited seven days to report since she was away at church camp.

> Andrea was being sexually abused by the camp counselor and had no access to a protective adult. Andrea reported her sexual abuse in the driveway of her home, minutes after she was deposited by the Sunday School bus. Common sense would suggest that Andrea made an immediate report.

In comparison, 61% of the MODERATELY TRAUMATIZED group reported within three months. If examining the large number of patients in the SEVERELY TRAUMATIZED group who never made a report, it seems that the patient's ability to make a report correlates with lessening the trauma.

Factor #3

Report Response

It is important to note, however, that many patients in the SECONDARY SEVERE category reported quickly as well, but something else happened. Reporting alone was not enough. The difference between those who were more traumatized, but reported immediately, and those who were less traumatized and reported immediately appears to be found in the response to the report. In all of the MINIMALLY TRAUMATIZED scenarios, the sexual abuse disclosure was handled in an extremely supportive and protective manner. It appeared that not only did the victims initially identify themselves as innocent, but the person to whom the child

reported held to the same ideas about identification of the players. Therefore, the children were able to see themselves as being wronged, abused, and victimized during the abuse. Additionally, the victim made a report to someone who held the same ideas about the victim status. The offender was clearly *the offender*, which perhaps allowed the patient to take another step toward rehabilitation.

There was an additional factor, however, that clearly emerged in this group differentiating the MINIMALLY or MODERATELY TRAUMATIZED patients from those in a more severe category. There was immediate reporting in some cases in other categories of trauma and there was also somewhat of a positive response to the abuse. However, a fourth factor seemed to emerge in the less traumatized group.

Factor #4

. . . And to the Future

Regrouping of the first three factors recalls that first, the identification of the victim and the offender occurred, thus allowing the second factor to emerge in an immediate report. Thirdly, the report was met with positive and supportive responses by those individuals who shared the same feelings about the offender/victim identification. Fourth, the patients who seemed to be MINIMALLY TRAUMATIZED clearly had access to appropriate information about the sexual abuse throughout their sexual development. In other words, it was not enough to simply make a report and have a positive response. The most important factor was a *continuation* of important information to guide the child through sexual development. The following case demonstrates the optimum opportunity for rehabilitation. This scenario is very typical of those cases found in the MINIMALLY TRAUMATIZED group.

Ruth is sexually abused, along with her sister, in a movie theatre during the Saturday Matinee. A stranger, unknown to both Ruth and her sister, positions himself in front of the children's ability to exit. Ruth, age 6, and Sandra, 8, learn the man has a knife which will be used unless the children are quiet. The man performs digital penetration on both girls while he masturbates himself to the point of ejaculation. He also holds the knife between their legs cutting the girls slightly. In her adult life, Ruth feels as though the sexual abuse and genital penetration took place for over an hour. Whether or not this is accurate is unimportant. It is significant to note that this situation contained elements of violence and additionally the probing was so severe that both children required medical treatment. In discussing the situation with Ruth, the following ideas and attitudes become clear.

This man was very frightening. He was dirty, he smelled bad, and we were afraid. During the entire abuse, our eyes were fixed on the neon sign,

QUIET, PLEASE. We knew we couldn't make noise in the theatre. We were obedient children. You can't talk in the movies or the library!

During the entire rape, and I do call it a rape, I knew the movie would be over. I knew the lights were going to come on, and I knew I could start screaming when that happened. When THE END came upon the screen, both Sandra and I began screaming as loud as we could. The man started running toward the emergency exit and we ran to the lobby.

It is difficult to remember the exact details. What I can remember is being picked up, cuddled, and placed on top of the glass candy counter. They told us to reach in and grab popcorn whenever we wanted. It was great! I remember the lobby filling up with people and the dirty old man being dragged to the lobby by two men who must have been some kind of security people. My strongest recollection is eating popcorn and the crowd cheering and clapping when the police arrived to take him away.

I can't remember exactly what my mother said or did, but I can tell you it was okay as soon as she got there. Both of us had medical exams and required brief hospitalization. But I cannot remember having bad feelings.

I can remember, as I proceeded through the next few years, that my mother was always willing to talk to us about what had happened. She always made us feel like our bodies were great and that we were so brave to tell. It seemed like whenever I had questions about sex, my mother was always there and the incident at the movie was openly discussed. I can remember laughing about it and our mom spoke of our courage in the same way she talked about when I got bucked off the horse or won an exihibitor's ribbon for my pot holder at the fair. It was a real bad pot holder, but she still talked about my tenacity.

I have always had good attitudes about sex and, this man, this horrible thing that happened to us, was just so unimportant. He was such a jerk — such a dirty old man. It seemed like there was no connection at all with what he did and my sexuality. He was always the **movie pervert** *nothing more, nothing less.*

Being able to proceed through sexual development with clear cognitions that allow separation between the sexual abuse and human sexuality seems to be an overriding effect or issue in those people who will be less traumatized by their abuse. Unfortunately, the small child who is asymptomatic often is neglected. It seems difficult for parents or professionals to recog- nize the profound effect sexual abuse is *going* to have on sexual development in the future.

A four-year-old child who has been brutally abused may appear to be *happy as a clam at high tide.* It is common to suggest that the child is somehow not traumatized by what has hap- pened and the child is often neglected from a therapeutic standpoint. Have the individuals who made these decisions carefully considered the difference in cognitive interpretation be- tween a four-year-old performing fellatio on her father and a 14-year-old? The changes children make through development is not a mystery or a secret to professionals. Somehow, however, the sexual development of children is a very neglected subject in understanding trauma. From this research, the impact that sexually abusive situations have on sexual development appears to be a more profound factor in deter- mining trauma than age at onset or frequency.

Development Damage

Sexual development of children from a sociologi- cal perspective is difficult. Ours is one of the few societies in the world which actually seem to punish puberty. It is not uncommon for fathers or other males to withhold attention and affec- tion from a female child when she begins to sexually develop. Males often find rejection from their parents who fear the prospect of causing arousal in their sons. Even children who have not been sexually abused in childhood often begin their sexual development with rejection, confusion, embarrassment, degradation, and misinformation. Most often, children are left on their own to try to make sense out of this unwelcome change in development.

These issues will be fully discussed in later chapters, but consideration of the profound effects on sexual victims in this already uncomfortable stage in development is important in opening the closed doors. How does a sexual victim respond when some fifth graders are excited about kissing boys and the victim is already having oral sex with her father? It would seem that the SEVERELY TRAUMATIZED patients proceeded through sexual development with the deviant acts involved in their abusive scenario as the developmental focus. When normal sexual development steps were taken with sexual abuse as the framework or springboard, it is no wonder that the SEVERELY TRAUMATIZED patients had profound sexual dysfunctions. If less trauma is to occur, a different course of action was taken, protecting sexual development for those patients who seemed to escape profound damage.

Hope

What the MINIMALLY TRAUMATIZED patients in this study demonstrate is the possibility of preventing the trauma of sexual abuse even when sexual abuse may be violent, may involve penetration, may occur to smaller children, and may happen on more than one occasion. First, if we could teach children to feel robbed, to feel like a victim — the same as they would if

someone had stolen their bicycle or taken their lunch — then the precognitions of the criminal aspects of the offender's behavior would be clear and the first step in reducing trauma would have taken place. Second, we need to encourage children to tell. And they will, if they feel robbed. If they feel responsible, they will be doomed to secrecy.

Then, if those children were met with positive and supportive feelings about their disclosure, the third step toward rehabilitation could occur. Children who were blamed, who felt guilty, who were ridiculed, who were traumatized by the system, who were not believed by the jury, etc., had very little hope of rehabilitation. Those children who were met with the same support given to a *bicycle robbery victim* would seemingly be less traumatized and have an easier road to recovery.

Finally, those children who continued to be given information in order to prevent trauma to their sexual development took the final and fourth step toward rehabilitation. It would seem that a better appreciation and understanding of the precarious nature of sexual development should be a priority for preventing trauma to sexual victims. Sexual victims are in desperate need of information that will help them separate their abuse from normal sexuality. The common cry from SEVERELY TRAUMATIZED adults was that in adulthood the sexual offender lies in bed with the victim and the victim's partner. Sexual abuse and sexuality seem to be in the same package.

I have a wonderful husband and I want to be sexual with him. There are certain conditions under which I can be sexual. If I masturbate, if the lights are on and I can see what's happening or if I am drunk, sex comes easy and feels good. When my wonderful husband wants to turn the lights out, wants to hold me in bed, and wants to have intercourse, I am suddenly there with my father feeling the same feelings, hearing the same words, experiencing the same disgust. In my head, I know it's Paul; in every other part of my body, it feels like I am sleeping with my father.

Obviously, Winona has not only taken her father to bed with her in her adult life, but she has taken her father and her sexually abusive situation with her through her entire sexual development. In her efforts to break this bond, Winona has developed self-abusive cycles and other symptoms which place her in the SECON-DARY SEVERELY TRAUMATIZED group. Winona's abuse by her father had terminated by the time she was eight. Questions can be raised about how much different Winona's sexual life and her resulting symptoms would be, had she been able to separate her sexually abusive situation from her sexual development.

In summary, it is important to understand the purpose of this data. Categorizing victims and examining their abusive scenarios is a difficult task and often less than objective. The purpose of this research was for understanding, not for complicated categorization or computation. As the legal community set about to establish guidelines for determining serious from more serious crimes, the therapeutic community has eagerly followed, and treatment plans have been developed according to that model. This research should hopefully stop us from heading in that direction and perhaps teach us to lean toward another, perhaps more appropriate, look at the trauma to sexual victims.

TRAUMA BONDING —
THE NATURE OF THE BEAST

Childhood is a process, a delicate development of a human being. If sexual abuse is not isolated or constant, what is the result of continual cultivation of trauma through a lifetime?

The Trauma Assessment

The research and data from the Trauma Assessment project can provide hope and also cause questioning of old ideas and traditional attitudes about trauma. The purpose of this publication was to provide a new look and to open minds toward new reflections in examining trauma. The Trauma Assessment is the vehicle for these innovations. With a better understanding of how victims are and are not traumatized, we turn toward a hopeful future.

And why is it important to understand how victims are traumatized? Of course, the answer is rehabilitation. If more comprehensive, more appropriate evaluation of the damage is con-ducted, better treatment can emerge. The Trauma Assessment then becomes an important solution to the rehabilitation of victims with two major purposes.

And, to the Future

The first purpose of the Trauma Assessment is to evaluate and *predict* for the younger patient what trauma is more than likely to occur in adolescence or adulthood. The small child who may appear to be functioning quite well will benefit from a Trauma Assessment predicting what data and research suggest will happen if an appropriate treatment plan is not implemented. In other words, the Trauma Assessment based on this research will assist parents, clinicians, and other professionals in being able to *prevent the cultivation* of trauma through the child's critical development. With the Trauma Assessment, damage may be prevented. The Trauma Assessment can raise flags, predict outcomes, and provide directions so that future trauma can be alleviated.

And, Backwards to the Past

The second purpose of the Trauma Assessment is tailored toward the adolescent or adult patient who is already symptomatic. Commonly, sexual abuse patients respond and behave in ways that are uncomfortable, degrading, and inappropriate. It is often this sense of being out of control, wanting certain things, and being unable to reach goals, that leaves the patient devastated. The adult seems to be caught up in a hook, a control, a *Trauma Bond* (Fillmore) with the sexual abuse. It is trauma bonding that allows the victim to be connected back to the abusive feelings, attitudes, or thoughts. Victims' voices tell us about this hold, this bonding, this connection back to the pain.

I have a four-year-old under my eyelids. Part of me is 34, but another part of me is four. The 34-year-old drives the car, but the four-year-old keeps wanting to stop for ice cream.

I just feel awful. I don't know where it comes from, but I know where it hurts. Sometimes I have a lump in my throat

that feels like my throat is going to explode. Sometimes I feel like throwing up in the middle of the Pinochle game.

I feel so suddenly sad for no reason, sad, very sad, just like I watched Bambi for the first time.

I sometimes feel frozen like I can't move. I can't care for my kids. I can't get out of bed. I feel stiff. I feel like if I move, something bad will happen. Somewhere on my body, I fear pain will attack.

Sometimes I feel frozen in a memory. I see myself at three, crying, next to my mother's shoes. I don't know why I'm there. I don't know why the shoes are there. I just feel sad looking at her shoes. It makes no sense.

I feel stuck, helpless to move in any direction, unable to commit, unable to feel, unable to care. My big part says, shame on you, get busy! My little part says, don't you dare.

I feel like a prisoner to my memory or my lack of memories. My big part says, you know what happened. My little part prays desperately, it isn't so.

I keep being attacked by this kid. I want to be confident, professional, and sexual. I am a survivor! This kid keeps kicking me in the crotch.

My body betrays me. I am attractive, perfect, and intact. My skin memories result in my body responses becoming totally opposite. In bed, with my wife, I feel like bees are chasing me through the backyard of the house where I lived when I was five. At work I feel like someone has purposely shut off the air conditioner in the courtroom so the pillow over my five-year-old face keeps me from breathing.

My big part says, respect your family, be nice, be good. My little Suzie part keeps saying, you hate me, you keep me a 45-year-old 5-year-old.

Flashbacks and Feelbacks

These voices from victims attest to an out-of-control *zapping* as the victim moves through life. The victim seems to be attacked by the memories or by unconnected events with piercing *flashback and feelbacks* from the abuse. Whether it is skin memories, visual memories, or verbal memories, it is a cruel pain for the victim to be rendered out of control by these experiences.

It is as though the victim has a memory bank like a computer. Unfortunately, this bank of memory can be accessed by a wide variety of stimuli, often without the victim's knowledge or desire. The victim has the hardware and must run the program of life. The software regarding how the data will be accessed is unknown to the victim and the victim is vulnerable. It is this stimuli in the environment that keeps accessing the memory bank of the victim's computer and forcing the victim to relive and re-experience the trauma. Trauma bonding is found in the access codes to the memory bank held by the victim.

Three Deadly Deals

Three issues from a general perspective make trauma bonding more understandable. First, it seems to be a natural human response to be attracted or focused on the negative. It seems typical for adults to remain connected to unpleasant incidents simply because they are significant. Something within people keeps connection with frailties or vulnerabilities.

As an example, returning to a class reunion finds most adults sensitive and perhaps more attentive to those individuals who were aware of our frailties. *The ninth grade girl who knew you put bobbie sox in your bra may be the one you purposely seek out at the class reunion, to whom you exhibit your svelte figure. The boy (now 45 years old) who stood you up for a date with "Ole Four Eyes" may be the object of your attention.*

It is common when errors are committed in a job, when testifying in court, making an irresponsible sales decision, or when finding a $100 shortage in the tellers till, that pondering over these experiences will occur longer than pondering over successes. Is it not common for the bank teller to balance 90% of the time and for those experiences to seem insignificant or beyond reproach, while the 10% rate of failures seems to be the focus of memory and contemplation?

It is understandable that the sexual victim who has uncomfortable experiences from sexual abuse may naturally focus on these memories. Even in families where more positive memories exist, it would not be uncommon for a victim or even a nonvictim to focus on these *feelbacks* to childhood which were negative. Typically remembered would be the broken arm, a profound illness, or the extreme punishment due to a specific misbehavior. It is not necessarily common to remember the guidance received for consistent teeth brushing or the encouragement to complete homework, which eventually resulted in a college scholarship. Like everyone else, the sexual victim may focus on the negative experiences of childhood.

Switch On — Switch Off

A second issue is important to recognize when understanding general issues of the trauma bond. Different than other kinds of abuse such as neglect or physical abuse, the traumatized sexual victim is required to *flip off* the terror and return to a similar scenario in adulthood to achieve *pleasure*. Hopefully, victims who have been physically abused or neglected do not need to repeat those same behaviors in the future. It is very different in sexual abuse. The sexual victim is required to repeat a behavior that has caused profound pain, trauma,

degradation, and upheaval. The message is *please enjoy this.*

Being a sexual partner in adulthood is a general requirement. Sexuality requires the victim to participate in the same kind of behavior that was horrible and degrading as a child, but one that should be extremely fulfilling and pleasurable as an adult. It is no wonder that a return to the trauma occurs as victims are asked to repeat the experience under a different affective modality (pleasure).

Stuck

A third important factor in understanding the trauma bond in general terms seems to be related to the issue of regression or fixation to stages of childhood. Clearly, sexual offenders regress or fixate back to a stage in sexual development where their abuse may have occurred. It is not uncommon to be empathic toward pedophiles because of the understanding that those experiences occurred in the pedophile's childhood. Understandably, the pedophile did not develop beyond a specific stage of sexual development. It is easy to understand pedophile's behavior as an adult if childhood abuse is examined. Is there a different standard or lack of standard for the sexual victim?

If it is understandable that the pedophile, due to childhood sexual experiences, is an adult trapped within a child development cage, why is not the same true for the sexual victim? Why would not the victim be trapped in a stage of sexual development, or even in a stage of general childhood development, due to the same experiences? Isn't it common for anyone who has experienced extremely negative events in childhood to have a fixation or regression back to that experience?

The same seems to be true for sexual victims. The raging battle between the adult and the child results in a fixation or regression back to a stage in development. As one woman stated, *The 34-year-old drives the car, but it is the 4-year-old who wants to stop for ice cream.* Much of trauma bonding is the battle between the four-year-old and the 34-year-old.

For the pedophile it seems more understandable. The pedophile who teaches school must operate on an adult level, correcting papers, attending faculty meetings, and renewing his certificate. The childlike characteristics of the pedophile are in constant battle with the competent adult. Pedophiles are often described as *adult children,* and the etiology for their problems is often due to childhood sexual abuse. The same is true for the sexual victim. To be stuck in a stage of development is one of the reasons the trauma bond so tightly and painfully controls the sexual victim.

These three issues, being naturally drawn toward unpleasant experiences, being asked to relive a horrible experience under the veil of pleasure, and having tendencies to be fixated or regressed to stages of childhood, explain why the sexual victim seems to be caught up in a bond with the unfortunate and uncomfortable experience of sexual abuse. More specifically, the nature of this bonding requires victims to be in a constant battle, faced with constant failures and constant reminders. These are general issues — related to human beings. More specific issues related to sexual abuse also plague the victim's future with bonds of trauma.

Trauma Bonding Generic — Virgins, Orgasms, Fantasies, Stud Horses, And The Big "R"

The ways in which victims are bound to their trauma comes in a variety of packages and compartments. For the sake of generic examination, several topics will be used for examples of trauma bonding.

Virgins

The issue of virginity is an example of a compounding traumatic bond, more specifically for the female victim. The topic of virginity is interesting since it would seem that sexual promiscuity is common. Jokes suggesting that virgins can only be found in the fifth grade violin class are common. Society's sexual promiscuity should set the stage for empathy and understanding about a female who was not entirely *sexually pure* on her wedding. Our society, however, seems to have another code of morality for the person who has relinquished her virginity through sexual abuse.

As discussed in the last chapter, one junior high school female discusses *getting it on* with her boyfriend in the backseat of the Chevrolet. Her cheerleader companion, another high school junior, does not discuss being sexually involved with her father, brother, uncle, or mother since age eight. The issue of virginity seems to be somewhat flexible in our society as long as virginity is relinquished under certain circumstances. There seems to be tremendous pain involved if virginity is lost through sexual abuse.

In the previous example regarding Linda, it becomes clear that death is more understandable and appropriate than reporting the loss of virginity from sexual abuse. The tradition of a white dress, chastity, and purity gives one message, while, in contrast, rock star, Madonna, sings gloriously about giving up her virginity. Adding even more confusion, couples who live together and who are obviously engaging in a sexual relationship nonetheless are allowed to have a wonderfully white wedding, complete with all the trappings of tradition. Something very unusual happens forbidding the tradition, however, if the sexual behavior involves sexual abuse.

The 14-year-old child who has been exposed to pornography, who has been required to perform oral sex on her brother and his friends, and who has been subjected to violent anal intercourse, asks the question, *Jan, am I still a virgin?* The answer she desires and the answer that will be most helpful may not be the same. The right answer, and the same answer which will be accepted by the rest of the world in which she lives, are sadly different. The issue of virginity is important to her because she lives in a fickle world. The answer can be given, *of course you are.* The question is, however, will her world echo that attitude? And is her question important? *YES*, is the answer we can give her, but only if she lost her virginity under certain circumstances.

It would seem that the issue of virginity in this case goes far beyond a hymen that is intact or not intact. Just as penises and penetration seem to have magical properties, vaginas and what has been in vaginas also seems magic. For cases of trauma bonding, the sexual victim suffers from the cruel traditions related to virginity.

Solutions, Solutions

Often, it is the solutions to problems that help determine and understand the original problem concerning the virginity conflict. The appropriate therapeutic response helps understand the power of the trauma bond in the case of virginity. A three-sentence letter from the medical doctor examining a sexual victim can have a profound effect on rehabilitation when the issue of virginity becomes important. From the victim's viewpoint, a sexual abuse examination is like sexual abuse. Their legs are spread, lights are shined, and another individual, perhaps similar to the abuser, probes, picks, and causes pain in the genitalia area. Evidence of trauma or damage is often rejoiced! Lack of trauma or damage is often met with disappointment. It is typical for the sexual victim patient to leave the medical examination feeling further traumatized and feeling as though whatever was seen and examined between the legs caused tremendous response from those individuals conducting the evaluation.

As a therapeutic contribution to prevent a trauma bond regarding this issue, a very brief letter written by the pediatrician conducting an examination can have a major contribution to preventing a trauma bond in the future. This valuable contribution may read as follows:

> *I am the doctor who looked at you and checked you to make sure you were okay. I want you to know you look just fine. There is nothing wrong with you. Everything is okay and you and your body look beautiful.*

In 30 seconds, an emergency room doctor can alleviate tremendous potential for grief, agony, and pain through a trauma bond in the future. Whether or not the hymen is intact is not the issue. Sexual victims leave the sexually abusive scenario feeling as though they are damaged goods, then an insensitive society confirms! When simple, four-sentence letters help alleviate trauma, but are uncommon, it is understandable why so many sexual victims are terribly traumatized who did not receive such information and support.

Orgasms

The issue of *orgasm* or sexual responsiveness during sexually abusive scenarios seems to have a profound effect on trauma bonding. The first, most obvious, area of concern is the victim's own sexual responsiveness during sexual abuse. As research indicated in Chapter Five, *the identification of the victim and the offender has a profound effect on how traumatized the victim may be.* When the victim has sexual pleasure or experiences sexual responsiveness, obviously the ability to identify the victim becomes confused and often impossible.

Remembering that sexual offenders need to deny or rationalize in order to find pleasure while children are being abused points to an issue of offender behavior that has tremendous impact on victims. One of the most important denial mechanisms for sex offenders is to concentrate on their victims sexual responses. It is not uncommon for sexual offenders to verbalize about sexual responsiveness of victims, which is either pretended or real in order to enhance their arousal and control their victims.

Innies and Outies

It seems to be extremely difficult for victims to contemplate their own responsiveness when their bodies may have responded, and seemed out of control. This is particularly difficult for males who have had erections or who have had ejaculations. Male genitalia sticks out, — *outies!* Female genitalia sticks in, — *innies!* Vaginal lubrication, clitoral erections, etc., are easier to deny than penile erections. The male's ability to recognize himself as a victim is often hampered in those sexually abusive scenarios where the male's body physically responded.

I hated it when he would come into my room. This only happened on the weekends because he was the night manager on weekend duty. I had to have the light on because I was afraid and he knew it. He would turn the light off, come into my room, and ask me what I would do to have the light turned back on. He knew the answer already. Each time I promised myself, I hated it, I hated it, I hated it. Each time he put his mouth on my penis, I couldn't help it. Soon, I had an erection and soon I had very nice feelings. The rest of it didn't matter.

He knew that it didn't take long to get me feeling that way. When he first came into my room, it was him that I hated. By the time he left, it was me that I hated.

A second kind of trauma bonding related to orgasm or sexual response is encased in what the child views in the offender's arousal behaviors. Penthouse or Playboy Magazines traditionally describe signs of arousal. Rather barbaric (in some sense of the word) human responses, such as moaning and groaning, sweating, hip gyrations, and huffing and puffing, are portrayed as signs of arousal that should trigger for adults, at least an understanding. These behaviors are recognized as arousal and often encourage arousal from the reader. A child's perception of these responses, however, without adult cognitions, creates a very different perception. Perceptions from the child may create the foundation for another kind of trauma bonding related to ORGASMS.

Consider a six-year-old child watching a perpetrator huffing, puffing, sweating, moaning, groaning, and ejaculating. The child may be horrified and feel responsible for perhaps inflicting pain, causing discomfort, or creating anxiety. From the child's perception, it is very difficult to understand what these responses mean. Pleasure does not seem to compute. The child may feel responsible for hurting the offender or causing pain because that may be the child's perceptions of those behaviors.

A more profound effect, however, concerns the child's developing years and associations of sexual abuse with adult sexual arousal. In the future when the victim's partner is huffing and puffing, or portraying any other responses known to be associated with arousal, the victim may be returned to the sexual abuse through a painful affective perspective.

It is very difficult for a female patient, as an example, to be attracted to her partner's responses if she is reminded of her abusive experiences in childhood.

I just couldn't stand it if he liked it. When he was tender, intimate, kissing me, and holding me, I did just fine. When he started to get that funny look in his eye, when he started to tremble, to breathe hard, I automatically turned off. I hated him. It was disgusting, repulsive. He looked like the barnyard dog. If he just didn't like it, I would be all right.

Obviously, Betty's relationship with her husband from a sexual perspective is doomed. Many years ago the early signs of Betty's trauma bonding surfaced, although no one understood the etiology or the appropriate treatment.

Betty was a reasonably contented adolescent excelling in sports, especially volleyball. One afternoon in particular Betty can recall being taken to the hospital in an ambulance after a severe panic attack at school. In adulthood, Data Collection exercises assisted Betty in understanding keys to her trauma many years ago. Previous to the panic attack, Betty realized that she had been vigorously engaged in volleyball with several of her teammates. She was standing next to several males in the drinking fountain line when she began to feel panic. In adulthood, Betty makes the connection between her male teammates, huffing, puffing, and sweating, to being forced to watch her father

masturbate. The first tragedy is Betty's abuse. The second tragedy is years of being connected to the traumatic bond of *knee jerk* reactions to any signs of male arousal.

What a tragedy for victims to be bound to the traumatic experiences they observed in the arousal of their perpetrator! What a cruel fate to befall the woman's husband who is responding normally and naturally in his sexual experiences! His partner is traumatically bonded to feelings she had watching her father masturbate. She has what could be considered a phobic reaction to male arousal.

Sexual Fantasies

Sexual fantasies of victims are another example of *generic* trauma bonding. A neglected area in the treatment of sexual victims seems to be the victim's arousal to deviant activities or to the perpetrator. In some cases, the trauma bond is the result of a repulsion or a phobic response to the sexual experiences, as in Betty's case. She is appalled by her husband's sexual responsiveness and the trauma bond is manifested in a phobic reaction. A contrary example can demonstrate how the reverse responses can cause a trauma bond for the patient.

Dear Jan,

I am finally writing this all down. I hope you will forgive all the errors and misspelled words because I don't have very much confidence in putting words down correctly. I hope this letter helps someone else because it is very hard to write. I just feel like I am going to explode inside so the whole thing has to be worth something to someone.

I remember growing up with a strange feeling about my family. We were the kind of family that you see on T.V. with everything going perfect, all the time. My mother always looked like the ladies do on television with perfect hair, perfect clothes and a perfect house. I have no idea what time of the day she would get going in the morning because I always remember everything being taken care of and everything in its place. I remember getting up in the morning with the smell of my father's ejaculation all over me and my pajamas. I felt dirty and ugly. I would look over to my dresser and there would be my clothes neatly laying in special little piles in order of how they were to be used. My matching ribbons, matching socks, and color coordinated outfit caused a rage to swell up inside of me. Those things were not there when I went to bed! Somehow I had this feeling that while my father was shoving his penis in my mouth, my mother was three feet away, smoothing out the wrinkles in my socks, smiling pleasantly, and planning a special casserole for dinner.

I can't remember the first time my father touched me sexually. He was so discreet with the things he did. I remember sitting on his lap and he would let me pretend that I was driving the car. His hands and fingers were all over me. It was a feeling of excitement. I always thought that these special times with dad were very, very exciting because of the things *he let me do,* when actually it was exciting because of what he was doing. As a teenager, I learned what I had done. I recognized that I was sexually excited and it made me furious at myself. I felt like a whore.

Everything my father did to me had a feeling of excitement and secretiveness about it. He would wink at me when my mother was scolding me — and this made me feel special. I knew that he was saying — *It's okay, you don't have to listen to her.* He had this way of making me feel underhanded and sneaky. I always had the feeling that I was dishonest and a cheat because of the special treatment he gave me. Sometimes when I was in trouble with my mother he would immediately take me off somewhere alone and touch me sexually. I remember one specific time he volunteered to punish me and took me to the bedroom. He smiled and said, *We will not punish a special, little girl like you. We will pretend to mommy that we got a spanking.* Then he would spread my legs and begin touching me. Instead of feeling violated, I felt very special and very close to him. He had a way to bring those sexual feelings to me and he would recognize my arousal and then smile at me. He would say, *You like that a lot better than a spanking, don't you?* When we came out of the bedroom, he would be firm and allow me to take part in his conspiracy. I had mixed feelings of being proud that I was special and feeling guilty about what I had done.

What all this taught me was that you *use* sex. He cheated me out of knowing any kind of intimacy or trust in sex. I hated him, I hate him, yet I would probably have sex with him today just to have him be close to me. I seek his love through every sexual relationship I have had. I seem to take him into each relationship with me. I am the whore in the family, I was the promiscuous teenage girl, I am the bad mother, I am the failure in the family — and my father is still in control and still the focus of my fantasies, and my mother is still perfect.

Before I was eight, I had every part of my body touched, examined, fondled, licked and violated. I had no privacy, no trust, no security. I loved what my father did to me while he was doing it but hated myself when it was over. I knew I was bad, I knew I was not like the other kids. I just never fit in, of course, except with him.

I know that you tell me in group what I should be feeling. The therapy has helped and I can put it all in the right perspective if I choose. I understand that I was the victim and that I am not to blame. I know all these things but I can't stop the swelling inside of me. It's so boring without him. You say it will continue to get better and I will continue. When I see what damage I have suffered, I want to scream. Instead of screaming, I will keep going like you say, but it's so hard not to give it up. It's so empty.

I think of all the chances I have had in life and of all the accomplishments I have made. In your groups, you talk about being a *B+* all my life and I guess you are right. I wonder if my need for excitement tells me that unless I have secret, illegal, scary sex I will never be fulfilled. My *B+* in life will always be my lack of excitement that probably only my father will be able to give me. I feel so numb when I think about what is coming up ahead, and so bored. I think the program has done me good and I plan to keep working, but I have this sense of depression when I think about laying to rest the feelings I have for my father. It is just horrible to have these feelings.

I need to stop writing. *Reprinted by Permission*

Rachel undoubtedly is caught in a trauma bonding with her father through the excitement, the intensity, and sexual stimulation that have become embedded in her arousal system. Rachel's sexual fantasy development is similar to the deviancy acts committed upon her during childhood. Unfortunately, Rachel has two battles to fight, thus resulting in her trauma bond.

The first battle is that Rachel is ashamed, embarrassed, and uncomfortable with her own fantasy development. On one hand, she absolutely hates her father for what he did; on the other hand, he seems to be the source of her arousal. In tender, kind, intimate relationships with adult men, Rachel is bored. When fantasizing about abusive, deviant, degrading, and hostile scenarios, Rachel is aroused. Her father continues to maintain control even though he is 73, a thousand miles away, old and decrepit.

Double Trouble

The second issue in Rachel's battle is the difficulty she finds in facing and eventually receiving help for her trauma. If Rachel had been involved in an airplane crash and survived, her friends, her marital partner, or her family would have no problem understanding her upheaval. If Rachel had been raped in the grocery store parking lot, Rachel's support system would rally around and assist in her needs for help. Will Rachel's friends, husband, and family understand that the residual effects of her sexual abuse are found in an arousal toward deviant sexual activity or toward a

deviant sexual person? Will her support system be empathetic?

Additionally, will the therapeutic intervention designed for Rachel give her comfort in this rather ugly trauma? If Rachel described phobic reactions, abhorrence, and resistance toward sex, more than likely she will be met with understanding and empathy. If Rachel talks about the enjoyment of her fantasies surrounding the deviant acts, will she be met by the same sense of empathy and support from learned professionals?

Not only do traditional ideas exist regarding how victims are traumatized, but the same guidelines mandate traditional symptoms. As an example, there appear to be acceptable symptoms and unacceptable symptoms. Some symptoms seem to be much more glamorous and accepted by professionals than others.

Victims who commit suicide or exhibit signs of depression or phobic reactions toward sexuality seem to be much more likely to receive empathic responses from professionals. Victims such as Rachel, whose trauma is related to an attraction toward the perpetrator, seem to be less acceptable, making Rachel's rehabilitation even more difficult.

The trauma bond, then, for those patients who have built their arousal systems around deviancy occurs much the same as in Rachel's battles. The guilt and rejection of self are profound examples of trauma bonding while the difficulties in receiving effective treatment compound the potential for trauma.

THE STUD HORSE THEORY

What is the Stud Horse Theory? — What the Stud Horse Theory is Not!

The Stud Horse Theory is not a common theory taught at traditional veterinarian schools. The Stud Horse Theory *is* a pervading attitude regarding sexual responsiveness in sexual consent. Founded in this society's belief is the idea that somehow men, and on occasion women, are driven out of control due to presentation of sexual stimuli. Rapists are often excused from their very violent acts due to the enticing clothing worn by the victim/seductress. Affairs in a marital arrangement are often forgiven with statements such as, *She was so attractive, I am only human* (which in actuality means *I'm only animal*).

The Stud Horse Theory should be used to understand or point out the difference between the human sexual response and more animalistic responses. The Stud Horse, as an example, does not stand in the field, look over to the mare, and contemplate, *Gee, she has nice withers* or *She's got a great tail!* Simply the smell from the mare's discharge, as a result of her ovulation cycle, finds its way to the nostrils of the stud horse, resulting in a desire, if not rage, to break through the fence and breed. Animals do not make responsible sexual decisions! Animals respond according to their sensory stimulation and their instincts. Human beings are a different matter.

Unfortunately, the sexual victim lives in a world that covertly condones the Stud Horse Theory. *Men just can't help acting on impulse* is an example of an advertisement suggesting that from certain sexual stimuli, a man, and in some cases a woman, is rendered out of control. From a very early age, sexual victims learn these messages even concerning the seductiveness of children. As an example, victims may see very small children advertising such products as Chanel #5 perfume or women's clothing. As will be further explained in Chapter Nine, in the development of the children, independent of sexual abuse, clear messages suggest that the attractiveness or the sensuality of one person can cause another person to be out of control.

In reference to the data of Chapter Four, it is clear that the identification of the victim and offender was extremely important. This process is inhibited as the victim becomes bound in a guilt-ridden response, feeling in possession of the *stimuli* that caused the abuse to happen. The trauma bond is guilt. Society increases the trauma bond by encouraging the victim to actually believe that adults can be rendered out of control due to the attractiveness of the child.

Compounding the problem of the Stud Horse Theory are sex offenders and their behaviors. Sex offenders typically want to create certain elements in the sexually abusive scenario that will reduce their guilt and responsibility. Effort may be exerted to have the victim feel as though he/she has caused the offender to act inappropriately. While this attitude may help the offender rationalize the deed, it has a profound effect on the trauma bonding felt by the victim. In consideration of the Stud Horse Theory, the following statements from sexual offenders have tremendous impact.

To Angela,
You know if your breasts hadn't grown, I never would have allowed you to touch me like this.

To Candice,
You're prettier than your mother. I just couldn't help it. It's a woman's job to be attractive to a man and your mother isn't doing her job.

To William,
You're a young man now and I have been watching you. I know you get hard-ons in class. The rest of the boys don't seem to have the problem you have. There doesn't seem to be much else I can do but to find out exactly what was going on.

The issue of feeling responsible or being caught in a traumatic bond because of sexual attractiveness is typically attached to the female victim. In the media, advertising, television, etc., females are portrayed as being seductive and the male as being seduced by female temptation. There have been some cases in this study, however, that involve abuse of a male

through teaching a child this same irresponsible, sexist attitude.

Rod can't remember when his father first began the discussions. Rod only remembers learning from a very early age that someday his father would tell him when the time had come. Rod reports that he knew this time was directly related to his sister's development. At 11, Teresa was held down by her father while Rodney attempted intercourse. Months and months of previous discussion about what would happen to him, when his sister's breasts developed, was clear in Rodney's mind. Rodney was punished for failing to maintain an erection at age 13 during the first abuse of Teresa. Rodney was told that his father would have nothing to do with him until he felt the next urge.

The next time you see your sister's tits or her pussy and it gets you a hard-on, you better act. It's her stuff that will do it. If you don't act when you first see it, you will never be able to be a man.

This situation caused extreme conflict for Rodney as he tended to be a passive, sensitive, young man. His father's teaching about Teresa's development causing him to act on sexual impulse enveloped Rodney in a trauma bond. Rodney did not continue molesting Teresa. He continued attempts at suicide, suffered from depression, and as an adult, struggled with homosexuality.

The Big R

The *Big R* stands for *responsibility*. The trauma bond is often encased in the ideations and attitudes that the victim has regarding responsibility for trauma as a result of the victim's disclosure or attempts at disclosure. As indicated in several of the categories in this data sample, many victims did report and the response was less than favorable. The resulting trauma appears to be encased in the responsibility felt by the victim *due to the disclosure*. This responsibility, or the *Big R* takes on many faces within the *post -disclosure arena*.

Wanda and her sisters, brothers, and mother spent each Sunday at the prison. Visiting hours were from 10:00-2:00. Mother and the other children spent approximately 1 1/2 hours in inspection waiting lines and paperwork, and approximately 1 1/2 hours with Wanda's father. Wanda had reported to her teacher about her father's sexual abuse. The military response was quick and deadly. Wanda's father was sentenced to ten years in prison. Wanda's mother never spoke to her again, and for the rest of Wanda's childhood her mother communicated only through Wanda's siblings.

Wanda was forced to wait on the steps of the prison in rain, snow, sleet, or shine while the family visited inside for three hours, each Sunday. Not only was the three-hour wait devastating to Wanda on the prison steps, but the other children who were forced to dedicate their Sundays to this ritual created tremendous trauma for Wanda.

Wanda's brothers and sisters were outraged at their Sunday obligation. It was Wanda who had caused them to forego their church activities, their athletic endeavors, and their social events. In her silence, Wanda's mother also told Wanda how she felt about the disclosure.

Had Wanda reported a criminal, stopped a crime from being committed, and rescued a young budding child from the horrors of sexual abuse by a 6'2" drill sergeant? In actuality Wanda became the criminal for causing tremendous trauma by her disclosure. Her father became the hero in the family, and Wanda became the perpetrator. The trauma bond is strong. If the father remains in prison, the family remains obligated and Wanda remains guilty.

Symbiosis

Another example of trauma bonding and the

Big R has to do with symbiosis. In symbiotic relationships, the victim and the perpetrator feed upon each other in a mutually nurturing manner. The role of the parent or the adult, and the role of the child are much the same in symbiotic relationships. The child seems to take on a parental or caring role while the perpetrator seems to be in a dependent role. Unfortunately, the relationship is not equal, thus allowing for disservice and damage to be caused to the victim, not the offender.

Two teenage girls present themselves to the emergency room of the local hospital. Both are suffering from severe cases of influenza, complete with dehydration, dizziness, and vomiting. Emergency room doctors recommend hospitalization but both girls resist. Much to the amazement of hospital staff, the girls contact their parents. Both parents are at home waiting for the notification. It does not appear to be a normal parent-child relationship. The children seem to be concerned about the parents and reluctant to stay in the hospital due to the needs of the parents. The parents seem to be reluctant to allow the children to stay in the hospital due to their own caretaking needs.

When the younger teenager agrees to stay and the older child returns home, depression becomes part of the younger child's attitude and local men-tal health authorities intervene. Sexual abuse is eventually reported. The findings involved in this scenario indicate that the girls have been told from a very early age that their mother, who is alcoholic, despises sex and will begin drinking if the father makes sexual demands. It is clear these children have been responsible for the sexual needs of their father, but the girls have also been responsible for protecting the mother and keeping her sober. Contemplation of disclosure often places children in a very precarious situation. In this case, father may be labeled and convicted as a sexual offender by the system, but the children may become responsible **(Big R)** for their mother's resumed alcoholism. It was only through depression and anxiety resulting from not being able to go home and take care of the parents that the younger adolescent disclosed the secret. Obviously, these children are plagued with tremendous responsibility.

In these situations, trauma bonding results in either the child feeling responsible for tremendous losses as a result of the disclosure, or the child contemplating disclosure and feeling so responsible that disclosure does not occur. In any event, the victim remains connected back to the sexual offender and the sexual abuse, due to tremendous guilt resulting from this responsibility.

CHAPTER SIX / 111

Trauma bonding concerning the **Big R** obviously takes place in childhood but may have lasting and traumatic effects in adulthood. Victims may survive by keeping secrets or protecting a parent or sibling but later become outraged when more clearly understanding the childhood dilemma. It seems that the victim has only two rather deadly choices. The victim either continues to be in a trauma bond through total dedication and responsibility to family members, or the victim is in a trauma bond of outrage toward the unfair situation in childhood. In either case, the victim continues to relive the feelings of the sexual abuse in the traumatic bond.

As will be outlined in the next three chapters, trauma bonding can occur in a variety of different situations relating to the sexual abuse in childhood. Feelings and attitudes about the abuse keep jerking the victim back to the pain. There are many more specific issues, however, relating to trauma bonding which have a more direct impact on organizing the Trauma Assessment itself. While *virgins, orgasms, fantasies, stud horses, and the Big R* seem to be generic issues for consideration in the Trauma Assessment, examination needs to occur on a much more specific level relating to the *players* within the dynamics of sexual abuse trauma.

THE POWER
OF THE OFFENDER

*Who are these people who not only perpetrate crimes against victims, but
also seem to have never-ending power in the victim's future? Is their power
developed? Cultivated? Accidental? Distorted? Unintentional?*

Considering the PLAYERS within the sexually
abusive situation, probably none are more
significant to trauma bonding than the offender. In many cases, it is the offender who
remains in control of the victim's life through
a *traumatic bond.* This is not necessarily due
to the offender's actual power as evaluated by
others. The trauma bonding or the *power of
the offender* is usually founded in events or
situations that took place during the sexually
abusive scenario. Examining this power is an
important issue in the Trauma Assessment and
will be the focus of this chapter.

Victim's Eye View

The first step in understanding the power
offenders have over victims is to delineate
between the victim's perceptions and the adult's
or clinician's perceptions. Those offenders who
may be repulsive or obnoxious often may have
the most power over victims. When professionals learn of incidents where victims are
brutally abused or horribly traumatized through
extraneous events, a common response is rejection of the perpetrator. In actuality, this is the
professional rejection of a perpetrator, without

carefully considering the victims' view. Sadly, this may be an insensitive response and one that is echoed by those individuals who are not necessarily professionals.

The community is an example of how the lack of appreciation for the *victim's view* causes problems. If the *burning shed treatment*, as described in Chapter Three, is revisited, clearly this response also comes from others not empathic toward victimology or the trauma to victims. Rather than understanding the victim's view, this response seems a way to vent anger toward individuals who commit horrible crimes against children. Unfortunately, if a trauma bond is in place, those actions taken against a perpetrator may be indirectly applied to the victim, who is usually the person the community attempts to protect through the *burning shed* mentality. Often trauma bonds have occurred between the perpetrator and the victim, resulting in the victim feeling responsible for the perpetrator and, therefore, if the perpetrator receives tremendous anger and punishment from the community, the victim may accept blame for the offender's pain.

Contrarily, community members may make decisions about the treatment of perpetrators in the opposite direction, suggesting that the crime was insignificant or unimportant. The lack of consequence for the perpetrator (or the reverse of the *burning shed treatment*) may also engage a victim in a trauma bond with the perpetrator, in the form of outrage. The community's response is extremely important in victim rehabilitation. Understanding trauma bonding begins with careful examination, through the Trauma Assessment, of the trauma bond between the victim and the perpetrator. The most important step in understanding the trauma bond is to recognize that the views of the community are not as important as the view of the victim toward the perpetrator.

We — Not Thee

The *burning shed treatment* allows individuals to laugh, to feel as though a solution has been created, and, most importantly, to stop *thinking*. The *burning shed treatment* is common in many areas because community attitudes concerning sexual perpetrators are believed to automatically coincide with the victim's attitudes. Nothing could be further from the truth.

It is not the community's, the family's, or the therapist's attitude, but the victim's perceptions, that are important. The four-year-old child truly believes the offender who says, *If you tell, Mom will go crazy and it will be your fault*. At 44, the victim still approaches disclosure with trepidation, not cognitively, but affectively. The offender does not need to be involved in the victim's life in order to have tremendous power and control. Just as a child who was forced to eat oatmeal, cold and soggy at the breakfast table, will always hate oatmeal, the child who was sexually abused will continue to feel the same feelings that the *oatmeal-phobic* 44-year-old bank executive feels when sitting in front of a bowl of Quaker Oats. How does this powerful source emerge? How does the offender keep such power, years and sometimes decades later?

Captain Hook(s)

The most powerful hook or trauma bond between the victim and the offender relates to the offender who is still in contact with the victim, who still demands a relationship with the victim, who still has power over the victim due to a continued relationship. In adulthood, the victim continues to respond to many of the affective responses of the four-year-old. Also traumatic is that often the offender improves in status and stature while the victim tends to succumb to the symptoms of sexual abuse and to manifest behavior that renders the *victim status* less possible.

The outrage or frustration with secrecy and continued pain combine with obligation and duty to the offender and entangle the victim in a traumatic bond. In most situations, it is the victim's frustration and symptoms which become the focus of the surrounding support system or family. Due to unflattering symptomatology, the victim often becomes the perpetrator, engaging in drug and alcohol problems, depression, suicide, and other self-abusive cycles. It is not uncommon in the years following the abuse to find the sexual offender enhancing his/her status in the family while the victim's status continues to disintegrate. The *good news* regarding this therapeutic situation is in the possibility of resolution and rehabilita-

tion because the perpetrator is still available. It is those scenarios where the offender continues to have power over the victim without a possibility of resolution due to absence, incapacitation, incarceration, etc., that evolves to a more bleak picture for resolution.

The Unknown Offender

As an example of trauma bonding, the lack of identity of the offender can cause victim suffering. The following scenario is a classic example of the power of the unknown offender, or the trauma bonding held by the offender when the victim has nowhere to focus anger, frustration, betrayal, pain, or *fear*.

Wilma was the middle child of seven children. There was nothing particularly profound about Wilma except that on a cold winter night, she slept closest to the door. This was a very poor family living in a one bedroom trailer, requiring all the children to sleep near the stove in the front room while the parents slept in the only bedroom.

An unknown assailant, perhaps confused of his whereabouts, stumbled into the living room, grabbed Wilma, and proceeded to rape her. Due to the fact that there were so many human bodies entwined on the living room rug, it was not until penetration occurred that Wilma was clear she was being assaulted. Piercing pain resulted to the point where Wilma nearly lost consciousness. By the time her rapist had completed orgasm, several of the children were sitting up crying, whimpering, and Wilma was able to focus on her assailant. The man fled the home with Wilma knowing only that he was Hispanic, had a stocking cap, and smelled of alcohol.

The resulting trauma for this child occurred because of the absence of a clear identity of the offender. The child lives in a community where 40% of the population is Hispanic. The child also lives in a community where the winter season is more than five months in duration. The trauma bond occurs because many Hispanic individuals wear stocking caps in close proximity of Wilma's home, her safety net, and her sense of security. The power of the offender results in the victim not being able to identify any specific individual. All Hispanic males, especially with stocking caps, cause the victim to develop agoraphobia. The victim is unable to leave her home, she is unable to feel safe, and eventually she is totally unable to function. The unknown offender has control due to the victim's lack of focus for her fear and outrage. Because of the trauma bond, Wilma is completely vulnerable.

The Deceased Offender

If the offender who is unknown to the victim can have power, what happens to the perpetrator who is *innocent* due to death? A strange but deadly arrangement occurs as death befalls the perpetrator and trauma befalls the victim.

Rarely do individuals who are deceased take on negative characteristics within families. Often, even the cruelest of fathers or mothers seem to emerge in a more positive light once they decease. It is easier for families to focus upon the positive rather than the negative following the death of a family member. Again, whenever the perpetrator's status forbids taking on the role of the guilty person, a traumatic bonding occurs.

Reality for the present does not seem to apply. Past attitudes and feelings pervade and lay the foundation for trauma bonding. At the time of abuse, the sexual offender is often a young, vigorous, or powerful individual, not only in the relationship with the child, but in the relationship with others connected to the child. During the time of the sexual abuse, the offender usually has the victim under control, enshrouded in confusion or secrecy. As children proceed through development, they are continually *looking backward* on their confusion, their powerlessness, and often their stupidity for not stopping the abuse. This evaluation by the victim usually encourages feelings of shame and degradation for being powerless. Even for sexual victims who recognize the abuse as inappropriate, but were unable to prevent the abuse, proceeding through development with a helplessness and hopelessness will be likely.

It is usually not until either late adolescence or adulthood that the victim attempts to regain some kind of power. Outrage often replaces helplessness. By this time, the offender's status seems to have gone in a different direction. Through the years, the offender may be in the process of losing power. Often, the death of the offender signifies the utmost in powerlessness. *How can anyone seem to have power in death?* On a surface level, it seems the answer is *there is no power in death*. Trauma bonding gives a different answer.

Tipping the Scales of Justice

Trauma bonding requires examination of the balance between the victim and the offender in the identification process of the *guilty and innocent*. If the offender dies either in old age or even in a younger time period, the offender is often eulogized and, as in this society's tradition, often viewed with respect. Even those individuals with shady character or questionable virtues are usually respected in death. Families commonly attempt to remember the positive aspects of individuals who have died. This creates a particularly difficult situation for the victim who, in adulthood or late adolescence, may be attempting to identify the perpetrator as the person responsible for the crime. A death on the part of the offender abruptly stops this process and prevents the victim from taking the first step toward rehabilitation.

Small children who have not yet recognized the significance of the sexual abuse may, at the time of the offender's death, be forbidden to view the offender as responsible. The victim may proceed through childhood in the accompaniment of individuals who continue to respect the offender. Had the offender remained alive and demonstrated human frailties, the victim could have perhaps carefully examined both positive and negative aspects of the perpetrator. A *process* could have occurred. Unfortunately, through the death of the perpetrator, the adult or the child victim is prevented from identifying the perpetrator as guilty and responsible.

Evelyn and her sister Evonne were both sexually abused during childhood by the family's favorite uncle. Upon return from Vietnam, this individual had become involved with the family through a marriage to the girl's aunt. Although this individual seldom obtained consistent employment, had substance abuse problems, and, often was unfaithful to his wife, he nonetheless cultivated a reputation of an endearing father to his children and to his nieces and nephews. Since Evonne and Evelyn's aunt needed to work outside the home, this uncle became a primary childcare provider for many nieces and nephews within the family, as well as for his own children.

At family functions, this individual always seemed to be the person who organized the children's games and orchestrated a positive and playful attitude. His social competencies were profound and family functions were disappointing without his presence.

Sexual abuse of the children took place over a four- to five-year period. Sexual abuse was encased in *games* but eventually escalated toward cunnilingus and fellatio. Abruptly, the uncle was killed in an automobile accident. Evonne and Evelyn had not yet reached a developmental stage that would provide them with an awareness of the inappropriateness of his sexual behaviors.

The victims attended the funeral and then participated in a year of extensive family mourning. The natural children of the perpetrator spent a great deal of time in the home of Evonne and Evelyn. Their sadness over the loss of their father permeated Evelyn and Evonne's household. By the time the victims had become aware of the improprieties of their uncle's behavior, the offender had been raised to a position of eloquence and respectability. None of his negative characteristics were ever discussed, and constant reminders of his heroic term in Vietnam were exhibited to the children.

As Evonne and Evelyn recognized elements of their sexual abuse, they also recognized the futility in identifying their uncle as the perpetrator. Anger and frustration were internalized and both victims began extremely self-abusive cycles. Antagonism developed toward peripheral family members as Evelyn and Evonne worried that perhaps the sexual abuse was known and not prevented. These girls remained in a *trauma bond* with the perpetrator since, because of his death, he was never allowed to accept the perpetrator role. The abuse remained unresolved.

The Incapacitated Offender

In death, the offender takes on an extremely powerful role, unable to accept any or very little blame. But what happens to an *alive* but incapacitated offender? Even more devastating to victims may be the perpetrator who becomes incapacitated and not only remains in a positive position through eulogizing from the family but may demand constant attention in a medical or *dutiful* way.

Perhaps worse than dying is the offender who becomes incapacitated and requires the family to organize themselves into shifts of constant care. Not only are the memories of the offender suddenly required to be positive, but the family is forced to be actively involved in the perpetrator's life while the perpetrator lies in a state of *innocence*. Additionally, it is considered highly improper to be critical of the handicapped or incapacitated, further stifling feelings of anger. In death, perhaps the perpetrator can eventually be forgotten to some degree or at least remembered less. In comparison, the incapacitated offender requires a constant vigilance from the family.

Children are typically raised to be respectful, empathetic, and sympathetic toward those who are less fortunate. The victim of the incapacitated perpetrator will have very little opportunity to recognize the negative aspects of the offender's abusive behavior. It is likely that the victim will be constantly reminded of the offender's continued power over not only the victim, but over the family from which the victim is desperately seeking support. Again, power goes to the offender.

In early adolescence, Jason finally reports to his girlfriend that his father has sexually abused him for the last five years. Jason's girlfriend is horrified and eventually reports to her parents, against Jason's wishes. Subsequent and follow-up reports allow the abuse to be known to the family and eventually law enforcement. An investigation takes place and initially Jason is protected. The family supports Jason as a victim. Jason's father is forced to leave the family and volunteers for the local treatment program. Frustrated, over his loss of power in the family, Jason's father violates the no-contact order and, after consuming a great deal of alcohol, visits the family home. Following a raging argument, Jason's father places a gun to his forehead and fires.

Jason's father does not succumb to the injury and instead remains in a coma for the next few weeks. Initially, Jason had been supported; however, as the life and death situation of his father remains in question, support for Jason diminishes, and support naturally gravitates toward the offender. In spite of the family sympathy Jason had received from many members, he is now forced to view constant vigilance and dedication to the man who had sexually abused him for five years. Pity and support for Jason's father permeated the family. Obviously, there was no prosecution, which could have affirmed Jason's victim status. Financial efforts that perhaps would have supported Jason's treatment endeavors were distributed among family members for medical attention for the father.

Approximately six months after his father became incapacitated, Jason reported, *I would rather have my dad back and have to give him head every day than live in my family the way it is now. If he dies, I don't think I can take it, and if he continues to live like this, I don't think I can continue.*

Unreported Offender

Often, the nature of the trauma bond occurs when the victim is unable to report the offender and clarify the abuse. This may occur in adulthood or late adolescence when the victim has finally recognized the improprieties of the offender behavior. In the *victim's mind,* the *identification of the perpetrator and the victim* has finally occurred. However, the difficulty and the *trauma bond* lies in the victim's fear of losing a position in the family if sexual abuse is reported. The trauma bond occurs because the *victim status* is impossible to share with others.

Sexual abuse remains a secret and the victim is often forced to be in contact with the sexual offender. The trauma bond occurs in the forced situation of *continuing business as usual*. The victim observes the offender being supported and a having a powerful position within the family or cycle of relationships. The offender does not necessarily need to be a family member but could be, as an example, a teacher who continues to be acknowledged in the local school system or a church member who has a powerful position in the victim's chosen religion.

As the victim attempts to weigh all the options, it is determined that reporting will be more painful and less rehabilitating than keeping the secret. The victim is in a trauma bond through forced participation with either the perpetrator or others who are connected with the perpetrator. A raging debate continues internally, as the victim wants to feel exonerated and protected, but at the same time feels impotent due to the perpetrator's powerful position. Even though the victim may have made the right decision in consideration of a society which is ill-prepared to protect the emotional safety of victims, nonetheless the victim remains in a trauma bond and under the power of the offender due to the secrecy.

Saundra is sexually abused by her Sunday school teacher at girl's camp. The abuse takes place *each* summer and occurs for a duration of approximately two weeks. During the winter months, Saundra attended church where her abuser had a powerful position and continued to teach Sunday school. Although no abuse occurred during Sunday school classes, Saundra was constantly forced to view this individual's power and control over others.

To increase Saundra's frustration as an adult, she was married in the same church and the perpetrator took part in the wedding ceremony as a church official. As Saundra gained strength in adulthood, she became more frustrated over the lack of consequence for the perpetrator. Saundra's bitterness toward her church mounted and eventually culminated in a rejection of her religion due to the fact that even her husband continued to talk in positive terms about the perpetrator. To Saundra, this individual continued to have power over her and, in fact, seemed to be invading her private life just as though the abuse was continuing. As Saundra contemplated reporting the abuse, she also contemplated her fears of rejection. Many of Saundra's previous feelings of being betrayed and dirty surfaced. Just as she had felt she would not be believed in childhood, she also feared disbelief in adulthood. The trauma bond continued to plague Saundra to the point where divorce became imminent. Saundra had become nearly sexually dysfunctional and extremely paranoid in regards to the protection of her own children. Although Saundra's decision not to report may have seemed best, nonetheless the trauma bond continued to victimize Saundra.

from sexual abuse suffered by her grandfather, Paula's grandfather was becoming weak, feeble, and aged. As Paula took painful steps toward informing her mother that she had been sexually abused, she was met with disgust and rejection for being antagonistic toward the *older gentleman*. In spite of the fact that the grandfather had sexually abused Paula's mother in childhood, Paula's mother now faced the prospect of *losing her father*. Paula's mother does not want the *father/daughter* relationship disturbed.

The Aged Offender

Through the natural progression of time, the offender may lose the ability to take on the role of the perpetrator. It is not uncommon in the aging process of the offender that conflict arises as the victim tries to view the perpetrator as responsible, deviant, and undesirable. Simply through the process of obtaining gray hair, becoming feeble, and losing capacity, the perpetrator is weakened and often pitied by others. The natural aging process robs the childhood victim, in adulthood, of being able to identify the *perpetrator and the victim*. As years go by, the victim may gain power and strength, but in proportion the offender often loses power, and thus another trauma bond emerges.

Unfortunately, by the time Paula was strong, assertive, and taking extremely healthy steps toward rehabilitation

For Paula's mother, the grandfather is now safe in his old age and she is attempting to renew a relationship with him that has been impossible due to her abuse as a child. As Paula's mother attempts to resolve her relationship with her perpetrator, she is desperately drawn to the perpetrator in a *hope* of finally being accepted. The *four-year-old* in Paula's mother wants a relationship because *daddy is finally safe*! The trauma bond for Paula strengthens. Paula's mother's coping skill regarding her own abuse turns Paula away since, if Paula had been sexually abused and was truly victimized, Paula's mother would need to be a victim as well. This resolution was absolutely impossible for Paula's mother and Paula was left *becoming the perpetrator* for attacking an aged and protected grandfather.

In-Maturity Offender Power

Some trauma bonding occurs not necessarily between the victim and the offender, but in the offender's entourage of supporters. As in Paula's case, it is often a family denial system that is deadly for the victim. This trauma bonding occurs in an attempt to become *mature* or in the desperate attempt of family members who have participated in a dysfunctional family to cope by denying abusive or dysfunctional family issues from the past. It may be family members' desperate attempt to maintain a fairy tale image of the family that may create the trauma bond between the offender and the victim. Even though the offender may be competent and capable of accepting the perpetrator role, it may be the family, in their attempts to become mature, that tightens the trauma bond for the victim.

Gwendolyn received therapy as an adult regarding the sexual abuse suffered from her father. Many elements of the dysfunctional family were also part of Gwendolyn's trauma. The perpetrator himself did not seem to be as important to Gwendolyn as her remaining family members. Gwendolyn had identified her father as the perpetrator and was not particularly interested in confronting him or establishing a relationship. However, the rest of the family was extremely important to Gwendolyn in her road to recovery.

As Gwendolyn attempts to take steps toward resolving family conflicts with her brothers and sisters, she is met with extreme resistance. Comments made to her illustrate family denial: *Why are you stirring this up now? Our parents did the best they could under the circumstances. You're only remembering the bad things.*

In actuality, Gwendolyn becomes the perpetrator for attacking the dysfunctional family in adulthood. Although the family members may not be directly supportive of the perpetrator or denying that the sexual abuse occurred, they nonetheless force Gwendolyn to be guilty for breaking a *hopeful harmony* of the family's denial system.

What is even more cruel for Gwendolyn is that her family quickly acknowledges that the abuse took place. There is no struggle or denial. In fact, by so easily acknowledging Gwendolyn was sexually abused and then denying the dysfunction of the family (or essentially, her pain), Gwendolyn's brothers and sisters are cruelly saying *So what?* This may make Gwendolyn even more helpless and in a tighter trauma bond than before her abuse was acknowledged.

Teetering And Tottering Under The Power Of The Offender

The sexual victim seems to vacillate back and forth on a deadly spectrum between two roles, but always under the power of the offender. Both of these roles adapted by the victim keep the victim under the power of the offender with a variety of trauma bond situations. The victim seems to range between two ends of the spectrum, tittering and tottering under the offender's power. At the core of this bonding is the inequitable situation between the perpetrator and the victim. The victim cannot be an adult, competent, in control, as long as vacillation between these two spectrum positions occurs.

The Raging Child

On one end of the spectrum is the raging child, angry, furious, and often *self-abusive* due to anger. The power given to the offender is one of *lack of control* on the part of the victim. In spite of the age of the victim, this is an outraged *child* furious at the reality of the sexual abuse. Unfortunately, due to the power and control of the offender, this outrage is hardly ever directed at the perpetrator. Instead, the victim may act out in school, abuse drugs or alcohol, become sexually promiscuous, etc., while the perpetrator remains intact, powerful, and often unscathed. It is common for victims to set up situations of self-abuse in their outrage toward the offender which prevent sympathy or empathy to the victim when sexual abuse is finally

reported. The trauma bonding occurs because the perpetrator controls the victim as a self-abusive status is adapted.

Although small children may not have the capabilities of becoming involved with substance abuse, marrying abusive individuals, or committing crimes, they can behave in ways that are a response to outrage. Similar to the adult, small children have nowhere to attach their anger since the perpetrator has control and power. The child's behavior, much the same as the outraged adult, forces the child to *become the perpetrator* through uncontrollable rage.

The Pleading Child

On the other end of the spectrum is the pleading, begging child wanting to be rescued, cared for, and finally loved. The figure of this child stands with outreached hands toward the perpetrator in hopes that wishes and dreams of the child will be met. Rather than the outraged, out of control child, this child is pleading and begging for love and acceptance.

The nature of the trauma bond on this end of the spectrum may result as the victim puts forth great effort to please the offender or to be accepted by the offender. Even though in adulthood the victim may be away from the offender or resist being in contact with the offender, the victim may adopt obsessive, compulsive, perfectionistic behavior as a hope to please the offender and finally become *worthwhile.*

Traveling to this end of the spectrum is a result of many years of developing the coping skill of accepting responsibility for the abuse in order to have some control. Through taking on responsibility, the victim becomes the reason for failures. This allows some resolution in the child's mind. In adolescence or adulthood, *the child within* may continue to please or to beg for the offender's acceptance. This may be on a subconscious level, but nonetheless the child is trapped in a trauma bond of *pleasing*. As the victim's obsessive perfectionism is processing, not for the purpose of personal growth or accomplishment, the trauma bond is in place through dedication and *hope* of final acceptance.

Teetering and tottering between the begging child and the outraged child is an example of perpetual trauma bonding. At times, the victim may become outraged when recognizing the damage that has resulted. The victim may become the raging child, with stomping feet and obnoxious language. The victim may write hateful letters, discuss the abuse in a confrontive or angry manner, or behave in an erratic way, much the same as a *temper tantrum*. Unfortunately, with the perpetrator's power intact, the result of this behavior is compounding feelings of guilt, shame, worry, or rejection. The victim has become the *bad child* for being out of control. The victim will often retreat after what may appear to be a very assertive and confrontive behavior to the other end of the spectrum where the victim is pleading and begging for forgiveness. Often, without any response from the perpetrator,

the victim will attempt to compensate for the *outraged child* previously exhibited. The victim may want to soothe guilty feelings by total dedication to the offender not only in the hope that forgiveness will occur for outrageous acts, but in an eternal *hope* to be loved and protected by the perpetrator.

As time passes, the *hopeful* victim heals and feels as though compensation has been made for the *outrageous* child. The pleading child takes over, soothing guilt. Eventually, however, when guilt is no longer an issue for the pleading child, the outraged child begins to be reminded of the injustices of the sexual abuse. Eventually, anger simmers to the point of boiling. The outraged child emerges, bringing the victim to the other end of the spectrum and the deadly cycle repeats.

Bouncing back and forth from one end of the spectrum to the other plagues many victims who were not allowed to resolve abuse in childhood. The nature of the trauma bond forces the victim to be *stuck* with many childlike feelings and attitudes. The vicious cycle from the outraged child to the begging child can keep the victim tied to the perpetrator and to the abuse, for decades. Resolution or recovery is somewhere between both ends of the spectrum but, most importantly, from a status as an *adult*.

The offender has the child hooked to being *a child* with similar childhood emotions and responses. Recovery requires breaking of the trauma bond through maturity and through an adultlike approach from an intellectual, as well as from an affective perspective.

Summary

Those who would suggest that resolution and recovery occur through the death of an offender, through incarceration, through punishment of the offender, or through separation of the victim and offender may need to reconsider. Trauma bonding keeps the power of the offender alive and usually has very little to do with the *actual* power of the offender. As described in many of the previous examples, even if the offender is losing power through death, incapacitation, or age, the victim also loses since the perpetrator is unable to take on the role of the perpetrator.

The inequities in the power system in the relationship triangle must be uncovered in a Sexual Victim Trauma Assessment in order to prevent trauma bonding from occurring in the future. Small children have *potential* trauma bonds that can be eradicated early and before deadly cultivation. Older patients need clarity and explanation of the strings tying the victim to the offender in order for recovery to occur. These issues and answers regarding the power of the offender emerge in the Sexual Victim Trauma Assessment.

YES, MOMMIE, WE HEAR YOU

And what about the mother in the deadly triangle of trauma bonding? Is she automatically caring, supportive, and empathic to her children, demonstrating undying love and selflessness? Or is she the NON-OFFENDING, but often OFFENSIVE, spouse?

In examining trauma to children, the power of the offender emerges as obvious. There may be other individuals within the scheme of players, however, who also have extreme potential for trauma bonding with the victim. Other hooks from relationships may occur, preventing the wounds of sexual abuse from healing.

Higher and Higher, Lower and Lower

Trauma Assessment research suggests that in many cases the most traumatic bonding occurs with family members or individuals who were perhaps more important than the offender. The mother in the incestuous family may be the primary owner of the trauma bond outside the power of the offender. There are several reasons, which will be described later, why the non-offending parent, being a mother, may be more traumatizing than perhaps a *set* of parents or a non-offending parent that is the father. The trauma bonding from the mother could actually apply to various other individuals within the incestuous or sexual abuse triangle. For particular reasons, however, the mother seems to be the most common form of trauma bonding, outside the relationship between the victim and the perpetrator.

What appears most profound in the mother/child trauma bond is the expectations

127

put upon the mother and the subsequent betrayal of the child's expectations (hope). Society has very clear expectations for parents, especially the mother. Whenever expectations are enhanced, the trauma bonding (the damage to victims from betrayal) occurs. With the elevation of expectations, betrayal of those expectations has profound effects.

A converse example may demonstrate this point. If an individual is perceived by the child to be unimportant and the child's perceptions are affirmed by society, or if an individual has low status and therefore low expectations, the child may be minimally traumatized. If a child is sexually abused by an individual for whom there are very few or no expectations, betrayal is almost non-existent. The betrayal becomes generic, and not specific, toward a person. Higher or lower expectations result in proportionate potential for trauma.

Sexual abuse is certainly a crime and unfortunate, but the betrayal of trust is not inherently profound. Often, sexual offending of a child is consistent with many of the other behaviors of the perpetrator. *It was normal for him* — could signal less trauma to a victim. No one expects children to be sexually abused, but if they are abused by someone whose behavior affirms the characteristics of a sexual offender, in all likelihood the trauma would be lessened or perhaps non-existent.

Lisa is sexually abused at age seven by a stepbrother who lived with the family for a short period of time. Lisa's father

regretfully allowed this young man, whom he had not seen for several years, to spent a summer with the family. Prior to Jack's arrival, the children were made aware that Jack had many delinquent tendencies and behavior problems.

Although the children were instructed to be empathic and respectful to Jack, they were made aware that he was not always to be trusted. Although the sexual abuse of Lisa lasted for three weeks before she reported, Lisa was nearly asymptomatic in adulthood. Jack's reputation and the expectations of Jack allowed Lisa to view her sexual abuse as one of his many inappropriate behaviors. Additionally, Lisa's surrounding family viewed Jack's behavior much the same. Lisa was clearly identified as the victim, resulting in minimal trauma for her at a later time.

In consideration of trauma bonding with a mother, a different pattern of expectation emerges. What are the requirements for a mother from a sociological perspective? And how does that affect trauma bonding for victims?

"M" Is For The Million Things You Gave Me

Who is the American Mother and what does her status provide the victim in consideration of trauma bonding? Before the question is answered, it must be recognized that *reality* does not necessarily betray the child. It is the mystical and mythical portrayal of *mothers* and what they *should* be that creates trauma bonding. Many victims can intellectually describe defects and liabilities concerning their mother's job as a caretaker. On a cognitive plane, it may not be difficult for victims to describe such issues as abandonment, emotional neglect, jealousy, and rejection. Affectively, however, victims are often unable to give up or to avoid trauma because of their *hope* in what their mother might have been, or should have been.

Is the American mother, the typical American mother, someone who automatically loves her children? *A face only a mother could love* is a common statement describing the unselfish and unconditional love mothers have for their children. Mothers are portrayed as being self-sacrificing and happily centering their lives around PTA meetings and the proper consistency of oatmeal. A great deal has been written about maternal instincts, the bond between mothers and their children at birth, and the tragedy of women relinquishing children for adoption. More uncommon are ideas of paternal instincts or the tragedy of men losing their children through adoption or abortion.

In earlier times, women were portrayed as being quite satisfied and fulfilled with rearing children and providing a home for their children. In more recent years, many women have left the home and family for careers, yet they are constantly reminded of the conflict between self-fulfillment and their maternal obligations. Articles in women's magazine regarding the joy of childrearing now must share pages with articles about the trauma women suffer when they cannot be a full-time mother. Tips are provided for career women on how to balance the selfishness of their careers with the expected *selflessness* of being a mother.

Love At First Sight

A mother is supposed to be a wife and a partner, but most importantly she is supposed to have unending and undying love for her children. From the moment children peek out of the womb, women are expected to forget labor pain, swelling ankles, and the grotesqueness of their bodies during the previous nine months. A blood covered, shriveled, shrieking, mound of flesh the size of a football is supposed to result in total amnesia from all previous discomforts. The past nine months are not only forgotten but her future happiness has now been provided. The mere suggestions that some women are angry at their children for birth trauma or that some women may be jealous of their children who receive attention from a doting father are absurd! To consider that women would be disappointed at the sex or the size or the attractiveness of their child is totally rejected. That's not the way real mothers behave!

Beyond birth, other expectations for mothers emerge. Women are believed to be the primary caretaker of their children, in charge of all childhood needs. Although during the child's early years nearly all needs are met by the mother, the level of need decreases as the child first toddles, then walks, and finally runs. To maintain control of her children, the mother must also become the primary disciplinarian. She must enhance her children's feelings regarding her control yet balance that control with the child's need for independence. The more capability children have to be on their own, the more control mother must exert.

I Just Know That's How!

Most children grow up believing, either because of direct teaching or indirect learning, that their mothers know everything. *I can tell when you are lying* is a common refrain from mothers attempting to control their children. Children who cut huge chunks of hair from their foreheads often conduct this exciting activity with the belief or the hope that mother will *never know.* The fact that the child is too young to see in the mirror and observe the obvious bald spot does not prevent the excitement. The child may bury the hair, flush it down the toilet, or create other pain staking activities to destroy the *evidence.* When mother states *I know you have been cutting your hair,* children are often dismayed at her brilliance and her ability to know and control everything. Most mothers delight in these opportunities so their children will mind and follow disciplinary rules. Unfortunately, the fact that mothers *should* know everything contributes considerable ammunition for trauma bonding at a later time.

The most common trauma bond is found with the mother's inability — or, God forbid, *unwillingness* — to know and protect her child. This kind of trauma bonding is focused upon the child's view that somehow the mother knew the abuse was happening. This is the result of other experiences where the child is actually quite clear that the mother knew everything else and, therefore, she not only must know sexual abuse occurred, but must also be affirming the acceptability of the abuse. Even in cases where the mother is brought into a resolution and clarification session at a later time and convinces the victim of her ignorance of the abuse, the victim may be in a traumatic bonding because the replacement for *I know everything that is happening* is *You should have known*!

This is a dilemma not only for the victim but often for the mother, who may have been, in fact, ignorant. This is a *no win* situation because if she did know the sexual abuse was occurring, she failed as a mother to protect her child or stop the perpetrator. If she did not know, her child was not worth protecting in the appropriate, mythical *American Dream* of motherhood.

The nature of this trauma bonding then, is in the expectations upon the mother for loving the child, caring for the child, and being totally, absolutely selfless in regards to the child's protection. An additional betrayal comes from the fact that the mother should have known, or from the fact that if the mother did not care to know, then somehow the child was worthless.

But . . . Why?

Are these myths accurate and worth the pain victims feel in the trauma bond? Why does such expectation and then failure exist in so many incestuous families? And perhaps the question could be asked, *How does sexual abuse occur in many families, sometimes for decades, without the mother recognizing the abuse?* Is the myth of motherhood inaccurate and therefore her lack of knowledge is explainable? Or, are there other reasons why the non-offending parent may be deaf and blind to the incestuous situation within the home? In order to fully understand the incestuous family and prevent trauma bonding, the mythical portrayal of mother and the mother's contribution to the incestuous family should be examined.

Cyclical (Sicklical) Issues

National statistics and this research concerning the Trauma Assessment suggest that the cycle of sexual abuse seems to follow the victim rather than the perpetrator. The result of the non-offending mother being a sexual victim herself may shed light on why the trauma bonding occurs and why there is such a wide split between *expectation* and *betrayal* for the victim. Treatment centers throughout the country report an extremely high rate of children who are involved as patients having a mother who was also sexually abused in childhood. What does the mother's childhood sexual abuse have to do with the cycle of sexual abuse and the

nature of the trauma that will occur between the victim and the betrayal of the mother?

It is commonly believed that the cycle of sexual abuse follows the perpetrator. Studies throughout the country suggest that anywhere between 70 and 95% of sexual offenders were sexually abused as children. Most of these studies consider self-report from sexual offenders who find themselves in treatment or in prison. Sexual abuse in childhood has been explained as an etiology or an accepted reason certain individuals become sexual offenders.

Some research emerging within the past few years has indicated perhaps a different perspective (Hindman)(Freund). These studies would suggest that offenders over-report being sexually abused as children to avoid being responsible for their crimes or to avoid further incarceration. When offenders are held to polygraph examinations on their sexual histories and when they are given immunity from prosecution concerning what those histories might reveal, sex offenders seem to report being sexually abused as children at a much lower rate.

The non-offending parent seems to have maintained an extremely high percentage of being sexually abused as a child, and although polygraph examinations are rarely, if ever, administered to the non-offending parent, the motivation for making false claims does not appear to be the same as for sex offenders. In fact, it is not uncommon for therapists to engage a mother into treatment who is not only resistive to discussing her abuse, but may be extremely resistive to recognizing the trauma her child is experiencing. Female non-offending parents who become involved in a treatment program due to the sexual abuse of a son or daughter may make such statements as *I was sexually abused as a child and I am just fine. I don't know why you people are making such a big deal.*

Janelle learns that her daughter, 10-year-old Amy, has been sexually abused by Janelle's husband for the last three years. Upon entrance into the treatment program, Janelle is hostile, resistive to intervention, and explains, *That kid of mine has always been seductive. We have never been able to teach her anything about modesty. From the time she was little, she would sway her hips and make passes to any man who was available. My husband is only human. Now, don't tell me I don't know what I am talking about. I was just like her as a kid and I had seven offenders. As soon as I figured out that I was the one causing the problem, everything was all right. She is the one that's causing the problem in this family and, quite frankly, if I have to pick between the two of them, I'll take him any day.*

In spite of agency intervention, Janelle continues to reject her daughter who was so physically traumatized by the abuse, that she needed hospitalization. In spite of the fact that Janelle's husband used excessive physical force on Amy and extremely traumatizing coercion techniques, Janelle continued to maintain that her daughter was responsible. Fourteen months later in family resolution and clarification sessions, Janelle continued denying her daughter's innocence. Both Amy and her father appeared to have resolved and clarified many issues regarding the offender/victim identity. It was Janelle who remained in an intense denial system. It was not until Janelle entered therapy on her own and participated in a formal Trauma Assessment that any productive resolution occurred. Twenty-two months later Janelle stated,

*In my own abuse, I couldn't make any sense of why I had been chosen to be brutalized. As a little girl, I must have figured out that if I was to blame, I could fix it. I seemed to take the hardline approach, accepting blame for what had happened and it seemed to fit nicely until Amy was abused. In therapy, I have realized I am so angry at that little girl within me, and I also realized I couldn't stand Amy either. My feelings toward my daughter can never be repaired. Just like my own mother, I abandoned Amy. What I did may have hurt her more than the sexual abuse. I hope she doesn't **mother** my grandchildren like I mothered her.*

Janelle portrays a common situation for adult

victims whose children have been abused. Mothers reluctantly present their own sexual abuse as children. They also are more likely to deny sexual abuse as children and often deny the potential trauma to their children. This is quite different than sex offenders who want to use their victimization as a child to elicit sympathy, empathy, a different course in treatment, or to avoid punishment. To be viewed as *a victim* would be much easier for sexual offenders who have committed crimes. The motivation for non-offending parents to be dishonest about their own abuse does not seem to fit in the same criteria or motive as offenders who have recently been arrested.

Within the general understanding of why the *cycle* follows the victim, not necessarily the perpetrator, are many reasons for trauma bonding between the victim and the mother. Why does a female who is sexually abused in childhood have an approximate 85% potential for having her own children sexually abused, usually by her partners? Why does the cycle follow the female victim? The first reason pertains to the way in which women choose partners.

Dear Ole Dad, Where Are You?

Children are often abused by a father or a father figure. Women who have been sexually abused may have a father or father figure as a perpetrator. Independent from that issue, women commonly choose a partner with their father or father figure in mind. It is not uncommon for women to marry someone who has many of the

same characteristics of their fathers. The role modeling of *the father* often provides the foundation for a female choosing her partners. If, as in many cases, the woman was sexually abused by a father or father figure, that woman naturally has a potential to choose a partner with sexual offender characteristics.

Intimacy Ignorance

Second, if a female victim was sexually abused in childhood, she has a greater potential for sexual dysfunction at a later time (Maltz). Children who have been sexually abused in childhood, especially untreated victims, often have very little understanding of intimacy. It is not uncommon for women to be either sexually dysfunctional or sexually promiscuous as a result of sexual abuse trauma. At a very minimum, sexual abuse victims seem to relive their sexual abuse during adult sexual experiences and have very little understanding of the beauty of sexuality. This second characteristic compounds the first. The female has a potential for marrying someone with sexual offender characteristics and entering into that relationship with a poor sexual adjustment.

Mommy, Help!

Third, women who have been sexually abused were rarely, if ever, protected by their own mothers. The result is a special handicap, which destroys a *potential* for appropriate mothering. This woman may be handicapped in knowing how protective mothers operate and conduct the family. If these women were not protected in childhood, it is likely they will have few skills in knowing how to protect their own children. The problem intensifies! Not only does this female marry someone with sexual offender characteristics and have a poor sexual adjustment in that relationship, but she also may have very little understanding, willingness, or interest in protecting her own children from sexual abuse because no one protected her.

Attitudes of Abusability

Finally, individuals who have been sexually abused often have an ABUSABLE attitude about themselves. If the female does not overtly choose someone with sex offender characteristics, her own *abusability* is extremely attractive to people with *abusive* qualities. As an example, it is not uncommon for sexual victims, during their first dating activities, to accept boys who lie, who are late for dates, or who demonstrate selfishness. This *acceptability* or *abusability* stems from being denied rights, privacy, or other respect in the female's childhood family. Commonly, the mother who was abused as a child accepts mistreatment. Unfortunately, not only is she willing to accept abusive behavior for herself, but she also may be very willing to accept and *expect* abusive behavior toward her children.

Like Mother, Like Daughter

These four characteristics shed some light on why the cycle seems to follow the victim rather than the perpetrator. Recognizing that not all scenarios are alike, this four-pronged approach simply points to the nature of the cycle. What is more important for this study is the damage caused by the cycle. The damage results in a trauma bond between the mother and the victim. The victim is living in a world where women are known to be protective, caring, selfless, and dedicated to their children. In the incestuous family, where the female was sexually abused as a child, the dynamics may be quite different and certainly shed light on how the trauma bond can occur. Perhaps the ultimate in damage from the mother/daughter trauma bond occurs when the child, who is betrayed by the mother, has a very strong tendency of becoming just like her mother and continuing the cycle.

Whose Big R?

A caution should be raised in regards to responsibility and blame. The aforementioned suggestion of a cycle is in no way intended to take responsibility away from the perpetrator for sexual behavior. In outrage toward the non-offending parent for failing in her obligations, some would like to divide blame among family members, especially looking toward the non-offending parent who has not fulfilled her *Great American Mother* potential. Awareness of cycles explains that *why* is different than *who*. Clearly, a difference exists between sexual responsibility and the cycle of sexual abuse.

If responsibility for sexual actions is given to someone else, offenders have an opportunity and perhaps an *open door* to reoffend. Many other men in this society find themselves married to dysfunctional women or abusable women and do not sexually offend children. It would be easy to suggest that the non-offending parent who has been sexually abused as a child may contribute to an atmosphere where the sexual offender can operate with ease. It may be much more difficult for a sexual offender to sexually abuse in a household with an assertive partner who has a nurturing and protective relationship with her children. The male who has the potential or interest in sexual offending may avoid a relationship with the assertive female and may find a female who fits into the *abusable* criteria. Although non-offending spouses are often responsible for allowing an environment to flourish where sexual abuse can blossom, actual sexual responsibility must always be with the perpetrator.

Clam Chowder Syndrome

In addition to the *cycle* of victim-to-victim, the profile of the non-offending parent has characteristics which may also provide important information as to the continuation of *betrayal in expectations*, resulting trauma bonding. The non-offending parent is typically described as being dependent, lacking in communication skills, and subassertive. Most importantly, the non-offending parent has a coping skill or an ability to rationalize or *fog* reality.

Part of this *fogging* or inability to look at issues realistically may result in a lack of understanding of the *way it should be*. Even though the non-offending parent may have watched

Leave It To Beaver, seeing June Cleaver mop in stylish high heels that matched her linoleum, she may not be able to see the difference in her own family of dishonesty and secrecy, and the perfect *made for television* family. She may choose to live in a fairy tale world of foggy reality. The non-offending parent often seems to have developed a coping skill or a *footprint* that allows information to be rearranged, diffused, or fogged in order to survive. A case example demonstrates the *clam chowder syndrome.*

Emma is an adult victim whose children have been sexually abused. In her sixth month of treatment, she anticipates returning to Pennsylvania to visit her family of childhood. She remarks in the group process, *I am so frustrated with the secrecy and fogginess that awaits me at home. Me and my brothers and sisters will return home for Christmas because it's tradition! My father is the pillar of the community. He matches the pillars that grace our front porch. He is the superintendent of a public school system and respected by everyone. All of us will dote after him, allowing him to dominate the conversation. We will attend to his every need. My mother will pretend to care for us while carefully interweaving, in all conversations, our misdeeds as children. She will pretend to care for the grandchildren, yet her pointed comments about her own child rearing will* *make it quite clear **we** adults are not making the grade.*

*The reality in our family is that my father has sexually abused all of us and is probably now sexually abusing the grandchildren. None of us will speak of the trauma we have suffered and we will all pretend as though he continues to be **Father of the Year.** We will allow him to be alone with our children knowing full well of the terrors we suffered in the same house, in the same bedroom under the same circumstances. What is most frustrating to me is that on Christmas Eve my mother will serve her traditional clam chowder. It is runny and it is awful. We will tell her that it is wonderful! She, like everyone else, will know how terrible it is, yet we will all pretend. She will be the leader of pretension in that we are lucky to be partaking of her clam chowder.*

The silent scream is often never heard from the incest victim. Much the same as the victim may vacillate from one end of the spectrum to the other in the power of the offender, the victim is *bonded* to confusion in the role with mother.

Did she know?

Did she care?

Was she even interested?

How could this have happened right under her nose?

How could she miss it?

The Clam Chowder Syndrome offers understanding why the victim would suffer this same confusion. Emma is screaming, *Why don't you see, why don't you protect us, why don't you care?* The hesitation to confront mother on her runny clam chowder and to confront her with the sexual abuse stems from the underlying childlike stance, *Please approve of me, please love me, please care for me like you should.*

The Non-Offending, But Often Offensive, Spouse

Another example of trauma bonding occurs from the residual effects of professional intervention in incestuous families. Often, professionals do not understand the dynamics of the victim-to-victim cycle and tremendous expectations toward the mother in the family are held. When *Mother* does not respond according to the great American dream, the result from professionals is often rejection, anger, or frustration toward her. If the victim feels adults outside the family harbor outrage toward the non-offending parent (the mother), the victim may respond in a very protective manner, needing to support the non-offending, but sometimes offensive, mother.

Many professionals make statements such as, *How could she do that to her child?* or *She just doesn't care.* If this information is filtered back to the victim, the trauma bonding occurs as the victim needs to become the protector of the mother. Mother's approval and acceptance is something the victim may desperately want. A symbiotic relationship may have already developed long ago forcing the child to be mother's protector. The rejection of the mother from other professionals provides the opportunity for the victim to rescue *Mom*. The result may be a victim who is resistive and uncooperative in treatment, a victim who may recant a report of sexual abuse, but most deadly, a victim who learns to be proficient in protecting those individuals who are abusive. The cycle may have come full circle.

Always, All and Then Some

Caution should be exerted in generalizing or suggesting that *all* victims of childhood will marry perpetrators and that *all* mothers who learn of sexual abuse will be nonprotecting. Whenever 25% of the population is included in a sample such as sexual abuse, obvious differences will occur, especially in family responses. Whenever an inappropriate response exists, however, the trauma appears profound.

In defense of non-offending parents, some traumatizing responses are unintentional. Even in cases where mothers care about their children and are outraged at sexual abuse, responses may be inappropriate.

Carol is a bright, intelligent woman who learns that her husband of two years has sexually abused his step-daughters Sandy, age 9, and Shelly, age 11. These children from Carol's previous marriage were very important to her and she seemed to respond appropriately when learning of their abuse. Due to Carol's apparent investment in the children, the *system* concentrated on prosecuting the perpetrator and enrolling Sandy and Shelly in treatment. Not until the girls seemed to deteriorate was Carol brought in for an appointment. It was discovered that Carol's behavior was traumatizing Sandy and Shelly, not due to Carol's insensitivity, but due to her lack of understanding.

In Carol's assertiveness and strength, she vowed to protect the children from her emotional upheaval. When the children returned from school, they were usually met with a sparkling, clean home, special treats for dinner and a vivacious mother who played with them in the backyard. It was only when the children were in bed that Carol sobbed alone in her bedroom. Shelly began acting out angrily in school and the younger child became rejecting and depressed. The Trauma Assessment revealed that Sandy and Shelly viewed their mother as being insensitive and, in the words of the younger child, *My mommy was happy he did it to us.* While Carol was attempting to protect her children from emotional upheaval, she was teaching them that the sexual abuse was insignificant. She gave a silent affirmation of the abuse. As a mother, Carol's intentions were protective and supportive, yet the result was an investment in a potential trauma bond in the future.

Additionally, families may be sensitive and caring toward a victim, yet, through ignorance, create more trauma for the victim. MaryAnne's family demonstrates this deadly dilemma.

MaryAnne's Trauma Assessment as an adult reveals trauma bonding with her mother. MaryAnne was sexually abused by her mother's boyfriend for over nine years. Although the offender is insignificant to MaryAnne other than in her outrage toward him, her mother's affirmation is extremely important. MaryAnne has spent most of her adulthood attempting to please her mother without mentioning the sexual abuse.

With family resolution and clarification organized, MaryAnne's mother, brother, and sister are presented with MaryAnne's Trauma Assessment. MaryAnne's mother's first response is anger. Her shrieks can be heard throughout the entire building *Why didn't she tell me? I did everything for her. Why didn't she tell me?* MaryAnne's brother and her sister wailed, *How could she do this, how could she keep it a secret so long?* One

brother remarked, *If she just would have told me, we would have had a reason to get him out of the house. Because she kept it a secret, we all had to suffer for nine years.*

Clinical preparation excluded MaryAnne from the family's first session. Additionally, MaryAnne was prepared for these comments by her therapist. Clinical impressions indicate that in actuality this family cares a great deal for MaryAnne and all family members were unaware of the sexual abuse. Eventually, the family worked toward an extremely effective resolution and clarification with MaryAnne. Nonetheless, the initial remarks certainly would have been painful for MaryAnne. Therapeutic intervention taught MaryAnne how ill-prepared family members may respond. Inappropriate responses through interventions into incestuous families, especially including the mother, contribute to continued trauma to victims. Although the non-offending parent, typically the mother, may be more traumatizing due to the expectations upon her, it appears that inappropriate responses from all incest family members are more common than not.

And More Trauma

For the non-offending mother, typical responses are denial of the abuse, foggy perceptions, or the inability to affirm the pain suffered by victims. However, there are other forms of traumatic bonding that may on the surface be appropriate responses, yet in actuality have disregard for the child's trauma.

It would not be uncommon for a mother to believe the child's abuse and become totally consumed with outrage. The result seems appropriate but, in actuality, is an alienation of the child. It is as though the mother's anger toward the situation becomes the most significant issue. Mother abandons the child as anger replaces empathy. The mother seems to be supportive of the child and acknowledges the abuse, but the child's emotional needs are neglected due to the mother's outrage. She may begin attending a variety of mental health services, she may participate in a campaign against the perpetrator, or she may simply become so symptomatic she cannot care for the needs of her child.

If the mother was a sexual victim herself, she may respond because she now has an outlet for the anger she was forced to stifle as a child. Because of the dynamics in her own incestuous family, she may not have been able to speak of her abuse, respond with appropriate feelings, or resolve. Now that her child has been sexually abused, her own needs can be met by total outrage toward the perpetrator. In this instance the child drowns.

Yours, Mine, Ours

Another example of the inappropriate responses from the non-offending parents creating a trauma bond is when the parents take on the symptoms of the child or the symptoms that the child *should* be allowed to feel. The non-offending mother may become symptomatic and demand attention for the recent sexual abuse. This is not to suggest that mothers who learn of their children being sexually abused are not rightly upset, perhaps depressed, outraged, and symptomatic. In this example of trauma bonding, the mother finally has an outlet for her own pain and she may be manifesting the symptoms she felt as a child. She now has a legitimate reason to be traumatized without being responsible for rejecting her own family. In her *pleading child* role, she can suffer without becoming the *guilty child* who caused trouble. She can now be in pain because she was denied avenues of pain previously. Again, her own child, the current victim, is often neglected and abandoned emotionally.

A word must be stated about the non-offending parent who may not be a mother but may manifest some of the same symptomatology. If sexual abuse occurs outside the family with a teacher, a neighbor, or a trusted friend, both parents may take on many of the inappropriate responses previously mentioned. Outrage, feelings of betrayal, and developing avenues of self abuse may occur not only with the non-offending mother, but with both parents. Additionally, children who report may feel responsible for upsetting their parents. Unsettled issues may be the result of the parents' inappropriate responses, but the child victim is responsible for the parents' upheaval. When parents take these situations personally, then the child victim is often abandoned, setting up a situation which results in trauma bonding at a later time.

Mirror, Mirror On The Wall

Some trauma bonding occurs at the finish line of the cycle races. This kind of trauma bonding occurs not with the victim's intentions, but as the end result. When victims are extremely outraged at their mother for the lack of protection in childhood, the issue of *no protection* may or may not be spoken, resolved, or acknowledged. Typically, the victim copes by exerting effort to avoid being the same kind of mother. This does not appear to be manifested with the male victim, but with the female victim who must accept or reject her role models and establish herself as a parent to her own children. The *scripting* that occurs may be more powerful than the victim's vows to be different than her own mother.

When the victim becomes a mother herself, armed with vows to be different, she may find herself evolving as a mother very much like her own mother. She may actually perceive her children being distant from her, much the same as she felt with her mother. Her relationship with her partner may evolve similar to her mother and father's relationship. By the time the victim has married and perhaps has children, she may be going through what was previously determined as the fifth *pothole*. She may find herself in a situation where she has become very much like her mother. This would appear to be the ultimate bond with her mother as she has become a mother, a wife, and a partner very similar to the woman that authored much of her pain.

Rosemary was emotionally abandoned in childhood by her mother, who appeared very pompous and proper, demonstrating no affection or attention toward Rosemary's father. Rosemary's father preyed upon the coldness in the marriage to engage Rosemary in sexual intercourse, beginning at age ten and continuing until Rosemary ran away from home. In actuality, Rosemary did not report because during the sexual abuse she received precious attention and affection not found anywhere else in her childhood.

Rosemary's early departure from the family resulted in an unfortunate marriage and subsequent divorce. Rosemary found herself in late adolescence divorced, overweight, and bitter.

With some tenacity remaining, she entered into a secretarial program and eventually became employed to the point of supporting herself adequately. Rosemary continued to be perplexed and pained by her mother's coldness and her father's feebleness.

Eventually, Rosemary married an individual much older than herself, but nonetheless a religious person who is extremely trustworthy. Rosemary vowed to break the cycle of incest and marry someone who was an unlikely candidate for sexual perpetration. As Rosemary checked her *grocery list* of sexual offender characteristics, she evaluated her husband as having a low risk factor.

Arthur attended church regularly, had a respectful position in the community, worked diligently, and seemed to be mature. Arthur certainly did not seem prone to behaviors Rosemary had experienced during her first marriage, such as intense sexuality and substance abuse. In fact, heading Rosemary's grocery list of low risk factors was Arthur's low sex drive.

After 12 years of marriage, Rosemary is involved in a sexual abuse treatment program for incestuous families. Not only has she learned that Arthur sexually abused her 10-year-old, but through introspection, Rosemary recognizes that she has become her mother. Her disinterest in Arthur or his disinterest in her began in the early stages of the marriage. What appeared to be a diligent, hard working man was an obsessive, compulsive individual who had little time for anything other than himself and his work. His religiosity, in fact, seemed to enhance his sense of power and pompous attitude. Sexual dysfunction for Rosemary occurred shortly after the marriage as she seemed to be *taking my father to bed with me* during each sexual experience. Arthur eventually turned away from Rosemary with cold-

ness, very much like Rosemary's own mother. The final blow for Rosemary was in recognizing that her daughter Jenny's statement to the therapist echoed from her own childhood and mirrored her feelings toward her mother, *At least we knew our dad liked us,* said Jenny. *With mom, we don't know for sure.*

Sadly, Rosemary has become very much like her mother even though tremendous effort was put forth to avoid that consequence. The vows of sexual victims to break the cycle may become so intense that the cycle continues due to the victim's lack of common sense and balance. Additionally, it must be recognized that by virtue of being a mother, sexual victims are commonly reminded of their own mother through day-to-day activities. Each time Rosemary fixed her daughter's lunch or read her a bedtime story, she was administering motherly duties. At each daily activity, Rosemary was reminded of her mother and her vows to be different. The bombardment of these thoughts may have distracted Rosemary to the point where she lost all perspective of what was actually happening in her family.

Greener Pastures

A manifestation of the *pleading child* in the deadly spectrum of responses from the victim may result from competition or jealousy that seems sometimes to accompany the mother/daughter relationship. Maturity and sensitivity prevent most women from being affected by a female child growing through adolescence, becoming extremely attractive and, in reality, much more attractive than the mother. This is a society where attractiveness of females is an important, if not *the* most important, commodity.

In incestuous families, sex offenders often drive wedges between the mother and the children. It is difficult to sexually abuse a child who has an open, honest, and supportive relationship with the mother. Offenders must therefore drive wedges in the mother-child relationship to prevent protection of the child and to enhance the mother's rejection of the child.

In the most common circumstances, mothers may feel some twinge of jealousy or competition with their daughters who become attractive or who receive a great deal of attention and affection from the mother's partner. This may be a normal reaction experienced by many women, but it is usually overcome. In the case of the incestuous family, however, jealousy between the mother and the daughter may result due to the enhancement of this conflict by the perpetrator in the *driving of wedges*.

When children are small, they will often respond favorably to the competition laid out by the perpetrator, *I like you better than your mom*, or *Mommy will be mad if she finds out what we are doing*. Activities that allow little girls to be *partners* with their fathers may appear to be quite exciting and pleasurable for the child. The younger child may enhance the feelings of jealousy because she is unable to understand. Unfortunately, this may lay the foundation for the mother/daughter trauma bond through jealousy.

As the female child grows older, competition may be enhanced by the perpetrator in other ways. *Your mother doesn't like touching me like this, Your mother is so cold to me, you'll have to take care of my needs*, or *You're much prettier than your mom*, may all be used by the perpetrator. If the victim does not respond in a competitive way, the victim certainly will respond in a helpless manner since the underlying message to the child is *because of your attractiveness you have caused me to do this*. Trauma bonding evolves from the victim's perspective in feelings of guilt over winning the competition or being a victim in the battle of competition. Trauma bonding occurs in adulthood as the victim wants to compensate by receiving acceptance from the mother and by soothing the pains of war.

Karla, age fourteen, reports being sexually abused by her step-father. This man was ten years younger than Karla's mother. He engaged in sexual contact with Karla from age five until fourteen when, in a fit of anger, she reported the abuse.

Karla's stepfather had always encouraged her to believe that she was more attractive than her mother and that in fact his inability to be sexually satisfied with his wife was due not only to her *bags and sags*, but because of

Karla's attractiveness. Karla was indeed physically endowed and very attractive. She believed her stepfather's statements.

The perpetrator was arrested and placed in a local treatment program. Although he appears to comply with the treatment program and take on responsibility for repairing the damage, the trauma bond emerges quite clearly between Karla and her mother. In fact, the relationship is much more positive between the perpetrator and the victim.

Karla wants her mother to accept her and understand why the sexual abuse occurred. Unfortunately, Karla's mother had spent most of her married life attempting to be attractive and please her husband. She was constantly reminded of her husband's ensuing frustration with Karla's attractiveness. Karla's mother's response was to become more attractive herself. This was a never ending, vicious battle and obviously the way in which the offender kept Karla and her mother at odds.

As an example, the offender would often bring home lingerie magazines and ask his wife to *please put in some orders* to help with his fading arousal. As Karla's mother exercised, used health foods, and purchased attractive clothes, she saw her daughter, without any effort, emerging as a beautiful young lady.

In clinical clarification and resolution sessions, the damage seemed reasonably resolved between Karla and her stepfather at least as far as responsibility was concerned. It became quite clear that Karla wanted the love of her mother who was cold and rejecting. Karla's mother seemed to feel much the same as she would if her husband had a mistress. The mother/daughter relationship was non-existent. This appeared to be, in the mother's eyes, two women who had sought the same man, with the mother obviously losing.

The epilogue reveals that at age 24 Karla weighs approximately 220 pounds. She has a toddler, is pregnant, and is chasing a three-year-old throughout the neighborhood. Karla had eventually married one of her father's friends who was alcoholic and 15 years her senior. Interestingly, Karla and her mother's relationship seems to have mended. Karla is dedicated to her mother, taking care of her mother's needs and constantly putting forth effort to please her. Finally and most importantly, Karla's mother is now the *most attractive* of the two. Karla may spent the rest of her life apologizing for winning the early battle, but obviously not the war.

If She Only Knew

Another trauma bond often occurs through *withheld affirmation*. The mother's own denial system is needed to protect her from recognizing that she was not able to protect her child, even in cases where it is quite clear that the offender was masterful in deceit. For this trauma bonding to occur, there must be profound evidence that the mother had every reason to suspect and to know about the abuse, but remained in denial and obviously in control. Rather than saying, *I should have known*, the mother places herself in a prominent position of innocence. The result is trauma bonding connecting the child, who is desperately searching for legitimacy, to a never ending *limbo*. This is particularly troublesome to those victims who have fleeting memories or have had amnesia.

Most profound to those victims who do not have clear memories is the fear that the sexual abuse may have been much more extensive, brutal, or traumatic than currently understood or remembered. Seeking some legitimization from the mother is a common request from the adult victim. Tremendous power is given to the mother as her adult *child* requests her acknowledgement or memory.

There may be profound evidence that the abuse occurred, such as the acknowledgment of sexual equipment, confessions from the mother that she was forced to participate in the same kinds of activities with the perpetrator, or partial confessions on the part of the perpetrator previous to dying or departure. This kind of bonding usually occurs when the perpetrator is not available to affirm or deny but the mother has that potential. The more desperately the victim reaches to the mother for some kind of affirmation, the more effort the mother puts forth to deny acknowledgement or affirmation to the victim. In this case, the victim is the *pleading child* asking the mother to acknowledge, affirm, or legitimize. Through the mother failing to affirm the abuse, the victim hangs in limbo. The mother's status (Great American Mother) is protected, but the victim is terrorized by *what may have happened* or plagued with feelings of craziness that the memories have been fabricated.

Shoulding On Ourselves

A final example of trauma bonding occurs when the victim becomes dutiful toward the mother. The victim listens carefully to society's messages about how *good* sons and daughters *should* behave. Feelings of outrage toward not being protected are stifled. The *child within* needs to be loved, picked up and held, but continues being neglected, since the sons and daughters, now in adulthood, must become the *parents* and take care of the mother. Trauma bonding evolves since the outlets for frustration must be manifested in other parts of the victim's lives. Good sons and daughters are dutiful and therefore rage cannot be directed against the mother *because we shouldn't*!

Ted was raised by his mother and three fathers. Ted's natural father was never known to him and subsequently Ted lived with three stepfathers, two of whom sexually abused him for a total of seven years. In adulthood, Ted's mother is alone, and Ted and his sister are the major focus of her life. As Ted's mother has gotten older and perhaps more desperate for companionship, she appears to be more dedicated to her children. As conversations drift toward childhood, Ted's mother is quick to discuss her past difficulties and struggles. In therapy, Ted discusses the pain he feels because of his sexual abuse. Ted would like to discuss his abuse with his mother and he would like to be outraged at her for placing him in these vulnerable situations where brutal abuse occurred.

Unfortunately, Ted is enmeshed in a trauma bond with his mother as she purports that he *should* take care of her, be nice to her, and protect her. He *should* not hurt her since, after all, she had a very hard life and did the best she could. Ted can intellectualize that his mother was quite promiscuous, often left the children abandoned with a variety of men, and, at one point, was made aware of sexual improprieties occurring to Ted's sister by a sporadic boarder. Cognitively, Ted is aware that his mother failed to respond to his basic needs and, in all likelihood, knew the sexual abuse was taking place. Ted spent so many years *hoping* his mother would finally protect him and care for

him that it is difficult, if not impossible, for Ted to confront her at this time. The fact that Ted *should* care for his mother outwardly soothes his wounds. Ted finds some peace in being dedicated to his mother and having a relationship with her now because he longed for her in childhood.

Unfortunately for Ted, his feelings of outrage, guilt, and unworthiness are manifested in his personal life. Ted has failed marriages, occasional substance abuse problems, and difficulties vocationally. Ted's mother has been placed on a pedestal with his dedication soothing some of his wounds. Ted's *bleeding* occurs outside of the relationship with his mother, and the result is traumatic for Ted's adult life. Ted continues to suffer and his mother continues to be protected by the trauma bond regarding how Ted *should* take care of her.

What seems to be clear in understanding the nature of trauma bonding is that tremendous control may occur between the sexual victim and the non-offending parent — most typically, the mother. Perhaps different than any other *player* in the incestuous scheme, the mother tends to have great potential for trauma bonding because of the tremendous expectations placed upon motherhood. The way mothers *should* operate and feel about their children lays the foundation for tremendous betrayal and the potential for trauma bonding.

Although this list is not conclusive, it nonetheless describes some of the trauma bonding that occurs between the mother and the child. It is often the mythical issue of the mother that traumatizes the victim. Breaking the trauma bond first requires dispelling the *mother* myth. Exploding that myth may require, as Iliana Gill eloquently states, *saying goodbye to the family (mother) you never had.*

COLLATERAL CLAMPS
AND CRAMPS

What cruel trauma for the victim — bonded to the offender, emotionally abandoned by the dream of motherhood. Where is safety, security, sympathy? The family seems so insensitive! Perhaps the world of the victim will provide a soft place to land.

The future of the victim will be caught in a trauma bond by the power of the offender or unresolved issues with the non-offending parent(s), especially mothers. A final example of trauma bonding concerns peripheral events or items (collateral clamps and cramps) surrounding the victim's world. Although the victim may not be in a trauma bond with a single person, the victim may be traumatized by a world of reminders, confusions, and haunts that continually return the victim to the feelings of childhood sexual abuse.

Trauma bonding is not isolated to families or family members. As the victim attempts to move about the world, certain events occur providing exposure to painful stimulus. There may be common, ordinary, everyday stimuli that *zap* and cramp the victim's peace. It is a cruel, non-empathetic world for the victim of sexual abuse.

Difficult for victims to understand is that sexual abuse continues to haunt them throughout adulthood even though there is a belief, *I resolved this before* or *I put this behind me.* Intellectually, victims may have felt that a resolution occurred. Unfortunately, resolution is not isolated to *people.* At the very best, our society is innocently insensitive to victims and continually supplies messages and information that traumatize. Resolution must include the world beyond people and families.

147

The cry from sexual victims either conscious or unconscious when exposed to these collateral clamps and cramps is:

I must have been responsible.

This was okay to do this to me.

My body must have caused this to happen.

Little boys should be sexual as soon as they can.

I must have liked it.

It's not okay to talk about sex.

This wasn't really abuse that happened to me.

This was the job of women.

Rape is common.

Males can't be victims.

Sex abuse happens all the time — it must be acceptable.

I am damaged goods.

Men are supposed to like all the sex they can get.

Even little girls can turn men on.

These conscious or unconscious messages teach victims to be either reminded of their abuse or be in turmoil about their responsibility in the abuse. If the identification of the victim and the offender is important in rehabilitation and indicative of continued suffering, clearly *trauma bonding* can occur as the victim receives messages from society that cause confusion about the offender/victim identity.

Be A Real Man And Be A Real Woman

Male/Female role training is one of the most common sources of trauma bonding concerning collateral issues. Male and female roles tend to teach males to be *perpetrators* or certainly to be sexually competent and sexually aggressive. If male role training is accepting of men *taking sex*, then certainly the female victim will doubt the victim status. If the male is taught to be sexually aggressive and sexually assaultive, a general acceptance of sexual abuse will occur. How can the perpetrator actually be responsible if, in fact, the message is clear that men *taking sex* is normal. And if females *give sex*, the male victim, abused by a female, *must have wanted this to happen.* Male/female roles also teach female victims to be victims and to be responsible for turning males into perpetrators.

A Real Man

How exactly is the male role portrayed in our society? For the purpose of simplicity, the male seems to be portrayed as somewhat of a combination between *John Wayne and a German Shepherd* (McQuirk). This term is not necessarily disrespectful of the late great John Wayne, as the figure Rambo or any *Macho Man* would suffice. The combination, however, suggests male role training purports that males should be strong, unemotional, powerful, and unfeeling. In fact, the only feeling that is legitimized would be a sexual one.

The German Shepherd portion of the profile portrays a slobbering, panting animal, legitimately responding to sexual stimulus. Certainly, sexual control or responsible sexual decision making is not a German Shepherd's strongest point. In actuality, regardless of the female dog's ears, her integrity, or her past relationships, the German Shepherd will pounce on her at the slightest hint she is in *heat*. The portrayal of men in this regard is deadly to the sexual victim.

Although not totally responsible, advertisers can be cited as one of the best examples of the John Wayne/German Shepherd profile exposure. The German Shepherd profile is matched with the strong, powerful male only interrupted by sexual feelings. If men are not strong, cool, and powerful, then men are seducing. Sexual feelings, are the only legitimate feelings allowed.

For cigarettes, there is the KOOL man, the MARLBORO man, and the CAMEL man, all pictured in strong, unemotional poses. The Surgeon General's warning looks silly next to

these isolated, powerful men who could never even catch a cold.

If advertisers need to suggest that men are interested in fashion, they are often portrayed in situations continuing the strong, macho image. A recent advertisement of red jockey shorts (B.V.D.s) on a very attractive man finds him in a hotel, shaving (adorned with his cowboy hat) with a pitcher and basin. Obviously, to wear red underpants would only be appropriate if the man was independent and strong enough to stay in a hotel without running water.

Another advertisement (nearly three pages away from a red-shorted man without the basic amenities of Motel Six) portrays a man wearing blue underwear (GREAT LOOKS). This scene, however, is not in a hotel without running water, but where the man has recently tamed a cougar (bare handed), flung the animal over his shoulders and is smiling, quite barefoot, next to a huge phallic shaped cactus.

Three boot advertisements in one magazine within about 20 pages show, first, a woman slipping the boots off while kissing the boot toes (TEXAS). In another ad six pages away (WRANGLER), the boot toe is lifting up a woman's skirt. And finally, if boot fashion is not for the purposes of seduction or being seduced, the scene portrays a man *roping a bear!* The 1200 pound bear is whimpering in submission to this 160 pound man. The ring on the muscled hand reveals *let's rodeo* while

NACONA boots are displayed with *Bear Taming* pride.

Often, to portray the strong macho image there is a play on words, suggesting strength, power, and control. The SOLO-FLEX ad for weight lifting equipment states, *A hard man is good to find (Hardness in what?!!)*

Male cologne (MUSK) is advertised with the phrase, *We help American men stay sexy because it's powerful, stimulating, unbelievable, and yet legal* ... The suggestion would be that the male who is powerful, stimulating, and unbelievable could tread very closely to being illegal and still be a *sexy American man.*

Common profiles for sex offenders indicate an egocentricity or selfishness (Hindman). Some ads encourage that self-centeredness to the point of glorification. As an example, in advertising a cologne (DENIM) the message is clear, *Tell her what you want.* Or in a cigarette ad (SALEM), *I don't let anything stand in the way of my enjoyment.* If sex offenders *take sex,* do these messages legitimize the robbery?

IMPULSE perfume advertises with the statement, *Men just can't help acting on Impulse* (neither, by the way, can German Shepherds).

A famous jean maker (GUESS) shows a quite powerful man's head from the backseat of the car (his jeans are either missing or unavailable at the moment). The suggestion is one of seduction with the darkness of the backseat. But the advertisement is not without a hint of violence because the window is shattered and the obvious sexual partner is nearby. The hint of violence is important in advertising fashion. This man's fashion is one of legitimizing sex and violence.

The same jean maker also advertises black jeans for men with two rather powerful gentlemen lying down on a grassy hill with a naked woman sandwiched between the two of them. The same could be observed for a group of male dogs corralling a female in heat. Neither man (or the German Shepherds) seems to be interested in the other, only interested in the task at hand — seduction (breeding).

KEORA cologne is advertised with a pose of a naked man sniffing at a female's pink bathrobe. The implication is that his partner has left for work (probably at the local diner), yet he is home *sneaking a snort* of her bathrobe (a German Shepherd couldn't have done better!).

ANDROSE perfume portrays what appears to be a 20 foot bottle of perfume (phallic shaped) with a woman worshiping upward toward the bottle. The caption states, *Makes men really want you.* Interestingly, this advertisement was found in a woman's magazine. Is the suggestion that total dedication to a phallic symbol is a woman's station in life?

The ultimate in the German Shepherd myth is the message on a perfume for females (WILD MUSK), *The essence of animal attraction.* Sadly, since animals do not make responsible sexual decisions, certainly the *the essence of animal attraction* would not necessarily be an ideal sexual consenting scenario.

So what impact do these rather humorous, but perhaps poignant, messages have for the male or even the female victim? If the male role is portrayed as strong, powerful, yet yielding to sexual stimulus in an *out-of-control* fashion, then the role of the perpetrator for anyone, male or female victim, has lost status. In the victim's effort to identify the perpetrator and the victim, confusion will occur since society's message condones males taking sex. Although these messages may be subtle, they nonetheless chip away at the perpetrator's status in the mind of the victim. These messages suggest that males being sexually out of control is much more acceptable than unacceptable.

Be A Real Woman (A Real Attractive Woman)

The typical portrayal of women in advertising may enhance traumatization to victims who are searching for their identity as a victim or an innocent child not responsible for sexual misconduct. There seem to be three major areas of portrayal of women in advertising with the first being an obsession with appearance. A single magazine cover portrays the following articles pertaining to appearance.

Looking Younger Longer

Make-Up to Make You Over

Get In Shape for the Holidays

Making a New You

Ten Pages on Staying Happy and Sexy

32 Tips to Ease Off those Hard to Lose Pounds

Presto! Prettier Hair

Is there Sex After Success?

How Women on the Top Find Time to Make Love

Go From Mousey to Magnificent

What Jealousy Made Me Do

Keeping Up With New Fall Fashions

If it is true that women are constantly concerned about their appearance, then the purpose of their appearance must be evaluated. If attractiveness is important, then what is the purpose? Sadly, the purpose for female attractiveness may be represented in advertising as *waking up the German Shepherd.*

There are many advertisements regarding women and their obsession with attractiveness - — *Would you go to your class reunion if it were tomorrow?* The ad portrays the dilemma of attending a class reunion if OIL OF OLAY has not been used religiously. The unacceptability of her appearance being imperfect would certainly keep any sensible woman away from the event.

Zoomie, Zoomie, Hurry. Quick, Change!

Women are bombarded with a variety of options for changing their appearance concerning such things as their breasts. Whatever size women's breasts may be, they must be changed. If breasts are too big, the OLGA BRA will hide *too much*. Breast enlargements or foam pads will be helpful to those who do not have *enough*. To compound the frustration, even those women who may be reasonably acceptable may be interested in the *MEDIUM BRA* (PLAYTEX). If women are portrayed in any resemblance of a natural state, a product advertising the tools of change will be presented.

Ordinary People?

Women are often exhibited cooking dinner (a rather ordinary task), but only in long, flowing robes of white satin, advertising silverware (LEGEND). Women mop their floors (MOP AND GLOW), but never without their pearls. Women clean toilets (COMET), but not without perfectly manicured nails.

The message is clear. No matter what women do, they must always be concerned about their appearence. Mopping, dusting, driving, buying a computer, or closing a multi-million dollar deal must always be secondary to her appearance. And why? Because her attractiveness has a purpose, an important purpose.

The Seductress

As women may be valued for their attractiveness, it seems clear that the purpose of their attractiveness must be to seduce. Women who are sexy, sexy, sexy are successful. The contrary message, however, is that to be sexual is inappropriate. Women are portrayed as needing to *turn men on* (into German Shepherds) through their sexiness, but something else happens beyond reducing the German Shepherd to slobbers. As an example, Miss America is judged for her beauty and her attractiveness in a variety of outfits ranging from swimsuits to evening wear. *Mrs.* America may be more noted for her jams and jellies.

Be Sexy, But Not Sexual

The issue of virginity screams at women. Women are placed in a seductive role, but certainly not to give up their virginity. Women are somehow rated as a *B+* following matrimonial sanctioning of sex. If attractiveness is a woman's best commodity, the next clear understanding is that the purpose of attractiveness is to seduce, to use sexiness to entice. This emerges as the second deadly message to women regarding their role as a real woman.

For the sexual victim, the message screams, *If I am concerned about my appearance, I must be sexy. I must have seduced or caused this to happen.* Since women are supposed to seduce, it certainly would seem to the female victim that she somehow caused sexual abuse since this is a natural response for females.

CALVIN KLEIN advertises body cream for women while the woman is in bed with a partner. One pose shows the partner turning away, and one pose shows him turning around and obviously sexually responding, but only after the *sniffs* of the BODY CREAM enter his nose. The final scene shows the bedroom empty of the man since his sexual needs have been fulfilled. The woman looks gratuitously at her BODY CREME.

In advertising a necklace (DWECK) (traditionally worn around the neck) the beads are suggestively placed either near the crotch or draped over gorgeous, shapely legs, which subtly accentuate the purpose for the decoration (pubic area).

In advertising raspberry colored underwear (GIVENCHY), a champagne glass filled with raspberries is held near the crotch where shadows portray pubic hair. A bulge in the beautiful lace underwear appears to be an erection grown from nowhere.

GUESS jeans advertise a pair of pants that is nearly out of the view of the reader. A female is straddling a motorcycle in a very seductive pose, advertising these *unseeable* jeans, barely able to contain the crotch of the woman.

MAIDENFORM advertises their beautiful underwear with women posed on golf courses, in shopping malls, or on streets, moving swiftly, seemingly naive to the fact that an entire troop of German Shepherds are usually watching (and slobbering!)

NINA perfume advertises an Amazon-looking, gorgeous woman holding her hand on the top of a male who has been reduced to a panting, Tarzan-type character. The caption indicates, *conquer your heroes*. Obviously, the woman has reduced this very strong, powerful man to a panting German Shepherd.

CHRISTIAN DIOR underwear is also advertised with a man's face (even though on a photograph) held between the legs of the beautiful woman wearing the sky blue lace garment. Everything about a woman seems to have a sexual purpose.

Special Seductresses

Perhaps most painful in the attraction dilemma of women in advertising occurs when children are portrayed as *seductresses*. Many victims fear that somehow they caused the abuse to occur or that they somehow seduced the perpetrator.

ANDREA CARRANO Shoes are advertised with a nine-year-old child wearing women's shoes while she is bending over with her buttocks nearly exposed. BON VOYAGE Fashions advertise in the *Oregonian* newspaper depicting what seems to be a nine-year-old child seductively thrown into a sexual pose. The caption illustrates *feel like a native* but information not included in the advertisement indicates that this store did not carry children's clothing!

AVON advertises a complete range of make-up for children with the caption, *dressing up for daddy*. Although this may not be traumatizing in the normal sense and perhaps was not motivated regarding sexual abuse, nonetheless victims may be traumatized as they view this material and question their own role in the sexual abuse.

CHANEL #5 advertised a complete display of a five-year-old *seductress* advertising perfume. This child is gorgeously prepared and photographed with her nipples exposed. The caption reads, *Fragrance speaks the language of flowers. Roses to express romance, Jasmine and Gardenia for seduction with just a hint of innocence.*

These advertisements may seem innocuous or harmless if taken separately or if presented to a society that had a much better track record regarding sexuality. To the sexual victim, these media *zaps* continue to raise questions about the female victim status as a seductress. If she seduced the perpetrator or is in some way responsible, the status changes. It is the collection of these messages on a continual basis that raises these extremely traumatizing and painful questions to the victim who is desperately attempting to find understanding and resolution.

The Acceptable Victimization — Violence Value

A third message traumatizing victims through advertising is one in which the acceptability, the commonality, or the constant acceptance of victimization exists. It is as though the victim is prevented from becoming identified as the victim because victimization appears to be *EVERYWHERE*. The subtle messages encourage the connection between sex and violence. They teach victims the acceptability of *abusability*. The constant portrayal and acceptability of victimization plagues victims and denies the first step in rehabilitation, which is to accept the *victim identity*.

AMERICAN BEAUTY LEATHER advertises a quite attractive (and incidentally naked) woman in the desert, but nonetheless carrying her purse. A photograph shows a background desert scene. The absurdity of the woman being naked in the desert (but not without her purse) should cause attention to be drawn to the advertisement. The advertisers, however, have completed the acceptability of sexual violence by strategically placing a cactus at the opening of the woman's vagina.

As CALVIN KLEIN advertises perfume (OBSESSION FOR MEN), naked women are photographed in piles of bodies. Although there are no men placed in the picture, the women appear to have been thrown into a frenzy and lie exhausted in a haphazard pile due to their contact with OBSESSION perfume. Certainly, there is a disregard for intimacy or for appropriate sexual decision making in this advertisement, but most important is the acceptability of a word commonly associated with deviancy — *Obsession*.

Traditionally, CALVIN KLEIN advertises jeans for men with a caption titled, *sport*. The picture portrays two men wearing CALVIN KLEIN jeans, obviously alternating for the sexual favors of a woman. Both men are taking turns, which seems to glorify sexual exploitation.

Concerning the issues of violence, shoes (BANDOLINO) are portrayed in advertisements with a woman's leg being violently grabbed by a man or legs lifted in the air with a photographic emphasis on the naked crotch. The caption reads, *You can't be in fashion if your shoes ain't smashin'.*

ORGANICALLY GROWN sweaters are advertised with one man being whipped into submission by two very seductive women. The caption reads, *Remember the passion, remember the sheik, let Organic embrace you with their summer mystique.* The hint is of violence and sexual slavery. The clear message is an acceptability of sexual violence.

A GLORIA VANDERBILT jumpsuit is advertised in *Newsweek Magazine* by a woman standing next to an automobile. She has a look on her face that borders between arousal and terror. A man's shadow graces the white Volkswagen, adding to the sense that a rape is about to happen. The caption reads, *Let the adventure begin.* (How many rape victims would call their ordeal *an adventure*?)

DANIEL MINK advertises watches *with character.* However, the character of the watches is portrayed as a rape scene in the shower is taking place with an almost terrorized, almost aroused female.

The BOHEMIAN SUN UP, SUN DOWN swimsuit is advertised as being *outrageously trendy.* The woman is being jerked and pulled in what appears to be a rape scene. The first color for the swimsuit is *virgin white* and the second is *sexy black.*

CANDIES shoes are advertised in a bedroom scene with, again, a rape either in the process or at conclusion. The woman on the telephone may be trying to get away from the man who is holding her leg or she may be calling out for a pizza to celebrate their simultaneous orgasms! Nonetheless, in order to advertise these shoes, the bedroom scene is coupled with a hint of violence.

GUESS jeans are advertised in a barnyard scene with a cowboy-looking character holding a woman's arm in the air in what appears to be either a hint of dancing or a rape about to happen. The fact that the woman's clothing is ripped, exposing her bra, hints of a rape scene. Questions are raised about whether the couple is beginning to dance or whether the cowboy character is about to fling the woman down into the manure of the corral.

Diamonds are advertised with a barbell held against a woman's throat while she is posed in a position of either being orgasmic or choking to death. The caption illustrates, DIAMOND DESIRES.

MONET JEWEL advertises jewelry with a woman seemingly chained to a man. Again, her expression is a curious combination of sexual pleasure and terrorized resistance.

Beyond advertising, television, movies, literature, or even video games also glorify the acceptability of capturing females in sexual escapades. As an example, tremendous controversy occurs as to whether or not children should be given the proper names of genitalia, yet it is quite common and acceptable to have one television show after another depicting violent rapes and sexual mutilations. In movies, at a minimum, sex appears to be easy, accessible, and something that everyone takes. For video games, it is common to have a female being attacked and absconded by a nasty character and the purpose of the video is to rescue the female. Although the sexual overtones for video games found in pizza parlors, grocery stores, or arcades seem to be at a minimum, nonetheless the taking of females has a common place in our society. The victim may ask, *How bad can it be if it happens everywhere? This must be the job of a woman.*

Reality Test

Is this trauma purposeful? Do advertisers intend to traumatize? Are advertisors, television producers, authors, and manufacturers responsible for sexual abuse or for the trauma victims feel. Unfortunately, victims are traumatized as they peer out into their world and view these clamps and cramps. Responsibility or the reality of blame, however, should not necessarily go to advertisers or to the media who manufacture these tools of trauma.

Advertising is not done haphazardly, nor are advertisers foolish. Sexual overtones with violence, aggression, and domination are used because these tactics are effective, primarily from a financial perspective. Advertisers do not use these methods unless the messages produce results. Careful cost analysis and marketing research indicate which modalities are most effective. It is our society which dictates what advertisers use.

Supply and Demand

In a society where there was an abundant supply of sexual information, these advertising techniques would not be as productive. Very similar to basic economics is the supply and demand curve. The greater the supply of sexual information, the less the demand. When sexual issues are filled with secrecy and shame in the home, the church, and the school, tremendous demand exists. The need arises for titillating sexual information. Advertisers, as well as the media, feed into the low supply of sexual information. Rather than blaming advertising, television, or the media for trauma felt by sexual victims, it may be more appropriate to recognize that due to the lack of appropriate information regarding sexuality, sexual victims are traumatized by the end result. The entire issue of secrecy and shame traumatizes the victim directly. Indirectly, the secrecy regarding sexuality enhances the need for advertisers to use these kinds of methods as effective tools to generate revenue.

Clamps And Cramps For The Male Victim

The male victim has a particular set of problems concerning trauma from the world. The most profound issue regarding the male victim is the fact that male victims report much less often than female victims. Some professionals suggest that perhaps males are sexually abused as often or perhaps more often than females. Sexual offenders report an alarmingly high rate of abusing males in their past histories. Treatment programs throughout the nation, however, are primarily directed toward the female patient and the male victim is highly under-represented. What is the reason for the lack of reporting and the lack of male victims involved in therapy?

The Unvictim

Many of these answers regarding the male's inability to report lies in the confusion felt about his identity as a victim. Additionally, much of this confusion lies in society's teaching regarding male sexuality and male victimization. There are four profoundly important reasons why males tend to report sexual abuse far less often than females and these reasons have a foundation in the sociological teaching of the male to deny his victimization.

Homophobia

First, males appear to be most often sexually abused by males. The result of this male-to-male sexual abuse is tremendous trauma to the male because of homosexuality. Even the smallest of children in a preschool or daycare center are vociferously shouting the words *faggot* and *queer*. From a very early age, children learn the significance of homosexuality and society's views. Males who are sexually abused by other males tend to feel a pervading sense of rejection by society. A young man who has been sexually abused by a male looks out into the world and sees homophobia. His fears of society's rejection caution him to withhold reporting. He sees persecution, rejection and abuse of homosexuals and his fear may deepen.

As well as fearing retribution from an insensitive world due to his homosexual contact, the male victim may also focus on the issue of homosexuality, which may traumatize his arousal system. Sexual development is an on-going process with one experience being built upon another. If a disruption in sexual development occurs, the male victim may become fixated upon an uncomfortable or unfortunate issue. The young man who looks into the world and sees homophobia may develop tremendous fear about society's rejection. The result may be that, through the fear, the male victim becomes intensely fixated on the homosexual incident. He begins to concentrate, to worry, and to focus. Rather than moving forward in his sexual development continuum, the male victim stops. In some cases, homosexual inclinations may be developed rather than rejected.

Not Mom, Sisters, Aunts, Grandmas???

If a male victim is sexually abused by a female, he may suffer from the *female role teaching*. Males recognize they live in a world where females are not viewed as perpetrators and sometimes viewed as being asexual. Women are portrayed as being sexy, sexy, sexy, but certainly never sexual. The young man who is sexually abused by a female worries he will not be believed nor protected. His world portrays women as sexual objects or as seducing men. Confusion develops about whether it is possible that the female was actually a perpetrator. The male victim may withhold reporting because he lives in a world that denotes a lack of sexual capacity for females — *not mom, sisters, aunts, grandma???*

A.A. — Aggressive and Accessible

The third issue preventing male victims from reporting their abuse occurs in the sexual role training of *Be A Real Man*. If young men are trained to develop into a combination between John Wayne and a German Shepherd, the message to the young male is to strive for sexual aggression and sexual accessibility. If the male is sexually abused, especially by a female, questions arise as to whether the male victim wanted the sexual contact to occur. Certainly, if a young man is to be sexually aggressive, then the door to being a sexual victim is closed since *all males should want any sexual contact they could receive.*

As an example, if a proud father toasts the birth of his son and makes comments such as, *I hope he is getting it in the sixth grade*, it appears sexual aggressiveness or sexual competency is an admired feature in the upbringing of males. Therefore, when sexual abuse occurs, the male has many questions about whether or not he was a victim, a willing partner, or a son who pleases his proud father.

> Alfred, a competent coach and teacher with two masters degrees, reports his sexual abuse for the first time in the therapist's office. As tears fall down his cheeks, Alfred is asked if he made a report about his abuse. *Yes, I reported. I told my father that the 18-year-old babysitter was sexually abusing me. My father's comment was, "What are you complaining about? She's a fox."*

Some male victims never report their abuse because they are confused about their own sexual identity and whether they wanted the sexual abuse to happen. The sexual aggressiveness and the sexual accessability demands on the male victim often prevent the report from ever occurring. If the report does occur, however, the response is often shock, disbelief, and ridicule much as indicated in the example of Alfred. Even if the courage was collected to make the report, male victims are often met with responses more traumatic than the sexual abuse itself.

Physiological Trauma

A final reason males struggle with reporting may be less connected to the collateral clamps and cramps of society, but nonetheless is a factor resulting from the lack of information and education in society. As indicated previously, the physiological differences between males and females cause particular problems for the male victim. Such sexual responsiveness as vaginal lubrication, clitoral erection, or even female orgasmic responses can be much more easily denied than an erection and ejaculation. Sexual offenders who touch the male genitalia can force males to immediately become erect and sexually respond. It is extremely difficult, if not impossible, to deny an erection. The physiological responsiveness of males often causes tremendous confusion about whether the male wanted the sexual contact to occur or whether the male was, in fact, a partner rather than a victim.

Although this may not be a direct response from society, certainly the fact that the male sexual response is unmentionable and never taught to males has a contributing factor within this category of trauma. If males, as an example, were brought up to learn and understand the inability to control erectile responses or even, at times, ejaculation, then this trauma might be alleviated. Unfortunately, most males have their first wet dreams, ejaculations, and erections on their own without any intervention or education from even caring and concerned patients. The male victim is even more profoundly traumatized due to the fact he will view his physiologi-

cal responses as an indicator of his partnership in the sexual abuse.

Sexual Saturation, Secrecy, Shame

Another trauma from society's teachings is experienced by victims in the conflicting messages of secrecy and shame, as compared to the fact that sex is absolutely everywhere. Victims, like most people, receive thousands of sexual messages each week. Sexuality is used to advertise everything from doughnuts to Play Doh. Objects that have absolutely nothing to do with sexuality or sexual attractiveness are often portrayed with a very seductive or sensuous model advertising the product. The problem does not seem to be with sexuality as the advertising modality, but with the fact that, on one hand, sexuality is so obvious and so over-worked, while, on the other hand, there is tremendous secrecy and shame felt by the victim in discussing sexual issues.

Many sexual victims go their entire childhood without reporting sexual abuse. If they had experienced another kind of trauma in childhood, the report would probably be made in a very matter-of-fact way discussing the trauma or the traumatic experience in factual terms. The theft of a bicycle or damage to a stereo are examples of crimes easily discussed. Those working in the field of sexual abuse recognize this is obviously not the case for the typical sexual victim. Many victims find it extremely difficult to report their sexual abuse even to a therapist in spite of tremendous symptoms that seem to be ruining the life of the adult patient. The second step of confronting the abuser or clarifying even within a family is often met with more shame, degradation, and resistance. What trauma occurs as victims are faced with the conflict of having *sex everywhere* and yet their own abuse, their own robbery of childhood is unmentionable and may be so, for the victim's entire life?

Hair It Is

Volumes of literature could be written on how the issue of sexuality is used to sell products. If examination of simply one item, *hair*, occurs, it is clear that sex becomes a common modality or focus for advertising.

As an example, hair products often have sexual overtones advertising *sexy* hair (FABERGE), *going all the way with hair* (FROST & TIP), or *turn'em on with frost 'n tip* (CLAIROL). Even an unattractive hair issue, such as *dead ends*, can be advertised provided a nearly naked female is combing her *dead ends* near the ends of her buttocks, which are seductively portrayed on a satin pillow (PANTENE).

Hair removal, which may be a bit disgusting, can be sold if portions of the body that are traditionally viewed as sexual can be portrayed, such as legs (NOXEMA). Removal of pubic hair can be advertised (BARE ESSENTIALS), provided that a very sexual picture shows the bikini tan line on parts of the body, other than the pubic area. It should be noted that it is acceptable to show the pubic area when advertising other products that do not belong to the pubic area, such as necklaces or shoes. If hair removal products, specifically designed to remove pubic hair, are advertised, however, another part of the body must be shown! To add to the absurdity, if facial hair is being removed, voluptuous lips must portray a very sexual pose on quite obviously a hairless face.

Nostril hair removal is rarely, if ever, shown in an advertisement due to the perplexing confusion for advertisers in how to make *nostril hair removal* SEXY. Even John Wayne, standing at a mirror in a hotel without running water, would not appear particularly sexual removing his nostril hairs. Unfortunately for nostril hair removing equipment manufacturers, hair removal products will remain focused on those advertising techniques which can be portrayed as sexual.

Endless documentation could be made regarding the use of sexuality in advertising and the media. The point remains that the sexual victim is traumatized by the fact that everyone else seems to be openly able to discuss sexual issues. The early feelings experienced by the child of guilt, shame and degradation are compounded in the secrecy of the sexual abuse, contrasting with a world that uses sexuality as a commodity if not a currency.

The Sex Fairy Myth

The Sex Fairy Myth is another example in the conflicts of secrecy and sexuality. The Sex Fairy Myth is not helpful to any child, but *it is traumatizing* to sexual victims. The Sex Fairy Myth is a belief held by parents, teachers, educators, clergy, or professionals that some-how sexual education and sexual training for children will be successful without intervention from adults. Even highly trained and intelligent parents often omit comprehensive sexual education from their repertoire of parenting. It is as though somehow children will move about in a world that is preoccupied with sexuality and they will magically learn morals, values, and information providing them with appropriate sexual decision making power.

Thousands of dollars can be spent on ballet lessons, or braces, and countless hours may be invested teaching children to be honest, or to become Mormons, Baptists, or Catholics. Somehow when it comes to S.E.X., society believes that the Sex Fairy will somehow *zap our children in the crotch when they walk down the isle to get married* and (without any help from their parents) they will turn into wonderful, happy, healthy, sexual human beings!!!!????

The result of the Sex Fairy Myth is an outrage toward openness about sex. Some state laws, as an example, prohibit schools from teaching anatomically correct names of genitalia to children. As another example, **A Very Touching Book** is banned in some states due to the fact that nudity is exhibited to children. Many prevention programs are rejected by school boards if genitalia is either shown or, *God forbid!!,* discussed. In actuality, the openness or positive information about sexuality is met with shame and rejection and, contrarily, sexual aggression, damaging sexual role training, sexual violence and exploitation are much more acceptable.

Thore Langfeldt of Norway delivered a presentation at the International Conference on Sexual Offenders, in May, 1989. He discussed how in other countries such as Norway, a little boy's erection would be viewed with pride and met with discussion, much the same as the same little boy learning to ride a bicycle or gaining competency in writing cursive. In the United States, Dr. Langfeldt reported, the little boy's penis would only be worth discussion if it had been cut off in a violent crime or if somehow there was a tragedy associated with this young man. The pride in his erection would certainly not be mentionable without being met with shame and outrage.

If Some, Then Bad

As far as schools are concerned, if discussions of sexual issues are allowed, it is usually only the negative issues of sexuality that are permitted. Junior high and high school subjects regarding sexuality are usually those relating to venereal disease, date rape, teen pregnancy, sexual abuse, homosexuality, or AIDS. If the sexual victim is looking for an avenue of assistance or discussion, the only access to sources of information are negative, criminal and degrading. Again, at the same time, society itself is extremely sexual, yet the information available that might provide some sort of help is either limited or entirely negative. On one hand, the victim recognizes the impact of secrecy and the fact that being open about the sexual abuse will be rejected. On the other hand, as the victim peruses sexual information available, more shame emerges since society seems to have only one perspective of sexuality, and that is one that is extremely negative.

Home Sweet Home

If the victim is traumatized by society's messages, the home scene does not seem to be more positive or more helpful in preventing traumatization through collateral issues. As in the schools, if sexual education is conducted at home, it is usually negative, with tremendous warnings being given to adolescents about what fate will await them should they become sexually involved. Underlying messages previous to parents' futile attempt at morality training are often just as negative.

Body Works

As an example, most children grow up with negative ideations about body functions. Little girls are forced to hide the Tampax or Kotex in their homes or certainly to avoid discussing their menstrual cycles with the males in the family. While the male's body seems to be more acceptable in a functioning way (men seem to approach toiletry activities and such behaviors as *passing gas* more comfortably than females), bodily functions are extremely unmentionable. Even if children are given the proper names for body parts by their parents, they are rarely told about how those body parts work.

Acceptance of bodily functions is particularly difficult for females who may respond sexually during sexual abuse yet are confused about the significance of that responsiveness. Vaginal lubrications, as an example, are signs of female arousal or indicators of different stages in the female's cycle. If we had a *Fairy Tale World* for our society, little girls would grow up being just as proud of their vaginal lubrication as boys seem to be proud of their erections. Although little boys rarely discuss their erections with parents, they commonly compare their erections with each other during childhood.

Let's see who has the biggest.

Oh, look at mine.

Let's show'em to each other.

See mine.

Look at you, you look like a chipmunk!

Little girls rarely compare their vaginal lubrications and rarely even discuss such bodily functions. The message is clear. *If you have those parts (and everybody does), it's bad enough; if those parts work, it's very disgusting.*

A nurse, Miriam Coppens, was quoted at a sexuality workshop in Portland, Oregon. *At least little boys get to touch themselves each day as they urinate. Little girls are told, Don't touch yourself, it's dirty down there, save it for someone you love!*

Pee Pees And Poo Poos

On a more simplistic level, children usually grow up in families learning silly, confusing, or negative words for their body parts. *Potties, poops, pee pees, cookies,* etc., are common names given to children by parents. As children grow, they adopt more vulgar names as *pee pees and potties* become *dicks and pussies.*

Out of apparent fear that children will become sexual, parents typically provide these names to create confusion or in order to keep children quiet or *innocent.* The idea that *innocence is ignorance* pervades most sex education within the home.

The fact that genitalia are unmentionable, even in the home, compounds the guilt and anxiety victims feel. The cleansing process or the therapeutic value of being able to discuss a painful event and receive support is well known within the field of rehabilitation. When children are sexually abused and recognize that they live in a world where even the *equipment* used in the molestation is unmentionable, guilt, anxiety, depression, and trauma are heightened. The clamping and cramping is in place.

Touching Trouble

Even with attempted sex education for children or adolescents, parents often avoid discussing the fact that the sexual parts actually collide or *touch* each other. Many children have seen explicit charts of reproduction with ovaries and ovum on one side of the blackboard, while spermatozoa and testicles cuddle together on the farthest side of the blackboard. It is usually with magical arrows or mystical lines that the *parts* converge in order for the process of conception to occur. Children often run home, disrobe, and examine their bodies, looking for the *arrows!*

The idea of sexual *parts* actually touching is most commonly avoided in discussions of sex. Tremendous effort is exerted to avoid telling children that sexuality involves not only spermatozoa and ovum for reproduction, but actually involves the parts touching (and, God Forbid, feeling good!). It is no wonder victims have difficulty talking about sexual abuse since the touching of sexual parts is taboo.

Cruelty To Animals

Due to parents' fear of discussing the sexual parts colliding or touching, a visit to the barnyard is often used to compensate. It is common for children to be taught sex education through the use of animals.

The first grade teacher who objected to the sex education curriculum explained at the PTA meeting that sexuality education was already being taught while children are attending school. The teacher indicated that her first graders receive most of the sex education they needed before the second grade since an appaloosa stud and a field of mares were positioned directly across from the first grade class windows. She explained that when the mares came into heat, the first graders were allowed to watch as she explained reproduction. (Imagine the six-year-old female child anticipating her honeymoon with an appaloosa stud and his 18 inch penis!)

Children are often taken to the garden and taught the magic of seeds and fertilizer in a hope that they will be satisfied with watching carrots grow, rather than asking why their teenage sister is pregnant.

After returning from a Sunday visit to the farm, five-year-old Brandon asked his mother, *Why does grandpa have the bull Henry come visit his cows in the spring?* After driving in the ditch on the freeway, Brandon's mother regains composure and attempts to remind Brandon of his earlier experiences in the garden. *Remember, Brandon, how we took the cucumber seeds and we put them in a pile in the garden. Then we took the fertilizer and we put the fertilizer in the seeds and remember, Brandon, the cucumbers grew! Well, that's how it is with cows.*

The cow has the seeds and the bull has the fertilizer and that's how baby cows are made. Brandon, a very precocious child, pondered. He then asked his mother (after imagining the prospect of cucumbers growing out of the cow's back), *How does he get up that high to poop on her?*

Again, it is the shamefulness and the degradation of sexuality that children learn at home or school. Not only is this devastating to the prospect of children having a positive sexual attitude in the future, but the sexual victim hears these messages as well. Rehabilitation for the sexual victim requires feeling as though a crime was committed and that something extremely valuable was taken. Obviously, the sexual victim has very little chance to feel robbed of something special when genitalia and sexual acts are enshrouded in secrecy, negativism, and mystical barnyard antics.

The Unpardonable Sin

Perhaps the ultimate in negativism learned in the home is the horror adults feel regarding the *sexuality of children.* For adults educating their children, uncomfortable subjects are typically avoided. None is avoided with such profound panic as the sexuality of children. Most adults would admit to telling lies, stealing candy, perhaps picking on their brother or sister when they were children. Describing or admitting to sexual activities in childhood seems to be an extremely painful prospect, however.

The way in which adults learn about sexuality compounds this negative attitude. Before children walk they learn one message, then they suffer from a quick reversal in sex education. Sensuousness or sexuality begins at an extremely early age, perhaps even before birth.

> It was dusk, the apartment was empty, save for the two of them. As they lay entwined in warm embrace, this room, this bed was the universe. She stroked the nape of his neck, he nuzzled her erect nipple, first gently with his nose, then licked it, tasted it, smelled and absorbed her body odor. Slowly he caressed her one breast as he softly rolled his face over the contours of the other. He pressed his body close against her, sighed and fully spent, closed his eyes and soon fell into a deep satisfying sleep. Ever so slowly, she slipped herself out from under him lest she disturb him, cradled him in her arms, and moved him to his crib!

Herman Belmont, in his lecture in Philadelphia on the sexuality of children describes extremely sensuous activities with children before they begin to walk. It is not uncommon for adults to kiss, caress, and carry babies. They are oiled, held, cuddled. Adults place their mouths four, three, two, one inches from children's genitalia without a thought. In fact, as the listeners in Dr. Belmont's audience exclaimed, the passage seemed to be a very sensuous, seductive scene between a man and a woman. In actuality, a mother was breast feeding her son, compound-ing the point that children, in the first year of their life participate in very sensuous experiences. Many adults pay sex therapists thousands of dollars to teach them to return to behaviors they experienced during the first few years of their life.

Unfortunately, when children begin to walk and talk, adults suddenly become appalled at the sensuality or the sensuousness *they* taught their children. Although hours were spent kissing, caressing, and stimulating other parts of the infant's body, the toddler who dares his fingers to venture within four inches of his crotch will often be met with repulsion, scolding and, at times, even punishment. It seems absolutely impossible for adults to accept the sensuality of children that was taught to them in the first two years of their lives.

A little girl rubbing her clitoris on a chair or with a Teddy Bear may bring panic and horror to a mother's eyes. A three-year-old little boy streaking through the house after his bath, smiling, and holding onto his erect penis may cause a nervous father to scan the yellow pages for a child sex therapist. Even the three-year-old who can proudly respond to directions *show Grandma your nose, show Grandma your eyes, show Grandma your ears*, knows **not** to show Grandma her pee pee if she wants Grandma to live through Thanksgiving Dinner!

Sex And Supermarkets

In 1975, St. Martin's Press published a book entitled, *Show Me*, which is a sex education book for children and adults. This very explicit book contains black and white photographs of every sexual pose and activity between heterosexual couples, *beginning* in childhood. Although the book only portrays children being involved with other children, adolescents being involved with their peers and adults being involved with adults, the book nonetheless has been banned in many states as being *obscene*. *Show Me* has explicit photographs of such obscenities as breast feeding, intercourse between consenting adult partners, and sexual discussions, feelings, attitudes, and behaviors between consenting partners. Nowhere in the publication is any hint of violence or sexual exploitation of children. What is the reason, then, that this book has been found to be so offensive?

What seems to be most painful for adults examining this publication is the fact that children are sexually involved with children. The book shows little boys touching their penises with glee and hope of the future. Little girls rub their clitorises as such captions discuss how these parts feel different and wonderful to be touched (actually, better than our elbows!). Yes, the book does have explicit pictures of intercourse and the birth of babies, but most unpardonable is the fact that children are exploring their bodies. They are interacting sexually with one another and, most obscenely, they are enjoying the pleasure of their own bodies. The world is not ready for *Show Me*, but the world is ready, accepting or perhaps at least willing to ignore other sexual messages that are commonly found in supermarkets.

At the local supermarket, children can be exposed to what is determined as *the acceptable* side of sexuality. *True Detective* types of magazines, showing women being murdered, raped and mutilated are apparently more acceptable than books about children touching their own genitalia. It does not seem uncomfortable for society to have children exposed to extremely violent sexual behaviors in magazines, complete with pictures of women being chained or their dead bodies strewn on roadsides in sexually compromising positions. This, according to the supermarket sexual comparison, is much more acceptable than children actually enjoying the pleasure of their own bodies and, most importantly, enjoying the sensuality that *we* taught them as infants.

There is some suggestion that the book *Show Me* should be banned because pedophiles find this book to be one of their favorites. It is not uncommon for search warrants to confiscate many copies of the book, since pedophiles have an extreme interest not only in children engaging in sexual experiences, but in photographs and pornography. Those who would suggest that *Show Me* was banned as obscene because pedophiles found the book so interesting should remember that pedophiles also find erotica in the Sears and Roebuck Catalog (children's jammy section). The pedophile may also find walking by the playground at the grade school erotic. If we are to stop the use of pedophile material from being printed, where, in fact, will it end?

So what is the result for the sexual victim? How is the victim traumatized by the fact that we live in a world that finds the *mutilation, rape ,then murder of a seductive three-year-old* more acceptable than children being sexual? Careful consideration of offender operational procedures gives an example of trauma bonding because of these controversies.

May I Have This Dance?

In many cases, if not the majority, sexual offenders make children feel like partners in the sexually abusive scenario. *I can tell that you like me to do this to you,* or *You liked it last time, and I will tell if you don't do it this time,* are words from offenders that hook children into feeling as though they are a partner rather than a victim. For the smaller child who is developmentally incapable of understanding the significance of the sexual contact, cooperation often occurs during the early stages of development. For those children, as well as for older children who are taught to be acquiescent partners, this unpardonable sin or attitude regarding children being sexual is a disasterous combination.

When the latency-aged victim hears parents discussing their horror at their three-year-old touching his penis or their hysteria from learning the grade school program may talk about roosters and chickens in the same day, victims look back on their abuse with feelings of shame at *their* involvement. If the child lives in a world where the sexuality of children is either nonexistent, or repulsive, then reporting sexual abuse or talking about it is impossible. Not only is secrecy likely to plague the child who becomes aware of these societal attitudes, but the victim is caught in a trauma bond of ongoing upheaval.

In summary, it would appear that sexual education in the home regarding body parts, bodily functions, and the sexuality of children is an extremely difficult issue for the sexually abused child. Child sexual abuse is not isolated, nor is the pain. Victims are continuing to take in information and apply it to their own behavior and activities. For children who have been sexually abused, walking through the mirage of negative attitudes and secrecy compounds the pain and develops a trauma bond.

And Closer To The Fire

Even more specific than the negative attitudes about sexuality and genitalia in the home is how victims are traumatized by attempts to prevent or discover sexual abuse. There are many *abuses* in sexual abuse prevention programs which actually compound damage to the sexually abused child or to future sexual abuse victims(Hindman).

The Boogeyman Approach

Because adults are outraged and frightened by sexual abuse, prevention efforts often have negative or fearful tone —the *boogeyman theme* is common. And even when this type of approach is not consciously employed, often negative messages are communicated in a non-verbal way to children.

Negative and fearful prevention efforts fail miserably because they make children avoid the topic of prevention altogether. When the tense, solemn adult gives children a prevention scenario full of dark and forbidden warnings, the frightening messages speak louder than the attempt to protect children. Negative approaches not only push children away from the idea of prevention, but they discourage reporting of sexual abuse. The white knuckled adult with clenched teeth is obviously not comfortable. Children who have been sexually abused and contemplate reporting fear being responsible for more *upset* should they make a report. Additionally, children take on even more guilt and responsibility for the fact that they were sexually abused and participated in this horrible activity. Many children do not directly compute, *I have been sexually abused and, if I tell, I will create more hysteria in this purple faced teacher,* but children subtly take on more responsibility when the approach is extremely foreboding and upsetting.

Underneath Your Swimming Suit

Another classic example of abuse in prevention programs is found in efforts to avoid genitalia. Sexual abuse involves body parts. Yet, amazingly, most prevention programs avoid the discussion of genitalia, and programs that men-tion genitalia often use ambiguous phrases such as *private and public zones,* or *underneath our swimming suits.*

The avoidance of genitalia may work well for adults with bright purple faces, but this approach traumatizes children and sends a mystical and confusing message. Adults can't say the *real word,* but they demand that children be more confident. They are telling children who have not been sexually abused, *If you are abused, you must be more confident than we.* The message is, *Be sure and come and tell us if someone touches your* **parts, stuff, deals, down there (gulp)**. Again, the child learns these parts are unmentionable; therefore, they are also unmentionable to anyone who may be able to help the child.

This Is Too Simple

Another way in which children are further traumatized by unplanned or insensitive prevention programs is in the area of the simplistic approach. *Just Say No* pervades many sexual abuse prevention programs. As the child who has been sexually abused for as long as she can remember hears the chant, *just say no,* an automatic sense of failure abounds. Is the child likely to raise her hand and say *not only have I been sexually abused, not only have I had my body parts that are unmentionable to you touched, but I didn't say* **no!**

The guilt and failure is compounded again by the child's inability to do something that is presented as a seemingly simple process. The fact that adults are bigger in size, intelligence, and have tremendous power over children is rarely mentioned in these well-intentioned prevention programs. The message is *this is simple, say no, tell*. Children are never told it is very, very hard to feel strong enough to say no.

Even if you can't say no, we'll still help you. Even if you haven't said no for a long, long time, we'll still help you.

Sexual victims who already have patterns of guilt and anxiety about what they have done are going to be re-traumatized if presented with this kind of prevention effort.

For Big People and For Little People

It should be noted that the damage through these collateral cramps and clamps regarding prevention is not necessarily limited to small children sitting in the fifth grade class at the elementary school. What about the female teacher who is providing the prevention program who was sexually abused as a child and still vacillates in her feelings of responsibility and outrage? And what about trauma to the father who was sexually abused, as he peruses the local PTA material describing the simple solution to sexual abuse as *teaching children to say no*. If the father participated in homosexual acts with the neighborhood Boy Scout Leader and didn't say *No* and, in fact, enjoyed his erections and ejaculations, has the trauma truly ended for the unresolved male victim?

Good Touch, Bad Touch

Most prevention efforts use a word like *bad* to describe sexual contact between children and adults. To understand why this terminology is abusive, the difference between the well meaning adult perspective and the abused child's perspective must be understood. Because adults understand the intricacies of legal consent and sexual development, they view sexual abuse as criminal or *bad*. Children, however, do not view sexual abuse from the same context. They don't always feel victimized during a sexual contact with an adult, because sex offenders put great effort into making children feel like sexual partners. When a child feels like a partner, the abuser encases the child in guilt and secrecy and a sexual conspiracy exists, involving two people, not a clear perpetrator and an innocent victim.

The mistake of describing sexual abuse with such words like *bad* becomes apparent. If an abused child feels like a partner in the sexual contact and the prevention program called the contact *bad*, the only conclusion for the child is taking on the *badness*. This approach actually helps the sexual offender make the child feel even more guilty and sealed into secrecy.

Additionally, if this poor choice of word is used, a contribution is made to the child's sexual development in the future. Not only are children traumatized while the abuse is happening or while children are children, but the victim's future sexuality is damaged.

Helen discusses her sexual abuse at age five and the subsequent intervention and education she received through a well meaning prevention program.

> *That's fine*, she said. *For them to say that what my father did to me was bad. They carefully explained to me that what he had done was a crime, against the law, and bad, bad, bad. But, they failed to realize what would happen to me as a sexual adult. How was I expected not take this **bad** idea of sexuality into the bedroom with me as an adult? As I look back, I am outraged that you said, "What your father did to you when you were five was bad, but don't worry honey, you'll have a good time when you are 25."*

One Touch, All Touch

Another prevention issue that seems to be abusive and certainly compounds the trauma bond suffered by sexual abuse victims is in generalizing all genital touching as being abusive. Children often loudly chant together, *don't let anyone touch your private parts.* How does the fifth grader feel when she returns from this kind of prevention program and watches her father change the diapers on her baby brother? What happens to Johnny when his mother or father attempt to help him with bathing after he has listened to a prevention program generalizing all genital touching between children and adults as abusive? What happens to unresolved adult victims when

children return from these prevention program and seem to feel uncomfortable or phobic about normal hygiene and healthcare activity? Again, there are more negative attitudes and ideations to pile upon the already guilt-ridden victim.

Portrait Of A Perpetrator

Some prevention programs delight in providing children with profiles of perpetrators. Often, this methodology goes even beyond the classroom or the prevention program into public education awareness where perpetrators are portrayed as a Snidely Whiplash, evil person who obviously never changes his underwear. As children learn about the profiles of perpetrators, they are often exposed to information that would exclude the person who is sexually abusing them or who has abused them in the past. Although fathers or father figures comprise a significant portion of sexual offenders, rarely is the word *father* listed in prevention program profiling. However, the male (not the father) is primarily presented as a perpetrator, leaving children vulnerable to father and females. If a child is being sexually abused by a female, the fact that the male is usually portrayed as a perpetrator will often prevent victims from identifying themselves as a victim and feeling as though the female was the perpetrator.

If the profile *(nasty person)* approach is used without gender, then children often are prevented from identifying themselves as a victim since their perpetrator may have extremely positive attributes assigned to them by the child. This is sad, since clearly if children were taught to protect their bicycles, they would rarely be provided with profiles of bicycles thieves. Children are taught *to like* their bicycles, to appreciate the expense involved in their bicycles, and they are taught how to protect their bicycles. By providing profiles to children, the people who are abusive to them rarely are included in the profile, but, more importantly in the child's effort to identify the perpetrator and the victim, the child again loses.

Again, there seems to be no difference between the pain felt by the adult victim or the *child victim* when exposure to these issues occurs. Adult victims have a terrified, frightened, guilty child *within*. When those unresolved adult victims send their children to a prevention program, both the fifth grader and the eleven-year-old child within the 44-year-old mother suffer. The confusion about the offender/victim identity abounds for both mother and daughter.

The Fairy Tale World Of Families

Very similar to the power of the offender and power of the non-offending parent, the entire issue of family seems to *zap* the victim back to the affective responses concerning the abuse. The collateral clamp or cramp is that the victim learns the way it was *supposed* to be in their family. When the victim is constantly presented with the ideal family, the victim continues to be traumatized.

Tuning into the Bill Cosby Show, or watching reruns of Father Knows Best, take the victim through a process of believing that the rest of the world functions in a manner similar to the Partridge Family. Family portrayals of the Christmas scene, with everyone gathered around the fireplace, everyone in the family the proper weight and experts in dental flossing, suggest that no one in the entire world has a family member who would even violate the **DO NOT REMOVE** label from a mattress. Victims are sealed into a sense that there is something wrong with them and again guilt abounds.

Not only is the family unit constantly portrayed as being perfect, but if on television or in the media there is a blemish within the family, there is always a workable solution. *Death or change* seems to be a solution that is prevalent in many scenarios. The lack of resolution for the victim is never portrayed. Americans want a happy ending. They want a resolution if a problem exists. The adult sexual victim who has no resolution regarding the sexual abuse not only continues to feel badly without a resolution, but the lack of resolution indicates failure on the victim's part. If the sexual abuse is not bad enough, the victim must also feel guilty because there is no resolution. The victim did not come from a happy, perfect family.

The Sensory Cycle

Finally, collateral clamps and cramps for the sexual victim involve activation of the sensory stimulation that is similar to the sexual abuse. Many times these are described as phobic reactions by professionals, although many are quite subtle. The victim, as an example, gagged or choked on the behavior of fellatio may simply have a *crabby day* when wearing a necklace. Although the choking sensation does not return completely or may not even be understood by the victim, scarves around the neck, necklaces, or turtle neck sweaters may cause the victim to have many of the *aftermath* feelings that surrounded the sexual abuse. As she laid in bed and cried after the offender had left the room, feelings of sadness and overwhelming depression may have engulfed the victim as seminal fluid ran down her throat. When sensors are activated by the throat or the neck, as an example, many of the affective feelings continue, often without the victim's knowledge.

Skin memories are often the only memory. Skin memories do not necessarily require cognitive awareness of the abuse in childhood. Many victims proceed throughout their lifetime being *zapped* by skin memories without the clarity of the cognitive understanding of the etiology of the memories.

If a patient, as an example, is brought to the therapist's office due to panic attacks from driving across bridges or attempting to participate in a back-packing campout through the church, therapists may be completely confused since the victim does not report sexual abuse. Even if the victim did report sexual abuse, the etiology of the panic attacks may be confusing to both the therapist and the patient. It is not until tremendous work has taken place that the patient finds skin memories that correlate with the cables on the bridges, holding the leather reins of the horse's bridle in the hands, or feeling straps of the backpack. These seemingly unrelated items make the victim affectively respond to *bondage* that occurred during the victim's abuse.

A wide range and variety of skin memories or affective *zappers* will be discussed in the situational portion of the Sexual Victim Trauma Assessment. Most importantly, the sexual abuse victim is often traumatized in moving about a world re-experiencing certain aspects of the abusive scenario. Seeing advertisements where body positions were the same as the abuse, smelling smells that were consistent in the abusive scenario, or even hearing words that occurred during the abuse will often take the victim back, often without a clear, cognitive memory of the abuse.

This seems to be an extremely neglected area in therapy for the sexual victim. Too often, therapists concentrate on the sexual activities that took place and do not consider other activations of the senses within the situation of the sexual abuse scene. Most therapists in adulthood recognize that hearing a teenage heart throb song from adolescence can actually cause a memory to occur regarding *old what's his name in the backseat of the Chevrolet.* Smelling an air freshener in a car that was the same air freshener in the Chevrolet during a therapist's very first sexual kiss can also bring those memories back. It seems odd that those issues are omitted from the therapeutic involvement with victims as patients are cruelly returned to be *cramped* by many collateral events, activities.

The trauma of sexual abuse is not isolated. Trauma bonding goes beyond the offender, the non-offending parent, and into a cruel and insensitive world. The world zaps, clamps, and cramps the victim's efforts to survive in peace.

TRIUMPHS OVER TRAGEDY — THE TRAUMA ASSESSMENT

The trauma for victims is a methodical maze of madness, giving birth to continual turmoil. Is there a methodical method of resistance to the trauma? If trauma is everywhere, so be it! What can be done? If we understand, what can we do?

What a bleak picture for the sexual victim! Seemingly each day in a victim's life is another reminder of the sexual abuse. Revisiting the pain is commonplace. Sexual victims seem to live in a world cruel to their suffering. There the offender appears to remain powerful, the non-offending family members are insensitive, and the general world of the sexual victim *reminds*. The victim seems in a traumatic bond with the sexual abuse, unable to go forward, unable to find peace, and unable to be released.

The triumph over this tragedy begins with a comprehensive examination of how the victim has been traumatized. The present, past, and the future must be evaluated. The Sexual Victim Trauma Assessment is the first step toward rehabilitation and recovery.

In the Beginning

The Sexual Victim Trauma Assessment not only becomes a road map toward the future of recovery and rehabilitation, but also provides information regarding the past travels of the victim. The victim remains traumatically bound in returning to the abuse and attempting to step forward into a future with many *potholes* and difficulties. The Sexual Victim Trauma Assessment becomes the framework for understanding where the patient has been and where the patient will be in the future.

For the Young . . .

The young, often asymptomatic child is examined following disclosure of sexual abuse. A lack of symptoms may encourage professionals to believe the child has not been severely damaged, and treatment is often brief or nonexistent. The Sexual Victim Trauma Assessment not only takes into account the younger child at the present level of feelings, attitudes, and capabilities, but also takes the courageous step of looking at what may lie ahead. Phobic reactions and cognitive distortions lurk in the child's future. The potential for proceeding through development and building upon sexual deviancy is tremendous. The Trauma Assessment for the younger patient evaluates what has occurred, but most importantly what may occur if treatment for these potential problems does not occur.

Should this suggest to concerned parents and overworked caseworkers that a five-year-old child needs therapy until adulthood? The answer is *absolutely not*. The lack of symptoms in the five-year-old child, however, should not indicate the victim will be safe from trauma. Victims will continue to *develop* thoughts, attitudes and beliefs just as other children move from Barbie dolls to bobbie socks. It is a *process* and by virtue of being children, the trauma *process* is not completed, therefore the estimates of the trauma are not complete.

This research suggests that children are not necessarily traumatized because they are young. In actuality, children are traumatized because they continue to proceed through development without an appropriate vehicle to help them. That appropriate *vehicle* is outlined in the Sexual Victim Trauma Assessment. The Trauma Assessment predicts what may lie ahead in the victim's future and designs the *vehicle* to be used for recovery.

Deadly Double

Miriam is a six-year-old child evaluated regarding allegations of sexual abuse by her father and several of his friends. With a competent investigator, Miriam describes being tied in extremely distorted positions, blood being extracted from her veins and dripped upon her body, the torture of animals, and hours of exposure to sexual material. Can we accurately examine this child as reflected in her wonderment and curiosity as she explains these horrible experiences? What lies in Miriam's future as a happy, sexual, competent partner appreciating the beauty of sexuality and intimacy?

Traditionally, Miriam may be ignored until she is symptomatic. Sadly, however, coupled with her presentation of symptoms in the future will also be the Deadly Double. Miriam will have a resistance to therapy and a heavily entrenched system of distorted cognitions about such issues as responsibility, guilt, and blame. She will have doubled her problems. The cultivation of her trauma is not only is now manifested in symptoms, but she also is *developmentally* unresponsive to therapy. The tragedy is in waiting until the problem is *double* and perhaps impossible.

The Trauma Assessment for Miriam will indicate very few symptoms at this time. She will, because of the Trauma Assessment, be given the opportunity to be placed in a treatment program where she can desensitize. Her recovery can prevent skin memories, amnesia, dissociation, and phobic reactions. At the same time, she will be given intensive education regarding the *criminal* aspects of this behavior and, additionally, the positive aspects of her own body and sexuality. Hopefully, through a Trauma Assessment, the depth to which Miriam understands her role as a victim and the perpetrator's role can be discovered. Distorted views can then be rearranged and clarified. Miriam's hope lies in the prevention of trauma bonding.

The Sexual Victim Trauma Assessment can also pinpoint additional areas of concern and important things Miriam needs to carry with her in her *baggage* toward the future. Just as if Miriam had been in an accident and her pancreas had been damaged, she would need to rearrange her healthcare activities and adjust for the potential of diabetes, the Trauma Assessment will plan for Miriam's future in teaching her how to compensate and make adjustments. Currently Miriam is ripe for intervention and she is asymptomatic! It will only be through the sensitivity of the Sexual Victim Trauma Assessment that therapy can assist Miriam to prepare for her future and the onset of symptoms.

And For the Not So Young

For professionals dedicated to the DSM III, the older patient is much more comfortable than asymptomatic children. Finally, as the patient proceeds through adolescence or adulthood, symptoms arise. With glee, diagnosis can be made and third party payments arranged. Unfortunately, many of the symptoms suffered by a victim, as a result of cultivating coping skills to deny victimization or innocence, may also render the victim resistive to therapeutic intervention. The adult victim screams, *I want to go on with my life* or *I have forgotten. Why is this still bothering me?* Now that the symptoms are present, professionals want to proceed. They were trained to rehabilitate and the time is now. Unfortunately, because so much time has been spent nurturing distorted views, phobic reactions, and deadly coping skills, the patient is often either resistive to intervention or so devastated by the process that recovery is extremely difficult.

For the *not so young patient*, the Sexual Victim Trauma Assessment provides an understanding and awareness of the previous travels through the trauma. Being able to return to the sexually abusive scene, and to understand what has taken place since the abuse, can be extremely helpful to victims in recognizing their present state of symptoms. Taking the *child within* back to the abusive scenario and then describing the journey to the future, with different perceptions, can provide the older patient with an awareness that is extremely important. It is nearly impossible to resolve problems that are unmentionable, uncomfortable, and misunderstood. The Sexual Victim Trauma Assessment provides the older patient with an understanding of the etiology of the symptoms so control can occur.

Just as the surgeon does not proceed into the operating room simply knowing that the patient has cancer, the recovery for the sexual victim cannot proceed simply knowing that the victim was sexually abused. The traditional components of **AGE, PENETRATION, VIOLENCE** and **FREQUENCY** will not provide enough information to pinpoint important steps for recovery. Just as the surgeon must know the kind of cancer, the exact location of the cancer, and specific techniques in eradicating the cancer, so must the therapist and the patient put forth effort into understanding the trauma before it, too, can be eradicated.

The Relationship Perspective

Looking Around

The Relationship Perspective of the Sexual Victim Trauma Assessment is the first of three components comprising the evaluation process. In this portion of the Trauma Assessment, the clinician and the patient need to examine relationships within a triangular approach. At the corners of the triangle are:

- The Sexual Victim
- The Perpetrator
- And Others Who Are Important to the Sexual Victim and Offender

In the Trauma Assessment, the clinician must assign pluses and minuses within, the triangle in order to determine the victims perceptions in viewing appropriate identifications of the victim and the perpetrator. As the child at the top of the triangle looks toward the perpetrator, decisions are made regarding the child's perceptions of guilt, responsibility, and blame. As indicated in this research, those children who clearly viewed themselves as being innocent and who viewed the perpetrator as being responsible had the greatest chance for rehabilitation. Those children who were confused about the victim/offender identity, because the perpetrator had positive attributes and the victim had a low self-esteem, demonstrated difficulty with recovery.

The victim also looks down through the center of the triangle and examines how the perpetrator is viewed by others who are important to the victim. The bottom of the triangle is the connection between the perpetrator and *significant others* (the non-offending parent, the siblings in the family, the community, the church, extended family members, etc.). As the victim looks through the triangle to the bottom, the victim makes decisions regarding how the *significant others* view the perpetrator concerning guilt or innocence. If victims see the bottom of the triangle with a minus toward the perpetrator, it would appear to the victim that *significant others* viewed the perpetrator as responsible. If a plus occurs on the bottom side of the triangle, the victim may be confused about whether others, who are important to the victim, can truly identify the perpetrator as being a criminal.

Finally, the victim looks to the left side of the triangle to *significant others* and attempts to make decisions regarding the *victim status*. Even if those *significant others* view the victim's perpetrator as being guilty, but do not view the victim as being an innocent, precious child who was robbed of sexual safety and security, trauma may occur. The most rehabilitating scenario would be if the victim looks down the left side of the triangle and was psychologically and emotionally rescued by *significant others*. The victim was identified as the innocent child, the victim of a crime and rehabilitation has already begun.

Scoring Scars

It is important to realize that in this portion of the Sexual Victim Trauma Assessment, the victim is *SCORING* the identity of the victim and the perpetrator. The clinician's views are not important, rather the victim's perceptions, or how others important to the victim view the triangulation. Even the most dangerous or disgusting perpetrator can be, in the victim's mind, an important person who cannot take on the role of the perpetrator. Additionally, the clinician's view of the patient may be extremely positive, but if the cultivation of negative feelings toward the victim has occurred, the message may be unclear. In spite of the professional's view, victims may not see themselves as innocent and free of guilt.

Developmental Perspective

Looking Backwards

The Developmental Perspective of the Sexual Victim Trauma Assessment addresses perhaps one of the most neglected areas in the trauma of sexual victims. As research indicated, the most traumatized patients appear to be those who are sexually abused when they were under the age of eight. Additionally, the data shows that the majority of victims who are asymptomatic or who had very little trauma were also younger children. Clinical impressions suggest that it is not necessarily the age at which the child is abused that is significant. What happens to the child's sexual development in the process of building upon sexually deviant impressions seems to be of primary importance.

As an example, if children are abused in pre-teens or in adolescence, there is some hope that sexual development has been partially developed previous to the abuse, providing a potential for a more positive sexual development foundation. For younger victims, when the sexual abuse was discovered and separated from normal sexual development, children seem to have a much better chance for rehabilitation than their counterparts who are sexually abused and proceed through sexual development without assistance. Smaller children seem to be much more accepting of intervention and may be better patients in therapy than an older patient who has spent time cultivating distorted cognitions and phobic reactions. The younger child who reports sexual abuse may have the greatest chance for rehabilitation since sexual abuse can be separated from normal sexual development.

If the Relationship Perspective of the Sexual Victim Trauma Assessment involved the victim *looking around*, putting forth effort to identify the roles of the perpetrator and the victim, the developmental portion of the Sexual Victim Trauma Assessment examines the victim proceeding through development constantly *looking backward* toward the abusive scenario and building sexual development upon those memories and ideations.

> Beth is on the playground in the second grade. She believes she lives in a *normal household* considering her family to be like all others. One of the children yells at the top of his lungs the words COCK SUCKER. The teacher promptly punishes the children for saying the word that describes what Beth does with her father most every evening. As the bell brings the children in from recess, Beth begins to *look backward*. Does she raise her hand and say, *Teacher, excuse me. If you spanked those children for saying the word that describes what I do with my father each evening, what kind of punishment should I get for doing that behavior?*

The postulation is absurd! Beth is stepping into a different stage of sexual development and becoming more aware of the significance of her involvement. Now, instead of proceeding toward third, fourth, and fifth grade anticipating kissing, chasing boys, holding hands, Beth will be looking backwards, not at what was done to her, but *My God, look what I have done!*

Generally, children anticipate *looking forward* in sexual development. They begin to wonder about their bodies and about the bodies of their opposite sex friends. They see kissing on television and they anticipate kissing. Normal sexual development proceeds toward the future. For the sexual victim, sexual abuse provides a foundation of deviancy and sexual victims travel through sexual development looking backward at their own guilt, shame, responsibility, and horror.

The Developmental Perspective of the Sexual Victim Trauma Assessment first evaluates how the child has perceived what has happened according to stages in development and then examines what information was available to the victim at the time of the abuse. Extraneous issues will impact the child's perceptions. Thirdly, the Developmental Perspective examines what has been lost in normal sexual development due to the fact that victims continue to look backward on their perceptions of the sexual abuse scenario. The damage to normal sexual development is a critical issue in the Trauma Assessment. Research indicated that those people who had access to information separating their abuse from normal sexual development had the best chance for rehabilitation. The research also indicates that those children who proceeded to build upon sexually deviant activities had little chance to rehabilitate and establish a normal sexual development.

The Situational Perspective

The Situational portion of the Sexual Victim Trauma Assessment returns to the sexually abusive *scene* and examines the victim's potential for establishing deadly patterns of coping that will take the victim toward the future. As the Relationship Perspective requires the victim to *look around* and the Developmental Perspective requires the victim to *look backwards*, the Situational Perspective of the Sexual Victim Trauma Assessment predicts how the victim will step toward the future, establishing distorted cognitions and phobic reactions. The *footprints* for the future will be conceived within the Situational Perspective of the Trauma Assessment. The Situational Perspective of the Trauma Assessment is one of the future and one of prevention.

If the issue of *consent* and why sexual abuse is a crime against children is reexamined, the incapability of children surfaces. Children are unable to understand the significance of sexual contact when they are children, thus setting about the reason why sexual abuse is a forbidden taboo. In the sexually abusive scenario, because of the child's incapabilities, the victim must set about establishing coping mechanisms in order to survive. It is from the sexually abusive scenario, smells, sounds, tastes, conversations, visual perceptions, etc., that the victim attempts to order the environment surrounding the sexually abusive scene. These details within

the situation of the abusive scenario become the foundation for establishing coping skills or *footprints*.

Deadly coping skills occur when victims view the sexual abuse as being beyond their capability to survive. If the victim is terrorized, as an example, beyond endurance, the victim may simply say:

> *This is bad. I will not survive unless someone else survives for me.* The patient is beginning the process of dissociation. *This is bad so I won't be here*, substitutes someone else to endure the pain.

Amnesia patients began to cope with their own situations as they left the sexually abusive scene or as they attempted to endure the sexual abuse.

This is bad, so I won't remember provides the foundation for the amnesia patient to survive. Unfortunately, the amnesia patient did not allow the skin memories or the affective responses to be plagued with amnesia, as well. Often, the Situational Perspective discoveries are made as to the keys of unlocking the memory. Since the patient could not survive with a cognitive memory, the patient keeps the affective responses, which will be stumbling blocks for the victim as the victim attempts to proceed through adulthood.

This research suggested that the two most common coping skills for severe trauma were dissociating or amnesia, (thus removing the cognitive awareness,) or *a self-abusive solution.* When the situation of the sexual abuse was unbearable for the victim, the victim may not have had any other way to survive than to take on responsibility for the BADNESS.

This is bad, so I will be bad and then it will match!

The coping skills or the *footprints* for the victim's future can be discovered and hopefully *undone* in the Situational Perspective of the Trauma Assessment. The senses that are activated for the child's computer are the first level of examination in the sexually abusive scene. Second, within the Situational Perspective, the *scene* beyond the senses are examined. Conversations, extraneous activities, sexual behaviors, etc., must be observed. Finally, the entire world of the victim, including post-disclosure issues, will provide information regarding how the victim will pack the baggage to be carried into the future.

The Triumvirate

The Sexual Victim Trauma Assessment will be a three-pronged approach in attacking sexual abuse and assessing trauma. The first portion will examine people and relationships and the identity of the perpetrator and the victim. Second, the Trauma Assessment will examine the lost child, the loss of development, and discover the child within that needs rescue. Finally, the sexually abusive scene will be visited in order to determine what patterns of survival skills will keep the victim entangled in trauma in the future.

It's All Relative —
THE RELATIONSHIP
PERSPECTIVE

Who is the offender and who is the victim? And why does it seem to matter?
Isn't the identification of the innocent and guilty easy to see, easy to score?
If not, what is the trauma from these scoring scars?

A Closer Look

The Relationship Perspective of the Sexual Victim Trauma Assessment examines the child's perceptions of relationships. Within a triangular approach the victim will identify the perpetrator and the victim. This chapter examines that portion of the Trauma Assessment from a philosophical approach in order to enhance administration of the Trauma Assessment. The intricacies of relationships are complicated and not necessarily what is typically perceived on the surface. Traditional ways of examining the victim and the perpetrator roles need to be dispelled in order to allow this new approach of examining trauma to be helpful.

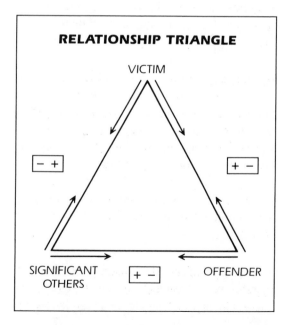

The Victim/Perpetrator Relationship

Relationships obviously involve at least two individuals. The diagram of the relationship triangle reveals that the first area for examination is the relationship between the victim and the perpetrator. The issue is the victim's perspective of that relationship. In examining the triangle, determinations of pluses or minuses between the PLAYERS will emerge to shed light on the offender/victim identity.

If a plus occurs, the victim has identified the perpetrator as having positive attributes, or at least more positive attributes than liabilities. A plus suggests that the perpetrator cannot take on the role as being the psychological perpetrator. A minus clearly indicates the opposite. A minus calculates that the offender, in the victim's view, is guilty and can be identified as the criminal.

It is important to recognize that the identification of the victim and the perpetrator is far more complicated than a superficial presentation. If the victim is asked whether or not the 18 year old babysitter who forced the nine-year-old boy to perform cunnilingus is the perpetrator, the answer might be yes. The 44-year-old man might intellectually respond appropriately, but the nine-year-old *child within* may doubt.

The psychological identification of the perpetrator role is usually unclear. In examining each side of the triangle in the relationship perspective, more than simple verbal identification is necessary. The victim may verbally report that the perpetrator is responsible. In-depth examination in the Trauma Assessment may force the clinician, however, to place a plus between the victim and the perpetrator because of other information. The perpetrator may have positive attributes that outweigh the negative role of being the actual criminal.

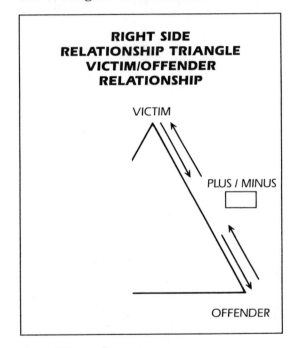

RIGHT SIDE
RELATIONSHIP TRIANGLE
VICTIM/OFFENDER
RELATIONSHIP

VICTIM

PLUS / MINUS

OFFENDER

Two-Way Street

If the purpose of examining this side of the triangle is to determine a plus or a minus, both portions of the relationship between the perpetrator and the victim must be examined. It is not a one-way proposition. If a plus is designated for the final tally on this side of the triangle, the perpetrator will not be able to take on the role of being responsible in the mind of the victim. A minus would indicate the victim views the perpetrator as being responsible for a crime and, therefore, rehabilitation may be easier. In order to determine what will be scored for the victim, the first issue in this two-way street must examine how the victim perceives the offender's attitudes in return. The final tally of how the victim perceives the perpetrator role will not occur until information has been gathered regarding how important the victim feels in the perception of the perpetrator.

Vera was sexually abused by her father who was a security guard at a local bank, working the midnight shift. Vera was the oldest child in the family and was left to be the caretaker of her younger siblings while her mother worked. During the summer months, Vera found herself in the kitchen being a mother and a caretaker of the family when her father awakened. Much the same as in many marriages, Vera's father would awaken and complain to his daughter/wife about the condition of the home, the fact that his meal was not prepared and he even took on the role of discussing his financial concerns with Vera. Soon, Vera became her father's object of sexual desires. Not only did Vera need to take care of the children and the home, but eventually she became her father's sexual partner.

Although as clinicians, this scenario may be painful and ignite feelings of dread and ap-prehension, the fact that Vera's father was critical, demanding, and obnoxious may have been one of the most positive contributions he could inadvertently make to Vera's rehabilitation, at least considering this portion of the Trauma Assessment.

It is important to note that if trauma appears to be minimal in an area within the Trauma Assessment, caution must be raised in recognizing there are several modalities, issues and areas of examination. In the case of Vera, the fact that her father was extremely critical and obnoxious to her may provide her with information that will assist her in identifying him as the perpetrator. It may seem that there is minimal trauma. Courage is needed to recognize trauma as it exists, but respect must also be given for trauma that does not exist. The fact that her father was particularly obnoxious may suggest that Vera is minimally traumatized *in this area*. Other areas of the Trauma Assessment must also be tabulated in order to complete a final and more appropriate Trauma Assessment.

If this side of the Relationship Perspective is examined, Vera first takes into account the fact that her father was critical of her and did not particularly seem to view her as being positive. Vera can describe his grunts and groans during his sexual abuse. He did not *wine and dine* Vera and, in fact, treated her very much as though he was involved in an acrimonious marriage. His continual harassment of her allowed Vera to recognize that he had little regard for her as a child. In fact, in examining her father's feelings toward her, Vera recognized that she had little to lose if she chose to identify him as the perpetrator.

The end result of Vera's case is a minus on the right hand side of the triangle going toward the perpetrator. In Vera's mind, her father was slovenly, critical, and demanding. Her father seemed to smell bad, talk bad, and look bad. Due to the father's negative responses toward Vera, it seemed easy for her to look down toward her father in this two-way street and recognize him as guilty. Vera clearly believed that her father was not accepting of her, nor was he positive about anything she seemed to do. This is not to suggest that Vera is not traumatized or damaged. In fact, other sides of the triangle will reveal that difficulty arises. If the first road on the right-hand side of the triangle reveals that the perpetrator had little regard for the victim, in most cases (in consideration of only this side of the triangle) the victim may have an opportunity to place a minus on this side of the triangle. A converse example may be more explanatory.

Douglas was sexually abused on a regular basis for three years by his mother. Douglas was born out of wedlock and his mother had no subsequent male companions. Douglas' mother's life revolved around him to the point of being intrusive. She was involved in every aspect of his life. Douglas quickly recognized that he was the most important person to his mother. She doted after him and made no attempts

to have a life of her own outside of the mother/son relationship.

Douglas has extreme difficulty viewing his mother as the perpetrator within a psychological and emotional realm. Yes, he can describe being sexually involved with her for as long as he could remember, since perhaps infancy. Yes, he can indicate *my mother was the adult and I was the child*. Years of training, however, remind Douglas that his mother cared for him, that she made sacrifices for him at her own expense. These thoughts may make it difficult for him to look down the right-hand side of the triangle and view her as a psychological perpetrator. As an adult, Douglas is a competent professional person. Intellectually, he recognizes his mother is a perpetrator. The fact that her relationship toward him was extremely positive makes it very difficult for him to take on the task of clearly identifying her as being guilty and responsible.

In examining how the victim views the perpetrator, the first step requires examination of how the victim saw the perpetrator evaluating the victim. The victim then needs to take the step toward identifying the perpetrator as the perpetrator, but obviously not without the previous perceptions having a great deal of impact. There may be some cases where the victim was able to identify the perpetrator as the perpetrator in spite of the fact that the perpetrator was unresponsive, abusive, or neglectful. Those cases appear to be rare. In other words, the most important issue in examining how the victim will eventually look down the two-way street and identify or reject the perpetrator's identification will depend on the opposite side of the highway, examining how the victim believes the perpetrator felt towards the victim.

The caution cannot be raised too often regarding clinicians who wish to put their own perceptions into this portion of the Trauma Assessment. Extremely obnoxious, manipulative, cruel offenders are often viewed by victims as being *saints*. This is not a clinician's perspective. This is the victim's perception, and most importantly, it is the victim at the age in which the abuse occurred. This is a test for the professional who feels exasperated at the victim's inability to recognize the role of the perpetrator and the victim. The importance of the Trauma Assessment is not to intervene or to correct, but to assess, to evaluate, and to be able to shed light on the victim's difficulties based on the childlike perceptions of the victim at the time the abuse occurred.

removed from the victim, but not necessarily unimportant. The victim will be able to examine the relationship between the perpetrator and others and consequently make diagnostic impressions regarding the *victim status*.

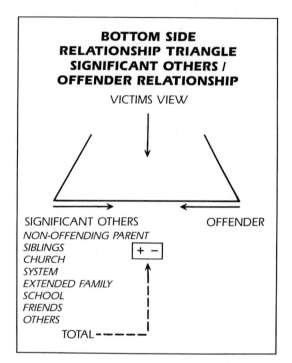

Offender/Significant Others Relationship

The bottom side of the triangle portrays a relationship between the perpetrator and others who are important to the victim. This is also a two-way street with the victim looking toward the bottom of the triangle, while others who are important to the victim look toward the perpetrator. The bottom of the triangle is the most

Significant Others Defined

Significant others include a variety of individuals, agencies, and perceptions on the part of the child. *Significant others* almost always include the victim's non-offending parent, siblings in the family, the legal system, the church, the community, extended family members, etc. On the same two-way street perspective, information must be gleaned in the Trauma Assessment regarding how the perpetrator views those *others* and, interacts with those people.

It should be noted that in the next phase of the Relationship Perspective, information will be gathered regarding the victim's relationship with *significant others*. If the perpetrator, in the relationship with *significant others*, seems to emerge as innocent, competent, and positive, the victim will obviously have more difficulties in the last examination of the relationship triangle. As the victim looks down toward the bottom of the triangle, the relationship between the perpetrator and others will be tabulated according to how the perpetrator responds to those individuals and how those individuals will eventually feel toward the perpetrator.

This portion of the Relationship Perspective is least likely to be predetermined by the victim's family. In other words, although the non-offending parent may be extremely supportive of the perpetrator, as may be the church and the church's pastor, there are unrelated contributors that may override other issues. As an example, if the *system* prosecutes the perpetrator, charges him/her with a crime, and processes the offender through the legal system, other issues in the family may be outweighed. Likewise, if parents are supportive, but the system fails, neglect of the victim by the system may overshadow family support. This side of the triangle has tremendous variables.

If the perpetrator is a positive community member, active in the church, supported by the family, it may appear that the victim will see a plus between the perpetrator and significant others. Should the *system* prosecute the perpetrator and hold a trial where the victim may be required to testify, results could vary widely. The child could be rejected for sending an upstanding citizen to jail or the child could become a hero for ridding the community of a criminal.

Additionally, in this phase of the triangle, the *two-way street* may be less significant than in any other area of the Relationship Perspective. The perpetrator may have positive ideations toward the community, may have positive feelings toward the non-offending parent, may have established a positive relationship with extended family members, but because of additional issues, the perpetrator may be quickly identified in the appropriate perpetrator role. This side of the triangle seems to have a *sweeping* effect. Unlike the other two sides of the triangle where pluses and minuses seem to be carefully calculated toward a tally with a clear end result, the bottom of the triangle seems to have a swift and overriding designation, different from any other aspect of the Relationship Perspective.

The end result requires the victim to look toward the bottom side of the triangle and determine whether others do or do not assign the role of the perpetrator. It would be more comfortable if the bottom of the triangle could be determined without examining any other phase of the Relationship Perspective. Unfortunately, this does not seem to be true. The victim, in examining whether or not others who are important to the victim view the perpetrator as guilty may not be able to make that decision until the left-hand side of the triangle is examined. Although preliminary findings will occur, this portion of the Relationship Perspective demonstrates the importance of the holistic approach in examining all sides of the triangle.

The final tally for the bottom of the triangle evaluating the relationship between the perpetrator and significant others (for the viewing of the victim) should determine a plus or a minus. A plus would indicate that in the victim's mind, significant others had positive feelings toward the perpetrator and, therefore, the offender status is unclear. A minus would indicate, that those in the victim's mind, who were significant to the victim, clearly viewed the perpetrator as being guilty and responsible.

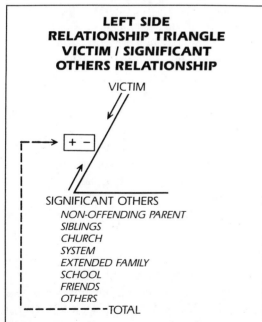

**LEFT SIDE
RELATIONSHIP TRIANGLE
VICTIM / SIGNIFICANT
OTHERS RELATIONSHIP**

VICTIM

+ −

SIGNIFICANT OTHERS
*NON-OFFENDING PARENT
SIBLINGS
CHURCH
SYSTEM
EXTENDED FAMILY
SCHOOL
FRIENDS
OTHERS*
- - - - - - - - TOTAL

Victim/Significant Others Relationship

The left side of the triangle is directly related to the victim and the victim's relationship with others who are connected to the perpetrator. Obviously, those individuals who have absolutely no bearing on the relationship between the victim and the perpetrator will not necessarily pertain to this portion of the Relationship Triangle. Research and data from Chapter Four and Five should be remembered.

Those children who clearly had precognitions of offender/victim identity even before the abuse occurred seemed to be minimally traumatized. This would suggest that those children who have a positive self-esteem and a sense of their own rights will be less traumatized by sexual abuse. In this portion of the Relationship Triangle, it is suggested that children are severely traumatized or are minimally traumatized based upon factors such as how others view the child. Consistency would suggest that only those people connected to the perpetrator would have a significant bearing on this side of the triangle. Unfortunately, the child's self-esteem, the child's sense of independence entering into the abusive scenario, will have a tremendous impact on how traumatized the child may be by sexual abuse.

Therefore, if there are *significant others* who are not connected to the perpetrator, but do have a bearing on the child's self-esteem, it would be suggested that a cause and effect exists. However, relationships that have a direct bearing or connection between the perpetrator and the victim seem to have the most significance.

As the victim examines the left side of the triangle, perceptions emerge regarding how the victim is viewed by others. Questions regarding how important the victim seems to be to those *others* must be examined. It does not seem possible for the victim to accurately examine his/her status as a victim without first examining the importance of those significant others to the victim.

If, as an example, a child is raised to be independent, to have a support system not necessarily connected to *significant others,* and if the abuse occurs within an arena that does not seem to permeate the support system, the child may have minimal trauma (in consideration of the left side of the triangle).

> Jeremy is a young man growing up as the only boy in a family of female siblings. Jeremy's parents appear to be extremely cognizant of such issues as personal protection and sexual abuse. Although Jeremy's abuse occurred over a nine-month period, several issues within the Situational Perspective prohibited Jeremy from reporting his own abuse. Jeremy's family was extremely close, but a very astute perpetrator used Jeremy's family as a way to enshroud him in secrecy. Upon disclosure, information was received regarding not only Jeremy's abuse, but

the intimidation that had taken place. The family support system quickly provided Jeremy with a *hero* designation. The category of *significant others* beyond the family unit seemed quite insignificant. The perpetrator who had abused Jeremy seemed to be insignificant and unimportant to Jeremy's family. Outside the relationship between Jeremy and his family, however, evidence emerged that would suggest the potential for trauma.

Due to the system's attitude toward this perpetrator, charges were not filed. The perpetrator had a tremendous support system in the school where he taught and the church where he attended. Uniquely, however, none of these individuals or agencies seemed to outweigh Jeremy's support from his family. In other words, Jeremy did not seem to view those other individuals as significant since his support system was so strong. Within the family unit, Jeremy was identified as the innocent child who quite courageously endured sexual abuse for the protection of a sibling. Outside of that family unit, there was very little affirmation of Jeremy's status as the victim.

As with other sides of the triangle, however, this is a *two-way* assessment. Although Jeremy did not receive affirmation for this status as a victim, he did not necessarily look toward that category of individuals as being necessarily significant. Had Jeremy received little support within his own *significant others* category, a different portrayal may have emerged. Many other children would have been severely traumatized by the fact that the system did not prosecute and that the perpetrator was actively supported by others. Jeremy, however, in the two-way perception, did not seem to *need* the affirmation of others, at least in consideration of this side of the triangle. It was Jeremy's perception of the importance of these individuals that determined how he would view their response to the perpetrator.

Hopeful Hurts

The opposite scenario, ripe for trauma, is obvious. Children who grow up in families where there is very little support, very little affirmation of their rights to sexual safety and security, will look toward the *significant other* categories with hope. The more the child needed affirmation from others, the more deadly the lack of affirmation will be. Often, the system, which includes prosecutors, defense attorneys, social workers, church members, and extended family members, can actually become the perpetrator and, in fact, be more traumatizing to the child than the sexual abuse itself.

Laura and Kathy are sexually abused by their father and by their uncle who is an attorney. The father immediately pleads guilty, providing affirmation for both children regarding their iden-

tification as a victim. The attorney, however, pleads *not guilty* and both girls are challenged in a criminal trial that is extremely sensational. Headlines shout the children's statement of being sexually abused for the past seven years. The children are portrayed as liars on the witness stand, to the glee of the cheering section organized for the perpetrator.

In spite of the fact that the father admits abusing the children for many years and testifies in the criminal trial as to having knowledge of the uncle's abuse, the attorney is acquitted after a lengthy trial. Superficially, this example would suggest that the children will be traumatized through the jury's actions.

Conversely, Mary is sexually abused for three years by her camp counselor each summer while she attends camp. In final desperation, she reports the sexual abuse that has been occurring. Developmentally, Mary is going to be a difficult witness, not due to her competency, but due to her age of nine. The perpetrator is an extremely important person in the community, as well as in the church. In fact, Mary's church members banded together to support the perpetrator. Previous to the trial, Mary is informed of the likelihood of an acquittal. Mary's support system organizes itself around Mary's ability to testify, not necessarily based upon the jury's decision. Mary enters into the courtroom believing that success occurs when she has completed *telling what really happened.*

Much to the rejoice of the perpetrator and his cheering section, the jury returns an acquittal. Due to the fact that Mary's support system prepared her for this option and due to the fact that her success or failure was not based upon the decision of the jury, Mary seemed to be minimally traumatized by the jury's decision. It cannot be ignored that someone outside the family may have less significance for the child in cases of sexual abuse. Nonetheless, because of the fact that the *significant others* became less significant to Mary before the legal involvement, her trauma appeared to be lessened. In the case of Laura and Kathy, this important preparation had not occurred and, therefore, the importance of significant others identifying the victims as *victims* was extremely important. Without proper preparation, those children were again damaged by the system.

A final word on juries and courtroom appearance should indicate an important factor. As mentioned previously, it is absurd for children to dictate their own treatment plans because they are unequal and unable to understand. The absurdity of the court system also exists. Children who have been sexually abused are at a profound disadvantage due to the fact they are children. The court system, however, demands there be no advantage given to children regarding their inequality. In other words, the system that says *We are not supposed to have sex with children due to their inequality,* demands equality once sexual abuse has been discovered. The courtroom is an adversarial position for children regardless of the competency of the prosecutors, interviewing techniques, or preparation. When children are taken into this adversarial arena without proper preparation, not necessarily for their testimony, but for the results of the courtroom decision, the potential for trauma will have increased. *Winning or losing* the prosecution may not be as important to the rehabilitation of children as the preparation for the adversarial arena of the courtroom.

In these two cases, acquittals from the jury had different effects. A two-way street in examining this side of the triangle determined how the child would respond to the offender's relationship with significant others. Those *significant others* who were extremely important to the child had a profound effect on the child's rehabilitation or trauma. Those children who had their own support system and could proceed independent of the significant others seemed to be less traumatized by the same behavior. Obviously, full rehabilitation and recovery could occur for those children who had a strong support system and also had affirmation by the category of significant others as to the offender/victim identity.

Introduction Of The Players

Good Morning, John

John is a perpetrator in this case scenario, and those professionals or therapists involved, would immediately identify him as such. John has been incarcerated in a state prison for homicide, as well as having an extensive criminal record for other crimes. John is exactly the kind of patient that is avoided by sex offender therapists due to his unwillingness to cooperate, his long history of criminal behavior, and his seeming lack of empathy. John has alcohol and drug problems, he has not established an appropriate relationship with Tara's mother, and, in all respects other than the victim's perspective, John would appear to be clearly identified as the perpetrator.

The victim, Tara, is an 11-year-old child who is obese. She seems to be somewhat developmentally delayed and has very low self-esteem. She has lived with her mother and a variety of *stepfathers* since John and her mother divorced when Tara was age three. Tara has very little ability to view herself as an innocent child robbed of something precious. In fact, Tara seems to view herself as unworthy of any attention or affection.

In examining the *significant others* category, Tara does not seem to fare much better. Tara's mother is interested in Tara only because she receives *SSI* funding. Tara has been sexually abused on two previous occasions by friends or acquaintances of Tara's mother and these abuses seemed insignificant to the mother. Tara is not popular at school, she is unkempt and, as a final illustration of Tara's sad situation, she has permanent scarring from bed sores as a result of sleeping on a urine-soaked mattress for many years. Obviously Tara has very little ability to feel positive about herself.

The sexual abuse scenario emerges when John returns to the geographic area where Tara lives. He asks for visitation and subsequently begins sexually abusing Tara approximately eight days after their first contact. Unbeknownst to Tara's mother, John continues his sexual involvement with Tara and eventually wins Tara in a custody battle. In actuality, John is determined to be the better parent. According to the court (who was ignorant of the sexual abuse) John seems more appropriate for Tara than her mother.

The sexual abuse of Tara is revealed *accidentally*. Tara did not make an overt report and, in fact, after the abuse was discovered and John was charged with a crime, Tara was extremely regretful. Her developmental delays allowed her to participate in an investigation simply because she was *following the rules*, not because she truly viewed her father as a perpetrator needing prosecution. When Tara became aware of the significance of her involvement in the investigation, she was devastated.

John presented himself for treatment for a short period of time. Eventually he was unable to follow the rules and was imprisoned with no opportunity to work toward a resolution with Tara. Tara was placed in foster care and continues to await John's return.

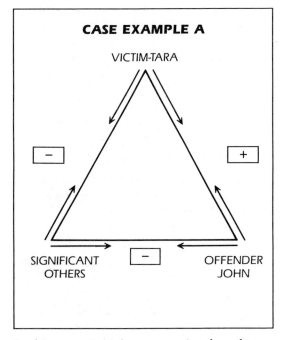

CASE EXAMPLE A

VICTIM-TARA

$-$

$+$

$-$

SIGNIFICANT
OTHERS

OFFENDER
JOHN

In this scenario, it becomes quite clear that as Tara looks toward the bottom side of the

triangle examining the relationship between her father and significant others, her father is identified as the perpetrator. He is arrested, prosecuted and convicted. The church excommunicates John and extended family members reject him, clearly labeling him as *the criminal*. This would seem to be an area of very little trauma since clearly Tara can see that the proper identification of the perpetrator exists.

Unfortunately, if the left side of the triangle is examined, Tara is a child who has very few attributes and has a nonexistent support system. Her obesity, her developmental delays, the fact that she was sexually abused previously, and the poor relationship with her mother all compute to force the left side of the triangle into a minus. Tara cannot possibly view herself as an innocent child robbed of something important since, in Tara's mind, there is absolutely nothing precious or positive about her in the eyes of others. A minus emerges on the triangle's left side.

The result, is that on the right side of the triangle, a plus emerges. With the left side of the triangle a minus, there is no opportunity for Tara to view her father as the perpetrator since Tara's support system has dissolved or was nonexistent. This may be the most deadly combination of all with Tara unable to see herself as being supported and obviously viewing her father as the *best thing I ever had*. Tara added, *He buys me real jeans*. If Tara was presented with an absent father under other circumstances, his involvement with her may have been insignificant. Due to the pre-existing situation with this child, Tara's perceptions relate that she has lost the most appropriate parent and her only positive support system. The fact that the *system* or the category of significant others viewed her father as a perpetrator became insignificant when the other sides of the triangle were examined. The insignificance of others' views becomes extremely important in looking at this example.

Meet the Family of Hope

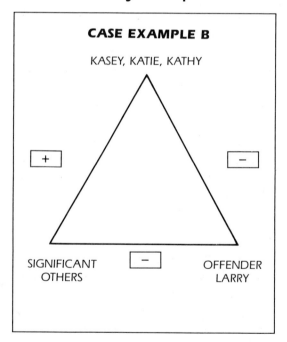

CASE EXAMPLE B

KASEY, KATIE, KATHY

+   −

SIGNIFICANT OTHERS   −   OFFENDER LARRY

The perpetrator is an individual who is a very important person in the community. Larry is the natural father of the victims and their brothers. Larry is an individual who, on the surface, is a very important person in the community. He has a very high-paying job and he is an active church member who takes on the role of youth leader.

The children in this scenario are three adolescent, natural daughters of the perpetrator who have been sexually harassed and abused by their father since birth. The children have grown up in a family where sexual abuse has occurred, but other important things have taken place in the children's lives to provide them with a positive self-image. In spite of the fact that they have endured their father's sexual harassment for many years, the children have participated in advanced studies in school, they have been active church members, they have taken ballet lessons and foreign language, and, much the same as the perpetrator, have had outward appearances that seem to be quite positive.

Concerning the opinions of *significant others*, the children do well in school, they seem to be supported by their mother, and they have developed a sense of *comraderie* within the sibling unit. The three males in the family seem to be quite close to the female children, Kasey, Katie, and Kathy.

The scenario unfolds with one child being chastised for a minor violation and inadvertently reporting the improprieties of her father. The sexual abuse has taken place with a great deal of voyeurism, exhibitionism, and fondling. The children have been sexually harassed on a constant basis. With the discovery of the sexual abuse, all three girls report being sexually abused for many years by their father.

The mother immediately responds to the girls' needs, contacting authorities and cooperating with the subsequent prosecution of the perpetrator. The male siblings in the family are also supportive of the three adolescent females. Not only is the mother supportive of the children through the investigation, but the children receive immediate support and counseling through the Catholic church they attend. The perpetrator seems to feel overwhelmed and immediately confesses. He is required to have no contact with the family and he applies for the local treatment program. His wife and children also enter into the treatment program, beginning therapy immediately.

Score Time

In evaluating the right side of the triangle, it becomes quite clear that these children currently (and have always) viewed their father as a perpetrator. In spite of the fact that Larry was superficially acceptable, the children were very cognizant of his deviant mannerisms and activities. One daughter explained, *He is a pervert.* When questioned about the identification of their father in that manner, she explained, *He keeps our pubic hairs in plastic bags in his office.* The father was a local realtor and the children had become aware that he collected their pubic hairs in plastic bags, and that these trophies were displayed in his office.

Although initially this behavior may be viewed as being disgusting to professionals or to the mother, factors such as these contributed to the children's minimal trauma. These disgusting behaviors provided information to the children throughout their abuse, identifying their father as a perpetrator. The nature of these activities may have had a rehabilitative influence on the children, allowing them to identify their father as the perpetrator and allowing the clinician administering the Trauma Assessment to place a minus between the perpetrator and the victim.

Enhancing this identification process is the fact that Larry seemed to be quite cold and insensitive to the children throughout their childhood. In spite of his appearances in the community, he seemed to disregard the feelings and attitudes of the children. Peeking into their bedrooms, forcing himself into the bathrooms while they bathed, grabbing their genitalia, fondling them, masturbating in the presence of the girls, allowed Katie, Kasey and Kathy to see their father as guilty and capable of accepting the offender identity.

On the bottom side of the triangle, as the children examined how *significant others* viewed the perpetrator, the good news seems to continue. The system swiftly prosecuted, the church acknowledged the victims' status, and therefore no other option existed than to acknowledge the offender's status. Even though in the two-way perception the offender was an important community member, once the abuse was discovered, his status faded and the identity of Larry as the perpetrator was profoundly clear in the eyes of the children, allowing a minus to occur in the victims' minds between the significant others and the perpetrator.

Finally, the left-hand side of the triangle again reveals positive support for the victims in what emerges to be the healthiest combination within the Relationship Perspective. Larry's support throughout their childhood has been minimal, and the children have leaned toward others. Due to the positive self-esteem and support, the victims identify themselves as innocent. Their mother's support is significant even though the children could not report the sexual abuse to her for many years. Placing the final touch on what would seem to be the best possible opportunity for rehabilitation (within this portion of the Trauma Assessment) allows a plus to occur on the left-hand side of the triangle. These children, from the beginning of their disclosure, recognized themselves as being innocent and not responsible for the abuse.

Triangulation Trauma

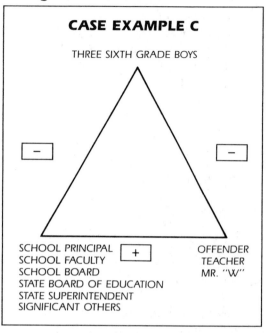

In this scenario, a civil case emerges after prosecution was abandoned. The male sixth grade teacher in this case sexually abused several children in his classroom and a combination of seven children reported sexual improprieties. Unfortunately, since the sexual behavior did not include skin-to-skin touching and since tremendous political effort was exerted to resist prosecution, charges against the teacher were dropped. Subsequently, the parents of three of the children filed a civil suit against not only the teacher, but also the faculty, the principal, the School Board, the State Board of Education, and the State Superintendent of Education. A Trauma Assessment was conducted to determine which group within the *significant others* category (or the offender)

was most responsible for trauma to these children.

In consideration of the right side of the triangle, involving the perpetrator and the victim, a minus seems to appear. These children were victims of a pedophile who enjoyed engaging them in constant sexual conversation, intrusive behaviors, and harassment. The children spent half of the sixth grade year dreading any contact from the perpetrator. He appeared to *leer* at the boys and his behaviors assisted the children in clearly identifying him as the perpetrator. Without considering other portions of the triangle, it would seem that because the boys could identify their teacher as guilty, rehabilitation is imminent.

The sexual behaviors were particularly degrading to the boys. *Mr W* forced the boys to sit on his lap when it was quite obvious he had an erection. *Mr W* whispered in the boys' ears, asking sexually intrusive questions and stimulating the boys' ears with his tongue. Other behaviors included watching the boys urinate, forcing them to kiss *Mr W*, and prolonged hugs that included genital thrusting. The victims seemed horrified and embarrassed by *Mr W's* behavior and had no difficulty viewing him as the perpetrator.

Unfortunately, the other sides of the triangle emerge and provide difficulty for the victims. This educator carefully chose children to sexually offend who already had difficulties with self-esteem and confidence. In fact, as mentioned in a previous chapter, this teacher provided personality testing to his sixth graders during the beginning of the year in order to determine which children had the lowest self-concept. This scientific process allowed him to appropriately target his victims. The perpetrator, therefore, chose children who were already struggling with confidence. These boys tended to be children who had many difficulties and, at the onset of the abuse, had very little ability to see themselves as worth protecting.

In examining the left-hand side of the triangle, the children already had difficulty. Although the boys' parents were supportive of their children at the time of disclosure, because of poor self-esteem the boys were in desperate need of support outside the realm of their family. The *significant others* category became very significant to the children as far as identifying the boys as being either guilty or innocent. In spite of the parental support, other factors within the *significant others* category became overwhelming and the source of severe trauma.

In consideration of which person or group of people appeared to be most responsible for trauma, the faculty of the school emerged as having tremendous impact. When the disclosure was made initially, the children were removed from the teacher's class and placed in classes with other teachers. In a collective fashion, those teachers confronted the children and in some cases allowed other children to confront the victims on the preposterous nature of their claims. In one class, the teacher gathered pupils in a circle around one of the boys who had reported the abuse. Through confrontation, the inquisition took place. In other classes, the children were placed in the back of the room or were given extra work loads. Some faculty members orchestrated investigations that allowed *Mr W* to interview the accusing boys. Outside the classroom, several teachers confronted the students on the playground and in some situations actually contacted the victims at home and requested an audience. Although several teachers were individually more responsible than other teachers for causing trauma, the faculty, as a whole, made tremendous impact on these young boys.

A decision was made to have a car wash and a baked foods sale on the school grounds in order to raise money for the teacher's defense. This event was publicized on the radio and the student body was encouraged to participate. Even though the teacher was eventually dismissed, his presence remained a never-ending threat and a form of trauma to the victims.

Data from the Trauma Assessment revealed that these boys demonstrated behavior permeated with fear. One boy nailed his window shut and requested permission to sleep in the garage. The victims avoided eating lunch, and several boys were found hoarding weapons. Fear demonstrated by the victims was not toward the perpetrator, but toward the faculty and the faculty's threats.

The result of this trauma is that in the children's mind, the bottom side of the triangle emerges a plus, indicating that *significant others* did not see the perpetrator as guilty even though the victims' individual parents were supportive. The tremendous outpouring of threats and negativism from the faculty suggested to the children that they were guilty and that the perpetrator was innocent. Even though the right-hand side of the triangle emerges as identifying the perpetrator, the bottom side of the triangle far outweighs the children's identification of the perpetrator as being responsible and therefore severe trauma occurs.

Who Won

The epilogue for this situation was disastrous. One young man never returned to an academic program after quitting school with half of his sixth grade completed. Another young man also quit school, but sadly has even more trauma. At age 17 1/2 he has two pubic hairs — the same two pubic hairs he had in the sixth grade. His entire sexual development appears to be arrested. The third young man took his own life at age 14. The civil suit was *a victory* with a large cash settlement. Perhaps a better definition of *winning* needs to occur.

Additional tragedy is found in the liability insurance dilemma. The civil battle was fought through lawyers representing insurance companies who have little regard for the problem of sexual abuse. Was the faculty ever made aware of the damage caused to these boys? Probably not! The responsibility of the school district was not to reduce trauma but to pay liability insurance premiums. When one of the boys took his life, was the faculty notified? Were they made aware of his death and their contribution to his trauma? The answer is no. Responsibility for trauma faded and the issue was monetary. And *Mr W* is probably teaching somewhere else, receiving Teacher of the Year awards from another faculty.

In summary, the relationship portion of the Sexual Victim Trauma Assessment examines the victim's ability to identify the perpetrator and victim status. Sexual abuse from decades ago often remains unresolved due to issues within the relationship triangle. Even when offenders are deceased, incarcerated, or incapacitated, victims can be kept in a traumatic bond due to pluses and minuses within this triangle of trauma.

LOOKING BACKWARD, STUMBLING FORWARD — THE DEVELOPMENTAL PERSPECTIVE

How do children perceive sexual contact? Is it the same at four as at 44? And, what is the impact of the child's perceptions on future sexuality? What is the damage to normal sexual development and what is normal?

One, Two, Three

In evaluating the trauma suffered by sexual victims, relationships are important, but other issues concerning trauma need consideration. The Developmental Perspective of the Sexual Victim Trauma Assessment examines three issues, with the first relating to how the child perceives the abuse according to two important factors. The child's perceptions will be based on the age of the child when the sexual abuse occurs, and upon what information was available to the child at the time of the sexual abuse. It is the child's perceptions based on these two issues that provide the foundation for continued sexual development. The foundation of the child's perceptions will be the vehicle with which the child will proceed through the next few years, which directly relates to the third component in the Developmental Perspective.

Since sexual development is an ongoing building process, a third consideration of the Developmental Perspective must examine what has been lost in normal sexual development due to the sexual abuse. As indicated in previous chapters, it was not necessarily the age at which the child was abused but the consequence of upheaval in the child's future sexual development that seemed to provide the most trauma.

Ages and Stages

Very little has been written about the sexual development of children, most importantly because children are not (hopefully) viewed as sexual. The *Sex Fairy Myth* pervades, and computes to very little need for scholarly work in the area of a nonexistent subject. Generalization of the sexual development of children can be made, however, in consideration of other child development frameworks. Certain *ages and stages* can be formulated, projecting information regarding the sexual development of children.

The Unaware

The *unaware child* is in a stage of development prohibiting a specific lack of understanding or awareness regarding the significance of the sexual behavior. Developmentally, children under the age of approximately eight years have very little ability to understand sexual abuse. Children in this stage of development often cooperate with the sexual act and may even initiate the sexual contact. If cooperation does not occur, as in the case of violent abuse or abuse that is painful, the child is nonetheless ignorant. Most children are confused about how to report the abuse or how to protect themselves.

It is important to note that children are often observed fondling their genitalia, even in the womb. Neuromuscular tensions in children's genitalia can be intensified and then released in orgasm (Haberle). Sexual arousal or sexual stimulation on the part of smaller children may often occur due to the child's lack of awareness during this stage of development.

Contrary to *Sex Fairy Mythology*, children often enjoy not only genital touching, but also the closeness, the warmth, and tenderness that sometimes accompanies sexual abuse. Striking horror in the hearts of juries are statements from children discussing pleasure in sexual contact. Somehow there is this sense that the touching of the genitalia feels horrible or is a *uh oh touch* or *confusing touch* (as described in many prevention materials). Because the body *works*, even at age two, and because of developmental limitations concerning this unaware child, younger victims often participate, acquiesce and may even initiate the sexual contact.

Examples of this lack of awareness can be demonstrated in several ways.

> Amanda's father has been arrested and convicted of sexually abusing two adolescent nieces. While he is incarcerated, Mandy's mother files for divorce and brings Mandy to a specialist. Mandy's mother requests that inquiries be made regarding Mandy's possible abuse by her father. Mandy is interviewed for three hours in a Sexual Victim Investigation. In many different ways, Mandy is asked whether or not her father had sexually touched her. Mandy denies and the therapist happily announces to mother that Mandy has not been sexually

abused. Leaving the mental health clinic, Mandy is happy with her popsicle and mother is relieved.

Forty-five minutes later, Mandy's mother returns to the mental health clinic in a state of hysteria. She has driven into the ditch after having a discussion with Mandy regarding her evaluation. *Did you have a nice time in Jan's office? Yes,* Mandy replies, *And Daddy didn't ever touch you in your private parts? No,* says Mandy, and after taking another lick of her popsicle, Mandy flatly stated to her mother, *but my daddy lets me suck on his weiner all the time!*

This is a classic example of a four-year-old child being unable to generalize. The interviewer had asked whether or not Mandy had been touched and Mandy rightly denied. Due to Mandy's lack of awareness regarding sexuality, she did not feel particularly guilty about what had happened and seemed rather nonchalant. Her nonchalant attitude encouraged the therapist to feel as though Mandy was not an abused child. Mandy's answers corresponded with the child who had not been sexually abused by the perpetrator touching the victim. Mandy had no reason to withhold the information about performing fellatio on her father. Developmentally, however, she was unable to generalize and report sexual abuse occurring not only from her father, but by her actions of touching her father.

Another example emerges as the lack of aware-ness demonstrated by the child's descriptions of sexual behaviors.

In the interview of four-year-old Samuel, efforts are made to ascertain if he is able to describe an erection or ejaculation. Samuel is asked, *What was his peepee doing?* Samuel replies, *Oh, it was sitting right up, big and wide awake. And what happened,* asked the examiner. Samuel replied, *I just kept touching it and touching it and touching it and touching it, up and down, up and down, up and down! And then what happened?,* asked the purple faced examiner, *It just blew up!* said Samuel.

A penis *blowing up* is probably the best way a four-year-old can describe erection and ejaculation. Samuel is developmentally unable to understand what he is describing and he is using his own developmental skills.

Another example of developmental limitations occurs when a child is asked if the sexual abuse happened *once*. The child replied, *yes.* The examiner indicated a one incident allegation to Law Enforcement. Later, the child is asked about the number of incidents and he reports several different and specific occasions. The child is perceived as being dishonest and changing his story. A mistrial is declared because of *discovery*. The defense had not been aware of more than one incident. However, when the child was questioned about the word *once*, the child answered, *Yes, I told you, it happened once in a while.*

Developmentally, children often find what is happening to them so confusing they cannot cope due to their inability to understand what is happening. The coping skills set about by children will be discussed in the situational portion of the Trauma Assessment. But, clearly, children cope according to their developmental capabilities.

Another child shows a final example of developmental stages and limitations in an interview regarding custody conflicts. This child makes a solution according to his developmental perspective.

> When Damian is asked about resolving where he should live, he looked at the examiner and indicated, *I would like to live with my dad, but have my mom be in the first grade.* Damian is questioned as to why he would advocate for this arrangement. *If I lived with my dad and my mom was in the first grade, I could eat lunch with her everyday and my dad wouldn't find out and be mad.*

The Unfortunate

The deadly effects of these developmental limitations is not felt until a child in the *unaware stage* begins to approach the next stage of development, which is titled, *the unfortunate.*

The unfortunate stage of development finds children becoming cognizant of the significance of sexuality and constantly looking back at a stage in development when they were cooperative, acquiescent, or, at a minimum, unable to stop the abuse. As children proceed through their development, they are continually looking back, criticizing themselves, and stumbling at attempts to go forward. As the example in the previous chapter indicated, children who begin to hear sexual words that relate to their own abusive behavior rarely become outraged at what the offender is doing. Most commonly, children become disgusted with *what I did.*

Punishing Puberty

As children approach nine, ten, and eleven years, they are becoming more aware of society's view on sexuality. In addition, they are also proceeding through an extremely difficult if not *unfortunate* time period for both victims and nonvictims. Prepuberty or early stages of pubescent development is a time when children become indirectly punished. This is one society in this world that actually seems to *punish puberty.*

Statements are commonly made to girls in the early stages of development *You are too big now to be sitting on his lap.* And, at the first sign that a son has had a wet dream, touching or affection stops. Parents tread lightly, fearing that they will arouse his senses even more than he is already aroused. Parents often pull away from children, perhaps not intentionally, when they enter into the early stages of sexual development. This creates more anxiety for children during what seems to be an already difficult time due to hormonal bombardment.

Most adults recall early stages of pubescent development with discomfort. Girls often have their periods before their mothers give them the usual, but very profound, four and one-half page pamphlet on Kotex. Many girls believe they are bleeding to death and if they do report to their mothers, it is usually with shame and embarrassment. Bright purple faced mothers often hand their daughter a Kotex and then state something intelligent like, *If you have any questions, be sure and come to me* (gulp!). Girls are then instructed to hide their Kotex from other family members as they learn words such as the *curse,* or *the rag* for descriptions of their menstrual cycle.

Boys, additionally, are forced to wander through their first signs of puberty or wet dreams with the same confusion and apprehension. *I am leaking* or *I peed on myself* are common phrases from hysterical males the morning after their first or second wet dream. Most young men are horrified at what has happened to them and, at the same time, feeling rather guilty about the pleasure they derived from the horror.

Utopia

In a better world with the Sex Fairy Myth laid to rest, parents would automatically teach their children about such things as menstrual cycles and wet dreams long before children are developmentally capable of understanding. As an example, in other situations, parents don't avoid explaining to children why they should not run out into the street long before they can understand the full impact of bone fractures, skull and head injuries, or quadriplegia. Parents teach children not to go into the street, and they may teach this lesson using a method pertinent to their child's development. Showing the five-year-old child a mashed cat on the freeway may be effective. Even though children are incapable of fully understanding what will happen to them if they go into the street, they can be educated according to their development. Simple! That is, except when it comes to S.E.X.

A perfect world would have a father organizing the pizza party and celebration for his daughter's first period. Should he wait until she is in the *unfortunate* stage of development, embarrassed, uncomfortable, and obviously experiencing cramps? The answer is *no!* The father from Utopia would explain to his daughter, *You know what, some day your body is going to work! And you are going to have something that is called a menstrual cycle. We'll call it a period because that is easier to say. Let's say it three times together,*

period

period

period

There, how did I do? Did I get it right? When you have this period, stuff kind of like blood is going to come from one of your wonderful body parts called a uterus (Let's say that one three times, uterus, uterus, uterus). The uterus is way up inside of you and will be the place where babies will first grow if you want to be a mother. When you get to be a little older, your body will start to work and get ready for the time when you might decide to be a mother. This is a very wonderful thing and I want you to be sure and come and tell us so that we can have a party when it happens. We will have to have pizza or something grand like that. It may happen to you in the middle of the night or it may happen to you at school. Be sure and tell us as soon as you can so that we can start the party.

Does the six-year-old child understand all of the complications of menstrual cycles? Obviously not, and is it important for her to understand? The answer remains *no*. What is important is that her mother or father can tell her about the miracle of her periods long before her periods start. She will listen and take in the information without embarrassment. She is ripe for the intervention due to her developmental limitations. If the unwise father waits until she is in an older stage of development, she may more clearly understand, but she will also be very uncomfortable. She will be in the midst of her sexual development, and she will very likely be too embarrassed, uncomfortable, and distraught to discuss anything. She may also be likely to tell him where he can put his four and one-half page Kotex pamphlet!

The same should be true for a boy's first wet dream. In the first grade when he is developmentally unable to understand, mother and sister should begin planning the pizza party for his *first wet dream*. His body should be thought of as a miracle about to happen and he should anticipate and plan for this celebration long before it happens. This would be a utopia or a perfect world because by the time the developmental stage occurred, children would be in anticipation and ready. Like other aspects of children's lives, there would be organization, consistency and preparation. Adults find no difficulty asking children *what do you want to be when you grow up?* Children approach their future of being a fireman with healthy anticipation. Unfortunately, sexuality is a different matter.

Sadly, this is not a perfect world. Most well-intentioned parents do not provide their children with any kind of information regarding body development or puberty until puberty begins. Most parents do not intervene in the *unaware stage* because they know children are unaware. Most parents wait until children are in the *unfortunate* stage of development and capable of understanding before they intervene. Unfortunately, children are not receptive to this kind of intervention, but would have been receptive earlier.

Double Dilemma

The same is true for the sexual victim. With the new awareness of the sexuality also comes the awareness of the previous activities of cooperation, acquiescence, or, at a minimum, inability to prevent the abuse from taking place. Just as the child who has not been sexually abused seems to fall apart during puberty, the child who has been sexually abused will also struggle during this stage of awareness from the process of *looking backward*. There is a double dilemma in play. Not only do children look backward toward the fact that sexual abuse happened, but they also look back to their cooperation or their acquiescence.

When Madelyn is approximately age four or five, her father tells her that she just doesn't seem to *get her hips up high enough for him*. Madelyn's father is attempting to engage this very small child in intercourse and rather than present himself as a perpetrator, he very cleverly uses the developmental limitations of Madelyn to encourage her to feel inadequate. She does not understand the significance of what is happening to her and she obviously has no understanding of adult male and female intercourse. Just as her father might say he was disappointed at

Madelyn's unkempt room, he is able to have Madelyn feel guilty because he cannot achieve full penetration for his total sexual satisfaction.

What does Madelyn do? Does she run to her mother and say, *My father is tricking me. He is trying to convince me to help him achieve full penetration.* The answer is obvious. Madelyn works hard. She practices, practices, practices. In spite of the pain each time her father has intercourse with her, she is most anxious for her report card to be positive. Each time her father gives her an assessment, *better, not as good as last time, that was really good, or you just have to try harder.* Rather than concentrating on the sexual abuse that is happening, Madelyn is working hard to get the final and ultimate approval from her father.

In spite of the fact that the damage to Madelyn rendered her unable to conceive children in adulthood, she proceeded from the *unaware stage* of development to the *unfortunate stage* of development being most critical of herself. At age 12, Madelyn became aware of what her father was doing. She was unable to stop the abuse and chose instead to simply survive. She no longer attempted to get her hips up high enough. Penetration could be achieved since she had cut off all feelings to her genital area. Madelyn recalls being most disgusted, not at her father, but at her stupidity.

When I finally got it, I was so pissed. I couldn't believe I was so stupid. I worked so hard. I remember once he took me to the Dairy Queen and we sat in the car eating our ice cream. He told me that he couldn't actually decide whether or not he was going to try it one more time since he was sure I wasn't trying hard enough. I can remember begging him to give me once more chance. How could I be so dumb?

This is a classic example of the victim looking backward and re-examining what has happened in the previous sexual abuse. Future steps toward sexual development can be severely traumatized because the foundation for sexual development has been laid in such negative, defeating, and disgusting activities.

Not only does the sexual abuse that occurred previously become even more damaging but, at the same time, this is a time of discomfort due to body changes and due to society's attitudes regarding sexual development. The victim is traumatized with a *double dilemma* because the child is abandoned by society and the family support system. The child is also looking backward toward the abuse with tremendous disgust. This seems to be a *no win* situation for children in this stage of development.

The Final Blow

The final blow to the *unfortunate* victims occurs because of another *normal* developmental change during this time. Part of the normal process for children in early adolescence or in the first stages of puberty is to begin cultivation of the attitude that anyone over age 21 is becoming terminally stupid! The process of rebelling, pulling away from adults who were once so comfortable and protective, seems to be a normal process, at least in this society. A triple trauma emerges. Not only are children's bodies suffering from hormonal rampage, not only are children looking back toward their early sexual experiences with disgust, but a third strike occurs as anyone over age 21 has become extremely suspect. To accept intervention, feedback and information from an adult during this time period is considered *uncool*. This final blow leaves the *unfortunate* victim in an extremely vulnerable position for trauma.

One Moment, Please

There are children who are not sexually abused during the *unaware* stage, but are abused during the *unfortunate* stage. For these children, the trauma may be somewhat less because they do not have to re-examine their own stupidity or inability to protect themselves previously. Nonetheless, these victims may be affected by strikes two and three.

For those children who were sexually abused during the early stages or during the *unaware* stage of development, their trauma will surface during the *unfortunate* stage. For those clinicians or parents who wish to disregard the asymptomatic child as not being traumatized, these are words of wisdom. Developmentally, the unaware child is unable to demonstrate the nature of the trauma. In other words, developmental delays and limitations prevent the child from being able to exhibit symptoms of trauma. The unfortunate stage will bring the onset of those symptoms and the *uncomfortable* stage will bring the *uproar* of those symptoms, and frustration to those around the victim.

The Uncomfortable Victim

The adolescent victim is determined or designated the prestigious title of the *uncomfortable* victim because the adolescent seems to make therapists, adults or professionals *uncomfortable*. During adolescence, victims who have suffered abuse during earlier stages of development seem to *break out* into behaviors that often are discomforting to adults. Normally, adolescence is a time of *putting frosting on the cake*. In other words, sexual development has generally been formed and adolescence is a time of adding morality and decision making to the sexual system. Information about the human body, bodily functions, and sexuality between men and women has hopefully been imparted to the adolescent. How the adolescent will actually use those tools or what limits and guidelines (the frosting) will be employed by the adolescent is pertinent to this developmental period. For victims of sexual abuse, this time can put the final touches on trauma.

Becoming the Perpetrator

If a book were to be written regarding the adolescent victim, the title should be *Becoming the Perpetrator*. Often due to frustrations, anxiety, and the inability to cope with years of guilt, degradation and shame, the adolescent attempts to survive by becoming very much like the abuser. Power and position is often given to the person who was deviant, manipulative, underhanded and controlling. For the adolescent, this seems to be a final solution. The adolescent, quite frankly, sees very little advantage in being *victim-like* and sees tremendous advantage in being like the perpetrator.

Many adolescents are discovered as being sexual abuse victims when they become involved in the *system* due to acting out behaviors. Adolescent victims tend to *make us uncomfortable* because they often respond in a manner very similar to behaviors of the perpetrator.

> Kathy is picked up by the police for shoplifting. She has problems with truancy, she is failing in school, and she has three previous *pick-up* orders for running away. The policeman, attempting to be empathic, inquires about Kathy's home life. Kathy's response provides clarity, but perhaps not the answer desired by the Law Enforcement officer. *If your dad fucked you every morning, you might run away, too*, is Kathy's reply to a rather bewildered policeman. Being *the victim* has gotten Kathy nowhere. Being ag-

gressive, violent, manipulative and powerful at least provides Kathy with some sense of choice.

Kathy makes us *uncomfortable*. Adults would prefer a teary eyed grateful victim thanking them very much for the intervention. Instead, in adolescence, an obnoxious, outrageous victim emerges telling us where to stick our treatment program.

The Race Ain't On

The adolescent victim is looking out into a world of peers who are making sexual decisions. Even the most prudish adolescent female is making sexual decisions by her dress, by her actions, by her language to perhaps not be sexual. The quarterback on the football team who lifts weights and carries his body with perfect poise is also demonstrating a sexual decision. Rock music, television, and adolescent literature all portray a theme of sexual decision making. Sexuality and sexual decision making is extremely important for an adolescent.

For the adolescent *victim* there are few decisions to be made. Decisions have already been made regardless of the adolescent's desires. Often, sexual abuse has occurred at a previous time where no choice or right to protection existed. In adolescence, sexual decision making is extremely important. For the victim, futility is an overriding theme. There is very little to decide when all decisions have been made. In essence, the adolescent is forced to *give up*. While other adolescents are trying to make decisions about

being sexually attractive, being sexually aggressive, or being sexually consenting, the adolescent recognizes the battle is over. The race isn't on. *Decision making* is a mockery! Competition is impossible due to the fact that the battle was decided before the adolescent had a chance to enter the race.

Cleansing Coping

In most cases, the adolescent response is one of outrage, of bursting out, of *becoming the perpetrator*. These adolescent victims recognize the battle was over before they arrived at the gate and, therefore, the most typical response is one of outrage. There are some adolescents who respond in a different manner, but from a very similar set of circumstances.

Some adolescents, due to circumstances found in the Situational Perspective, respond in a perfectionistic or more self-defeating process. The *I will cleanse myself from the abuse* is a cry for a minority of adolescents. The obsessive/compulsive adolescent who uses perfection as a way to *keep out of the race* is also an example of the *uncomfortable* victim. These adolescents make adults uncomfortable, but in a different way than the outraged, obnoxious adolescent. These adolescents strive for perfection. They are constantly working, working, working, not for self-fulfillment but for a cleansing process they believe will rid themselves of the pain. The obnoxious adolescent recognizes they have not even been able to enter the race, let alone compete. For the *perfect* victim, there is hope that the race will be reconvened. This may be even more deadly.

The obsessive/compulsive adolescent remains hopeful that if success is achieved and if the adolescent is *perfect*, somehow the sexual abuse will be resolved, disappear, or, more importantly, the race will be restarted with the adolescent being at the starting gate. This adolescent is obviously hopeful, but nonetheless uncomfortable for adults. None of the accomplishments seem to be for the sake of accomplishment, but seem to be rather a game, a race or a brutal competition. This adolescent struggles with intimacy. This adolescent is self-abusive through obsessive/compulsive behaviors and an unrelenting desire for perfection.

The Unvictim

The male victim was carefully described in Chapter Nine with emphasis on societal teaching. The male victim has a great deal of pressure from the world in which he lives to discount his victimization. Fears of homosexuality, anxiety over the rejection of the female perpetrator identity, the impact from the *John Wayne/German Shepherd* profile, and physiological betrayals provide the male with even more confusion about his role as a victim. For this reason, the male child is described as the *unvictim*.

From a Developmental Perspective, these four issues continue to force the male to worry, to second guess, and to be frustrated over his attempts to establish himself as a male. There

is little opportunity for the male to be positive about his future as a male sexual partner. As the male attempts to develop, each step causes a struggle of blame in efforts to identify himself as a victim.

Males struggle through the previously mentioned stages in the *unaware, unfortunate, and uncomfortable* just as females. In other words, the *unaware* six-year-old male victim may be hearing words such as *faggot or queer*, but he remains unaware of the significance of those words. As he proceeds into the next *unfortunate* stage, he will not only become more aware, but he will be suffering an additional issue of trauma as described in the *unvictim* category. In other words, chronologically males are proceeding through the same steps as females and experiencing the same struggles from one age to another. To compound the difficulties in the male viewing himself as an innocent victim are special considerations, which result in the title of *the unvictim*.

The Unresolved Victim

Finally, attention should be given to the adult victim who remains in a trauma bond with sexual abuse. Those adults who are traumatized by abuse seem to remain connected to their sexual abuse throughout adulthood. The adult victim is developmentally the age at which the abuse began. A 35-year-old woman in the therapist's office is in a sense a five-year-old child concerning attitudes and feelings regarding sexuality and sexual abuse. Therapeutic demands require that the precious *child* be rescued and that the undeveloped *child* feel protection, nurturing and acceptance by the *adult* counterpart. Childhood sexual development needs to be rekindled for the five-year-old inside the 35-year-old. Developmentally, the child has stopped and was never allowed to proceed to adulthood. As an example, the final blow for the adult female victim is that each time she attempts to be sexual, she takes this obnoxious five-year-old brat to bed with her, in addition to her 35-year-old partner.

No Child Is An Island

Damage in the developmental area is not only determined by the age of the child when the abuse takes place. Children do not develop in an *age vacuum*. They develop first with the foundations of their age, but they also perceive and evaluate according to information available to them at the time of the abuse. This information significantly impacts perceptions of the victim. Often, not enough attention is given to the sexual environment. Sex education for children is thought to be extremely unintentional. As an example, words coming from a parent's mouth are often insignificant compared to the messages given to children in a household by a variety of different *sex educators*.

The Family Plot

Examples of how children are influenced by their environment would include such issues as family constellation. Children who grow up with older siblings may have opportunities to witness advanced stages of development. By having older brothers and sisters, children's developmental process may be accelerated. Exposure to the bodies of older siblings, listening to older siblings' social interactions regarding sexuality, and observing bodily changes provide important information to younger children. When a 13-year-old earns the right to wear a training bra, the entire family becomes aware — even the curious five-year-old.

If the child is the oldest sibling, the process of sexual development may also be accelerated as the older sibling is in a position of caretaker and may be involved in some activities with a younger child concerning sexual behavior. The older (but sometimes frustrated) sibling may need to correct his younger brother for touching his *pee-pee* in the presence of the older brother's girlfriend. An older sibling may be involved in health care activities of younger siblings, such as bathing or changing diapers which may also speed up the developmental process.

Building Codes

Another factor that influences children within the family environment is the general codes or protocols within the family regarding sexuality. If children, as an example, are being brought up in a family that is extremely religious or chaste, the child's sexual development is influenced.

Mary Linn is being brought up in a

Mormon household. She has been taught strict codes of chastity requiring a marital process to take place in the Temple where she will be sealed to her husband in the spirit of chastity. At eight years of age, Mary Linn is cognizant of the religious attitudes regarding chastity. The family fails to recognize that since Mary Linn has been sexually abused, she is building her sexual development upon clear and crisp understanding of her *unworthiness*. No one has stopped to teach Mary Linn that she is innocent and that she did not make any sexual choices in her sexual abuse. Rather than separating Mary Linn's sexual abuses from her own sexual future, Mary Linn is building upon an image of her sexuality with the traditional Mormon doctrine in hand. Although certainly not desirable, Mary Linn may have fared better in a household that was perhaps even more sexually promiscuous or sexually *free*. Without separating Mary Linn's abuse from the church's teaching, she is prepared for a deadly future.

The modesty codes of morality within the family teach children very specific messages. Independent of sexual abuse, it is extremely important for these codes of morality to be established. Unfortunately, the sexual victim hears the same codes or messages in the same family and uses those messages to build upon a sexual foundation. Messages themselves may be quite appropriate, but children will not separate sexual abuse from those messages. As in Mary Linn's case, she is building an understanding of her abuse upon the modesty and morality codes of the family and the result is traumatic.

Limitation Liabilities

Without understanding the intricate nature of sexual development, many parents close the door to discovering sexual abuse or close the door to the rehabilitation of the child should abuse happen. Children who are developing in an extremely *child-centered* household may have a limited likelihood of reporting sexual abuse if encased in that general family atmosphere is a lack of specific sexual abuse information. When parents spend thousands of dollars on their children's ballet lessons, when they take organized and structured vacations to Yellowstone, when they seem to put forth every effort possible to center their lives around the children, but limit sexual information, those children are often the most unlikely children to tell their parents about sexual abuse.

To Ginny,

Tell me some of the reasons you didn't want to tell your mom you were being sexually abused.

From Ginny,

I knew how much she cared for me and I knew how important I was to her. She did everything for me. I didn't want to hurt her feelings by telling her that she had failed.

Had this mother presented a different family atmosphere with unlimited sexual information, such as having a new sexual partner on the family room couch each Sunday morning, Ginny may have told immediately about the abuse. Keeping the couch busy is certainly not recommended, but it may have provided a lackadaisical attitude about sexuality and may have resulted in Ginny's report. Ginny didn't need her mothers' promiscuity, she needed specific sexual information.

From a Developmental Perspective, children learn messages important to their sexual development by parents' omissions, or limitations of sexual information. Children see parents put forth tremendous effort in every other area, but when sexual information is omitted, they learn an important lesson about sexuality. The message screams loudly through the silence, *Sex is unmentionable. It is unspeakable.* That message shatters the silence and makes deadly contributions to the child's sexual development.

Profoundly Peripheral

There are other events, activities, or items in the periphery of a child's environment that make contributions to the child's sexual development. Most of these issues are so common that the impact on sexual development is often overlooked. Some of these elements are more blatant or obvious while others are much more subtle.

As an example, those families who pay for cable television (Home Box Office or Showtime) make a contribution to the sexual development of children. Parents themselves may avoid the sexual explicit material and pronounce proudly at PTA Meetings, *We mostly watch the Disney Channel.* Unfortunately, while mother and father are attending the PTA meeting, children may be home watching sexually explicit material. This does not suggest that the family need to subscribe to the *Playboy Channel,* because movies with such titles as *The Biggest Little Whorehouse in Texas* provide messages to even a preschooler. The subtle message is, *We can't talk about anything between our belly button and our knees, but whorehouses are okay.*

More explicit examples occur with sexually explicit printed material. If Playboy and Penthouse magazines are lying on the living room coffee table, children will certainly be influenced by this material. Music that plays in the family home also provides sexual information. Some parents become horrified when they carefully peruse the album covers of their teenager's rock music. Parents may take a stand against the sexually explicit lyrics of their teenager's rock music and take comfort in only allowing country and western music to be played while the younger children are present. Unfortunately, there is a much greater chance that small children will understand the words of country music while people are sliding off *Satin Sheets* or posing the question, *If I Said*

You Had a Beautiful Body, Would You Hold it Against Me? Lyrics that may be drowned out by electric guitars or drums may have made no contribution to the preschooler's sexual development, and may have been better than the much more wholesome *cowboy stuff.*

The Immaculate Conception

Another example of subtle sexual messages occurs as parents teach their children through the parents' sexual behaviors or lack of behaviors. The most common way children learn male/female interactions is through observing their parents. Children who see mother and father patting each other on the *buns* at the breakfast table or sleeping in separate bedrooms learn a great deal about sexuality. If parents withhold information regarding their sexual relationship, most children grow up believing their parents to be asexual.

I remember the exact day I realized that my parents were sexual. At approximately age 12, pieces of information finally merged together with the result being that I recognized my parents were probably doing it. I was horrified! I had listened to jokes about such things as caves and flashlights and I had seen the cats, hissing, clawing, and spitting. Later, I learned that something went in something and that was how babies are made. Finally, it became clear that when my mother and father went to bed, they probably were putting something in something and, God forbid, they were probably liking it. I saw some stuff on television and I had even read some books about romance. It never, up until that horrible day, dawned on me that my conception occurred with my parents huffing and puffing. I could not conceive of them being sexual. Perhaps my father, perhaps he might like it a little, maybe! But my mother, she was too, too, too, too, I don't know what the word is. I just know that I cannot conceive of her getting all sweaty and being sexual. And most important, God forbid, I couldn't imagine her liking it. I can still feel the repulsion and disgust on the day I figured it out. I can remember the smell in the house and I can even remember a song that was playing on the radio that started the process of me making this final revelation. Without any trouble at all, I can return to those feelings of disgust. How dare them!

Conversely, children grow up in households where tenderness and affection is demonstrated between their parents. These children may learn very quickly that their parents are sexual and in cases where parents do not hide this information, the parents are subtly educating their children about the beauty of intimacy. These unintentional acts provide positive information to the child. Obviously, the opposite side is true. In other words, if children view anger, hostility, or such things as domestic violence, they are learning about the role of men and women, and certainly the roles of men and women have an impact upon their sexuality.

Rules for Roles

Children who grow up in a household with extremely different rules for boys and for girls also learn about sex. The different rules for sexual roles tell children something about the ways they will establish relationships in their sexual futures.

If girls in the family are treated with disrespect and boys are given a sense of power, sexual messages are gleaned from that teaching. The message may be, *Boys are powerful and take sex*, and *Girls are weak and give it*. If girls' position in the family is elevated or threatened, most likely the males in the family will choose females and establish relationships in the same manner. Even rules concerning such issues as nudity that are different between females and males teach about sex. If a male's body is much more acceptable in its natural form or even in its natural functioning state, interest in or rejection of the female body may be the lesson learned.

Let's Talk

Another way children learn about sexuality is through the overt efforts of their parents to teach sex education. Unfortunately, children learn usually the exact opposite of parents intentions through their *talks*. Although it is clear that parents must spend years teaching children how to be honest, how to be Catholics, or how to be a good mechanic, somehow parents believe that one white-knuckled talk about sexuality will suffice. The message or the underlying learning is usually disastrous.

An adult when questioned about his sex education, states, *I didn't get any sex education*. This man is answering from a place of ignorance. Withholding information is very educational and certainly just watching the relationships between a mother and a father is very important sex education. Although no one talked, he still learned.

Of course, the story is common about the little boy who asks where he comes from. The bright purple faced mother brings a podium into the living room and gives the young man a lecture on reproduction that would pass for a college course. He shrugs his shoulders and walks away stating, *That's funny. Kevin came from Kansas!*

The idea pervades that sex education must be verbal and in a *talk*. Adults believe that sex education must be formal and if a formal lesson about the *birds and the bees* was omitted, no learning took place. Actually, most of what individuals believe to be sex education is a very small part of the total educational picture.

Boys are often taken on excursions with their father about the time their underwear is examined and a hysterical mother thinks her sweet, darling boy is having wet dreams! On a hunting trip, the crimsom-faced father may bring up a subject with sweating palms. He may ask about the *birds and the bees*.

Well, son, I suppose it is time we had a talk about, well, you probably know.

You mean about sex, Dad?

Well, er, yes, that is what I meant. How much do you know already?

I think I know pretty much about all of it.

Good, I am so glad we had this talk.

These *formal* sex education talks are often thought to be something that passes for sex education. By the time children are demonstrating to parents that they need The Big Talk, usually children are so far into their sexual development that the Big Talk is meaningless. The Big Talk is really to give parents some sense that they fulfilled their obligation. The Big Talk usually does nothing but further separate parent and child and usually does not provide any information (except that their parents are extremely uncomfortable and a very unreliable source of information regarding sex).

The loudest messages do not come from the Big Talk on the hillside while deer hunting with dad. The loudest messages are the ones that occur around the household on an ongoing basis. The messages come from codes of modesty. The messages come from the way in which mother and father relate to each other. The messages come from the television, the radio, sleeping arrangements, or even decisions about knocking on the bathroom door.

The Whole Child

Before the questions can be answered regarding how the child perceived the sexual abuse, an examination must occur concerning the body of information available to the child at the time of the abuse. As the research indicated, children who were sexually abused with a clear, crisp awareness of the offender/perpetrator role appeared to be far less traumatized than children who were confused. Children's sexual perceptions are very important in clarity or confusion.

It would be important to avoid the assumption that a lack of information indicates no trauma. Ignorant children are not necessarily less traumatized. Likewise, children who have tremendous information, but who may have the wrong information, may also be traumatized. Sex education is extremely subtle and usually unintentional. Much education occurs before parents even realize what is happening. Children will be sexually abused during different stages of their development and they will perceive the abuse differently as they are proceeding through sexual development attempting to make sense of the information available to them.

Debits and Credits

A third issue in the Developmental Perspective of the Sexual Victim Trauma Assessment examines what has been lost in normal sexual development due to the sexual abuse. Before trauma to normal development can be assessed, *normal* sexual development needs discussion.

Is it true that we all grow up sexually safe and secure? Is it true that we all grow up believing that our pee-pees and wee-wees are the nicest parts of our bodies and that when we make decisions to share our wee-wees and pee-pees with someone, it is a wonderful, wonderful thing? Is sexual development a process of one positive event occurring after another? Is it common for bodies to be perfect, never betraying us, breasts being exactly the size girls want them to be and boys never once getting an unwanted erection in math class?

Is it accurate to assess trauma to sexual victims because they did not grow up sexually *normal*? Perhaps sexual development in this society is already traumatic and very painful for children. Is *normal* development perfect?

A perfect world, of course, does not exist and therefore in order to understand this portion of the Trauma Assessment, it must be clear that trauma to sexual development must go beyond the seemingly normal painful process. Adult patients wandering in and out of therapy, being evaluated in mental hospitals, and suffering from their third or fourth marriage can provide us information that will help understand what trauma to the normal sexual development appears to be.

Beyond Norms

Perhaps most obvious is the damage to sexual development when sex has become intolerable. Rating scales for the trauma assessment research indicated a PRIMARY SEVERE rating if the patient was asexual or, if given a choice, would like to live in a world where the sex fairy had zapped everyone into total avoidance of sex. Although it is clear that adults fail to educate children about the positive aspects of sexuality, most adults find sexual behaviors pleasurable and, if given the opportunity, would like to continue to be sexual throughout their lives. For some patients who are severely damaged by their sexual abuse, sex was intolerable and they would actually choose to live in a world where sex did not exist. In rating scales for conducting this research, sexual victims appeared to have a difference in their rating or attitudes regarding sexuality as compared to non-victims. However, those *normal* individuals had negative attitudes about sexuality in many areas. In other words, it seems impossible or extremely unique for individuals to have totally positive feelings regarding sexuality. The difference seems to be not in whether negative attitudes exist, but to the level or to the extent of those negative atitudes with the most obvious level being those patients who would like to live the rest of their life asexually.

Intolerable Limitations

On the opposite end of the spectrum, compared to those people who find sexuality intolerable, are those people who disregard intimacy and become either sexually promiscuous or sexually aggressive. It is difficult to determine who is more traumatized, the 25-year-old female who allows 15 men to have intercourse with her at a party, or the sexual victim who would avoid all social interactions in fear of the possibility of being sexual. Certainly, the middle ground is desirable, appreciating sexuality and being positive toward sexual experiences, but also being self-protective. The victim who is totally *abusable* and has absolutely no regard for his or her rights to protection is severely traumatized, as is the patient who has been robbed of the opportunity to appreciate and anticipate intimacy. The result is either a total shunning of any effort to be sexual or a total disregard for privacy or consent.

The first step in deciding what has been lost in normal sexual development is to make predictions about what a reasonable development should be. The best way to approach this *hope* would be a categorization of those things which would be present in a normal sexual development, as well as those issues which should be absent.

Bon Appetit

At a minimum, normal development should include a sexual appetite. Obviously, individuals vary on the depth of sexual desires and such issues as frequency. It would be safe to say that normal sexual development would require some kind of sexual appetite or a sense that sexuality was at least something desirable and an important component of a person's repertoire of activities. Such issues as frequency, behavior, or partner choice could be considered on an individual basis. At a minimum, then, normal sexual development should at least include an appetite of sexuality.

Canoe Theory

It would seem that normal sexual development should also include an acceptance of body image in order to balance the issue of being vulnerable due to society's perpetuation of perfection. In other words, The Canoe Theory emerges.

> The Canoe Theory suggests that *good sex* is being able to ask your partner to have sex with you standing up in a canoe, yet knowing that should you fall in, your partner won't let you drown.

This quaint analogy suggests that *good sex* occurs if, with imperfections, bags, sags, etc. (total vulnerability), the adult is totally and absolutely safe snuggled next to a partner. Being able to ask your partner to have sex with you standing up in a canoe is taking tremendous risk, just as adult partners risk being vulnerable with their body imperfections. This is a world where the human body is constantly portrayed in magazines, television, etc., as being perfect. Most adults with bags, sags, beer bellies, and dimples on their buns are less than perfect. The analogy of asking your partner to have sex with you standing up in a canoe is comparable to the tremendous risk for partners who enter into a relationship being quite imperfect.

But knowing your partner won't let you drown signifies the issue of being completely safe. Whether or not partners actually want to have sex standing up in a canoe is not the issue. Being free to ask and then knowing that if you fall in, you won't drown, signifies the ultimate in safety. Good sex is the beautiful combination of being totally vulnerable and totally safe.

Bod Squad

For normal sexual development, and for the canoe theory to operate, there must be a reasonably positive sense of body image. Not suggesting that everyone looks like Playboy foldouts or competitors in a weight lifting contest, but that the person who has perhaps developed normally has a reasonably positive body image in the sexual experience with a partner. Quite clearly, this comfort level is not necessarily how people feel they look in the shopping mall or at the bowling alley. This is a sense of safety in a sexual experience with a partner.

Caution should be raised about the suggestion that most *normal* individuals have a positive sense of body image. The average American adult tends to be overweight and the proud owner of many imperfections. Worries about sexuality are more common than not.

I wonder if she can feel my beer belly.

I wonder if my breath is okay.

I hate it when he touches my sides, I have so many rolls.

My legs are so flabby. I am glad the lights are out.

I hope she doesn't care about my little penis.

My stretchmarks hopefully don't show.

I wish she wouldn't run her hands through my hair that is no longer there.

Are these people normal? Do they have commonly held worries about their body image? The answer is *yes*, but something happens beyond the worries and that is a sense that they are acceptable in a sexual relationship. Worrying about a beer belly or stretchmarks does not suggest an abnormal body image. Recognizing the acceptance of the body image in a sexual relationship tends to be normal, otherwise adults would spend most of their time in weight loss clinics or aerobics classes.

For Boys and For Girls

An important contribution to normal sexual development is an *acceptance* of sexuality for both males and females. Recognizing that sexuality is the involvement of two individuals, both seeking their own standard of pleasure, is an important component in normal sexual development. There is a wide variety of understanding and beliefs regarding sexual role development. Questions are raised regarding whose job it is to initiate sex, who should be the first person to have an orgasm, or who gets to be on the *top or bottom*. No one can determine normalcy within the framework of those questions. What is clear, however, is that there should be a basic understanding that both men and women have sexual capacities for pleasure. Sex is not necessarily an unequal proposition, reserved for only one sex.

Talk, Talk, Talk

Another ingredient in what would seem to be a normal sexual development would include the ability to communicate about the sexual relationship. Sex is not something that is necessarily simple. The Sex Fairy does not exist and sexual discomfort, confusions, and difficulties occur. As with mortgage payments, child rearing decisions, or vocational concerns, adults need the ability to discuss these issues in order to make decisions. Without the ability to at least communicate, most problems are unsolvable and continue to fester. Human sexuality, whether it be a *one night stand* or a 50 year relationship, is always enhanced and stands a greater chance for success if both partners have the ability to communicate regarding their behavior.

This is not to suggest that each sexual experience needs to be accompanied by a panel debate in the bedroom, complete with podiums and microphones. A list of minimal standards for normal development should dictate at least some ability to discuss sexuality with the partner who is looking for a canoe.

An assignment often given to professionals further demonstrates this dilemma. In training seminars teaching professionals to proceed through the process of introspection requires a particularly difficult assignment. Professionals are often asked whether they feel they are competent to interview victims of sexual assault if they are not comfortable enough to discuss their own sexual behaviors. Certainly, this assignment does not suggest that the 210-pound law enforcement officer interviewing a three-year-old must discuss his problems with premature ejaculation, but it does ask the same, very large policemen, *If you cannot discuss your own sexual behavior with your partner, how comfortable will you be discussing sexuality with a three-year-old stranger?*

Participants are asked to take their partner (the person they are most intimate with) to an *unsexual* place for a casual experience such as eating a meal. McDonalds or Burger King is highly recommended due to the lack of sexual props such as candlelight and wine. The assignment should be completed in the brightly colored room (about as sexual as the police station), and it is particularly helpful if the fifth grade bowling team's birthday celebration is also taking place. Professionals are simply asked to tell their partners three things they enjoy when the couple makes love. They are instructed to say,

> *Sweetheart, I don't know how long it has been since I have told you that one of my favorite things for you to do to me when we make love is . . .* (and then he takes a bite of his Big Mac). He then says, *and in all of these 17 years we've been married, one of my really favorite things for you to do is . . . and what really knocks my socks off is when you. . .*

Most law enforcement officers, social workers, or other professionals exhibit curled toes, white knuckles, and crimson cheeks when this challenge is presented. For some adults, talking openly to their partners of 17 years is extremely painful and difficult. Sexual communication appears to be very, very difficult but it certainly is a prerequisite to a compatible sexual relationship. Marital partners often hump and bump and huff and puff in the darkness of the night, often, assuming, hoping or wanting, and yet sometimes feeling bewildered. Communication in any other area demonstrates the competency of the couple. When it comes to S.E.X., however, lips quiver, palms sweat, and tongues thicken.

These issues are very general and basic. They would suggest the minimum standards for positive attitudes and sexuality. In order to have a reasonable opportunity for sexual success, these aforementioned ideas should exist. Indicators of those things which should be absent from the sexual laundry list point to the possible areas of damage for the sexual victim. The residual effects of sexual abuse are often found in this portrayal of those things which must be excluded in order to have sexual success.

Issues of Trauma

The Knee Jerks

Phobic reactions to certain sexual behaviors certainly suggest areas of abnormally. Phobic reactions are very much different than personal taste or preference. The male who, as an example, finds anal intercourse repulsive may not have a phobic reactions at all. He may simply have a preference excluding that behavior. Somewhere in this individual's mind, a decision has been made to exclude that behavior from his preferred laundry list of sexual preferences. If this man, however, had been anally raped as a child and did not make a decision, but is responding to a past behavior, then he has a phobic reaction.

Phobic reactions are cultivated and born in uncomfortable or horrifying experiences. Phobic reactions are a response to a previous behavior, some of them more overt, such as an anal rape. But others are traumatizing to the victim because they had the capacity to be pleasurable in adult life but, due to sexual abuse, potential pleasure has been shattered.

> Veronica reports that she finds sex acceptable. *I don't mind doing it and it really has never been a problem for us.*

If I lived alone, I probably wouldn't miss it, but it isn't all that bad. I like intercourse, but, I can't stand to have him touch me. If he will just put it in, it's just fine. Veronica is asked to define *just fine.* Questions are asked about Veronica's pleasure or her definition of the term, *Oh, what I mean by that is, it doesn't hurt. It's not a problem for me. He can put it in and it is just fine. There is no pain and no memories. That's why I like to do intercourse and nothing else.*

In actuality, Veronica rated her general sexual attitude as being within the normal range. For Veronica not to be feeling pain during sex and not having the panic from phobic reactions meant sex was acceptable. Obviously, Veronica has no idea about normal, pleasurable sexuality.

War and Peace

A second component that is commonly found in sexual victims has to do with the ideation that sex has a potential for weaponry and conflict. Again, this issue is something that has a somewhat normal component, but for the sexual victim this normal component is completely out of proportion. It is not necessarily the existence of this issue, but the extent which the issue is used.

On a more normal level, sexuality can be a method of communication. Feeling particularly positive about a partner and feeling aroused can be a normal and positive way of conveying an attitude. Sending a message to a partner regarding the depth of caring can result in sexuality being used as a method of communication. Contrarily, but perhaps still within normal range, is the opposite response when sexuality can be used to communicate a negative message. Sleeping on the couch may be a way in which one partner can communicate frustration and anger to the other partner. Under some circumstances, this can be a helpful method of communication, especially if it is followed with verbal communication, *I cannot be sexual if we are fighting all day long. I don't feel safe being sexual with you when I don't feel safe at the breakfast table.*

When sexual communication becomes sexual weaponry, tremendous damage has occurred. Rape, as an example, is certainly a way to communicate aggression. Using sex to be powerful or using sex to humiliate certainly seems to have taken the issue of communication far beyond normal realms. To use sex as a weapon, to use sex to hurt people, or to gain control over people are examples of damage due to sexual abuse.

River of Many Returns

Another issue in comparing normal sexual development to severely damaged patients pertains to arousal. Damage to arousal system occurs as the victim develops arousal patterns in a response to the sexually abusive experience. In some cases, this may be the development of an arousal system as a rejection of events that occurred during the sexual abuse, and in other instances damage to the arousal system may be building arousal upon sexually deviant activities. As explained in Chapter Six, trauma bonding often occurs in the arousal to the deviant activities or to the offender. This is particularly damaging to the arousal system of the victim because the victim becomes fixated toward certain activities and people, that intellectually, the victim abhors.

Consider the conflict for a sexual victim who has developed an arousal pattern around the sensuousness of his sexual experiences with his mother. Her soft, tender caresses performing fellatio on him were extremely arousing. As he performed cunnilingus on his mother, he had *control* in a very *out-of-control* family. The sensuousness of his mother's attitude toward him even in nonsexual experiences caused him to be aroused.

As an adult, Mark's arousal patterns remain fixated on the feelings he had in his involvement with his mother. His mother is psychotic, abusive, and manipulative. He abhors the sexual abuse that she committed. He is disgusted with her attitudes and her current situation. On an arousal level, however, Mark danced with her again and again. His fantasies toward his mother provide him with ultimate masturbatory excitement coupled with subsequent revulsion. In his mind, Mark remains chained to his mother's sexual experience due to the fact that his arousal patterns were strongly developed toward the sexual abuse.

There are some theories indicating a tendency toward homosexuality or arousal to the same sex as a response to sexual abuse. Some women report that through their sexual abuse by males and through the absence of their mother's protection, they feel drawn toward females for sexual experiences.

As one of two girls in a family of eight, I learned very early what men need from females. Three of my brothers sexually abused me, as did my father and my grandfather. I learned that men sweat, they grunt, they groan, and they come. I associate the smells of my father, brothers and grandfather with the smell of all men. I hate penises and I find men in general intolerable within a mile of the bedroom.

For me, women are soft, nurturing, tender. They smell good and they feel good. I feel safe with women and I also feel very, very sexual.

In this example, severe damage has occurred as Jill was unable to establish anticipation and excitement toward interactions with the opposite sex. Instead of learning to anticipate male/female interaction, Jill learned torture, pain, and fear in direct relation to sexual contact with males. Her knee jerk response is to turn toward females.

However, the same end result can emerge from an opposite set of circumstances.

I was sexually abused by my sisters perhaps before I walked. They delight in adulthood at telling me about the sexual things they did to me. As a toddler and as a small child who was unaware of what was happening, I responded. They were left as caretakers for a great deal of the time and boredom ended with a wide variety of sexual experiences. Reciprocity occurred. I performed sexual favors for them and they gained control over me through my own sexual pleasure. My primary sexual interests remain with females. I hate my sisters and what they have done to me. Being gay is not a picnic. I have attempted marriage and I have two children. I have a college degree and, in spite of all of those things, I still have sexual attraction to females and I believe I am a lesbian. I never had a chance to develop normally. It was too late once I figured it out.

This is certainly not to suggest that the cause for homosexuality is sexual abuse. Some individuals who are homosexual and sexually abused as children may have been predestined to be homosexual in spite of the abuse. Certainly, many people are homosexual without being sexually abused. In the Trauma Assessment, a discovery must be made regarding a response or an impact on the sexual arousal system due to the sexual abuse that has occurred. If the abuse occurred as in the case of Jill, the damage to the sexual arousal system was a rejection of what happened in the sexually abusive situation. In the second example, an attachment of the sexually abusive situation to arousal occurred. In any event, sexual abuse that occurred for both of these patients caused the patient to deviate from the paths or the journey toward normal sexual arousal development.

Sexual Identification

There are additional examples of things that may occur in the sexual abuse situation that cause damage to the development of sexual arousal systems. Sexual identity is an example. Transexuality or transvestism could be the result of certain specific behaviors, such as being forced to dress in women's clothing, or being involved in a homosexual experience posing as a partner of the opposite sex. These events can have tremendous impact on the development of arousal. Sexual ridicule and humiliation occurring at the same time when arousal is taking place is another example of a disastrous effect on the victim's arousal system.

Too often, the evaluation of a sexual victim occurs with adult perceptions complete with adults attitudes about crime, loss, age of consent, etc. Sexual arousal during sexual abuse situations for victims is perhaps one of the most neglected areas in understanding what has taken place. All of the issues, events, activities, etc., will be carefully considered in the situational portion of the Sexual Victim Trauma

Assessment in order to understand how the victim viewed the sexual abuse. Clearly the connection between abuse and arousal, from children's perspectives, can appear quite different to adults.

In terms of arousal development, it is important to look in the developmental perspective at how the victim was impacted by certain sexual behaviors at the time the victim was aroused and experiencing pleasurable sensations. Certainly, pain and lack of sexual stimulation is prevalent, but the neglected frontier of arousal of victims is evident as well. Whenever sexual victims are feeling sexual pleasure and an event, such as being forced to cross dress or perform as a member of the opposite sex occurs, tremendous damage to the arousal pattern of the victim is likely to take place. It is the coupling together of something occurring in a sexual way and sexual pleasure that has such great potential for causing sexual identity problems.

Exit Only

A final example of traumatization to sexual development occurs when the victim rejects the sexual experiences and, in many cases totally rejects sexual arousal. Even if sexual arousal does occur physically, the victim rejects his/her participation. The victim has made a subconscious effort to forbid or exclude arousal. The damage is not the coupling of arousal to the sexually abusive scene, but the coupling of *resistance* to sexuality. This damage occurs in

several different levels, with the first being one of distraction.

When sexual abuse occurs, the victim may put forth effort to avoid inclusion or prohibit involvement through the process of distraction. The victim may not completely dissociate, but attempts to become removed from *feeling* during the sexual abuse situation. The result of this distraction technique is that the victim survives with the response of distraction. During sexual experiences, the victim may be experiencing pleasure and may be feeling positive, 30 years after the abuse. When the same sexual behavior occurs, such as the beginnings of intercourse, penetration, or breast fondling, there is often a reaction of distraction. Immediately the victim feels overwhelmed to make a grocery list, think about tomorrow night's dinner, or consider closing the deal on a real estate proposition. It is not necessarily a feeling of panic or returning to the affective responses of the sexual abuse, but is a detachment, a distraction, or a numbing of feelings when the sexual pleasure begins. The arousal for the victim is carefully encased in total control through distraction. *Thou shalt not be aroused* has shattered the entire sexual arousal system of the victim.

Another example occurs when the victim actually attaches the affective responses felt during the sexual abuse into sexual encounters at a later time. This is evidence again of damage to the sexual arousal system of the victim. In adulthood, the victim may have made an emotional commitment and may have the potential for positive sexuality. Intellectually and cognitively, the victim is sexually safe and secure. Unfortunately, when sexual touching begins or when arousal is imminent for the victim, all of the affective responses felt during the sexual abuse return. In other words, rather than attach arousal to the reaction of distraction, in this case the victim attached the affective responses felt in childhood to arousal.

This seems to be prevalent in many situations where the victim makes a decision to be asexual for a long period of time. The victim may have masturbated, but recognized that masturbation was wrong, deviant, unholy, and immoral. The fact that the negative responses occurred during this disgusting behavior may not have bothered the victim and the victim may have reinforced arousal to negative feelings of anxiety, panic, degradation, and humiliation. Even though the victim may be responding orgasmically, the victim nonetheless is continuing to connect sexual pleasure with negative affective responses. The victim seems to rationalize by hoping for the future when perhaps *a sanctioned relationship* (Pothole #3) or a marriage in the church will somehow separate these negative feelings of arousal and sexuality. This unfortunately is not the end result.

I lie down at night with my beautiful wife. I look at her and I feel aroused, sexual and anxious to make love. When we start to touch, I feel like I've just sat down to take the Bar Exam, or I feel the same as I did when I was in the third grade without my spelling book. In my head, I know it is her and she cares for me and this should be wonderful, yet I feel just like I did when I was five. I am taking my offender to bed with me. There has always been the three of us.

What has occurred is that arousal is coupled with all of the affective responses suffered many years previous. Damage to the sexual arousal system is one in which any sign of arousal is an automatic precursor to feelings of victimization. To be sexual, the victim must return to the sexual abuse on each occasion. What a deadly contribution to something that had the potential for pleasure.

The Commitment

Also included in the laundry list of things that should occur in normal sexuality is a general attitude concerning sexual commitment. If sex is totally intolerable, it indicates that severe trauma has occurred to normal sexual development. Many patients indicate a desire to be sexual or a desire to break the deadly bonds of their own traumatization of normal sexual development. The most SEVERELY TRAUMATIZED patients, however, indicate a desire to be asexual. Sex is absolutely intolerable to some victims; no commitment to change exists. People who divorce, or who lack interest in having children, or have vocations that prohibit potentials for sexual encounters are not necessarily abnormal. However, when sexual abuse is the author of these decisions, trauma has occurred.

Sexual Taking

On the opposite end of the spectrum are those individuals who have a total disregard for sexual consent. These individuals have been traumatized in their sexual development through believing or learning that sexuality is not a prized possession or something to be held with respect. These individuals would suggest that sex is something to be disregarded and taken. It is meaningless and perhaps no more profound than brushing of teeth every morning.

Sex is just no big deal to me. Ever since I was a kid, sex is just something you do. I've done it with the cats, the kids in the neighborhood, with prostitutes, or with basically anybody I can find. To me sex is just like scratching an itch. I don't know why people get so excited about it. I've lost more relationships with women over the fact that I had relationships with other women. I just don't get it.

The idea, of course, is that sexuality is viewed as something that has potential for providing pleasure, intimacy, nurturing, etc. The same could be said about a hot tub, but hot tubs break down and there are times when they are not appropriate. More importantly, hot tubs can provide tremendous value. Most individuals walk along the middle road, having sexuality be important with controls, guidelines, and rules. When sexuality is viewed as either totally intolerable and therefore to be avoided at all costs, or when sexuality is viewed as being totally worthless and no more significant than changing socks, obviously the middle ground is not available to these sexual victims.

Human sexuality is something of value. In a chaotic world of *zoomie, zoomie*, intimacy and sexual pleasure, regardless of personal preference and desires, can be a treasured experience. Whether through masturbation, homosexuality, a commune, or a traditional long-term marriage, human beings have a potential for sexuality to provide a source of nurturing, pleasure and affection. Trauma to sexual victims in the whole area of sexuality is profound. Struggling with the positive aspects of sexuality may occur for many individuals who are not sexually abused. Somehow, survival occurs. The sexual victim is in a situation where tremendous impact can occur to what may be an already difficult area. Without appreciating the impact of sexual development damage, a Trauma Assessment cannot be accurately completed and rehabilitation for a sexual victim is not likely.

HABITS OF THE HURT —
THE SITUATIONAL PERSPECTIVE

How can children survive sexual abuse? How does a five-year-old **compute** *information only appropriate for a 25-year-old? How do children cope and, more importantly, what* **habits** *develop from the coping? And what* **hurt,** *from those habits, creates suffering in the future?*

Footprints to the Future

Habits of the hurt is an eloquent way of describing the situational perspective of the Sexual Victim Trauma Assessment. The *habits* are more specifically designed as coping skills used for survival. The trauma suffered by victims, or the *hurt,* forms the foundation for how the habits emerge. Footprints take the victim away from the sexually abusive situation and it is the development of those footprints that set lifelong patterns of adjustment for the future.

The Senses

There are three major areas for examination in the situational portion of the Trauma Assessment. First and most basic, sensory activation is examined. Through the senses, information is provided to the child's computer. The memories will often be in sensory activation and, in cases of amnesia or dissociation, affective memories may be absent. The habits or the responses taking the victim away from the abuse and returning the victim to the pain of abuse

229

have a foundation in sensory activation. The first basic level of examination, then, is the discussion of those senses which were activated and the subsequent memories stored within the senses.

The Scene

A second issue for examination involves the sexually abusive *scene* where the sexual abuse occurred. Environmental influence, the locality of others, lighting, conversations, method of coercion, etc., are examples of elements providing further input into the child's computer.

Not only is sensory involvement important, but also those elements in the *scene* provide information concerning development of the victim's coping or survival skills. Children are not capable of responding to behavior beyond their capabilities. If a victim watches the molestation of an animal, is exposed to pornography, endures intercourse, or is forced to perform fellatio, it is unlikely that the victim perceives and computes that information in the same manner as an adult.

> *Oh, dear, I am being sexually abused! Heavens, this is against my consent due to the fact that I am only eight. Therefore, it is entirely inappropriate that this is taking place. I will check the yellow pages for the nearest sexual abuse prevention program.*

The example is obviously absurd. No eight-year-old child could make those computations. Un-fortunately, adults often believe that children are abused with the precognitions of adult understanding. Nothing could be further from the truth.

While a child is being fondled, manipulated, or molested, the environment of the sexually abusive scene permeates the child's computer. The conversations of the perpetrator, artifacts in the room, the locality of others, and other extraneous elements bombard the child's mind. If children could compute from an adult perspective, the temperature in the room, the dog barking outside, or a mother being on a couch next to the perpetrator would not seem to matter. Part of developing from a child to an adult is developing the cognitive processes. As cognitive processes become fine tuned, more basic observations and computations fade.

As an example, an adult rape victim may frantically contemplate screaming, running, or using her rather rusty martial art skills. Also going through the rape victim's mind may be thoughts of escape, outrage toward the sex offender, and contemplations about the future or thoughts of loved ones. The intellectual capabilities of the adult rape victim may be the focus rather than extraneous events. For children, without competent, cognitive development, more basic focusing occurs.

The Situation

Finally, examination of the sexual abuse situation does not end when the offender walks out of the room and the child is left in tears. It is extremely important to understand the *habits* that occurred 30 minutes after the abuse as the child lies in bed computing and contemplating. Additionally, the child may walk from the bedroom into a room of people which will provide additional information for the child's computer. Living in an alcoholic family, a secretive family, or a very moralistic family will also provide information to the victim. Thoughts of disclosure, residual effects of disclosure through investigations, court experiences, or traumatic therapeutic interventions make a final contribution to the victim's memory bank. Just as sexual abuse is not isolated to sexual behaviors, the sexually abusive situation is not isolated to contact between the perpetrator and the victim. Children are not isolated or independent.

Children who attend school with seminal fluid in their vaginas or pain in their rectums incorporate feelings of sexual abuse with their everyday lives. Because of these extraneous events, computations are impacted. Survival skills depend on computations, and computations occur as the child fits together the pieces.

In summary, the situational portion of the Sexual Victim Trauma Assessment will be divided into three components. The first and most basic circle will include sensory activation. Reaching out further from the basics of sensory involvement are the elements of the actual sexual abuse scene. A final circle examines the child's world and how computations will be made according to extraneous dynamics in the child's world.

Let's Make *Sense* Out of This

Sensory activation has tremendous potential for returning the victim to affective responses of sexual abuse. Phobic reactions occur as the senses are stimulated. Phobic reactions or sensory activation goes far beyond sexual behaviors and may include a variety of elements.

Rochelle finds herself clinically depressed after moving into a new home. The old colonial mansion was in need of repair, but Rochelle and her husband were very excited about the prospect of refurbishing. Rochelle began to notice feelings of depression and anxiety when her children were at daycare and she was home alone. Eventually, she became so despondent that medical attention was sought. Sexuality became intolerable. An outraged Rochelle was heard throughout the neighborhood screaming at her children. What appeared to be a life of contentment turned into one of depression and upheaval.

After eighteen months of therapy, a more clear picture emerged. Through sensory deprivation exercises, Rochelle was able to focus upon each individual sense for the purpose of gathering baseline data regarding her bouts of depression. A correlation was discovered between Rochelle being in her new home and her depression.

Without drawing an immediate correlation, Rochelle realized she was living in a home very similar to her home of childhood. Specific to sensory stimulation that seemed to stimulate Rochelle's depression were smells of the basement. The musty odor of the basement, the size of the house, the high ceilings and even the same type of coal furnace rekindled many of the senses involved during Rochelle's sexual abuse as a child. During her adult life she was plagued with depression but made no attempt to uncover the source. The stimulation of senses was a key to Rochelle's bouts of upheaval. The same sensory stimulation, however, became a key to Rochelle's total recovery.

Sexual Stuff

Perhaps most basic in understanding the sensory activation during sexual abuse is examination of the sexual behavior. Watching the offender be orgasmic, feeling penetration, and experiencing the pain of body contortions are obvious examples of sensory activation. From a sexual perspective, consideration should be made for any sexual experience where the senses of the child are involved, such as tasting, smelling, seeing, touching, or hearing. In order

for the Trauma Assessment to be conducted, looking into sensory memory is important.

Beyond Sex

The second step in examining sensory activity requires sight, sound, smell, touch, and taste to expand beyond penises and vaginas. A brightly lit room may require the victim to see each move of the perpetrator and may result in a more clear view of the child's participation. With the lights off, the victim's senses may be bombarded and terrorized since sight is prohibited. Tactile terror would be obvious if the victim was unable to see. In a darkened room, the offender may be probing for a child. A simple touch on the elbow or arm might signal terror.

The differences in therapeutic considerations for the child who was abused in light or in dark may be quite different. One patient may need to learn pleasure and safety in darkness, while the other patient may require learning to be comfortable with visual stimulation. Certainly, the sense of sight will have a profound impact on the victim, but it is important to understand that the deprivation of sight may also have traumatic effects. This may be true for many of the senses, but sight most particularly.

This portion of the examination, like many others in the Trauma Assessment, needs additional inquiry for most issues. In an unrelated example, it would seem improper to assume that because the offender did not use a weapon, no trauma occurred. The lack of a behavior such as a coercive modalities on the part of the perpetrator may have computed a more disastrous message. *I was so easy he didn't have to say a thing. He just abused me like it was expected and a common thing to do.*

It may also be possible that a single sexual activity may activate many senses. Forcing a child to perform fellatio activates the sense of taste. The tactile responses are also obvious, as well as perhaps the sense of sound as the offender covered the child's ears while holding the child's mouth onto his penis. The *muffled* sound of hands over the victim's ears has a tremendous potential for phobic reactions at a later time.

In summary, it will be the activations of the senses, sight, sound, smell, touch, and taste that set patterns for future *knee jerk* phobic reactions. The keys or triggers for the victim's future begin with sensory activation, but they do not end with sensory activation. It is almost impossible to isolate sensory input from the second component of the Situational Perspective. In other words, examining the peripheral elements of the sexually abusive scene would be impossible without ears, noses, and eyes. Sensory activation provides a basic cornerstone and should proceed into the next portion of the examination.

Cruel Cognitions and Coping —The Sexually Abusive Scene

Why Not One

In taking courageous steps toward clear understanding of trauma, old ideas must be discarded. For review and for preparation of this portion in the Trauma Assessment, the reason children must rearrange reality needs examination. It must be remembered that the minimum reason for readjusting reality occurs because of developmental differences between children and adults. As indicated in previous chapters and as echoed throughout this publication, the inequality of children requires adjustments. Even though children generally know that anything between their knees and belly buttons is unmentionable, they do not understand the significance of their 37-year-old aunt performing cunnilingus. Those who question why the victim does not compute like adults should recognize that the first reason of *why not* pertains to *I am not capable.*

Why Not Two

Secondly, sexual abuse is often painful, terrorizing, uncomfortable or, at best, incongruent from children's perspective. In other areas of concern, children are known to respond inappropriately because they lack cognitive preparation. Without this preparation, children may not be able to survive or cope unless reality is rearranged. Not only are children developmentally unable to deal with what is happening, but also in cases where terror, pain, or discomfort occurs, children may be forced to adopt a coping skill to survive the terror.

Pain that is understandable is always more bearable. The broken leg on the four-year-old is painful. The affirmation of the pain, the nurturing that is attached to the pain, and the ability to at least see the bright, white cast will soothe the pain. For sexual victims, pain may not have a beginning or an end. It may be intolerable because children are not capable of understanding. The confusion compounds the pain. Children will need to rearrange pain in their mind, in order to survive.

If sexual abuse is particularly terrorizing, the terror is impacted because the child is unable to have control. If a child is taken into a haunted house, terror will occur. Ghosts, goblins, and secret trap doors will terrorize. The confines of the terror provide understanding and control. Children have the cognition of reality in the haunted house. Children know there is a beginning and an end.

When sexual abuse is terrorizing, the child cannot cope. There is an inability to understand. As an example, for adult survivors of torture during war, one of the most commonly reported elements of trauma is the uncertainty. Prisoners often report being more traumatized by blindfolds or inconsistencies in treatment. It would seem that the *unknown* is particularly traumatizing to adults and certainly, because of developmental delays, is more traumatizing to children.

I am writing this letter to you because I found your views on trauma particularly interesting. As a prisoner of war in Vietnam, I was tortured for two and one-half years. Because of some of my treatment, I have permanent damage and I am forced to change careers. I am finding this *social work stuff* interesting and, therefore, I attended your conference.

I found your comments about the difference between children and adults profound. While I was starving to death, being tortured, humiliated, and ridiculed, I watched fellow prisoners die around me. So much of my survival is related to my ability to detach myself. I could always focus on other things and keep my perspective. Don't let it sound like what they did to me didn't hurt. It's not what I am trying to tell you. The difference in my survival and the death of others was in the way *I thought*. So many of them were like children, believing what our torturers told us, hoping and then being betrayed. It reminded me of your lecture on sexual trauma to children. They were dependent on those people and those bastards loved it.

Keep up the good work.

Sincerely,

Name Withheld. Reprinted by Permission.

Clearly, this soldier describes the difference between children and adults, although he is pointing out childlike characteristics in adults. His ability to detach himself, through a cognitive process, allowed survival to occur. Sadly, the men who perished did not have the cognitive strength. The example accentuates adults, who could not use their adult potential, clearly pointing to limitations in children's potential.

Why Not Three

The third reason children are not able to respond like adults pertains to the issue of dependency. Children in the most miserable family situations experience some inconsistency of positives and negatives. Children who are beaten at home may attend school with a teacher who is loving and nurturing. Sexual abuse is often both humiliating and tender. Conversations during sexual abuse may discuss frightening issues, such as threats that the child will be jailed, while at the same time sexual stimulation may be taking place. The offender may be president of the PTA in the afternoon, while at home during the evening her son is tied up while she performs fellatio. Since children are dependent and do not have a sense of choice in these situations, some resolution must occur.

> How does a child *match mommy performing fellatio and mommy passing out doughnuts at the Halloween party?* The answer is *he doesn't!* The result is *he copes!*

Expanded Horizons — The Sexually Abusive Scene

Clearly understanding a child's needs to rearrange reality or cope, the task emerges to evaluate the information received by the child's computer for the purpose of understanding specific footprints. Without abandoning the senses, the next step is to look out into the sexually abusive scene and evaluate the computer input. What did the child hear and subsequently think? What did the child feel and then understand? What cognitions were founded in the child's sense of taste and smell?

Temperature is, as an example, an immediate sensory stimulation providing a vehicle for footprinting in the future. Hot and cold temperatures, covering or uncovering, or the body being naked can affect the victim's skin responses throughout adulthood. None of the footprints would have been established, however, unless cognitions were taking place in addition to the sensory activation.

> The sexual offender was required to complete a resolution and clarification session as part of the victim's rehabilitation. He described particularly brutal and humiliating sexual behaviors. The seemingly calloused therapist felt queasy. When the offender left the room, the victim carefully explained *but he left the worst part out.* For the victim, nothing brought her more ter-

ror than the way in which she and her sister would be carefully unwrapped by the perpetrator before the sexual abuse. Forced fellatio seemed less important to the victim than the terror of hearing her father get up in the morning, use the restroom, and eventually make his way upstairs into the girls' room after he had milked the cows. The first noise of their father arising would cause both girls to wrap themselves tightly in sheets and blankets. Listening, knowing and waiting terrorized them. But the ultimate discomfort occurred when the girls were being unwrapped and forced to lie naked in a cold bedroom with their legs spread apart. Certainly, other elements within this scene impacted the children. The temperature is not the sole issue of trauma. Likewise, the issue of temperature should not be neglected.

Often, the sense of hearing is activated, but the cognitions keep the memory intact. In this example, the victim puts forth effort to concentrate on more familiar surroundings such as her mother's voice.

Twyla recalls sexual abuse while her diapers were being changed. As a toddler, she had no understanding of what her father was doing. As a 24-year-old, however, her most vivid memory was recalling her mother complaining about the dysfunction of the back burner on the stove in the kitchen.

Twyla can hear her mother shrieking and complaining about her kitchen equipment. As an adult, Twyla feels the intensity of the scene. She feels anxious and frightened, but these feelings are attached to the sense of touch since her father was masturbating next to her vulva. And what does the stimulation of Twyla's vulva bring her in her twenty-fourth year? She hears her mother shrieking about the *goddamn back burner.*

The preceding examples are specifically activated by the senses. More subtle examples may not be activated by a specific sense, but many senses, providing a cognitive awareness that becomes traumatic.

Pizza Profound

Following a presentation at the junior high school on personal safety, Jane approaches the speaker with tears. She reports being sexually abused by her uncle for the past few years. After formalities have taken place, Jane was asked *tell me some of the reasons why you had the courage to tell today.* Jane replied, *because of pizza!*

Jane related how she would be sexually abused by her uncle and after he had dressed her, he would ask if she wanted pizza. With horror, Jane reports, *I told him yes, and I ate it, and I liked it.* In the personal safety program, children had learned that bribery was a common modality used by sex offenders to entice children into keeping secrets. The instructor had explained that the acceptance of these items (pizza) was meaningless as far as responsibility was concerned. During the abuse, Jane's computer had taken in ideations that suggested she was a whore. She had decided to take on the responsibility of the sexual abuse in order to make sense and to survive.

Jane had developed extremely poor self-esteem and self-image. She was already self-abusive. Jane was responsible because she had taken the pizza. Because she was responsible, she found herself unacceptable. The pizza following the sexual abuse seems to be as traumatic as anything that occurred sexually. Because of developmental differences, because of her need to have control, Jane made decisions based on the pizza. This was a profound pizza, indeed!

Before

A methodical approach to examining this portion of the situational perspective would have three basic steps. The first perspective would be to examine what took place before the sexual abuse began. Often one of the most profound questions to ask victims is *what happened 30 minutes before you were sexually abused?* As indicated in the research, terrorizing activities often took place in anticipation of sexual molestation.

I can remember crying on my pillow when I would come home and find the *note*. The note from my mother would be cheerful, telling us that she would be home in a few hours. She always had great notes, informing us that she would bring home something special for dinner or explaining that she was shopping for *someone's birthday*. She always put XXXOOOs at the bottom to signify hugs and kisses. What the note really signified was that my brother would screw me when he got home. I can't even play Tic Tac Toe without thinking of my mother's notes. It wasn't her fault, but it was so sad to wait for him to get there.

During

The second perspective should examine what actually takes place during sexual abuse. Concentrating on many issues other than the sexual behavior should provide important information for understanding the victim's perceptions and eventually the victim's coping skills regarding those perceptions. Such issues as conversations can be deadly for the sexual victim. *If your breasts hadn't grown, I never would have let you touch me like this* could result in profound trauma. The footprint may be *because my breasts grew, I was sexually abused.*

Just Fondled

A classic example of a *just fondling* experience points out the importance of looking at the sexual scene, not necessarily at the sexual behavior. The following patient has been traumatized to the point of receiving a categorization in the PRIMARY SEVERE group. Was it the sexual behavior, *just fondling*, or were other issues responsible for this patient spending very few years without being hospitalized?

Frank would enter Lisa's room each evening while her mother was working. First, Frank would turn the lights on. In the brightly lit bedroom, Lisa saw Frank kneel beside her bed. His hands traveled under the covers and he would fondle her vulva area in a very sensuous and pleasurable manner. Lisa's body betrayed her. She hated the smell of alcohol on Frank's breath and she hated the disgusting knowledge that this behavior was unacceptable. She hated waiting for him to come into the room, knowing that he would be there each time her mother was away. Yet the touching of Lisa's clitoris was pleasurable.

Unbeknownst to Lisa, Frank would also masturbate himself to orgasm. Lisa could not see Frank touching himself and therefore her visual perceptions concluded that her father was *giving her pleasure*. When Frank ejaculated and composed himself, he would look at Lisa and say, *Do you want me to stop?* Lisa reports that she would nod, *yes*, and Frank would state, *That's a good girl. It's about time you told me to stop.*

It should be noted that Frank never asked Lisa if he could *start* and Lisa had no idea that Frank was giving himself sexual pleasure. If the sexually abusive scene is evaluated, Lisa is in control. Frank's closing comments, congratulating Lisa on stopping the disgusting behavior, put the final touches on Lisa being forced to compute that she was responsible for what has happened.

Just Say No!

Becky, on the other hand, was sexually abused for approximately a three-year period. As she became more developmentally able to understand what was happening, she contemplated resistance. Finally, her father made the error of molesting her when she was frustrated. Becky shouted at her father and resisted for the first time. Her father's cool response congratulated her as he said, *It's about time you said no. I would have stopped any time you would have wanted me to.*

Unbeknownst to Becky, this was a consistent pattern for her father. He molested each of his daughters until they resisted. Then he would begin molesting the next oldest child.

Without the knowledge of her father's behavioral pattern, Becky was left with total responsibility for three years of abuse. In therapy, she tearfully stated, *If I only would have said no sooner!*

Where Are You?

As the second modality examines the sexually abusive scene, consideration should also be made to influential peripheral issues. The sexual behavior is one component, and what is happening between the offender and the victim is another component, but extraneous events occurring around the sexual abuse may also provide an important component in the victim's perceptions.

Lana would be fondled in her crotch area and on her breasts in the living room. This behavior would occur on the outside of her clothing. Lana's mother was usually around the corner in the kitchen cooking dinner for the family. Consistently, Lana's brother would begin a conversation with the mother. Usually the conversation would contain elements of flattery or positive feedback toward the mother. Often, Lana's offender would inquire about something that was important to Lana's mother. Lana heard her mother's response in positive terms. Lana's mother seemed delighted by the fact that her son, an adolescent who tended to be quite selfish and belligerent, was actually paying attention

and seemed to be interested in something other than himself.

The fact that Lana's mother was so near the abuse and seemed to be verbally involved with the abuse provided a silent affirmation of her acknowledgment. On one hand, Lana was terrified that her mother would walk around the corner and see what was happening. Lana was also traumatized by the fact that her mother might be condoning the abusive behavior. Most importantly, attached to the sexually abusive scene for Lana is her mother's voice of harmony and pleasure. As an adult, Lana cognitively believes her mother was not aware of the abuse and did not condone it. Unfortunately, Lana spent her remaining 12 years at home believing her mother was a *co-perpetrator*. The damage to the mother/daughter relationship may never be repaired.

God Save The . . .

Another example of how peripheral elements can be traumatizing occurs when the victim must save, or protect another individual.

Andrew was forced to lie down next to the babysitter for bedtime stories. Andrew's younger brother would lie next to the babysitter on her right side, while Andrew laid on the left. The female baby-sitter forced each boy to hold one side of the book while she read Dr. Suess or Snow White. Her hands would grope for Andrew's penis and she fondled him throughout the entire bedtime story. For Andrew, many feelings provided information for his computer. *If I let her do this to me, maybe she won't touch Danny* or *Does Danny know I am doing it, too?* or *I should be stopping this from happening.*

Andrew does not know if his brother is being sexually abused. Whether Danny is being abused is not as significant as the damage to Andrew worrying about his brother. Different than Lana's mother, Danny does not provide an affirmation or acceptance of the abuse. What Danny does provide is the trauma of neglected responsibility on the part of Andrew. He is not protecting his brother. Also, he may be showing his brother that he is disgusting.

And After

The third perspective in examining the sexually abusive scene raises questions about the information provided to the child's computer following the incident. Children connect extraneous issues to the sexual abuse, which are often not connected. Because of the cognitive limitations of children, events completely unrelated to sexual contact may impact the child regardless of the actual connection.

Robin was walking home from school and a family friend gave her a ride. Instead of taking Robin home, he drove to the state park where he attempted to rape Robin. Although she resisted actual penetration, it was nonetheless a very humiliating experience. Eventually, the family friend dropped Robin off several blocks from her home.

Robin ran home in a state of panic. She was hoping to find the comfort of her parents, but instead found an irate father and a hysterical mother. *Where have you been?* Robin, a usually obedient child, was horrified at her parents' anger. Even more trauma occurred when Robin's father pulled her pants down and spanked her in the living room.

Robin's abuse by the perpetrator was traumatic, but because of other issues discovered in the Trauma Assessment, her trauma was inconsistent. The relationship perspective would suggest that the perpetrator was not important to Robin and trauma was lessened. The developmental perspective would suggest that at age eleven, Robin was at least aware of the significance of his sexual behaviors, which may also be helpful. Unfortunately, at age eleven, Robin was also very concerned about her body and her sexual development. Being disrobed in the living room for a spanking seemed to be an ultimate humiliation. Robin has been more traumatized by her father's behavior than the behavior of the perpetrator. Had the Trauma Assessment focused only on the sexually abusive scene, this level of trauma would have escaped.

Post Trauma

Post-disclosure issues are extremely important and will be the final phase of the Situational Perspective. The *big picture* will discuss the family scene and dynamics of the child's life in order to determine suffering. Post-disclosure issues are important within this far reaching area, but care must be given to recognize that many patients suffer without a disclosure.

Robin certainly was unable to tell her father about his friend's abuse. Robin's father was outraged at her tardiness and chose to humiliate her. Certainly, trauma occurred following the abuse, but not necessarily as a post-disclosure issue. The reason for withholding disclosure is the most important consideration.

In summary, the sexually abusive *SCENE* is examined from three components. The first step is to examine what happens before the sexual abuse takes place. The second step examines the actual scene in order to understand input into the child's computer. Finally, *post-abuse* elements need consideration. Whether or not disclosure has occurred is not as important as what takes place in the child's mind thinking about disclosure. Children cannot separate and isolate. They gather percep-

tions as they enter the abusive scene. They perceive issues during the abuse and they pack their baggage to carry them, from the abuse into a typically insensitive situation.

The Big Picture — The Situation

Beyond the actual sexual abuse arena, a larger picture of the family, the atmosphere, and the world needs consideration for input into the child's computer. Not only do children make computations according to what is available, but later in childhood perceptions often change and reality is rearranged. The old software is replaced. This portion of the Situational Perspective examines the dynamics within the family and the community and requires a return to the attitudes and feelings of the child in childhood. The new, rearranged realities of adulthood are more cognitive than the affective considerations of the victim during the abuse.

Laundry List

If a laundry list of issues pertinent to this portion of the situational perspective is prepared, the following items would be indicated.

- Family Finances
- Family Vocational Issues
- Family Health (mental, physical)
- Family Substance Abuse Issues
- Family Communication

- Family Disciplines Systems
- Family Mobility
- Family Morality (religion and values)
- Family's Relationship With Community
- Post-Disclosure Issues

These issues go beyond the *thirty minute relief period* following each sexually abusive scenario. Certainly, what happens immediately following sexual abuse is important in understanding the first impact on the child's computer access. The ongoing process of the family, however, is even more important as the child continues to cope and, most importantly, as the child continues to develop. A sexual victim may become much more cognizant of the realities of abuse as the years have passed. Unfortunately, the victim may also be living in a family situation that completely discourages reporting and discourages victim rehabilitation. Subtly, and perhaps unintentionally, families may be traumatizing victims.

The health or lack of health of a parent, the family's financial situation, family mobility or issues relating to the family's involvement in community provide important information to the victim. A sexual crime in one family may result in a completely different response in another family. Children are dependent upon their families and that dependency intensifies the importance of family dynamics as the victim attempts to make sense of the abuse. Leigh's case is a classic example of how an original *family financial problem* becomes the foundation for severe trauma.

Dollars and Sense

Leigh's father is in an accident and faces a year of recuperation. His hospital bed is in the living room. The once middle class family is financially squeezed. The entire family is forced to sacrifice. Most perplexing to Leigh is the cancellation of her preschool program. Leigh's mother is forced to find other, more financially acceptable babysitting arrangements. Leigh's aunt and uncle volunteer to babysit for a small fee. Leigh was a bright child who enjoyed the daycare interaction. She is saddened by the change in plans.

Each day Leigh is dropped off at her aunt's and picked up each evening. Although her father's condition improves and the family is recovering, Leigh's status deteriorates. Within eighteen months, a very bright, contented child is now depressed, hostile and demonstrating erratic behavior. Most significantly, Leigh seems to detest her parents and her family. Her behavior deteriorates to the point where a decision is made to postpone her entrance into the first grade. Psychologists are baffled since all testing exercises (from neurological to academic) reveal nothing. Halfway through the first grade year, Leigh is allowed to enter school. Changes occur. Leigh appears to function very well within the academic realm and, in fact, school becomes her only source of success. At home, Leigh remains belligerent, acting out, and abusive. At school, her teachers report an acquiescent, studious, successful child.

Generally, this pattern continues throughout grade school. It is not until the fifth grade that Leigh's uncle is arrested for sexual abuse of other children his wife babysat. Investigation revealed that Leigh was also sexually abused during the eighteen month period while her father was recuperating. It is also suggested that she may have been abused several times during the first and second grade. Although the sexual abuse apparently stopped due to lack of accessibility, Leigh continued to be traumatized in the manner dictated by her uncle and suffered by her parents. In this example, the entire environment for the sexually abusive family has tremendous impact on the victim.

During the sexual abuse, Leigh's uncle took her into his shop in the basement and molested her. The abuse was painful and humiliating. Leigh's uncle seemed to be a rather sadistic person who enjoyed meticulous and complicated preparations for the abuse which Leigh was forced to endure. For Leigh, her uncle's behaviors seemed to be *tasks*, but most damaging were her uncle's statements, which fit perfectly into the family scenario.

Leigh's uncle told her before, during, and following the sexual abuse *Your parents are paying me to do this*. Most significantly, Leigh's uncle made her watch the exchange of money each Friday night in the kitchen. For adults, the exchange of money was payment for babysitting. For Leigh, her parents were paying for her torture.

The entire financial situation of Leigh's family allowed her to make sense of what her uncle was saying. Tremendous resentment resulted toward Leigh's parents. Leigh chose to mold coping skills of anger toward her parents. The resentment did not stop the sexual abuse, but was fortified by each statement or activity in the family regarding financial issues. Leigh observed the family being deprived of cable television, she saw the family make changes from the luxury of Fruit Loops to inexpensive hot cereal. She saw family picnics on the weekend substituted with total exhaustion from Leigh's mother who was forced to take on an extra job. In Leigh's mind, the financial situation was real and her parents were paying for something dreadful. Additionally, the family taught the children to *be brave and sacrifice*. Since Leigh was the youngest in the family, she lived with several *pseudo* parents who continued to give her messages about frugality and sacrifice.

Can Leigh's attitude toward her parents, after five years of hate, be repaired? Sadly, when the sexual abuse was discovered, no one examined the entire family dynamics. The sexual abuse behavior provided information to therapists for treatment planning. Leigh entered into a generic program. Now, her parents were able to pay for treatment to correct something that, in Leigh's mind, they had *paid* for originally. The damage did not stop for Leigh, but continued to fester throughout adolescence. No one had asked about the uncle's conversations nor about Leigh's following perceptions. By the time Leigh reached the *uncomfortable* stage of development, she was an acting out, promiscuous, angry teenager. In Leigh's thirty-fifth year, she enters therapy due to residual effects of unresolved anger. The trauma to Leigh could have been found in the situational portion of the Trauma Assessment. Certainly, the damage caused between Leigh's abuse and the discovery of the abuse was profound, but opportunities for resolution and undoing of tremendous damage between Leigh and her parents existed, but was ignored.

The Sobering Effects of Sobriety

Kristen and Kathy are two adolescent females being sexually abused by their father. Mother is alcoholic and has been sober for two years. Father im-

plies knowledge to the girls of their mother's sexual promiscuity when she is drinking. Father reminds Kristen and Kathy of the traumatic effects of mother being absent from home for long periods of time. In what appears to be *family counsel*, the girls' father portrays mother as an individual who needs to keep her sexual arousal under control at all times. Should mother become *ignited*, father relates, the family becomes vulnerable.

The girls become partners of their father in order to take care of their mother. Father continues to perpetuate the vicious cycle by placing six-packs of beer in the refrigerator even though he does not drink. He reports during one family meeting, *It is important to tempt your mother so that she can continue to know she is being strong.*

Kathy and Kristen are constantly reminded of the precious nature of their mother's sobriety. The children have become caretakers in their symbiotic relationship. None of this could have happened without specific issues within the family framework.

Sex offenders are quite clever individuals who recognize the need to control children in order to protect secrets. The deadly nature of that hold is often where trauma occurs. Family dynamics and specific situations often provide the tools to be used by the perpetrator.

Adoption of Trauma

Diedra is being sexually abused by her father during the *unaware* stage of development. Diedra cooperates until she enters the second grade. Accidentally, Diedra reports her involvement with her father. The offender is an important person in the community and church. The situation is handled informally through the counseling department of the large corporation where the offender is employed. In three sessions, the problem has been alleviated. At age eleven, Diedra's father again abuses her.

Different during this abuse is Diedra's continuing cognitive development. Additionally, the family is anticipating or attempting to adopt a handicapped child. Jolene has Downs Syndrome and many complications. The family adores Jolene and the adoption will be final once she has lived in their household for one year. Due to her medical complications, Jolene continues to be rushed to the hospital and eventually returned to her doctors in a nearby city. Jolene is usually gone from the home four to six weeks before she has rehabilitated, thus foiling the opportunities to complete the adoption.

The sexual abuse of Diedra continues because she is aware that if she should report, the adoption would fail. *I knew they checked everything carefully at the adoption agency. I also knew my mom told me not to tell about what my father did when I was in the second grade or we wouldn't get to keep Jolene. She didn't say what to do about the abuse that was happening now!* By the time Jolene is three and one-half, she is finally an official member of the family. The sexual abuse of Diedra has escalated and Diedra now feels *safe* to tell. Diedra's report is met with disbelief. The family scolds her for seeking attention. She is accused of being jealous of Jolene and making a similar claim to what had happened in the second grade. As Diedra sacrificed herself for Jolene, Jolene now becomes the reason Diedra is emotionally and psychologically expelled from the family.

Outside Home Sweet Home

Some effort needs to be made in the situational portion of the Trauma Assessment to examine the dynamics of trauma outside the family. It is often educational endeavors (as mentioned in Chapter Nine) that may traumatize victims. Stepping from the family environment into the child's world is important in assessing additional information used to formulate footprints.

An example of this expanded perspective of the victim's world is demonstrated in education.

Steven was sexually abused by the Boy Scout Leader who was an obsessive pedophile. Before Steven was able to understand what was happening, he had engaged in many of these activities over a long period of time. On occasion, Steven viewed himself as a partner.

Questions should be raised regarding how Steven will respond in his adolescence high school class on the topic venereal disease, especially AIDS. Is this a neglected issue as children are allowed to proceed through educational years learning of the horrors of venereal disease? How will Steven feel sitting in his high school classroom where AIDS is discussed and where he also learns that the homes of children who have AIDS are burned to the ground by a society that abhors homosexuality? Certainly, the body image of Steven is impaired and his entire attitude about sexuality may be traumatized as he learns how the rest of his world views his body contamination.

Post-Disclosure Issues

Perhaps most glaring in the situational portion of the Trauma Assessment are post-disclosure components. What happens to the child who tells about sexual abuse? The relationship perspective of the Trauma Assessment examines people, relationships, and the identification of the perpetrator and the victim. The developmental perspective examines the cultivation of sexual issues over the child's developmental span. Neither of those two perspectives would stand isolated without examination of post-disclosure issues. Would the relationship triangle change regarding disclosure or lack of disclosure? Would developmental issues and the potential for cultivating negative ideations regarding such issues as body image be more profound according to disclosure? The answer is Yes! Although it is important in the Trauma Assessment to be clear and to isolate issues, obviously no component of the Trauma Assessment stands alone. Post-disclosure issues are extremely important not only in the situational part of the Trauma Assessment, but throughout the entire examination.

In the case of Diedra, she anticipated disclosure and then reported. Would Diedra have survived better had she withheld the report? Empathic professionals shout NO! The reality may be that Diedra might have suffered less if she had withheld the report. Her contemplations regarding reporting and her subsequent report had a profound effect on Diedra's level of trauma.

Waiting Room Only

I remember the door opening and my fourth mother walked in the room. For the fourth time, I had been adopted and for the fourth time, someone in the family abused me. For the fourth time, I was caught.

I can't remember exactly what happened except that I was scolded and told to go to bed. I don't remember anything happening that night, except the next morning she came back to the room. She told me to get dressed and took me to the Welfare Office. As an adult, I recognize that this may have been hard on her and perhaps it was hard on my caseworker since this was the fourth time it had happened. I sat in the waiting room for six hours. No one really talked to me and no one cared whether I had something to eat or whether I was frightened. I saw men coming in and out with police uniforms, badges, and guns. I watched parents come in and scream at the receptionist, and I watched other children be reunited in the waiting room with their lost parents. Some cried and kissed, while some cussed. Nothing much happened. After six hours, they came out to get me and a new caseworker took me by the hand. I never saw my fourth mother again nor my fourth perpetrator. I remember I passed out in the parking lot and the caseworker slapped me for being disobedient. After she put me in her car, she took me to the grocery store and made me wait while she bought groceries for her family. The car was full with groceries while I sat quiet. I could smell luxury items of potato chips and cinnamon rolls. I hadn't eaten for nearly twenty hours. After she had picked up her son from Boy Scouts, she took me to my fifth mother and eventually my fifth perpetrator.

The System As Perpetrator (Revisited)

Post-disclosure issues seem profound, especially concerning the system of prosecution, criminality, and case work. There are situations, however, where disclosure occurs but trauma is reserved for family dynamics.

Pammy Jo becomes angry with her father. He is critical because she has not dusted properly. She decides to run away. On Sunday morning, she leaves the house, taking refuge with a favorite aunt. Aunt Bertha inquires and eventually learns that Pammy Jo is being sexually abused by her stepfather. Hoping mother will be supportive, Aunt Bertha contacts her sister. Pammy Jo's mother is furious, accuses Pammy of lying, and subsequently brings her home. Pammy Jo is forced to disrobe in the living room after her mother has confronted the *innocent perpetrator. In pelvic exam style,* Pammy Jo is examined by her mother and father. She is told that she is obviously lying (although Pammy Jo never discussed intercourse) and she is threatened within an inch of her life.

Unfortunately, Aunt Bertha made a report to Law Enforcement and a legal investigation took place. Eventually, Pammy Jo was removed from the home and eventually deserted by her parents. It was not until after criminal conviction of the perpetrator that the case was *resolved or sort of resolved*. Pammy Jo never regained her status in the family and she will always remember the degradation of her post-disclosure.

Sounds of Silence — So What Does All This Mean?

The sensory activation, the sexually abusive scene, and finally the *whole* situation of the child, collectively provides information for the construction of footprints. If it is important to examine each of these components, what conclusions can be drawn?

As indicated previously, victims cannot survive unless they rearrange reality. They cannot maintain under the same cognitive framework as adults and they will constantly seek some sense of control and order. The result of the situational perspective is not necessarily limited to phobic reactions, but to the development of these coping skills or footprints.

Some coping skills have already been mentioned, especially in the research. For the purposes of review, a variety of footprints or coping skills will be discussed.

Exit Memory — Amnesia

Sexual victims who are placed in the severely traumatizing scenarios gather information and compute *this is bad*. Nearly every computation during sexual abuse begins with some form of

this is bad or this feels bad. The footprint of amnesia occurs when the victim resolves by stating, *this is bad, so I won't remember.*

Someone Else, Please — Dissociation

The second component of this footprint relates to dissociation. The first initial computation is made regarding *badness* and then a decision to be removed from the memory. For unknown reasons, amnesia does not appear to be an option. Changing the personality or splitting away may be the only available survival technique. Dissociation is deadly for victims at a later time, but certainly understandable as a child's way to solve the problem. An extremely high percentage of those patients with dissociative disorders have suffered severe childhood sexual abuse. When the situation becomes absolutely unbearable, victims must remove themselves and *someone else* takes over.

If You Can't Beat 'em, Join 'em — Self Abuse or Abuse Responsive

There are two coping skills directly portrayed by an abusive response. When children are sexually abused, they may choose between two abusive roles. As indicated previously, it is not uncommon for victims to indicate *this is bad, so I will feel bad* and, thus, self-abusive cycles develop. Two opposite responses occur to the abusive issue.

One rather unattractive footprint established by victims is the *ABUSIVE* footprint. The victim clearly recognizes *this is bad* and adopts the profile of *I will be bad*. Unfortunately, the victim becomes abusive to others and actually quite self-protective. The victim takes on the role of the perpetrator directly or indirectly.

In other cases, the victim becomes self-abusive. *This is bad, so I will be bad,* results in drug and alcohol abuse, failure in school, criminal behavior, etc. The victim becomes the perpetrator of self and subsequent revictimization results.

The Really Big R — Obsessive Guilt, Responsibility Avoidance

Through information given to the victim through sexual abuse, the raging debate over responsibility emerges. In order to survive, victims often accept responsibility for what is happening in order to have control. This may be somewhat more subtle than *this is bad, so I will be bad* because the victim finds peace in accepting responsibility. The footprint occurs as the victim becomes hyper-vigilant in responsibility. The result is an obsessive-compulsive, neurotically responsible victim. The victim is obsessed with responsibility. The victim will appear to take on the world. Just as an anorexic patient gains control by food intake, this patient develops a footprint of being totally responsible for not only the abuse, but also perhaps the weather.

Reversible Responsibility

On the opposite end of the responsibility spectrum is the footprint from the same computer printout, but with different responses (reverse responsibility). *I am responsible; therefore, I will never be responsible again.* In retaliation against the horrors of abuse, the victim chooses a footprint of irresponsibility. The cultivation of the footprint may be a rejection of the victim's responsibility in any situation. The risk in attempting to be responsible in any other way is too much for the victim. The victim feels safe in being irresponsible since perhaps the first and only situation where the victim was responsible resulted in sexual abuse.

Shhhhhh . . . Footprints of Secrecy — Obsessive Secrecy, Privacy Avoidance

Another example of footprints relates to the issue of secrecy. Some victims who have been robbed of privacy and enshrouded in secrecy may adopt the footprint of secrecy in an obsessive manner. Even when being straightforward would be helpful to the victim, in adulthood, secrecy remains. The victim may not be able to share on any personal level and may find others' attempts to engage the victim in trusting relationships as offensive. This may affect the victim's ability to be a productive employee since a victim who adopted this footprint would withhold even information that may enhance communication in the work place.

On the opposite end of the secrecy continuum are those individuals who have been traumatized by the lack of privacy and, therefore, adopt the footprint of no privacy. If risks of privacy are avoided, trauma will be avoided. This victim emerges with no boundaries whatsoever. Nothing is sacred. The milkman may learn of the victim's ovulation cycle if he is not careful.

Soap Opera Syndrome/Obsessive Affective Focus, Affective Avoidance

Some victims feel badly about what has happened and establish a footprint in the opposite direction. Affective Avoidance computes to *this feels bad, so I won't feel*. The opposite is the obsessive affective focus; the victim states, *this feels bad, so I will control by feeling badly about everything*. This is entitled the Soap Opera Syndrome due to the manifestation of the victim feeding upon the feelings of others. In this instance, the victim becomes obsessed with the misery and suffering of other people. It is as though the victim has shut off personal feelings and becomes soothed only through the feelings of others.

A very unfeeling victim may find solace or comfort in feeding upon the sorrow and pain of others. Since the victim was unable to feel and survived by dissociating from feeling, in later years the victim may be drawn toward feelings. The footprint is, *I can't feel for myself, so I will feel for you*. This victim would appear to be a *Teflon Person* with emotions, sorrow and misery seeming to slide off without sticking.

There is a syndrome cited in psychological literature regarding individuals who feed upon the misery of themselves or their children. Cases have been cited where parents actually sabotage medical treatment of children in order to present themselves as dedicated parents, sorrowful in regards to their children's medical condition. In this case, the sexual victim is obsessed with the sickness, sorrow, and misery of others, even to the point of being homicidal.

There are times when the female non-offending parent (who has a high potential for being a sexual victim) may have adopted this footprint in childhood as a result of her abuse. If she decided as a way to survive her own abuse, *This feels bad, therefore, I won't feel*, it may be understandable why she is cold, insensitive and uncaring to her daughter or son who has recently reported sexual abuse. Not only may this non-offending, but sometimes offensive, mother avoid being empathic, but she may thrive on her children's abuse.

> Evelyn was sexually abused in childhood by seven different offenders. Two of her perpetrators' crimes resulted in sensational trials. Evelyn was extremely abused by the system and by her family in post-disclosure issues.

> In adulthood, Evelyn's children have been sexually abused by all four of Evelyn's husbands! A pattern seems to emerge with Evelyn as she behaves in this dramatization.

> An attractive gentleman asks if she knows the location of paper plates in the

supermarket. In six minutes, Evelyn has introduced herself, discussed her sexual abuse, introduced her children, provided a profile of her children's perpetrators, and asked this bewildered gentlemen if he would care to see the children's gynecological exam records.

Unfortunately, Evelyn seems to thrive not only on her own abuse, but on the abuse of her children. She has tremendous needs for intensity and seems to have these needs fulfilled by her children's abuse. Before her daughters would graduate from high school, two more perpetrators would come into their lives.

Additionally, there seems to be a response to dissociation in this footprint. Rather than being able to dissociate and develop a personality, this person recognizes the *badness* and decides to dissociate feelings. If the victim is forced into extremely ritualistic, brutal, or terrorizing experiences, screaming, yelling, or protesting is not allowed. Stifling of emotions during sexual abuse may lay a foundation for continued stifling of emotions.

Barbara has been diagnosed as having a dissociative disorder. She endured many years of ritualistic abuse by teachers in a small, rural community. Barbara's *personalities* do not seem to have names or ages. They seem to be categorized according to the emotions Barbara feels. As an adult, Barbara has

a *personality* that is Barbara's age, but is her source of love. She has the ability to nurture, to be soft and sensitive. Unfortunately, this face of Barbara has no other emotion. She is dreadfully abused in this stage of her personality.

Another face or personality of Barbara is her anger. She is extremely violent, controlling, and outrageous. This face of Barbara is the same age, has the same name, but like the preceding Barbara, has only one emotion, that of anger.

The continuum of emotions is varied, but all of Barbara's emotions are separate. She can only operate from one emotional strata at a time. There is no incorporation of a total person for Barbara. Her life is in shambles due to her lack of balance. While Barbara lay immersed in animal blood, she did not scream or express emotion. She was forced to postpone her feelings. In order to live, Barbara needed to make nice tidy packages of feelings. She soothed herself during the abuse by organizing and categorizing all emotions. The outrage she felt was placed into another box to be used at another time. Her feelings of betrayal were also categorized and scheduled for another day.

Tremendous fear pervades Barbara at the prospect of opening all of her boxes at the same time. The only way Barbara could survive was to categorize and eventually control. Being totally out of control, Barbara was forced to establish a footprint of affective avoidance.

Helpless Hurts — Obsessive Helplessness, Obsessive Aggression

Another example of footprinting occurs as a result of feeling helpless. Some sexual victims, in recognizing their sense of helplessness, decide to control or cope by becoming eternally helpless. The adaptation of this footprint evolves to create a coping skill of smoothing over situations by being inactive, helpless, and without risk.

Betrayal is extremely important to the trauma suffered by victims. When expectations of an individual are elevated, there is tremendous betrayal when sexual abuse occurs. The incongruency of sexual abuse between a positive person and a negative behavior may render victims absolutely helpless and hopeless. The risk was taken to trust and the trust was betrayed. The victim becomes helpless and chooses to never risk again. The footprint is manifested in a pattern of sabotaging relationships through a very passive approach. The victim may fail in what appears to be a purposeful pattern, but in reality, it is simply a coping skill by being helpless and avoiding taking risks. Through passivity and helplessness, the victim finds consistency and control.

On the other end of the helpless spectrum is the footprint of power. In this case, the victim says, *I was helpless and, therefore, I will take total control in order to survive.* The coping skill is one of aggression. In some instances, the control will be more internal, such as with eating disorders, abstinence from relationships, etc. In other situations, the footprint is the development of a controlling, aggressive individual.

Symbiosis Spectrum — To Trauma Bonding

Symbiosis is the process of feeding upon one another. In the case of sexual abuse, a symbiotic relationship develops when the role between parents and children is undefined and the boundaries have dissolved. The footprint of symbiosis may be a total dedication to the perpetrator, as described in Chapter Seven. Trauma bonding may occur because the victim has taken on the protection of the perpetrator. Total dedication occurs. The perpetrator who may have been brutal, dehumanizing, and humiliating to the victim is now a saint to be worshiped. This footprint evolves from the eternal hope of the victim that somehow if the victim takes responsibility, the suffering will stop.

On the opposite end of the symbiosis perspective is the victim who comes under the power of the perpetrator. Different than being in a symbiotic relationship and in dedication to the perpetrator, this footprint evolves overtly as a campaign against the perpetrator, but covertly the victim is still in a punishing modality. The victim may continue to live in the same town as the perpetrator or the victim may withhold success based on the perpetrator's wishes. A son who was abused by his father, as an example, refuses to use his engineering degree because his perpetrator contributed money to the college fund. The male victim finds some sense of peace in knowing that the perpetrator has *NOT WON*. On the other hand, the question can be raised regarding who is actually suffering.

From Terror to Terror Terrified

When victims are terrorized, it is possible to establish a footprint revolving around terror. On one end of the spectrum, the victim who may have been terrorized feels that consistency is the only survival option. The inconsistency in the time period between terror and peace comes unbearable. The victim learns that when peace happens, the overriding feeling of impending terror makes peace unbearable. A constant state of intensity or terror is better than feeling peace, but knowing that terror is about to occur. Intellectually, the victim may be seeking peace, love, and kindness, but affectively the victim is drawn toward terror so that the periods of peace are not shattered by terror.

On the other end of the terrorizing spectrum the victim copes with terror by thriving on terror. The victim finds consistency in becoming very much like the sexual abuse situation or like the perpetrator. Through exerting terror and fear on others, the victim finds consistency and safety. Sadly, this approach is commonly adopted by male victims. There is an en-

couragement in males' sociological training to become strong, controlling, and aggressive. The potential for the male victim to adopt terror as a coping skill may be common.

Perfect Plus or Minus

Another example of a coping skill is the victim's tendency toward the cleansing process. As the victim computes, *this is bad, I will make up for it*, the available footprint is obsessive-compulsive perfection. It is important to note that this is an external process, not internal. The victim does not receive excellent grades, get accepted into medical school, or take on neighborhood projects for the benefit of self or community. The victim is attempting to cleanse the abuse away. *Maybe if I just do more or become better or . . .*

An off-shoot of the obsessive-compulsive footprint is the obsessive-compulsive failure. Very similar to the footprint of *this is bad, so I will be bad* is the person who becomes obsessed with failure. The footprint may be manifested in less overt ways as compared to drug and alcohol abuse or criminal behavior. This coping mechanism will result in the individual carrying his failure slips of junior high eighth grade science class in his wallet as an adult. A female victim may delight in discussing her burnt brownies in the fourth grade baked food sale contest. Another victim may lament how she was always chosen last for the physical education volleyball teams. Although this footprint may be manifested in other forms or in combination with other footprints, the obsession with failure is nonetheless an adaptation or footprint for sexual victims.

The footprints are a result of the victim's computation. Footprints cultivated by victims do not necessarily come in these nice, tidy packages. Footprints may be similar to, or a combination of, these examples. Evaluation and categorization of the victim's FOOTPRINTS is not for the purpose of satisfying professionals as to whether as the proper diagnosis occurs, but for understanding the victim's future.

INTIMATE INQUIRIES

What are the tools for the Trauma Assessment? How can this delicate subject emerge without revictimization of the patient? And, if distorted cognitions are common for sexual victims, how valuable is an assessment based on the perceptions of those traumatized? What inquiries can be made of this most intimate pain?

Process Not Product

The Trauma Assessment begins with inquiries of the most intimate nature. Feelings, behaviors, acknowledgments, attitudes of the victim need examination. The Trauma Assessment is not a purely scientific, standardized test to determine levels of trauma consistent with a slide rule or calculator. The Trauma Assessment is an inquiry of the patient's most intimate, but often confused, thoughts. The purpose is to find the road map to recovery. Most commonly, victims are blinded by their pain as far as etiology is concerned. The Trauma Assessment searches for cause and

points toward the future. The Trauma Assessment is a process not a product, and the process has many purposes.

As previously discussed, sexual victims are constantly looking forward, looking backward, and looking around, making assumptions that result in tremendous pain. For the older patient, tremendous denial systems and distorted cognitions have become the cornerstone of survival. The Trauma Assessment will provide a map for recovery after those distorted cognitions and denial systems have been revealed. The victim will be able to travel the road back to the pain with a guided hand. The

Trauma Assessment is a process that provides that first painful step toward treatment.

The Trauma Assessment is, in fact, therapy, because of the *process*. Many victims who have developed an obsessive-compulsive perfectionist footprint will be much more interested in a product. *Yes, let's get this Trauma Assessment done and get on with this.* The coping skill is a distraction to avoid the pain. Without care, the Trauma Assessment could become a vehicle to avoid resolution by hurrying quickly toward a product. On the other hand, the Trauma Assessment can become a vehicle with which the victim returns to the scene, returns to the trauma and, with guidance and protection, emerges whole.

Additionally, many victims have developed coping skills of avoiding self-preservation or avoiding trauma. Victims may have spent their entire lives avoiding feelings and emotions. The residual effects of that avoidance brings the patient to therapy. The footprints of avoidance may make the patient resistent to a Trauma Assessment. With guidance, the Trauma Assessment will take the victim through a journey back to the pain, but, for the first time, the journey will be purposeful and hopefully productive.

Caution

A caution should be exerted in first approaching the Trauma Assessment. In most testing situations within the subjective realm, the patient's responses are noted and taken at face value. This may be a disastrous clinical approach when conducting a Trauma Assessment. Distorted cognitions and resulting footprints do not disappear in the safety of a therapeutic intervention. Information from the victim is the most important information, but perhaps not at a superficial level. Victims are continuing to suffer from distorted views and it will be important to conduct the Trauma Assessment with not only the victim's information, but also with a diagnosis of the victim's ability to provide that information.

FROM TAMARA: *My mother did the best she could. She was a victim herself and there was no way she could have protected the children in the family. I don't blame her and I don't view her as being responsible.*

Notations could be made that the patient has healed, especially concerning the mother/daughter relationship. Tremendous errors may occur, however, if this statement is taken at face value. Tamara may demonstrate an extreme emotional response and may have abandoned her own children as they have been sexually abused. She may struggle with night terrors regarding homicidal ideations toward her mother. She may also be showing tremendous signs of trauma bonding with her mother that are unclear to her at the present time.

I couldn't believe what was happening to me. I really didn't hate him, but I hated her. All I wanted was her to love me during the day and, at night, I dreamed about cutting out her tongue. Blood would spurt all over me and I just laughed at her. I was forced to be the dutiful child, even at 45 years of age. I couldn't believe what power she had over me.

It is very difficult for someone who has been robbed of childhood to understand normal or acceptable childhood. This same person who has limited understanding of the way it should be for children will be asked questions about attitudes and feelings regarding normal childhood. Questions will be raised, in the Trauma Assessment, regarding families, normal sexual development, healthy responses to tragedy, possible limitations, and hopes for the future. For someone who was forced to rearrange reality, personal perceptions may be a traitor to rehabilitation.

This is not to suggest that the victim's responses are unimportant. The victim is the primary reason the Trauma Assessment is conducted. A combination of both the victim's responses and the victim's symptomology will provide important information for Trauma Assessment diagnosis.

Listen, Listen, Listen

In order to carefully diagnose and disseminate information provided from an individual with distorted views, the skill of listening will be extremely important. Not only will the victim's responses be important, but cataloging the victim's statements and assessing the changes in the victim's statements will be extremely important. The Trauma Assessment will contain a collection of information to be documented and *then* diagnosed. Conclusions will need to be drawn from a variety of modalities. Disseminating information received from the parent will require a different kind of listening.

Clarity, Please

The Trauma Assessment is purposeful in many ways. In most cases, the Trauma Assessment will be presented to the victim, the victim's parents, or to other professionals who may be providing intervention and treatment. The purpose of the Trauma Assessment is to clarify the pain and provide a road map to recovery. The Trauma Assessment should provide that clarity. An excellent assessment of trauma could be made without writing a Trauma Assessment. Unfortunately, clinical impressions are not profound for the victim, nor for the victim's parents. Case consultation by correspondence or telephone also lacks the clarity needed for victim recovery. Even though clinical understanding has taken place, the victim or the victim's family needs to see, to feel, to understand and clarify the pain.

The clarity of the Trauma Assessment is extremely important. In most cases, Trauma Assessments will be written in what can fondly be described as *psycho babble*. Psycho babble is professional jargon. Terms such as *cognitive distortions* and *phobic reactions* are understood for processing, but should also be important for others reading the Trauma Assessment. The importance of making the Trauma Assessment *official* must be understood.

Officiality

In most cases, pain suffered by victims is personal, intense, intimate, and extremely burdensome for even the smallest child. There is a tremendous sense that somehow what has happened to the victim is unimportant or, at the very best, insignificant. The first step in the Trauma Assessment is to make the victim's suffering important, profound, official.

A Utopian world would exist if each time a child was inappropriately touched, a felony conviction of the perpetrator would magically occur and the victim would be honored and idolized in hero fashion. Obviously, this is not the case and many patients involved in a clinical Trauma Assessment have been abused decades previous. The cry from the waiting room where adult patients wait is, *This wasn't important, no one cared.*

The Trauma Assessment must take on the sexual abuse in an official or formal capacity. It is a time to treat the abuse with the importance of a prosecution. If the response is official, the importance of the Trauma Assessment is enhanced and the pain suffered by the victim becomes significant.

Susan is employed as a waitress in a truck stop on the border of two western states. She was sexually abused by a variety of individuals throughout her entire childhood. Due to Susan's abuse, she was never able to finish high school and she has struggled vocationally because of her lack of education. With resulting suicidal attempts and eventually losing her children to foster care, Susan is required to participate in a therapeutic intervention. Through the Trauma Assessment, Susan is forced to journey back to her child abuse. Susan's first statement indicated that the abuse was unimportant and that there was very little need for therapeutic involvement. Many of Susan's *footprints* were developed around the issue of discounting feelings and minimizing pain. Through the Trauma Assessment, Susan became suicidal. It appeared to be very painful to return to her abuse and put forth effort to discuss hidden feelings and thoughts. Not only were questions asked about the perpetrator, but the *little Suzie* inside was asked to describe her feelings of being trapped in an incestuous tragedy.

When Susan was presented with her very *official*, ten-page, typewritten Trauma Assessment, she was overwhelmed with the vocabulary. *I can't read the goddamn thing!* Susan's reactions to her frustration became the focus of therapy over the next few weeks. Susan began to describe her feelings of frustration. Yes, she was frustrated with the words, but when a *process* put the words in terms understandable to Susan, she became even more traumatized. The trauma she had so bravely endured on a private basis was now official, with black letters on white paper. When the words were explained to Susan, she seemed even more upset than when her Trauma Assessment was incomprehensible. Eventually, therapy resulted in Susan rewriting her own Trauma Assessment.

I can't tell you how I felt when I read the whole thing on paper. At first, I was mad because I didn't understand the words. It was just another abuse, I said. Then, when the words became clear, I was mad again because I knew what the words were saying. When I didn't completely understand everything I felt better. Then, when I had to rewrite my whole evaluation, it seemed as painful as the abuse. What I know now is that I understand it. It's under my control. It's on black and white paper and I know every single word. The good news is I can put the paper in the drawer and I don't have to take it to work, to the shopping mall or to visit my kids.

The same will be true for parents of children who must read the Trauma Assessment. Parents may be overwhelmed by the vocabulary in the Trauma Assessment, but will eventually benefit from the same process as Susan. Parents can benefit from the sense that their child's suffering was indeed official and as important as a bill introduced into Congress. Parents who may be less than supportive or doubting of their child's pain may also benefit from the official nature of the Trauma Assessment. Parents, very much like victims, may want to discount, minimize, or alleviate the abuse. It is very difficult to avoid the reality of pain through the Trauma Assessment in its official form.

From *Officialdom* to Intimacy

Susan's initial response seemed to be a continuation of her own abuse through intimidation. She could not understand the *officialness* of the Trauma Assessment and, therefore, responded with anger and frustration. Eventually, Susan benefited from the grand presentation of her pain. The Trauma Assessment should begin with a very official document providing the opportunity to bring the victim or the victim's caretaker in contact with suffering. The next step is to allow either the patient or caretakers of the patient to bring this very official pain under control. In reality, when the Trauma Assessment becomes manageable, the implication that the pain may be manageable surfaces. It is a previously insurmountable task that has been overcome. Through this process, important steps toward recovery have taken place.

Order, Please!

When conducting the Trauma Assessment, it is important to appreciate the order in which the Trauma Assessment emerges. Purposely, the

Relationship Perspective begins the evaluation. As the victim is asked to describe, not centimeters of penetration or descriptions of bestiality, but how the family felt about each other, competency emerges. Traditionally, victims have very little confidence in being able to describe what happened sexually. Sexual descriptions are not only difficult for victims initially, but compound archaic ideas that seem to have deadly connotations to victims.

There is an inherent bias that trauma is related to sexual behavior. It seems abusive to a patient struggling with trauma to immediately turn to sexual events or issues. The implication is traumatic. For those patients who have not had brutal or, under traditional terms, *extensive* sexual contact, there is an automatic feeling of disappointment since the clinical effort seems to be focused on sexual behavior. For those victims who have had extensive sexual behavior, but who may be suffering in other areas, the implication requires concentration on perhaps a meaningless or very painful issue. If the data of the Trauma Assessment research is accepted, sexual behavior may be unimportant in assessing trauma. By initially avoiding sexual issues connected to the perpetrator's behavior, tremendous comfort may be provided to the victim and a much greater chance for success emerges.

Additionally, the comfort level of the victim is greatly enhanced through the order of the Trauma Assessment. Most victims feel disgust, rejection, and repulsion from professionals regarding their abuse. Victims commonly feel they will cause professionals discomfort through discussing sexual issues. From the specific order in the Trauma Assessment, victims can learn that sexual behaviors are not necessarily significant and that other issues will be the immediate focus. Tremendous relief for the patient is a typical response. The order of the Trauma Assessment was designed not only to enhance the process of conducting the assessment, but to make the contribution to the victim's emotional safety during the assessment.

The order of the Trauma Assessment is also purposeful in the area of rekindling memories and focusing upon important issues of trauma. By allowing victims to discuss what may seem less painful, a comfort level is established. Most important, victims who suffer from amnesia, dissociation, clouded or *smeared views* of sexual abuse will be relieved to learn that many memories will resurface while concentrating on other areas of the Trauma Assessment.

Memories, Memories

The Relationship Perspective, as an example, is important since victims are asked to discuss, on a peripheral level, the sexual offender. A coping skill of amnesia may have distorted the memory of sexual abuse, but discussing the perpetrator in unrelated areas may not be limited by amnesia and may rekindle memory, providing the victim with an opportunity for success.

Lucy agreed to have a Trauma Assessment conducted as a formal part of her therapy. She expressed, *I will tell you right now I don't remember hardly anything about what he did.* The response to Lucy indicated, *It doesn't necessarily matter what he did sexually; that's not the important part. First, what we need to talk about is who liked him. We need to discuss how little Lucy felt about him and how she felt about other people who liked him or were mad at him. That's the most important part in beginning the Trauma Assessment.*

For Lucy or for *precious Lucy*, the Trauma Assessment process is pouring concrete into Lucy's footprint, *I won't remember.* The message to Lucy is *It doesn't matter whether or not you remember. You really can't use that footprint any more because we are going on with your rehabilitation whether you remember (your footprint is stuck!) or not. The real Lucy is important to us and she needs some help. We are going to find her, love her, and rescue her regardless of whether or not she can remember.*

Not only does Lucy's footprint become cemented, hopefully into oblivion, but Lucy can now go in the back door and commence discussing feelings, attitudes, hopes, dreams, confusions regarding the sexual abuse. She is free from the battle of remembering or not remembering. The footprint becomes ineffective. The disappearance of the footprint is an important component for Lucy. She will be able to discuss those individuals in her triangle

without the protection of her footprint. She will discuss those individuals who have caused her pain without the protection of not remembering. What will happen is obvious. As Lucy gets closer and closer to her memories through the process of approaching sexual abuse peripherally, she will gain strength. Lucy's footprints have instructed her not to remember the sexual abuse. Lucy did not establish footprints regarding memories of her feelings and attitudes as a little girl, abandoned and unprotected. Those affective memories will surface if the order of the Trauma Assessment is appreciated.

It is common for victims who initially indicated they could not remember their abuse to accurately remember many previously undiscovered aspects of the sexual abuse by time the sexually abusive scene was visited in the situational portion of the Trauma Assessment. By arranging the Trauma Assessment with the Relationship Perspective first, many memories about what occurred will be rekindled in the proper section and the victim will have a sense of accomplishment.

Return to Childhood

The Developmental Perspective is strategically placed second to the Relationship Perspective in the Trauma Assessment. After discussing the intricacies of relationships, a return to childhood occurs. It is important to discover what information was available to the victim at the time of the abuse in order for decisions to be made regarding the child's perceptions. The victim will be asked about the childhood that has been robbed. The desensitization from the developmental process can have a profound effect. It is the child's perceptions that are extremely important. The Developmental Perspective requires a rekindling of the *child within,* but this time with the safety of a guided hand.

The Developmental Perspective requires examination of sexual issues in the child's life such as sexual education, sexual activities, and sexual input. The victim will be asked to describe such things as body development and body functions. The Developmental Perspective takes another step toward the sexually abusive scene, but with the protection needed. As an example, if the victim is asked to describe the names used for genitalia in childhood, the answer on the surface may be comfortable. Two important steps are taking place, however. First, discussions about the taboo subject of sexuality provide a valuable desensitization process. Secrecy and shame regarding sexual issues are alleviated. But, second, *childhood* is revisited. The adult patient struggles in a battle with the *child within.* Feelings of anger may pervade toward that child who did not protect or who acted inappropriately. The Developmental Perspective of the Trauma Assessment allows the patient to rekindle childhood memories in a protective situation. The combination of returning to childhood and discussing sexual issues accomplishes a great deal of value in the Developmental Perspective.

The Developmental Perspective is an example of how the Trauma Assessment is a process, not a product. The product is the answer to the questions. It is important to find out if the family attended church, if the victim learned *pee-pees and wee-wees* rather than *poops and potties,* or exactly how boys were treated differently than girls in the family. The product is the answer to those questions. The process of returning to a secretive subject and returning to childhood *safely* is as valuable as answers to the questions.

As the third portion of the Trauma Assessment is approached, the senses will be activated and the final approach to the actual sexual abuse will be much more successful. If the first two portions of the Trauma Assessment have been successful, it will become clear to the patient that the most dreaded portion of the Trauma Assessment is not dreadful at all. Hopefully, the baggage has been packed in the Relationship and Developmental Perspective. Childhood is now much more under control and the feelings and attitudes experienced by the child in those areas can now more appropriately examine the sexually abusive scene. The order of the Trauma Assessment has become an important tool and an obvious vehicle for success.

But What If?

The order of the Trauma Assessment is important to follow. However, information from the patient does not always emerge in a nice, tidy, orderly processes. It would be a lovely world if patients divulged information for documentation and diagnosis in proper categories. Generally, that is not the case. An important coping skill adapted by victims is often to avoid order and demonstrate *tangential* or compartmentalized thinking. Patients may be working in the opposite direction of order as a coping skill. A simple question regarding the relationship between the perpetrator and the community may result in a complete dissertation on the patient's upcoming bowling tournament. From the word community emerged a full circle discussion to the present-day community activities of the victim. The order of the Trauma Assessment may be painful for the victim, so the victim attempts to *disorder* as a coping skill. Not only is disarray important for the victim, but it is also a challenge to the clinician as well.

The purpose of the Trauma Assessment is to clarify and resolve issues that have been out of the patient's control. Focus has not been possible in the past, but can be possible with the Trauma Assessment. The Trauma Assessment needs clarity, order, and preciseness, which will seem to be in opposition to the victim's purpose of disorder. Patients tend to *leak* information or be redundant. Since the purpose is to clarify, the task of order may be the professional's task and one that is impossible for the patient.

Double Up and Catch Up

Concentrating on the issue of processing, not working toward the product, will provide consolation for a bewildered professional attempting to make clarity and order from disorder. Yes, it is important to pose the questions of the Trauma Assessment and receive answers. Yes, it is important to order the Trauma Assessment

from the recommended design. And, yes, the patient may be working hard to cope through disorder, confusion, or compartmentalization. But if two processes will actually take place, both the victim and the Trauma Assessment purpose will benefit.

Pecans

Felicia is a highly motivated professional who appears to be somewhat compulsive. Background information questions provide endless opportunity for verbiage. What appears to be a rather simple question regarding the mother/daughter relationship emerges in a complicated discussion of soccer.

How did my mother and I get along?, Well, I will tell you. She just never seemed to be there for us. Now, I said when I left home, I was going to be a different kind of mother. I always had to babysit other kids and I had a good look at how a mother should be. With my kids, it is different. I am involved in everything they do. I attend all of their activities and, right now, I am very involved in my son's soccer. You know, the coach we had last year never communicated with the parents. This year he has a coach who seems to be much more interested. Last Saturday at the soccer game, the coach gathered all of us around and told us how we could be involved. That reminds me, we are having a potluck for the team this Saturday and I need to see about getting my pies ready. I make a great pecan pie.

Exasperation may overtake the clinician attempting to organize the Trauma Assessment. If only one purpose is in mind, and the purpose is only *answers* to the question, Felicia may be receiving her social security check by the time the Trauma Assessment is completed. Felicia is an obsessive-compulsive woman who has chosen to cope by staying above the issue. The simple question concerning the mother/daughter relationship results in discussions of pecan pies. Most important for the purpose of the Trauma Assessment is diagnosis that Felicia is demonstrating her coping skill. Even though the evaluation is diverted by Felicia, important information is provided regarding Felicia's coping skill or footprint. Clinical diagnosis is important and even though a frustrated professional may be *out of order*, important information is being presented.

You're Out of Order

Even for patients who seem to focus on questions and answers and are much more inclined to maintain themselves under the direction of the Trauma Assessment process, information will rarely be provided in the exact order of preference. It will be important to gain skills in allowing patients to continue dialogue, comfort level, and rapport, without destroying the assessment process. A clumsy clinician would state, *Hold on a minute, slow down, we aren't ready for that part yet, you're out of order!* Even when the patient is answering questions in the order provided, important information from a peripheral perspective may emerge. Ordering the patient's information needs to occur, but from the clinician's perspective, protecting the patient's ability to respond comfortably.

Peggy is proceeding through the Developmental Perspective of the Sexual Victim Trauma Assessment. She is discussing the sex education she received within the home. Peggy reports, *we learned that the human body was nasty, dirty, and awful. Every time I see a commercial on television that contains any messages of seduction, I feel and think about my sexual abuse.*

Peggy is describing a phobic reaction. She is describing a collateral *clamp or cramp* that returns her to her sexual abuse. But (*God forbid*) Peggy is describing her phobic reaction (Situational Perspective) in the Developmental Perspective of the Trauma Assessment. It is important to protect Peggy and to encourage her to continue the dialogue. Criticizing her for being out of order would be inappropriate. Discounting the information would hamper the evaluation process. Peggy needs to continue her thoughts and the clinician needs to organize the information at a later time.

No Sex Allowed

Perhaps one of the most difficult tasks in ordering of information in the Trauma Assessment pertains to background information. Sexual abuse usually permeates the entire life of victims. Unfortunately, the Trauma Assessment dictates that sexual abuse information be omitted from the background information section. The patient may have a difficult time answering background information questions without discussing the sexual abuse. Generally, the information provided by the victim (in this out of order fashion) is extremely important and should not be discouraged. Clinical intervention will need to reorder the valuable information.

> George is asked to describe disciplinary techniques used in the family during his grade school period. George's answer begins appropriately. *My mom was always in charge of punishment. My father never seemed to do anything as far as controlling us kids. In fact, when I told my mom about being abused, the first thing she did was wash my mouth out with soap. That was one of her favorite things to do. Months later I told her again, but this time she had a different punishment. I was sent to a mental hospital.*

George provided important information concerning disciplinary techniques of his mother. From that question, however, he divulged important information for the post-disclosure section of the Trauma Assessment. Hours later in the assessment, George would be asked about his report. The information George provided in background information must be placed in the proper section. Since sexual issues are not part of background information, George's responses will be noted elsewhere and he will continue to respond as he chooses with a *sanctuary* atmosphere. Victims need a safe place, a sanctuary for the painful discussions. The task of ordering the information will be left to the professional as the safety zone for victims remains throughout the evaluation.

Pitfalls

Two pitfalls emerge for administration of the Trauma Assessment. The first tendency will be in discounting information that is improperly ordered. Since George is *out of order,* the tendency may be to omit very important information regarding post-disclosure issues. A second pitfall is to include George's important information in both sections. While the first pitfalls omits the important information, the second pitfall dilutes the information. George's post-disclosure issues become less significant as a result.

Again, victims need clarity before resolution can occur. Coping skills developed by victims for lifetimes often prevent this clarity. A valuable Trauma Assessment emerges and places trauma in three categories, allowing each to emerge in its own importance. If information is either omitted or presented in all sections, the value of the evaluation is lost.

Variety Is the Spice of...

A typical status of victims beginning the Trauma Assessment process is one of minimization, withholding and resisting. The *P.P.* (Practice Principle) is in operation. The victim has been *practicing* avoidance of the abuse and, therefore, avoidance of the pain. Now, a brilliant professional has asked the victim to return to the pain and meet the suffering head on. Even small children who have not fully developed their *practiced footprints*, playing with toys in the play therapy room would be more comfortable than talking about *poops and peeps*. Avoidance may be more subtle for adults, but both children and adults have a repertoire of resistive techniques.

With the P.P. (Practice Principle) intact, as well as a variety of coping skills, the Trauma Assessment from a question-and-answer perspective may be doomed to failure. Simply discussing the sexual abuse may not be sufficient. The issue of secrecy and *don't tell* pervades the subconscious for even the smallest victim. Now, in the Trauma Assessment clinical environment, secrecy is to be discarded and sexual abuse is to be discussed openly. This may be very difficult from a verbal perspective.

Because of these difficulties, the Trauma Assessment requires a wide variety of modalities to enhance the assessment process. The information needs to be extracted from a patient who has been forced to *practice* (P.P.) withholding that information. Through creativity, a large pool or repertoire of modalities needs development. The success of the Trauma Assessment will be based on the variety of modalities available to victims as they accept the task of shattering the silence.

As an example, an eight-year-old child may not be able to understand the concept of *assets and liabilities* concerning the perpetrator. It may also be ridiculous to ask the eight-year-old child *how do you feel about your father?* The nature of the question, *How do you feel?* is preposterous for victims since it is obvious that affective responses are misconstrued, smeared, reorganized, and confused. By asking the question about feelings, the message to the patient is, *You should have one feeling, one clear, crisp feeling that can be easily described in an answer to my question.*

Neither the confused eight-year-old child who is attempting to decipher the words, *assets and liabilities*, nor the frustrated adult patient who has *ten thousand feelings* toward the perpetrator will be successful with the question. There are, however, a variety of modalities or activities that could be implemented to provide the patient with success.

Let's pretend like you are me and I'll be you, Megan. You can ask me all the questions and I will pretend like I am you. I will answer the questions for you, but you will have to help me. Let's trade shoes and you sit in my chair. You can wear my high heels.

Eight-year-old Megan is now sitting at the clinician's desk with high heels dangling from her feet. Silence pervades. In whispering, Megan is instructed to repeat the question to the *new Megan*. In a whisper, Megan hears,

Ask me what I think of my daddy. With the competence of a psychiatrist, Megan asks, *What do you think of your daddy, Megan.* Now, it is important for the examiner to resist, to ponder, to twist, and to fret. The clinician behaves like a child bound to secrecy. The question is not answered. Dr. Megan's questions continue. After a few minutes of uncomfortable silence, Megan again hears in a whisper, *Tell me it's okay to say what I think of my daddy.* Dr. Megan will then encourage the *patient/therapist* to answer the question. *It's okay. You can say what you think of him.*

As this behavior is repeated, *Dr. Megan* is encouraging another child to express feelings about Megan's father. Each time encouragement occurs, resistance follows. The victim (the real Megan) has taken on the role of cheering for the *other Megan.* The child is encouraging disclosure about feelings toward herself, but from the perpetrator.

Go ahead, you can tell how you think he feels. You can say whether he likes you or not. As resistance heightens through Dr. Megan's encouragement, a point is reached where the question can be whispered *What shall I say your daddy thinks about you?* If sufficient resistance and encouragement has occurred, Dr. Megan may be very anxious to provide the information relating to the father/daughter relationship in order to solve the problem of the resistant patient (*therapist*).

This technique is a simple example of how role playing can provide an important modality in assessing trauma. Megan may be quite disappointed in her assessment of her father's opinion. She may have spent a great deal of time worrying about his rejection. The clinical interview may have been impossible for her and may have been painful. Role playing activities allow Megan to answer the question for the purposes of evaluation, but also provide her with the desensitization process so important for undoing the damage in the father/daughter relationship. As Dr. Megan whispers, *Say he is mad at you for telling*, the little victim Megan may take the first step toward discussing the pain she feels at the perpetrator's rejection. This first step may not have been possible for Megan in the traditional clinical interview.

For the older patient, switching chairs and high heeled shoes may be inappropriate, but role playing on certain levels may be a valuable technique.

If I had your mother on my couch twenty years ago, and I asked her to tell me about her daughter Sherry, what would she say? How do you think she would describe you if I was a friend of hers and asked her about you? And, if I had Sherry's father, Sherry's teachers, or her brothers and sisters, one-by-one on this couch, what would they say about little Sherry when she was in the fifth grade?

The 47-year-old Sharon may find it too painful

to discuss the disintegration of relationships within the family. She may be unable to disconnect herself with her coping skills of minimization and rationalization. From a personal interview, she may not be able to answer these questions accurately. From a projection perspective, she may be able to use an indirect role playing technique to be successful in this endeavor.

Your Toys, My Toys

There are a variety of modalities to be used through the Trauma Assessment process. Footprints and denial systems have a cognitive framework. The acts of doing, playing, drawing, cutting, and creating often have not been fortified by footprints. As an example, such techniques as art therapy, letter writing, sentence completion inventory, role playing, memory recapturing exercises, or the use of tape recorders, videos, or other electronic equipment provide a wide variety of modalities to ensure success in the Trauma Assessment.

In some cases, the clinical interview may suffice. But, most often, success will depend upon creative modalities to avoid confrontation with the footprints, finding other modalities to reach the *child within*.

The Trauma Assessment is a collection of information. It is not a scientific, standardized test to separate valid from invalid complaints or to categorize victims on a comparative level. The purpose of the Trauma Assessment is to extract the victim's internal pain. Through the process of externalizing, therapy will have already occurred. The additional value of ordering the information, clarifying, and dissecting the trauma provides a foundation for treatment planning. Nothing can be eradicated or controlled without understanding. Although a great deal of therapy occurs through the Trauma Assessment process, it will only be through the results of the Trauma Assessment that treatment plans can be organized and the road to recovery planned.

STEPS TO SUCCESS —
ADMINISTRATION OF THE
TRAUMA ASSESSMENT

If product is not as important as process, what is the process? How can something as unique as trauma be organized in a clinical format? What questions will divulge dimensions of destruction?

As indicated in the preceding chapter, the clinical Trauma Assessment is a specific process defined to organize discovery. For the purpose of evaluating trauma, the Sexual Victim Trauma Assessment Data Collection Form is reproduced in this chapter. A Data Collection Form is designed to guide the clinician as the clinician is guiding the patient. Information elicited in these most *intimate inquiries* should be organized in a fashion that is helpful to both the patient and the clinician. The purpose of the Data Collection Form is to accomplish both of these goals.

Steps to Success

Clinical Category

The Sexual Victim Trauma Assessment Data Collection Form is organized into three categories moving vertically from top to bottom. The CLINICAL CATEGORY appears on the far left hand side of the Data Collection Form. These categories will be represented in outlined boxes, designating categories to be used in the formal evaluation organization.

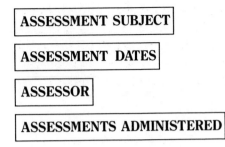

These boxed titles are examples of clinical categories to be used when preparing the final Trauma Assessment. These categories throughout the Trauma Assessment Data Collection Form will always indicate the clinical category to be listed on the formal evaluation.

Clinical Issue

The category of CLINICAL ISSUE is found in the middle of the Trauma Assessment Data Collection Form. In the shaded boxes, directions will be provided to the clinician for assistance in examination. The information contained in shaded boxes, under the category of Clinical Issue, should never be revealed to the patient or used to formulate questions to the patient. Clinical Issues are designed to provide the clinician with information and techniques in organization.

Clinical Response

One-half of the right-hand side of the Data Collection Form is reserved for patient responses. Categories are organized and writing space provided. Some areas under the CLINICAL RESPONSE category request diagnosis of the patient's response, but, in most instances, the Clinical Response is to organize and record the patient's responses.

Genesis

The first clinical categories ASSESSMENT SUBJECT and ASSESSMENT DATE begin the Trauma Assessment with specific information needing very little explanation. It is recommended, however, that all sessions directly or indirectly relating to the Trauma Assessment result should be listed under the *Assessment Date* Clinical Category. As indicated in the preceding chapter, the Trauma Assessment that is official and formal will have the most impact. The amount of time spent administering the Trauma Assessment varies widely from three to ten hours. The formality of the Trauma Assessment may be enhanced if the patient or the patient's caretakers recognize that several sessions and dates were included in the Data Collection process.

Clinical Category of ASSESSOR(S) should simply record the primary therapist involved and any additional collateral assistance. If consultation occurs, notations should be made. Collateral information received will be recorded in another category. This portion of the examination requires documentation of professionals who participated in the assessment, directly or indirectly.

The Clinical Category of ASSESSMENTS AD-

MINISTERED requires documentation of any other collateral testing modalities employed in the Trauma Assessment process. This categorization should include specific evaluations of adjunct components. Assessment modalities, such as play therapy or role playing, will not be included in this category but will be documented later. ASSESSMENTS ADMINISTERED requires documentation of specific tests, such as the Minnesota Multiphasic Personality Inventory, Mental Status Exam, and others.

ASSESSMENT REFERRAL

The clinical category of ASSESSMENT REFERRAL requires the clinician to record only referral information available at the time of the initial intake. Background information should be avoided and saved for other categories. ASSESSMENT REFERRAL should provide a thumbnail sketch of how the patient has been presented for a Trauma Assessment. Information regarding who is making the referral, what has been done in the past regarding the reason for the referral, or the information regarding the legal situation should be included. Objective data concerning past situations, present aspirations, and future goals should be designated.

One of the most important issues in the ASSESSMENT REFERRAL clinical category pertains to the purpose of the assessment. There is often confusion and perhaps controversy regarding the purpose of the Trauma Assessment, especially where conflicts between the patient and the referring person exist. In the case of children, there may be a discrepancy between what the child feels is the purpose for the assessment and those purposes belonging to the parent, caretaker, or caseworker.

Randy is presented for a Sexual Victim Trauma Assessment by his mother. Randy's father has been arrested for sexual abuse of Randy's sister and subsequently the victim was removed from the home. Randy's sister, Dana, has been in foster care for a total of twelve days. Randy is scheduled for a Trauma Assessment as part of the intake process for an incestuous family. Even though Randy's father has been incarcerated, Randy's mother has been reluctant to provide emotional support for her daughter and, therefore, Dana was placed in foster care. Concerns were raised about what appeared to be Randy's depression and lethargic attitude.

In the intake process, Randy's mother and Dana's caseworker indicate that the purpose of the Trauma Assessment was to evaluate Randy's suffering, as well as to consider the potential that Randy was sexually abused. In other words, the *referring person* indicated that the purpose of the examination was *to assess the damage to Randy as a result of being a member of an incestuous family and to examine Randy's possible victimization.*

Unfortunately, this was not Randy's understanding of the purpose for the Trauma Assessment. When Randy was asked about the evaluation, he reported that the purpose of the Trauma Assessment was *to talk about rape.* When asked to describe the term *rape,* Randy explained, *Rape is when you have your throat slit on the street and you bleed to death.* Through further inquiry, Randy was asked if he knew anyone who had been raped. Randy indicated in the affirmative. Randy reported that Dana had been raped by his father. The question then posed to Randy was, *Is your sister dead?* And Randy replied, *Yes!*

The trauma to Randy is unimaginable. He spent twelve days believing that his sister was dead. He believed her throat had been slit and that she had bled to death on the street. Since no one talked to Randy about Dana, he formulated thoughts and ideas that were untrue, and sadly those thoughts have caused tremendous trauma. If Randy had spent twelve days believing his sister had died at the hands of his father, how successful will the Trauma Assessment be if this information was not known to the clinician? Most importantly, how honestly would Randy answer questions about his possible sexual abuse?

The most important issue is not whether Dana is dead, has been raped, or is alive. Randy's belief or ideas are profoundly important. It would have been extremely inappropriate to attempt the Trauma Assessment with Randy unless these issues were resolved.

ASSESSMENT ENVIRONMENT

The clinical category of ASSESSMENT ENVIRONMENT is designed to establish a base of documentation. There will be three paragraphs in this category, with the first reporting collateral information used in conducting the Trauma Assessment. Documentation should occur regarding such items as newspaper articles, mental health records, letters from the perpetrator, court documents, police reports, etc. The author of each of these collateral documents should also be listed.

To Do, or Not to Do

A decision must be made by the clinician regarding perusal of the collateral information. Since traditional methodologies of evaluating trauma tend to be inappropriate, there may be danger in examining collateral information previous to making diagnosis and documentation with the patient. Innovative methods of examining trauma are contained in this publication, as well as documentation that traditional methods of evaluating trauma are ineffective, but nonetheless common. It is likely that collateral information will view trauma under traditional avenues. The clinician may be *less than objective* if this information is perused prior to the involvement with the patient.

The second paragraph in the clinical category of ASSESSMENT ENVIRONMENT describes the process, number of hours, sessions, and types of activities or modalities used in the clinical experience. This paragraph should document time frames and describe the atmosphere and modalities from which the Trauma Assessment information was collected.

The final paragraph of the ASSESSMENT ENVIRONMENT category describes the patient's demeanor or attitude. Diagnosis of any change in attitude or demeanor would be important for the final conclusions. As an example, if the patient began the assessment extremely apprehensive or resistive, but demeanor changed throughout the evaluation process, reporting this change may provide important clinical diagnosis. If the opposite is true, such a diagnosis may also be important.

Although the ASSESSMENT ENVIRONMENT clinical category occurs at the beginning of the Trauma Assessment, many of these issues or answers may need inclusion at the closure of the involvement with the patient. Following referral information, but previous to background information, the ASSESSMENT ENVIRONMENT information assists in the process of reading the evaluation at a later time. The clinician will need to return to the ASSESSMENT ENVIRONMENT category at the close of contact with the patient in order to complete this category adequately.

A Word About Legal Issues

There will be times when the Trauma Assessment is used in a legal framework. In some cases, the Trauma Assessment's purpose may change from a clinical or therapeutic perspective to one of legality. As an example, the victim who is being evaluated concerning the abuse of one offender that is not within a legal framework may report being sexually abused by another offender that requires legal intervention. Civil litigation may also result following administration and presentation of a Trauma Assessment. If the Sexual Victim Trauma Assessment is conducted in an ethical and *legally appreciative* framework, there should be very little concern about the possibility of legal involvement.

There are obligations, however, whenever involvement with the legal system becomes a possibility. Guaranteeing objectivity, avoidance of contamination, and requirements of documentation are important requirements in preparation for the legal arena. Documentation in the ASSESSMENT ENVIRONMENT is very important in anticipation of possible involvement within the legal system.

Step By Step

For those specific cases where it is apparent that information contained from the Trauma Assessment will be the subject of legal intervention, obligation to the clinician unfolds. Many children who have been sexually abused participate in contaminated, inappropriate, and disorganized interviews. The result may be that the child was sexually abused, but due to the inappropriateness of the intervention, the claim is viewed as invalid and the victim is further traumatized by the *system*. Clinicians who may be examining sexual traumatization from an *investigatory* modality may benefit if a specific protocol is implemented. *Step-By-Step: Sixteen Steps Toward Legally Sound Investigations* (Hindman) is an example of an acceptable process. If alleviating trauma to sexual victims is the primary purpose for the Trauma Assessment, then certainly protecting the victim from trauma through the system will be important as well. The clinician untrained in legal ramifications may contribute more trauma and sabotage the purpose of the Trauma Assessment. If a possibility exists that sexual abuse is undisclosed and that the clinician may need to report sexual abuse, the Trauma Assessment should not be discontinued, but rearranged within the confines of an appropriate legal protocol.

Before inquiring about the trauma or damage to victims, validation needs to occur in cases where the legal system may be involved. A protocol, or the protocol outlined in *Step by Step*, should be implemented between ASSESSMENT ENVIRONMENT and BACKGROUND INFORMATION of the Trauma Assessment outline.

BACKGROUND INFORMATION

The first task in outlining the background of the patient is to provide a *family tree* diagram beginning in the middle of the *family tree* with the patient's natural parents at the time of the patient's birth. Siblings from the natural family should be recorded, as well as siblings' ages.

Next, information should be obtained regarding the victim's parents' *previous* relationships and children. Additionally, if the patient's parents have subsequently divorced, remarried, and produced children, those items on the *family tree* should also be recorded. It is important to see the genealogy of the family, since the victim's family becomes extremely important in understanding potential for trauma during the Relationship Perspective.

Chronological Designation

The most appropriate method of describing BACKGROUND INFORMATION is a chronological designation of the preschool, grade school, adolescent, and adult time periods. Within each of these time frames, the following issues should be considered:

- Geography and/or Family Mobility
- Family Structure
- Living Situation
- Caretaker Employment
- Academic Issues
- Medical/Mental Issues
- Religion/Moral Issues
- Substance Abuse
- Financial Concerns
- Self-Esteem Issues
- Family Discipline
- Significant Events

A background sketch of the child's life during each of the chronological periods should include some information about each of the previously mentioned issues. Obviously, some items will not be applicable or some information may not be available. These items should stimulate discussion between the clinician and the patient and not be used as a checklist or a method of intimidation. Examples of questioning strategies would include:

- Tell me what it was like before you went to school. Who lived with you? *AUNT MARIA*

- Can you draw a picture of the house and tell me how many houses you lived in as a little boy?

- Where did dad work?

- Did mom stay home? *YES*

- Was anybody ever sick in your family? *YES*

- What did you learn about church and about God when you were growing up? *DON'T KNOW*

- Tell me about Christmas when you were five. *HUH?*

- Was anyone ever allowed to say *goddamnit* to you? *YES*

- Did anyone in your family drink alcohol? *YES*

- How happy were you and what were your favorite things to do before you were six? *PLAY TALK SING READ EAT HAPPY*

- When recess time came what did you like to do most? *BE ALONE*

- Did you have any pets when you were in school? *NANCY*

- What did you think about in adolescence when someone asked you *what will you be when you grow up? SADNESS*

- How did you handle your homework? *?*

- If I had one of your high school cheerleaders in my office and I asked them about you, what do you imagine they would say? *NOTHING*

- What would have been your three wishes in the fourth grade and what would have been your three wishes when you were 14? *TO DIE*

It is extremely important to avoid sexual issues in the BACKGROUND INFORMATION section of the Trauma Assessment. Not only should sexual issues be avoided, but also those issues relating to trauma should be reserved for other portions of the examination.

As an example, the patient may describe substance abuse problems in the family household. Certain notations may be made during the grade school chronological period. If the patient goes on to explain that his mother became sexually involved with him because his father was alcoholic and left her alone a great deal of the time, that information is pertinent to the Situational portion of the Trauma Assessment. Substance abuse, as a family issue, should be mentioned in the chronological designation categories, but the issue regarding trauma from manipulation should be documented later in the evaluation.

In examining the adult chronological time period, marriages and/or LAS (living as spouse) relationships should also be included. Adults should be asked to expand on their marriages and children, as well as readjusting the aforementioned factors for consideration of the adult's life. For adult patients, their childhood is extremely important, and they should be encouraged to provide as much information during the preschool, grade school, and adolescent periods as they provide for the adult time period.

Some Trauma Assessments will be conducted with children who have very little background information. When custodial parents or guardians provide information, caution should be exerted regarding prejudicial information. If information must be obtained from caretakers, that information should be used after diagnosis from the victim's perspective. The Trauma Assessment is based upon the victim's feelings, thoughts, and attitudes, and reality may not be as important as the child's perceptions. Caretakers may provide accurate information regarding reality, but the victim's perspective, even for an eight-year-old, is more important.

SYMPTOMATOLOGY PERSPECTIVE

SYMPTOMATOLOGY PERSPECTIVE of the Sexual Victim Trauma Assessment occurs in two separate stages. The first process inquires of the patient a perspective of symptoms within three areas. Questions regarding how the patient functions in Relationships from a Psychological Perspective and within the Living Skill arena will be asked. These categories were included in the Trauma Assessment research and seemed to provide an organization for understanding how the patient functions. It is important to examine these three areas in two separate steps.

Some limitations will occur when interviewing children since, by virtue of being children, they may be incapable of understanding symptomatology. An interview with the custodial parent, caseworker, or guardian may be required. Questions should be formulated inquiring how the pain or trauma appears to be manifested in the child. Again, caution should be raised regarding prejudicial information. The symptomatology information received from a caretaker or parent should be used to re-examine the child victim and should not necessarily be taken at face value.

Stop, Do Not Enter

It is also important during an interview (with an older patient who is describing symptoms or a caretaker who is describing symptoms of the child) to avoid therapeutic intervention. This is the time for the clinician to listen, listen, listen. It is not a time to intervene or to change the cognitions.

I don't seem to have any problems in my marriages. Although I have been divorced four times, I still get along very well with my husbands.

This may be an overt example of a patient who is obviously having difficulties within the relationship realm but is not aware of those problems. The patient's statement is very diagnostic and should be recorded, but not confronted. When the second step of symptomatology examination occurs, the true meaning of this statement can be analyzed.

It is also important to recognize that patients are often unable to describe symptoms, which may be diagnostic in itself. For an adult, perhaps the most deadly response indicating symptomatology would be *no symptoms*. Due to heavily entrenched distorted cognitions and denial systems, the patient may not be aware of how other individuals function in positive relationships. Questioning strategies should include tangible or specific issues, such as *how many times have you been married* rather than *are you happily married?*

The second step in examining symptomatology occurs at the completion of the examination. During the SUMMARY portion of the Data Collection Form, the clinician is asked to revisit symptomatology and diagnose the patient's ability to *diagnose.* Just previous to this section, the clinician is asked to diagnose distorted cognitions or the development of *footprints.* When discovery is made regarding how the victim has chosen to cope with trauma, information can also be revealed regarding the patient's ability to diagnose symptoms. This is an important step in recognizing the victim's distorted cognitions and obviously an important step in rehabilitation.

As an example, problems within the living skill dysfunction area may be manifested in the development of a coping skill, *This is bad, so I will be bad*. The patient may be self-abusive through vocational failures, problem solving techniques, anger mismanagement, etc. The patient may *need* to fail in the living skill area in order to cultivate the coping skill learned in the past. The patient, during the first step of symptomatology examination, may need to report *NO symptoms* in order to hang on to the footprint. Collateral information revealed in the Trauma Assessment may paint a different picture. In re-examination of symptomatology issues and diagnosing the patient's ability to accurately perceive symptoms, important information is revealed.

As far as diagnosis is concerned, the more clearly a patient recognizes symptoms and residual effects of abuse, the more likely rehabilitation is to occur. Certainly, a painful step in treatment takes place for those patients who are not aware of their symptoms or residual damage. For the aforementioned patient, the ignorance of her symptoms has a traumatic effect. Recognition of the etiology of those symptoms may be painful but is obviously a key to her rehabilitation.

Another important issue in the second phase of diagnosing symptoms pertains to the situation where a caretaker describes symptoms.

Underlying motivations may exist for caretakers of children in providing symptomatology information. As an example, a parent who wishes to discount sexual abuse may describe *no symptoms* for a small child. The non-offending parent who has not resolved his own abuse may need to soothe his pain by discounting the pain of his son. In Step II of the SYMPTOMATOLOGY PERSPECTIVE, the clinician will revisit and re-examine the non-offending parent's statements for diagnosis.

Sonia is presented for a Sexual Victim Trauma Assessment by her mother. Sonia's mother understands that Sonia has been sexually abused by her father from ages seven through nine. The father is incarcerated and Sonia's mother is desperately seeking treatment.

During the SYMPTOMATOLOGY PERSPECTIVE, one of the symptoms reported by Sonia's mother describes Sonia being unable to survive in a classroom with male teachers. It is reported that Sonia has a phobic reaction toward men and her mother is concerned about her future dating and eventually Sonia's fear of being married.

As the second step was completed, re-examination of Sonia's mother's statement revealed a different picture. It is true that Sonia has been unable to survive in classrooms where the teachers were males. Careful examination, however, within the Relationship and Developmental Perspective reveals that Sonia typically runs her hand up the inner thigh of her male teachers' pants. Sonia has been traumatized within the Developmental Perspective by recognizing that her sense of value and her sense of worth is sexual. Sonia views sex as a way in which she can receive attention, nurturing, and affection. Sonia is not developing a phobic reaction to men. Men are terrified of Sonia since she is quite seductive. This is a difficult situation for male teachers and the natural solution, without causing extreme controversy, is to transfer Sonia into other classes. If the SYMPTOMATOLOGY PERSPECTIVE had not been revisited, the most important symptom would have remained a mystery.

Contained under the Clinical Issue section of the Trauma Assessment are lists of considerations for symptomatology within the Relationship, Psychological, and Living Skill dysfunction area. Many items contained on these lists can be found in the research design, although many more issues are suggested for consideration. Lists contained in the Clinical Issues area should not necessarily be inclusive nor limited. Additionally the patient should not be asked to answer *yes or no* to the items. As indicated previously, these issues are for the clinician to consider and to use in developing questioning strategies.

In discovering symptomatology, informality is most important. Being able to ask questions in a way that is comfortable for the patient is an art. The following is a very brief list of examples that can be used with both children and adults regarding symptomatology examination. The purpose of these examples is to demonstrate the informality of inquiries into very significant symptoms.

- When you were little, what were the jobs you had to do around the house? Did your parents need you? Who did you think was the boss and who wasn't the boss? (Symbiosis) *DISHES CLEANING* *N-O* *MOM NOT DAD*

- What do you think good wives should do? (Relationship Dysfunction) *NOT BE WIVES*

- When you were little, who did you think was the most wonderful person in your family? (Relationship Dysfunction) *NANNY*

- Describe your best sexual experience. (As A Partner) *CLAYTON*

- Who did you like most in the whole world? Who would you like Batman to stomp out? (Anger Mismanagement) *NO ONE* *MEN*

- Describe your worst sexual experience. (As A Partner) *STEVE*

- If you were put on a deserted island, who would you want to be with? (Relationship Dysfunction) *ANIMALS*

- Do you have times when you feel just rotten? (Depression) *YES*

- What happens when you dream? (Sleep Disorders) *BREATHING*

- If there was a sex fairy who could stomp out sex, would you like that? (As A Partner) *SOMETIMES*

- When you're in school, who do you think most about in your family? (Symbiosis or Academic Dysfunction) *SID*

- Do you ever have hot flashes that you cannot describe? (Psychological Dysfunction) *NO*

- Do you ever break the rules at school? (Academic Dysfunction) *YES*

- Do you ever have dreams in the daytime? (Sleep Disorder) *YES*

- Could I make you mad enough to hit me? (Anger Mismanagement) *YES*

- What would you do if you lost your paycheck? (Living Skill) *FIND ANOTHER*

RELATIONSHIP PERSPECTIVE

The Data Collection Form includes the first paragraph recommended for the RELATIONSHIP PERSPECTIVE category. Recognizing that the Sexual Victim Trauma Assessment must clarify, resolve, and teach, it becomes important to begin each of the three main portions of the Trauma Assessment with an educational paragraph.

The RELATIONSHIP PERSPECTIVE of the Sexual Victim Trauma Assessment evaluates the relationship between the victim and the offender, the offender and others who are important to the victim, as well as the relationship between the victim and others who are important to the offender. Positive and negative ratings within this triangular approach provide information regarding the *victim/offender* identity. Those patients who perceive themselves as innocent and who view the perpetrator as guilty have a much better opportunity for rehabilitation. Those patients who are confused about the offender/victim status tend to be more traumatized.

For the purpose of summary, the Relationship Perspective will be examined in three sections examining all three sides of the relationship triangle. Tabulations will occur as the victim's perceptions designate the offender/victim identities. Caution should always be exerted remembering that the victim's perceptions are the most important issue. Reality is second place compared to the child's perceptions of the offender/victim identity.

Right Side Perspective Offender/Victim Relationship

Chronological Involvement

The first task in examining the right hand side of the triangle is to record chronological involvement between the victim and the perpetrator. Many victims are abused by a variety of offenders and in different time periods. The chronological involvement with the perpetrator needs to be documented between the categories of preschool, grade school, adolescence, and adulthood. Documentation should be made regarding the type of involvement only. Affective considerations or issues relating to trauma should not occur in this section of the Trauma Assessment. The clinician can evaluate the potential for trauma based upon the offender's importance in the child's life from this chronological perspective. Diagnosis of the chronological *impact* on the victim will be made by the clinician and diagnosed later.

Victim's View of Offender

Remembering that each side of the triangle is a *two-way street*, the first task examines the victim's importance to the perpetrator in order then to evaluate the offender's value to the victim. Although not listed on the Data Collection Form as a reciprocal issue, the underlying message is one of reciprocity. The technique most often used is to examine the victim's view of the offender by designating the assets and liabilities. During the *victim's view* portion of this side of the triangle, the offender's assets and liabilities from the victim's consideration will be examined. All aspects of the offender's power should be designated.

Examples of questioning strategies for adults or for children are as follows:

> When you were seven, what did you think of Uncle Joe when he would come to pick the kids up to go fishing?

> I know now you are an adult who has been traumatized by what Uncle Joe did. The adult part of you is quite clear that Uncle Joe was wrong. I want to know what that precious, little boy thought of Uncle Joe each time he waited on the porch for Uncle Joe to take him fishing.

Offender's View

Additionally, it is important to examine the other side of the two-way street concerning how the victim was viewed by the perpetrator. A follow-up question to Bart, the adult victim of Uncle Joe, would be as follows:

> If Uncle Joe were here today, what would he have told me about the seven-year-old little boy? Would Uncle Joe tell me Bart was an ornery kid or would Uncle Joe go on and on about Bart being a great kid?

For very small children, role playing is an extremely effective technique requiring children to describe themselves from the offender's view. Play therapy modalities, art therapy, or a variety of other techniques can be used. It is important to examine *the child's view of the offender's view of the victim.*

The Envelope, Please . . .

A final tabulation is made from clinical impression and from information contained in the patient's answers. A plus indicates that the offender has more positive attributes than negative in the mind of the victim, resulting in the offender's inability to accept the offender status. A minus indicates that liabilities outweigh the offender's assets in the mind of the victim. With a minus, the offender is identified by the victim as being guilty and as being responsible.

Penciled In

Advice for the clinician is to *tentatively* provide a plus and minus at the conclusion of this portion of the evaluation. Without examining the other two sides of the triangle, it may be premature to officially designate a plus or minus. Relationships for the child are not isolated to one side of the triangle and it may be helpful to withhold absolute designation until the next two portions of the assessment are completed.

Bottom Side Perspective: Offender/Significant Other Relationships

The bottom side of the triangle examines the offender's relationship with others who are important to the victim. An aerial view of the triangle would imagine the victim looking down at the bottom of the triangle and examining the offender's status according to other individuals. As with the other sides of the triangle, a two-way street or reciprocity exists.

Reciprocity, Again

The clinician should first assess the victim's view of reciprocity in the relationship between the offender and *significant others*. This task requires evaluation of the importance in the relationship from the victim's perspective. As an example, if the victims' step-siblings were extremely important to the victim but not necessarily important to the offender, the step-siblings' identification of the offender as a perpetrator may still be important to the victim when the left hand side of the triangle is examined. The reciprocal examination examines the weight with which the child will view the tabulation from *significant others*.

The Finer Details

The next task in evaluating this side of the triangle requires inquiry into specific relationships between the offender and *significant others*. The offender's relationship with the victim's mother, father, siblings, family, community, and the system need assessment. Again, it is important to remember that reality is not as important as the victim's perspective. As an example, a child may view her father as being extremely important in the community due to his boasting or other behaviors in the home. A realistic picture may reveal an obnoxious, rude person whose presence is dreaded even at the grocery store. His *actual* devalued position in the community will not be as significant as how the offender's importance is viewed by the victim.

Working toward the final assessment of the offender and *significant others* relationships, clinical diagnosis must be made regarding the final computation of the offender/victim status. The group of *significant others* needs to be tallied. As indicated in Chapter Eleven, one component of the *significant other* category can have an overwhelming influence. As an example, *the system* could deny or accept the status of the perpetrator and impact all other individuals within the category. If the criminal charges were dropped against the perpetrator, the therapist may withhold treatment, parents may forbid treatment, or the child may be chastised at school due to media exposure. It may be important to tally both pluses and minuses to find an average or sum of the pieces.

Scoring Scars

A final assessment is made concerning the offender and *significant others* relationship. A plus indicates that the victim views, as a whole, those individuals as believing the offender is innocent and not capable of accepting the offender status. A minus indicates that, in the victim's view, those individuals who are important to both the offender and the perpetrator have designated the perpetrator as a criminal.

Left Side Perspective: Victim/Significant Others Relationship

Victim Self-Image (Independence)

The first step in examining the left hand side of the triangle relating to the victim/*significant others* relationships is to determine the level of self-esteem or independence of the victim. The victim's need to be accepted by *significant others* will be directly related to the victim's sense of self and the victim's comfort with independence. For smaller children, independence and self-esteem will be directly related to the family as a whole. As in a previous example, the child's support system within the family overshadowed the rejection of the victim status from the *significant others* group. The two-way street issue is examined in this step of the assessment. Lower levels of independence and self-esteem result in more significance in the reciprocal response from *significant others*.

One By One

The next portion of the triangle's left side examines individual relationships between the victim and the mother, the father, siblings, extended family members, community members, and the system in general. Information must be gathered regarding each of these relationships with an importance pertaining to how these individuals view the status of the victim. The perpetrator's relationship with these individuals should have already been examined. One by one, these relationships should be examined, diagnosing possible support or rejection of the victim status.

Talley Ho!

A final tabulation is made concerning the left side of the triangle. A plus indicates the child has been vindicated, viewed as innocent, and worthy of the victim status designation. A minus reports to the victim that significant others demand that guilt and responsibility to be accepted by the victim. As with the bottom side of the triangle, the tally considers the weight of the entire group of significant others.

Changes Upon Changes

A final tabulation of the entire triangle may need to occur at this point in the evaluation. Returning to all three sides of the triangle may assist in re-examining the RELATIONSHIP PERSPECTIVE. Information gathered in the bottom of the triangle or on the left side may impact the original rating in the offender/victim relationship on the right side.

Finally, it may be important to speculate in the Trauma Assessment about changes that have occurred or may occur in the future. As an example, decisions regarding the offender's involvement in treatment, or lack of involvement, may need consideration. Recommendations to prevent a triangular perspective that is currently positive from becoming traumatic may also need explanation.

DEVELOPMENTAL PERSPECTIVE

The DEVELOPMENTAL PERSPECTIVE of the Sexual Victim Trauma Assessment evaluates three components, with the first concerning the victim's DEVELOPMENTAL PERSPECTIVE. How victims perceive, evaluate or understand the sexual abuse depends upon the victim's stage of development at the onset of abuse. Secondly, it is important to assess what sexual information was available to the victim at the time of the abuse in order to carefully evaluate the victim's perceptions. Finally, assessment must be made regarding what has been lost in normal sexual development due to victimization. This portion of the examination will be divided into these three segments with the first approaching the victim's perceptions based on chronological or age development.

Ages and Stages Revisited

Chronological information must be obtained regarding the age at onset and the age at the final encounter of abuse. This provides information as to the developmental *segment* having a potential for trauma. The issue of frequency is also important to discover since developmental impact would occur based upon sporadic abuse as compared to ongoing abuse.

To continue the chronological perspective, assessments must be made concerning the victim's stage of sexual development, coordinating with Sexual Development categories as outlined in Chapter Twelve.

- The Unaware Victim
- The Unfortunate Victim
- The Uncomfortable Victim
- The Unresolved Victim

Since the Trauma Assessment should educate and clarify, it is important not only to describe the victim's stage of sexual development, but also to include information about what would be normal or abnormal if sexual abuse had not happened. Sexual development is a neglected topic because very little is known. Therefore, this portion of the Trauma Assessment should educate and provide needed information. Diagnosis will be made later regarding trauma or losses in normal sexual development. In this portion of the Trauma Assessment, establishing what *should* be normal will be more appropriately compared to the later portion of the evaluation regarding what has been lost in normal sexual development.

Environmental Influences

Generally, no conclusions can be made based on the developmental stage of the victim in isolation. The next step in the DEVELOPMENTAL PERSPECTIVE is to examine environmental influences, which in turn influence the victim's perspective. The following issues will be examples for consideration:

- Family Structure Influences
- Morals, Values, and Religious Influences

- General Family Communication Level

- Available Sexual Information (informal)

- Sexual Relationship of Parents

- Male/Female Role Training

- Formal Sex Education (parents/school)

- Sex Activities with Peers

- Body Development/Education of Body Image

The purpose of this inquiry is to carry information about the child's developmental stage into the child's sexual environment. Just as the RELATIONSHIP PERSPECTIVE evaluates the child's perceptions of the victim/offender identity, this portion of the assessment evaluates the sexual perceptions of the child based on available information.

Richard grew up in a household where both his mother and father used drugs extensively. There were many instances where Richard was forced to care for his sister even when he was a pre-schooler. Not only was drug use rampant, but sexual activity was commonplace. In the first seven years of Richard's life, he witnessed a great deal of sexual activity, some of which included his own abuse by several

males. Richard, in turn, began to be sexually active with his sister Tracy.

In the third grade, Richard's father severely beat his wife. She was hospitalized and the father was incarcerated. Eventually, the couple was divorced. After a period of hospitalization, Richard's mother changed her lifestyle. She became fanatic about religion and subsequently fanatic about morality. The message to Richard about sexuality during the third grade to the seventh grade was one of *evil*. Richard's mother changed her addiction from drugs and alcohol to religion. Richard's perceptions were forced to change as well.

It is important to note these changes and compare the changes to the developmental stage from a chronological perspective. As Richard proceeded through the latency stages of development, a change in his morality code had disastrous effects. Richard's eventual suicidal ideations and attempts could be understandable from the DEVELOPMENTAL PERSPECTIVE as Richard proceeded into his freshman year of high school believing he was a sinner unworthy of redemption. In one stage of development, Richard's sexual acting out was acceptable. Later, Richard was an evil criminal.

What Has Been Lost

This portion of the DEVELOPMENTAL PERSPECTIVE first requires assessment of what should have occurred in normal sexual development. Reference could be made to Chapter Twelve regarding normal and abnormal sexual development. In order to understand trauma suffered by victims in sexual development, a discussion of normal development must be made.

Those issues which suggested some normalcy as compared to other issues that signify traumatization are listed on the Trauma Assessment Data Collection Form. The list requires inquiry into a variety of areas.

- Sexual Appetite
- Body Image
- Body Function
- Attitude
- Male/Female Role Influence
- Sexual Communication Skills
- Sexual Phobias
- Sexual Purpose
- Sexual Arousal
- Sexual Identity/Acceptance
- Sexual Goals for the Future

Each one of these issues should be carefully examined for *EXCESS*. As described in Chapter Twelve, it is not necessarily the presence of these elements, but extremes, which cause trauma.

A Trauma Assessment of eleven-year-old Dawn is requested. Dawn's natural father is currently serving life in prison for raping and murdering a neighbor child. When Dawn was four, her mother married the perpetrator who sexually abused Dawn from age five to nine. Dawn told her mother on many occasions that she was being sexually abused. In the intake session, Dawn's mother reports being aware of Dawn's abuse but helpless to intervene. *There were times when the screaming was so loud we had to leave the house.*

Dawn's second father has also served time in prison, but not for a sexual crime. He and Dawn's mother were married shortly after Dawn's natural father was incarcerated. The *new* father is alcoholic and seems to have already begun a pattern of domestic violence. Although Dawn denies being sexually abused by this individual, she recognizes that the potential exists and that she and her sisters are vulnerable.

Obviously, Dawn's role model training is traumatized. Through inquiry, it becomes clear that Dawn views the female role as one of acquiescence and acceptance of brutality. Although Dawn can express anger toward her mother for not protecting her, she has tremendous potential for establishing herself in the same mold.

When Dawn was asked *what could your mom have done?* Dawn's only answer was, *she could have called the police.* Through further inquiry she is asked, *What if the police didn't come?* Dawn's second solution was, *Call another police station in Texas.*

Dawn saw her mother as totally inadequate and unable to protect the children. Clearly, Dawn's mother was not a resource. Unless Dawn's mother was able to secure a policeman, safety in the home could not be assured.

Dawn's role model for a father or a partner is also an area of trauma. If Dawn was asked, *What do good dads do?*, she replied, *they don't hit their kids very much.* It would seem that Dawn may be accepting of a male partner who simply controlled his domestic violence and did not become obsessive.

Courage

The three portions of the Developmental Perspective are summarized and diagnosed. Some victims are outraged when their lack of normalcy is revealed. Other victims may be angered at criticism toward their childhood family. Younger victims may feel a need to protect a parent or family member. It may take courage not only to define trauma and losses of normal development, but to predict what will be lost in normal development unless therapeutic intervention occurs. This is an important part of the assessment, but a controversial part as well.

SITUATIONAL PERSPECTIVE

The SITUATIONAL PERSPECTIVE of the Sexual Victim Trauma Assessment evaluates the environment where the sexual abuse occurred in order to determine the patient's potential for developing phobic reactions and cognitive distortions. Issues from sensory input in the sexual abuse *scene* and from subsequent environmental reactions provide information to the victim's computer. Those pieces of information allow the victim to develop lifelong patterns of coping for the future.

For review, this section of the Trauma Assessment evaluates three levels, *sensory* activation, the sexually abusive *scene*, and finally the child's general *situation*, in order to determine the foundation or potential for phobic reactions and cognitive distortions. Purposely, sexual behaviors that occurred during the abuse have not been discussed previously. Now, for the first time the victim will be asked to revisit the sexual abuse in a very methodical and calculating manner.

Laundry List Sexual Abuse

The Data Collection Form requires consideration of a checklist of sexual behaviors. The clinician should record only sexual behaviors that occurred. The patient should be allowed to acknowledge or deny behaviors. Different than other *lists* designed to guide the clinician, this is a checklist. This process should be used for the purpose of desensitization, as well as for gathering information. *Yes* or *No* answers are the most comfortable way to look at the sexual abuse. It is important to record not only behaviors that occurred by the offender to the victim, but by the victim to the offender. Extraneous or affective issues should be avoided. The checklist should be a laundry list of inquiries regarding only sexual behaviors.

The second laundry list pertains to a variety of extraneous sexual activities that could have occurred. As an example, a child who reports being fondled may not be developmentally competent to report that he was forced to dress in black nylons and a garter belt during the fondling. For this reason, another laundry list of sexual behaviors can be used for obtaining information.

The desensitization process is extremely important. The clinician should examine the potential that a variety of deviant activities occurred. Caution! The victim should be protected from feeling as though this checklist indicates no trauma or insignificant trauma if certain scores are not given. This process is to discover, not to categorize, trauma.

Sensory Activation

The next step in the SITUATIONAL PERSPECTIVE examines very specific sensory activation. Sound, sight, smell, taste, and touch should be considered without affective considerations. Clinicians should anticipate assessing phobic responses but avoid examining the patient's *thoughts*. Questioning strategies that would be helpful are as follows:

When you think of your sexual abuse, what can you smell?

As you move about in your daily life, what do you hear that makes you think of your father?

Does your body have responses that render you out of control because of something you sensed?

When you close your eyes and think of the abuse, what do you see?

Sexual Scene — Cognitive Connections

This portion of the Trauma Assessment evaluates the sexually abusive scene from the time period before the abuse occurs, through the abuse, and following the abuse. This section would not include post-disclosure issues, but would examine a reasonably short time period following sexual abuse that is generally used by the victim to rearrange reality. This portion of the assessment should include both the sensory activation *and* the cognitive process. It will be important to return to the *laundry lists* from the first portion of the SITUATIONAL PERSPECTIVE in this inquiry.

Those issues for consideration in the sexually abusive scene are:

- Environmental (physical)

- 30 Minutes Previous to Sexual Contact

- Precognitions Offender/Victim Identity

- Position Locality of Others

- Lighting

- Sexual Conversations

- Issues of Coercion (verbal/nonverbal)

- Victim Sexual Response

- Offender Sexual Response

- Extraneous Items in Victim's Perceptions

- Compliance Issues Terror — Violence, Consent, Cooperation, Etc.

- Victim's Cognitions Concerning Disclosure

- 30 Minutes Following Abuse

It is also important in this portion of the Trauma Assessment to describe several specific examples of how the sexual abuse evolved from beginning to end. Many victims have had ongoing abuse and may have many instances. The assessment requires the patient to relate a specific scene or incident in order to provide the best opportunity for total understanding. It will be important for the clinician to repeat the scene back to the victim for the purpose of accuracy and desensitization. This process will not only assist in desensitizing the victim, but will provide important information for the clinician in evaluating the final portion of the SITUATIONAL PERSPECTIVE.

Phobic Reactions Summary

At the completion of this stage in the Data Collection Form, a summary should be made concerning phobic reactions. As the third phase of the SITUATIONAL PERSPECTIVE is examined, cognitive issues are of primary importance. The combination of the sexually abusive scene and sensory activation forms the foundation for phobic reactions. A summary can be made at this point concerning phobic reactions that exist or, in the Trauma Assessment of younger children, the potential for phobic reactions in the future.

Sexual Abuse Situation

The final expansion of the SITUATIONAL PERSPECTIVE examines the child's world including the dynamics of the family and the community. This portion of the examination requires evaluation of general environmental issues beyond the sexually abusive scene. These issues must be considered as influencing the victim who is about to establish footprints or coping skills for the future. Those influential issues are as follows:

- Family Finances

- Family Vocational Issues

- Family Health (Mental/Physical)

- Family Communication

- Family Discipline Systems

- Family Mobility

- Family Morality (Religion/Values)

- Family's Involvement with the Community

Special consideration should be made in recalling some of the issues in the RELATIONSHIP PERSPECTIVE. This portion of the Trauma Assessment examines the footprints or the coping skills the victim uses for the future. Obviously, the identity of the victim and the offender will have a profound effect on the etiology or foundation of those coping skills. It is important at least to consider the pluses and the minuses from the triangular examination, but caution must be taken in interpreting the results of that *offender/victim identity* process.

As an example, if the victim is not viewed as an innocent child worthy of protection, a variety of coping skills can be manifested. Since the victim is not a victim, a coping skill of *becoming the perpetrator* may exist. On the other end of the spectrum, a victim who feels guilty and responsible may become self abusive, involved in body mutilation, eating disorders, or substance abuse.

References to Chapter Thirteen will assist in designating footprints. Combination of footprints or creativity of unique coping skills not listed may need consideration.

Post-Disclosure Issues

Finally, post-disclosure issues must be examined within the criteria of legal responses, community responses, and the family responses. If disclosure did not occur, the victim should contemplate disclosure in order to determine the psychological ramifications of disclosure. If disclosure did occur, the following issues should be carefully considered:

- Prosecution

- Criminal Trials

- Legal Investigations

- Visitation

- Incarceration

- Foster Placement

- Hospitalization

- Medical Response

- Divorce Separation

- Therapeutic Intervention

- Death

- Distorted Cognitions (Footprints)

With special consideration to the RELATIONSHIP PERSPECTIVE, diagnosis of the victim's footprints or coping skills must occur. Although diagnosis of the footprints occurs previous to a summary of SYMPTOMATOLOGY PERSPECTIVE, it is obvious that symptomatology issues may need consideration previous to final diagnosis of footprints.

At the close of the SITUATIONAL PERSPECTIVE revisiting symptomatology and assessing the patient's ability to diagnose symptoms is important. Gross misinterpretation of symptoms or discounting of symptoms by the patient will have an important bearing on the clinician's diagnosis of footprints.

Summary

If the coping skills or footprints have been diagnosed and symptomatology has been revisited, a summary should occur. For the benefit of the clinician, revisiting each of the three sections of the Trauma Assessment is recommended. Summary and Recommendations should include a wide variety of clinical interpretations and interventions.

The next step is to prepare the Trauma Assessment in official form and present *a piece of the pain*. The process of administering the Trauma Assessment has allowed the patient to externalize the abuse. The clinician's responsibility is to take the externalization process one step further by placing the trauma in an official report to be presented to the victim or to the victim's caretakers.

SEXUAL VICTIM TRAUMA ASSESSMENT

DATA COLLECTION FORM

An instrument for evaluating Trauma and Treatment Planning. This evaluation form should be used in conjunction with the publication Just Before Dawn, available from **AlexAndria Associates.**

by Jan Hindman

Additional Copies Available Through:
AlexAndria Associates
911 S.W. 3rd Street
Ontario, Oregon 97914
(503) 889-8938

AlexAndria Associates
Ontario, Oregon 97914

Sexual Victim Trauma Assessment
Data Collection Form

CLINICAL CATEGORY   **CLINICAL ISSUE**   **CLINICAL RESPONSE**

ASSESSMENT SUBJECT

Name _____

Date of Birth _____

Chronological Age _____

ASSESSMENT DATE(s)

1. _____   2. _____

3. _____   4. _____

5. _____   6. _____

ASSESSOR(s)

Record Primary Therapist or
Collateral Assistance

| ASSESSMENTS
ADMINISTERED |
|---|

Record Specific Assess-
ments as Adjunct Compo-
nents. Assessment Names
Only.

Record only information pertinent to intake process. Avoid issues relating to trauma or background. Provide objective data concerning past situations, present aspirations and future goals. Clearly designate purpose of assessment from referral or patient perspective, if applicable.

Referred by _____

_____

Present Living Situation _____

_____

Present Legal Situation _____

_____

Present Therapeutic Situation _____

_____

Past Therapeutic Situation _____

_____

Purpose of Assessment (Referral) _____

_____

Purpose of Assessment (Patient) _____

_____

**ASSESSMENT
ENVIRONMENT**

Record collateral documents, list title and author.

Record process, types of involvement, number of hours, and assessment modalities.

Record affective descriptions of patient including attitude, cooperation, demeanor, etc. Record changes during assessment period.

Collateral Information _____

_____

_____

_____

_____

_____

Assessment Process _____

_____

_____

_____

_____

_____

Affective Assessment _____

_____

_____

_____

Family Constellation

Parents at Birth _____

Location _____

Mother's Previous Marriage	Father's Previous Marriage
_____	_____
_____	_____
_____	_____
_____	_____

Patient's Mother   Patient's Father

Offspring

_____
_____
_____
_____
_____
_____

Divorced

_____	_____
_____	_____
_____	_____
_____	_____

Record background of patient from "family tree" perspective. Record natural parents, step parents, siblings, step siblings & "half" siblings. Record subsequent marriages of parents to obtain continual portrayal of "family tree."

Record background information from chronological perspective dividing into "lifetime" sections. Avoid sexual abuse issues or related trauma. Consider FACTORS from next page within each chronological section.

Chronological Designation
PRESCHOOL _____

_____
_____
_____
_____
_____
_____
_____
_____
_____
_____
_____
_____
_____
_____
_____
_____

GRADE SCHOOL _____
_____
_____
_____
_____
_____
_____
_____
_____
_____
_____
_____
_____
_____

Continue to assess issues
within each chronological
area according to FACTORS.

ADOLESCENCE _____
_____
_____
_____
_____
_____
_____
_____
_____
_____
_____
_____
_____
_____

FACTORS

Geography / Family Mobility
Family Structure
Living Situation
Care Taker Employment
Academic Issues
Medical / Mental
Religion
Substance Abuse
Financial Concerns
Self-Esteem
Family Discipline
Significant Events

ADULT _____
_____
_____
_____
_____
_____
_____
_____
_____
_____
_____
_____
_____

Expand on marriages and
children for adult patients.
Readjust FACTORS for ex-
amination of adult's life.

Record patient's symptoms in each category. Focus of patient perceptions of symptoms. Avoid professional interpretation or intervention until assessment completed.

For Relationship
Dysfunction Consider:

Symbiosis
Abnormal Attachments
Abnormal Rejection
Domestic Violence
Passive / Aggressive
Superficiality
Dishonesty / Secrecy
As a Parent / Child
As a Partner
Sexual Dysfunction
Communication Dysfunction

For Psychological
Dysfunction Consider:

Mental Health Involvement
Mental Health Diagnosis
Schizophrenia
Delusional Disorders
Psychotic Disorders
Mood Disorders
Anxiety Disorders
Somatoform Disorders
Dissociative Disorders
Factitious Disorders
Impulse Control Disorders
Personality Disorders
Eating Disorders
Clinical Depression

Relationship Dysfunction _____

Psychological Dysfunction _____

Living Skill Dysfunction _____

_____

_____

_____

_____

_____

_____

_____

_____

_____

_____

_____

_____

_____

_____

_____

_____

_____

_____

_____

_____

_____

_____

_____

_____

_____

For Living Skill
Dysfunction Consider:

Problem Solving
Vocational Problems
Criminal Behavior
Run Away
Substance Abuse
Academic Problems
Anger Management
Residential Placement
Self-Abusive Behavior
Sleep Disorders
Mobility Problems

Describing Person (Clinical Impressions) _____

_____

_____

_____

_____

_____

_____

Record clinical impression of describing person's ability to diagnose symptoms of patient.

Patient's Ability to Diagnose (Clinical Impression) _____

_____

_____

_____

_____

_____

_____

Revise symptomatology perspective at completion of assessment. Diagnose patient's ability to accurately diagnose symptoms.

The Relationship Perspective of the Sexual Victim Trauma Assessment evaluates the relationship between the victim and the offender, the offender and others who are important to the victim, as well as the relationship between the victim and others who are important to the offender. Positive and negative ratings within this triangular approach provide information regarding the victim / offender identity from the perspective of the victim. Those patients who perceive themselves as innocent, and the perpetrator as guilty, have a greater opportunity for rehabilitation. Those patients who are confused about the offender / victim status tend to be more traumatized.

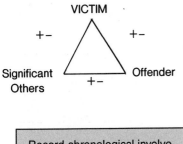

Record chronological involvement between victim and offender. Avoid affective considerations.

Triangle – Right Side
Offender / Victim Relationship

Offenders Name _____

_____

Chronological Relationship With Offender _____

_____

_____

_____

Pre School _____

_____

_____

_____

Grade School _____

_____

_____

_____

Adolescent _____

_____

_____

_____

Adult _____

_____

_____

_____

Victim's View of Offender

Record importance of offender to victim. Evaluate offender's assets and liabilities from victim's view. Consider all aspects of offender's power according to victim.

Assets _____
_____
_____
_____
_____
_____

Liabilities _____
_____
_____
_____
_____
_____

Offender's View of Victim

Record importance of victim to offender. Evaluate victim's assets and liabilities from offender's view according to victim's perspective.

Assets _____
_____
_____
_____
_____
_____

Liabilities _____
_____
_____
_____
_____
_____

Make final assessment of offender / victim relationship. Plus indicates the offender is more positive than negative, resulting in lack of offender status. Minus indicates victim has identified the offender as guilty and worthy of offender status.

Final Calculation - Triangle Right Side

☐ Explanation _____
_____
_____
_____
_____
_____
_____

Assess victim's view of reciprocity in offender / significant / other relationship. Evaluate importance of relationships from victim's perspective.

Assess specific relationships between offender and significant others, from victim's view in order to make final tabulation regarding identification of offender status.

Make final assessment of offender / significant others relationship. Plus indicates victim views significant others as identifying the offender in positive terms, not capable of offender status. Minus indicates that, according to victim, significant others identify the offender as guilty.

Triangle Bottom Side
Significant Others / Offender Relationship

Reciprocal Issues _____
_____
_____
_____
_____

Victim's Mother / Offender Relationship _____
_____
_____

Victim's Father / Offender Relationship _____
_____
_____

Victim's Siblings / Offender Relationship _____
_____
_____

Extended Family / Offender Relationship _____
_____
_____
_____

Community / Offender Relationship _____
_____
_____
_____
_____

System / Offender Relationship _____
_____
_____

Final Calculation – Triangle Bottom Side
☐ Explanation _____
_____
_____

Assess victim's self image, independent of evaluation of significant others in order to determine value of significant others' response.

Assess victim / significant others relationship in each listed category. Assess from reciprocate perspective, examining not only how significant others view the victim, but the importance of that identification from the victim's perspective.

Make final assessment of victim / significant others relationship. Plus indicates the victim has been identified as innocent and worthy of victim status designation. Minus indicates victim has been rejected for victim status designation.

Triangle Left Side
Victim / Significant Other Relationship

Victim's Self-Image (Independence) _____
_____
_____
_____
_____

Victim / Mother Relationship _____
_____
_____
_____

Victim / Father Relationship _____
_____
_____
_____

Victim / Sibling Relationship _____
_____
_____
_____

Victim / Extended Family _____
_____
_____
_____

Victim / Community Relationship _____
_____
_____
_____
_____

Victim / System Relationship
_____
_____
_____
_____

Final Calculation Triangle Left Side
☐ Explanation
_____
_____
_____

DEVELOPMENTAL PERSPECTIVE

The Developmental Perspective of the Sexual Victim Trauma Assessment evaluates three components. First, the victim's stage of sexual development at the onset of abuse must be examined to determine how the victim perceives, evaluates or understands the sexual contact. Secondly, it is important to assess what sexual information was available to the victim at the time of the abuse in order to more carefully examine the victim's perceptions of the sexual contact. Finally, assessment must be made regarding what has been lost in normal sexual development due to sexual victimization.

Record chronological information to include rate of frequency. Determine stage of development most impacted by abuse.

Describe developmental stages indicating liabilities and limitations within categories impacted.

Stage of Sexual Development — Chronological Issues

Victim's Age At Onset _____

Victim's Age At Final Encounter _____

Frequency _____

_____

_____

_____

Unaware Stage _____

_____

_____

_____

_____

Unfortunate Stage _____

_____

_____

_____

_____

Uncomfortable Stage _____

_____

_____

_____

_____

Unresolved Stage _____

_____

_____

_____

_____

Sexual Information Available

Examine potential for influence from siblings or family constellation considerations.

Family Structure Influences _____
_____
_____
_____
_____

Examine moral influences and value codes within environment.

Sexual Values, Morals, Religion _____
_____
_____
_____
_____
_____

Examine general communicative level between victim and parents. Make comparison with sexual communication and non-sexual communication.

General Sexual Communication Level _____
_____
_____
_____
_____
_____

Evaluate "formal" education and victim's perception following intervention.

Available Sexual Information (Formal) _____
_____
_____
_____
_____

Evaluate informal influences such as cable television, music, pornography, literature, etc. Include influences beyond child's home environment such as media information.

Available Sexual Information (Informal) _____
_____
_____
_____
_____

Evaluate influences from victims's observations of parents' sexual relationship.

Sexual Relationship Of Parents _____
_____
_____
_____

Sexual Information *(Continued)*

Sexual Activities With Peers (Non-Abuse) _____

Evaluate victim's peer sexual influence including siblings. Describe not only overt sexual behaviors but other influences such as sexual discussions, sexual games or masturbation.

Puberty Development Issues _____

Evaluate body development education and information. Describe learning from development of others as well as personal development.

Male / Female Role Training _____

Evaluate role training within environment. Include cultural, ethnic or religious issues when applicable.

Arousal Development _____

Evaluate victim's arousal development from childhood. Discuss fantasies, masturbation, opposite sex interest, etc.

Losses or Trauma in Normal Sexual Development

Evaluate sexual appetite or interest recognizing individual differences as "normal." Assess what decisions regarding appetite are influenced by trauma.

Sexual Appetite _____
_____
_____
_____
_____
_____

Evaluate patient's attitude regarding body image. Record only those issues related to trauma. Evaluate potential for eating disorders.

Body Image _____
_____
_____
_____
_____
_____

Evaluate patient's attitude regarding body functions from aversion perspective. Carefully relate responses to trauma, recognizing "normal" responses to body functions.

Body Function Attitude _____
_____
_____
_____
_____
_____

Evaluate sexual attitudes influenced by role training. Consider environment influences on victim's arousal.

Male / Female Role Influence _____
_____
_____
_____
_____
_____

Evaluate victim's ability to communicate regarding sexuality. Consider as a partner, as a parent, as a patient.

Sexual Communication Skills _____
_____
_____
_____
_____
_____
_____

Losses or Trauma in Normal Sexual Development
(Continued)

Evaluate sexual phobia connected to trauma. Carefully separate "preferences" from phobic reactions.

Sexual Phobias _____
_____
_____
_____
_____
_____
_____

Evaluate patient's **use** of sex. Assess range of sexual purposes from intimacy through weaponry. Assess sexual criminal potential.

Sexual Purposes _____
_____
_____
_____
_____
_____

Evaluate arousal as related to trauma. Examine not only partner relationship but masturbatory activities as well. Assess issues of rejection of certain behaviors or fixation to certain behavior. Assess fantasy development as well as sexual behaviors.

Arousal Assessment _____
_____
_____
_____
_____
_____
_____
_____

Assess patient's potential for sexual identity trauma. Transexualism, homosexuality or distorted views of sexual identification must be considered.

Sexual Identity/Acceptance _____
_____
_____
_____
_____

Evaluate patient's desire or ability to change. Finally, assess sexual future for patient.

Sexual Goals/Future _____
_____
_____
_____
_____
_____

The Situational Perspective of the Sexual Victim Trauma Assessment evaluates the environment where sexual abuse occurred, in order to determine the patient's potential for developing phobic reactions and/or cognitive distortions. Issues from the sensory input, from the sexual abuse "scene" and from subsequent environment reactions provide information to the victim. Computation from those influences allows the victim to develop life-long patterns of coping skills for future survival.

Examine first and last experience. Use exercise for desensitization.

Record only sexual behavior that occurred. Allow victim to acknowledge or deny. Use for desensitization. Record not only offender to victim behavior but victim to offender behavior. Avoid discussing extraneous issues. Use as "check list" of behaviors that took place. Inquire for all behaviors.

Sexual Specific Information

First Incident _____
_____
_____
_____

Last Incident _____
_____
_____
_____

Fondling

Vulva _____	Buttocks _____
Breast _____	Legs _____
Penis _____	_____
Testicles _____	_____

Penetration (Digital / Penile / Object)

Anal _____
Vaginal _____

Oral Contact _____
Fellatio _____
Cunillingus _____
Anal _____
Other _____

Continue to desensitize and proceed through "check list." Use for clinician and patient.

Ejaculation _____
Photography _____
Orgasmic Response _____
Bestiality _____
Cross Dressing _____
Group Sex _____
Exhibitionism _____
Voyeurism _____
Obscene Phone Calls _____
Bondage / Restraints _____
Sexual Apparatus _____
Pornography _____
Masturbation _____
Urination / Defecation _____
Fetishism _____
Weapons _____

Sensory Activation

Tactile Responses _____
_____
_____
_____
_____

Olfactory Responses _____
_____
_____
_____
_____

Visual Perceptions _____
_____
_____
_____
_____

Audio Perceptions _____
_____
_____
_____
_____

Taste Perceptions _____
_____
_____
_____
_____

Evaluate sensory activation. Avoid cognitive considerations. Anticipate assessing phobic responses. For adult patients, examine connection between sensory responses in adulthood to sensory activation in childhood abuse. For children record sensory activation and predict phobic responses in the future.

Evaluate sexual "scene" proceeding from time period before abuse occurs to victim's contemplations following abuse. Clinician should attempt to return to scene and examine abuse from perceptions of victim. This assessment should include both sensory activation and cognitive process. Reconsider patient's checklists on previous pages.

Sexual Scene — Cognitive Connections

Environment (Physical) _____
_____
_____
_____
_____
_____
_____

30 Minutes Previous To Abuse _____
_____
_____
_____
_____
_____

Precognitions "Offender / Victim" Identity _____
_____
_____
_____
_____
_____
_____

Position Or Locality Of Others _____
_____
_____
_____
_____
_____
_____

Lighting _____
_____
_____
_____
_____
_____

Sexual Scene — Cognitive Connections *(Continued)*

Sexual Conversations _____
_____
_____
_____
_____
_____

Compliance Issues — Terror, Violence, Consent, Coercion,
Cooperation _____
_____
_____
_____
_____
_____

Extraneous Items In Victim's Perceptions _____
_____
_____
_____
_____
_____

Victim's Sexual Response _____
_____
_____
_____
_____
_____

Victim's Contemplations Regarding Disclosure _____
_____
_____
_____
_____
_____

30 Minutes Following Abuse _____
_____
_____
_____
_____
_____

Continue to evaluate scene.

Sexual Scene Scenarios

Describe and summarize sexual abuse scenarios. Use this portion of assessment to compensate for multiple or ongoing sexual abuse. Use narrative form.

Phobic Reactions Summary

Recap phobic reactions. Clinician should avoid cognitive issues but potential for phobic reactions can occur beyond sensory activation and can be found in sexual scene.

Evaluate general environment of victim beyond sexual abuse scene. Consider variety of family issues that will provide information to victim for establishing coping skills (footprints). Although sexuality provides etiology — these issues will generally be non-sexual environmental issues.

Sexual Abuse Situation

Family Consultation — Adoption, Divorce, Separation, Remarriage _____

_____

_____

_____

_____

_____

_____

_____

Family Finances _____

_____

_____

_____

_____

_____

_____

Family Health (Mental / Physical) _____

_____

_____

_____

_____

_____

_____

_____

Family Vocational Issues _____

_____

_____

_____

_____

_____

Family's Level Of Communication _____

_____

_____

_____

_____

_____

Sexual Abuse Situation *(Continued)*

Family Discipline _____
_____
_____
_____

Family Mobility _____
_____
_____
_____

Morality Influences _____
_____
_____
_____
_____

Family's Situation In Community _____
_____
_____
_____
_____
_____

Post Disclosure Issues

Legal, Community, Family Response _____
_____
_____
_____
_____
_____
_____
_____
_____
_____
_____
_____
_____
_____
_____
_____
_____

Evaluate Post Disclosure trauma. Include such issues as:
- prosecution
- criminal trials
- legal investigation
- visitation
- incarceration
- foster placement
- hospitalization
- media responses
- divorce / separation
- therapy
- death

If disclosure did not occur, allow victim to contemplate what may occur. Use Relationship Perspective issues for recap and summary.

Distorted Cognitions (Footprints) _____

_____
_____
_____
_____
_____
_____
_____
_____
_____
_____
_____
_____
_____
_____
_____
_____
_____
_____
_____
_____
_____
_____
_____
_____
_____
_____
_____

Diagnose victim's distorted cognitions and the development of coping skills. Consider sexual abuse "scene" as well as sexual abuse "situation." Consider the following:

Amnesia
Dissociation
Self-Abusive
Abusive Responsive
Obsessive Guilt
Responsibility Avoidance
Obsessive Secrecy
Privacy Avoidance
Obsessive Affective Focus
Affective Avoidance
Obsessive Helplessness
Obsessive Aggression
Symbiosis
Terrified
Terrifying
Obsessive Perfection
Obsessive Failure

SUMMARY

Symptomatology Summary _____
_____
_____
_____

Relationship Dysfunction _____
_____
_____

Psychological Dysfunction _____
_____
_____
_____

Living Skill Dysfunction _____
_____
_____
_____

Referral Success / Failure _____
_____
_____
_____

Continue to summarize including information from all categories. Examine success or failure of evaluation.

Relationship Summary
   (I.D. Victim And Offender)

_____
_____
_____

Development Summary
   (Victim's Perceptions, Losses In Normal Development)

_____
_____
_____

Situational Summary
   (Phobic Reactions, Cognitive Distortions)

_____
_____
_____

Recommendations _____

Provide specific recommendations. Consider the following:
• Child Protection Issues
• Legal Issues Criminal / Civil
• Medical Intervention
• Custody Issues
• Substance Abuse Issues
• Domestic Violence Therapy
• Family Therapy
• Sex Therapy
• Couple Therapy
• Individual Therapy
• Parent / Child Therapy
• Offender / Victim Therapy
• Group Therapy
• Sexual Abuse Prevention
• Sex Education
• Resolution Scrapbook

_____
_____
_____
_____
_____
_____
_____
_____
_____
_____
_____
_____
_____
_____
_____
_____
_____
_____
_____
_____
_____
_____
_____
_____
_____
_____

COMPLETED EXAMPLE OF THE WRITTEN TRAUMA ASSESSMENT
OF
RANDALL ALLEN KYLE

SEXUAL VICTIM TRAUMA ASSESSMENT

ASSESSMENT SUBJECT

Randall Allen Kyle
DOB: 08/08/76
Chronological Age: 15

EXAMINER

Jan Hindman

EXAMINATION DATES

September 3, 1989
September 11, 1989
September 26, 1989

EXAMINATION REFERRAL

Randall Allen Kyle is a 15-year-old, white male child who was referred for a Sexual Victim Trauma Assessment by his family's attorney, Katherine Brady-Michaels. Civil litigation is pending regarding the sexual abuse of Randall by an elementary teacher. A suit has been filed by the parents of three of Randall's schoolmates against a variety of defendants. Ms. Michaels requested a Sexual Victim Trauma Assessment in order to secure information regarding trauma suffered by Randall, and to determine opinions regarding those individuals most responsible for Randall's trauma.

EXAMINATION ENVIRONMENT

This examiner was presented with depositions of Mr. Raymond Fuller, Principal of Fruitdale Elementary School; Ms. Angela Sweet, Faculty Representative; as well as depositions from Arnold Richards; Maryanne Saunders; and Julia Davidson, who are teachers at Fruitdale Elementary. Psychological reports and case notes were also provided by Dr. Arnold Miller, Mercy Medical Center. It should be noted that those providing intake information were cautioned to avoid providing this examiner with information of a prejudicial nature. Only a basic background sketch of Randall's childhood was provided by his mother and Ms. Michaels also refrained from providing specific details previous to this examiner's involvement with

Randall. None of the aforementioned depositions were perused by this examiner until all interactions with the patient had been completed.

Randall participated in approximately five hours of involvement, which included clinical interviewing, role playing, as well as subjective testing. Randall completed several written assignments during the interim time between assessment dates. It also should be noted that previous to the Trauma Assessment administration Randall participated in a protocol, as outlined in *Step-By-Step: Sixteen Steps Toward Legally Sound Investigations*, to determine validity of sexual abuse.

Randall Kyle is a 15-year-old, attractive, young man who appears to be somewhat small for his age. Randall seems shy, withdrawn, and during the early portion of the assessment, Randall had difficulty making eye contact and feeling comfortable. Randall is observed having nervous twitching of his fingers and pulling at his hair. Although Randall became more comfortable as the assessment proceeded, he nonetheless appears to be an anxious child who talks softly and avoids asserting himself.

BACKGROUND INFORMATION

Randall Allen Kyle was born to his parents, Charles and Claire Kyle while the couple lived in Austin, Texas. At the time of Randall's birth, his parents were not officially married, but made a matrimonial commitment approximately one month after Randall's birth. Randall's mother, Claire, worked as a waitress and his father had a variety of jobs, most consistently indicating vocational interests in the area of carpentry or construction work.

During Randall's preschool years, his mother and father apparently developed an acrimonious relationship. Randall's mother was disappointed at Charles' lack of interest in not only Randall, but in general family activities. Randall's earliest memories include pictures of his parents fighting, and of scenes where both he and his mother stand in vigilance, waiting for Charles to return home. Alcohol appeared to be a problem for Charles, but not necessarily for Claire. Religion was not a part of the normal family routine, nor was advanced education for either parent. According to both Randall and his mother. Claire was often away from the home in efforts to support the family and, when she was at home, she either doted on Randall or waited patiently for Charles to return. By the time Randall was four, the couple relocated to Oregon.

With a relocation to the West Coast, matrimonial conflicts seemed to intensify. Mr. Kyle was rarely at home and the family seemed to border on poverty. Mrs. Kyle did not date other men and continued her patient vigilance for Charles. Both Randall and Claire describe these early years in Randall's life as being one of scarcity of both tangible items, as well as emotional support. Finally, just before Randall entered the first grade the couple was divorced, with custody being given to Claire.

An abrupt change seemed to occur in Randall's life when his father married a woman named Phylis. Phylis had three children from another marriage and she and Charles quickly had a female child of their own. Charles appeared to become much more stable in the relationship with Phylis and eventually established himself in a position where visitation with Randall was not only possible, but also a demand of Phylis.

The first three years of grade school occurred with Randall visiting his father one or two times per month. As visitation occurred, there appeared to be obvious differences in the households. Life with Claire was scarce and barren for Randall while visits with his natural father took place in a suburban home, complete with other children, a great deal of activity, and most important to Randall, a swimming pool. From grades two, three, and four, Charles continued visitation with his father and the difference of the two households was constantly accentuated.

During the summer between Randall's fourth and fifth grade, he learned that his father was moving to Montana. Randall's visits were abruptly discontinued, except on a sporadic basis. During Randall's entire fifth grade year in school, he saw his father only on holidays. Previous to the fifth grade, Randall's academic abilities were marginal, but nonetheless adequate. Randall appeared to be somewhat shy in school, but was able to make some friends. The relationship between Randall and Phylis' children seemed to enhance his peer adjustment. There appeared to be tremendous loss to Randall with his father's relocation.

In the fifth grade, Randall was described as being *depressed* by one of his teachers and his academic abilities lessened. By the time Randall entered the sixth grade, he had barely passed the fifth grade. Eventually, Randall was placed in a sixth grade class that specialized in students who had unique difficulties, but could not be classified as handicapped.

Randall's life with his mother continued to be barren from a physical standpoint. Claire continued to work in the food service area and earned a meager wage. Claire provided for Randall's needs and she seemed to provide him with emotional support. Claire, very much like Randall, is sub-assertive and seemingly dependent. Just as Randall continued to wait for his father's visits, it seemed that Claire continued to wait for Charles' attention. Claire did not date other men and seemed to revolve her life around Randall.

Randall's adolescent period has been plagued with many problems, which are related to the intricacies of his sexual abuse situation. Currently, at 15, Randall is not involved in an academic program and he is manifesting many symptoms of trauma. It appears that his adolescence has become a time of turmoil and upheaval.

SYMPTOMATOLOGY PERSPECTIVE

The Symptomatology Perspective of the Sexual Victim Trauma Assessment evaluates the patient in three major areas: the Relationship Perspective, the Psychological Perspective, the Living Skill Perspective. These three categories of symptoms should provide information regarding the current functioning of this patient. The purpose of these three categorizations is to first examine the patient's ability to function with other individuals, secondly, to discover whether the patient is suffering from psychological problems, and finally to learn how the patient is managing on a day-to-day basis.

Within the relationship symptomatological realm, Randall is obviously having many difficulties. Randall is described as having no peer relationships whatsoever. His only social activities include involvement with males who are at least 23 years of age or older. Randall is not involved in social activities outside the home and since he has ended his academic involvement, he is extremely isolated. Randall's relationship with his father has deteriorated and Randall's mother describes him as appearing to be resentful and hostile toward her. In general, it would seem that Randall has very few positive relationships at this point in his life.

From a Psychological Perspective, Randall has been diagnosed by Mercy Medical Center as *clinically depressed*. Second diagnosis indicates that Randall appears to be suffering from paranoid delusions in his fears of retribution concerning those individuals connected with the sexual abuse. Additionally, Randall could be diagnosed as *agoraphobic* since he rarely leaves his home and seems to be frightened at even the most innocuous social situations, such as going to the store or venturing outside his yard. Although Randall's stay at Mercy Medical was brief (ten days), it appears those diagnoses are accurate and that Randall is suffering from psychological disorders that seem to be serious.

Within the Living Skill Dysfunction area, Randall is also having difficulties within the academic realm. Randall has never returned to school since he left Fruitdale Elementary in the sixth grade. All vocational/academic efforts have failed to reinstate Randall in a program. Randall also appears to be having difficulties with anger mismanagement as reported by his mother and confirmed by Randall. Since Randall has severed all ties with peers and suffers from *agoraphobia,* he has very little contact with anyone except his mother. Randall is observed having outbursts of anger to the point of destroying items in the home and, on two occasions, Randall harmed himself through body mutilations. Suicidal ideations have occurred for Randall, although he reports never actually making plans to take his own life. Finally, within the Living Skill Dysfunction area, Randall and his mother report night terrors and sleep disturbances of a profound nature. Currently, Randall is on medication to assist him in sleeping.

ASSESSMENT VALIDATION

In anticipation of legal involvement, effort was exerted to validate sexual abuse. Randall proceeded through the protocol outlined in *Step-By-Step: Sixteen Steps Toward Legally Sound Investigations.* After careful analysis, it appears that Randall is accurate in his statements regarding sexual abuse and that there is no reason to doubt his claims. It does not appear Randall is motivated to make false claims.

RELATIONSHIP PERSPECTIVE

The Relationship Perspective of the Sexual Victim Trauma Assessment evaluates relationships between the offender and the victim, the victim and others who are important to the offender, as well as the relationship between the victim and those individuals who are important to the sexual offender. Pluses and minuses within this triangular approach provide information pertaining to the victim's perceptions of the offender/victim status. Those children who clearly see themselves as innocent and free from guilt, tend to rehabilitate at a faster rate. Those children who are confused about the offender/victim identity tend to be more traumatized.

Randall was sexually exploited by his sixth grade teacher, Mr. Donald Williams. Randall reports no sexual abuse prior to his involvement in the sixth grade with Mr. Williams. Randall also denies subsequent abuse and, therefore, Mr. Williams is Randall's only perpetrator.

Concerning the right hand side of the relationship triangle, information suggests that Randall viewed Mr. Williams as the perpetrator. This would seem to be the most positive side of the triangular approach since Randall can quite clearly discuss Mr. Williams in negative terms. It has been nearly two and one-half years since Randall's sexual abuse, but he seems to have been consistent in his ideations about Mr. Williams. Randall's statements through interviewing, subjective testing, and role playing indicate *he was really weird* or *I hated being around him.* Randall describes Mr. Williams as disgusting, repulsive, and clearly the perpetrator.

Randall's views of Mr. Williams would suggest a rehabilitating status, especially considering the fact that Mr. Williams plays an important part in the relationship triangle. It is on other sides of the triangle, however, that trauma seems to emerge.

On the bottom part of the triangle relationships between Mr. Williams and significant others are evaluated. The *offender status* of Mr. Williams becomes blurred. It is Randall's view and this examiner's opinion that Mr. Williams receives tremendous support from those who are significant to Randall. In order to understand this portion of the relationship triangle, those individuals supporting Mr. Williams will be examined separately.

Aside from Randall's mother, all other individuals in the *significant others* category believe Mr. Williams to be a positive person with many attributes. Randall's peers, as an example, have been extremely hostile toward him and the other two boys who reported sexual abuse. Randall is aware that these boys and girls think highly of Mr. Williams and they continue to make their support known to Randall.

From the school administration's point of view, Mr. Williams also fares very well. Mr. Williams has received the TEACHER OF THE YEAR award three out of the last six years in the district. In Randall's mind, the school originally doubted the identify of Mr. Williams as the perpetrator and continues to doubt. Randall talks at great length about the friendship between Mr. Williams and the school principal, Mr. Fuller. Randall is aware that the two men spend vacations together and they are socially dependent upon one another. Randall sees tremendous power in Mr. Fuller and Mr. Fuller's rejection of Randall is also very powerful. Randall is aware that the legal system discontinued the prosecutorial processes against Mr. Williams and, therefore, Randall does not view the legal system as believing Mr. Williams to be a perpetrator. Randall was interviewed by the prosecutor and eventually told that the prosecutor did not believe the case merited prosecution.

Finally, within the Relationship Perspective, Randall seems to be most traumatized by the school faculty who continue to have undying support for Mr. Williams. Many of Randall's night terrors appear to be related to the faculty members who contacted Randall and his mother urging him to recant or shaming him for *making up the story*. Randall seems to be most fearful of retribution from the faculty who, in Randall's mind, have undying support for Mr. Williams. It should be noted that collateral information found in depositions confirms Randall's ideations. Quite clearly, those involved on the periphery and in the faculty of the school continue to support Mr. Williams and denounce the allegations against him. It is also important to note that Mr. Williams does not deny that the behaviors described by Randall have taken place. Mr. Williams denies that these behaviors have traumatized the boys, but does not deny Randall's claims. In spite of Mr. Williams' acknowledgment, the faculty continues to be supportive of Mr. Williams, which Randall computes to forbidding Mr. Williams to take on the role of the perpetrator.

Finally, on the left hand side of the triangle examining the relationship between Randall and others who are significant, it becomes clear that Randall's support from his mother is outweighed by the lack of support from all others in the triangular component. Randall does not view himself in positive terms and he does not view others as seeing him differently. The principal of the school, the faculty, the system, (including a law enforcement officer, a social worker, and a prosecutor) in Randall's mind, have denied the existence of the perpetrator status for Mr. Williams. Therefore, in Randall's mind, these individuals do not view him as innocent, as wronged, and as the *victim*. Randall does not feel supported by anyone in the *significant others* category except for his mother and his mother, in her sub-assertiveness and dependency, is far outweighed by other individuals. Even though Randall clearly views Mr. Williams as the perpetrator, the *significant other* category refutes Randall's opportunity for rehabilitation in the Relationship Perspective.

DEVELOPMENTAL PERSPECTIVE

The Developmental Perspective of the Sexual Victim Trauma Assessment evaluates how the child perceives what has happened, according to the child's sexual development at the time of the abuse. It is perceptions of the child at the time the abuse occurred, that provide information to the child and have a lasting impact on the child's development at a later time. Secondly, the Developmental Perspective of the Trauma Assessment examines what information was available at the time of the abuse in order to more fully understand the victim's perceptions. Finally, the Developmental Perspective examines what has been lost in normal sexual development or what will be lost in normal development due to the sexual abuse that has taken place. It is the early perceptions of the abuse that provide a foundation for sexual development and cause trauma to normal development.

Randall was sexually abused during what this examiner determines to be the *unfortunate* stage of sexual development. During this time, children are usually becoming aware of the significance of sexuality and, at the same time, hormonal development is taking place. This can be an *unfortunate* time since the child is perceiving an unfamiliar sexual world at the same time that body development may be enhancing discomfort.

In addition to Randall's stage of development at the time the abuse occurred, it is important to understand what information was available to Randall at the time of the abuse. Not only is the stage of development important, but the sexual information available to balance the developmental stage must be examined.

Randall reports having absolutely no sex education whatsoever from either his mother or his father. Randall has not received any sexual information from a formalized school program, but he did have some basic knowledge regarding sexual jokes from his friends. Randall reports playing what appear to be normal sexual games with two of his father's stepchildren when the children were in the third grade. It does not appear that these scenarios were abusive and it is important to note that these experiences seem to have provided Randall with most of his knowledge regarding sexuality up to the time Mr. Williams abused him.

In careful examination of male/female role understanding, Randall again appears extremely naive and lacking in any knowledge whatsoever regarding normal male/female relationships. Randall's first few years of his life were met with conflict and controversy viewing men as being dominant, controlling, and far more assertive than Randall seems to feel about himself. Randall's image of women is one of dependency and weakness. Randall seems to have disappointed feelings about himself as a male since his portrayal of his father is one of strength and control.

Concerning the issue of homosexuality, there appears to be profound trauma. Randall has very little information available to him, except through slang words, crude jokes, or his father's interpretation. Randall has lived in a household where homosexuality has been a favored topic of his father. Randall's father professes extreme hatred and ridicule toward homosexuals and this information has escalated since Randall's disclosure.

Most significant, in discussing what information has been available to Randall is the lack of information available to Randall. He is the only child and, therefore, has had very little opportunity to learn from younger or older peers. He has absolutely no knowledge of positive aspects of human sexuality and, in fact, his sexual abuse appears to provide the only specific information. Randall has no information to teach him to separate normal sex play from what has occurred with Mr. Williams. Randall has very little understanding of his own arousal, or understanding regarding deviant sexual arousal. In summary, Randall Kyle seems to have been traumatized by an overt lack of information, which results in his sexual abuse being his only source of information.

In examining what has been lost in normal sexual development, a most significant issue involves Randall's arousal. During many of the sexual abuse scenarios, Randall recalls erectile responses and genital stimulation. This is particularly significant since Randall had particularly negative feelings toward the perpetrator yet seemed to feel *out of control* with his bodily responses. Randall was extremely embarrassed and humiliated by his responses and has tremendous fear of his *partnership* with Mr. Williams. Randall's bodily responses in conjunction with his father's attitude toward homosexuals have a profound effect on Randall's normal sexual development.

Male and female role identity and acceptance seem to have been devastated by Randall's sexual abuse. Normally, sixth grade boys are in a process of anticipating kissing, holding hands, and engaging in anticipatory sexual interactions with members of the opposite sex. Randall has been severely traumatized by his abuse since none of those activities have taken place. Randall's sexual abuse and his subsequent ridicule have forced him to discontinue all activities with peers, including females. This issue is compounded by Randall's fears that he is homosexual due to his bodily responses during many of the sexual encounters. Unfortunately, the last two and one-half years has compounded Randall's problems as he seems to have become fixated on homosexuality and he has lost tremendous opportunity to engage himself with members of the opposite sex.

Finally, concerning sexual phobias Randall seems to have been traumatized in many areas. Randall describes certain smells of his teacher involving a specific aftershave. Randall has had difficulties with his ears since several of the sexual behaviors involved whispering in Randall's ear. Masturbatory activities for Randall occur, but, unfortunately, Randall confesses that he is concerned about his thoughts during masturbation. Although they are not necessarily related to Mr. Williams, some of his masturbatory thoughts focus on the arousal experiences involved in the sexual abuse. Many of Randall's body mutilations have been afflicted on his genitalia in his repulsion and disgust at his masturbatory activities connected with Mr. Williams.

Finally, Randall Kyle's sexual development appears to have been arrested. At 15 1/2, Randall reports he has very little pubic hair and that he has had no other bodily changes. Medical reports from Mercy Medical Center confirm that there appears to be a retardation in his sexual development. Most concerning is the fact that Randall's sexual development seemed to be in the early stages as he entered the sixth grade, but had absolutely no progress in the last two and one-half years. Medical intervention is being contemplated through hormonal medication. However, Randall is currently resistive and unwilling to take part in this intervention due to his embarrassment and frustration.

SITUATIONAL PERSPECTIVE

The Situational Perspective of the Sexual Victim Trauma Assessment evaluates the environment or the sexual abuse that occurred in order to determine the patient's potential for developing phobic reactions and/or cognitive distortions. Issues from sensory input from the sexually abusive *scene* and from subsequent environmental reactions, provide information to the victim. Computation from those influences allow the victim to develop lifelong patterns of coping for future survival.

Randall Kyle was sexually abused by his teacher, Mr. Don Williams, for approximately five months. From August through January, Randall was submitted to sexual harassment and sexual abuse on a daily basis. The abusive behaviors included grabbing Randall and forcing him to sit on Mr. Williams' lap while Mr. Williams had an obvious erection. Mr. Williams would force several of the children to hug him before they were allowed to leave the room for recess. During these hugs, the boys were pulled up to the waist of Mr. Williams and their legs were spread apart while Mr. Williams pulled children's genitalia onto his genitalia. Mr. Williams also forced Randall to urinate in the lavatory in his presence. What seem to be most uncomfortable for Randall are the sexual discussions. Mr. Williams would make Randall come up to the front of the room each day and report whether or not he had *jerked off*. Very intrusive questioning occurred each morning, often while Randall was forced to sit on the lap of Mr. Williams. During the school day, Mr. Williams would approach Randall's desk and, again, whisper in his ear about Randall's body, about his erections, or about his masturbatory activities. Randall reports that Mr. Williams would often run his tongue around Randall's inner ear and Randall would be questioned about whether or not he enjoyed those activities. Randall believes that, at least three to four of these sexual activities occurred during *each* school day for a four to five month period.

In consideration of sensory involvement, Randall's ears appear to be most impacted. Randall demonstrated panic attacks during the assessment as he described feeling Mr. Williams' tongue in his ear. Randall also describes discomfort in the tactile responses of his own erections, as well as the fear of being forced to sit on Mr. Williams' erections. Certainly, the sense of sound was also impacted by listening to Mr. Williams' questions. From a general sensory input, it becomes clear that Randall developed school phobia and has never entered into another academic or vocational program since January of his sixth grade year.

The sexually abusive scene appears to be one of profound humiliation and degradation. Randall expresses extreme embarrassment regarding the fact that most of his sexual behaviors took place while others were present. Randall fears that the other children were aware of not only Mr. Williams' behavior, but also of Randall's erectile responses.

It is also significant that Randall reports vomiting in the lavatory before school in anticipation of proceeding into his classroom. Randall also reports being nauseous on the school bus as he left school. The impact of the abuse seems to have been profound pre and post abusive scenarios for Randall.

Randall's contemplations regarding reporting the abuse are intensely involved with his arousal responses and Mr. Williams' power. Randall reports that he observed Mr. Williams' status in the school and in the classroom and, at the same time, he observed his erectile responses. Randall felt as though he would not be believed and he also felt that he was somewhat responsible. Randall felt *trapped* in the classroom and felt there was no opportunity for him to escape as a victim. In Randall's mind, he was a *partner* and he would not be supported.

If Randall's entire situation is examined, it becomes clear that he had very little support from his father and that he missed his father a great deal. Randall was a young man who had few social skills and, therefore, did not have a sense of assertiveness or self-protection when the abuse took place. Randall's family's financial situation was destitute and in Randall's mind, there seemed to be very little opportunity for rescue.

Post-disclosure issues seem to have compounded the negative responses observed by Randall during the sexual abuse scenario. First, Randall's report did not occur until he recognized that he could not return to school following the Christmas vacation in January. Randall's night terrors and anxiety had increased to the point where he felt unable to return. Randall's first effort at disclosure came with a request to be put in another classroom, which was investigated and eventually the abuse reported.

It is also most significant that seven children reported the same behavior as Randall reported. Investigations took place in the school counselor's office with Mr. Williams present. This seemed to be extremely humiliating for Randall since four of the young men, following a three hour confrontation session, recanted their claims. Randall and two other young men continued to make allegations, but were obviously traumatized by the confrontation with the perpetrator and various faculty members.

Following the confrontation session between the counselor, Mr. Williams, and the reporting boys, a Law Enforcement investigation took place. Randall reports being interviewed in the presence of his mother and eventually in the presence of his father. Randall recalls his father being extremely outraged at Randall's inability to stop Mr. Williams and it should be noted that since the day Mr. Kyle participated in the interview he has refused to talk to Randall via telephone, correspondence, or in person.

Eventually, Randall was interviewed by a deputy prosecutor who reminded Randall of Mr. Williams' accomplishments over the past two years. It should also be noted that the interview took place at the school in an office adjacent to the counselor's office where Mr. Williams was then stationed. School administrators had made a decision to transfer Mr. Williams from a teaching position to a counseling position. Randall reports seeing Mr. Williams and the prosecutor *chatting* following the interview with the prosecutor and following the prosecutor's decision to withhold the prosecutorial process.

Most significantly following disclosure, the faculty of Fruitdale Elementary School seemed to take on a campaign against Randall and his friends. Randall reports being accosted by several teachers on the playground inquiring about why he had *made up the story*. Randall's home was visited by several teachers and telephone calls were prevalent. Randall was placed in another classroom and forced to sit in the back of the room. During social studies, the case was discussed and, in confrontational style, Randall was berated for his allegations.

Finally, Randall's home is one block away from the Fruitdale parking lot. Randall observed many activities taking place at the school to raise money for Mr. Williams' legal defense. A car wash, a baked food sale, and an auction took place within Randall's view demonstrating extreme support for Mr. Williams on the part of the faculty and school administrators.

Concerning distorted cognitions and coping skills Randall has made a decision to take on the role of the perpetrator. Randall has become self-abusive in suicidal ideations, body mutilation, and excessive failure. Randall also has adapted an affective avoidance coping skill as he presents himself as a young man who *feels nothing* and who will take very few risks. Randall's arrested sexual development is a classic example of his avoidance survival skill. It is also clear that Randall has taken on a paranoid stance feeling extremely frightened and helpless due to the retribution from others which has resulted in his agoraphobic tendencies.

SUMMARY AND RECOMMENDATIONS

In summary, Randall Allen Kyle is a young man who has very little opportunity to view himself as a victim. Even though his mother is supportive, her support is outweighted by the negative response from the system, from significant others, and, most importantly, from the faculty at Fruitdale Elementary.

From a Developmental Perspective, Randall has been extremely traumatized. He is becoming fixated on homosexuality, he has a distorted view of the male/female role, and he has absolutely no interest or understanding of normal sexual patterns.

From a Situational Perspective, Randall Kyle is extremely phobic toward school, toward relationships with adult males, and of his own erectile responses. He has developed coping skills of helplessness, paranoid delusions, and avoiding affective responses. Randall seems to be shrinking into an extremely small world in his desperate attempt to find safety.

Randall is in need of a comprehensive and intensive therapeutic program. Randall will need sexual counseling and perhaps medical intervention for his sexual development problems. He is a suicide risk and he will be in need of careful monitoring. Resolution needs to occur regarding Randall's role as a perpetrator and this may come from sexual education and sexual identity therapeutic involvements. Randall is in need of desensitization exercises in order to deal with his phobic responses and finally, he is in need of some kind of resolution process in coordination with the legal system, the school faculty, and his father in some therapeutic modality. Two and one-half years have gone by and Randall has continued to be traumatized. Unless these suggestions are taken and unless these patterns are discontinued, Randall has very little chance for rehabilitation.

THE MOURNING AFTER — ASSESSING THE ASSESSMENT

So that's it! Now, that the trauma is out, ordered, clarified, and classified, what can be done with it? What happens when trauma, once stifled and tucked away, emerges with powerful force?

Regrouping

The Trauma Assessment will not cure abuse. There are two results from the Trauma Assessment. The first is a map of rehabilitation and the second is a valuable treatment contribution. Although these two results are positive, the immediate residual effects from the Trauma Assessment process are not always positive. Negative responses following the Trauma Assessment tend to be primarily for the adolescent or adult patient. A different response seems to occur for the younger patient.

The purpose of the Trauma Assessment for children is to pinpoint difficulties that lurk ahead in the child's future. The *process* of the Trauma Assessment can be rehabilitating to smaller children through the desensitization process and through positive interactions with a supportive adult. Again, by virtue of the developmental limitations of children, they are not capable of understanding their trauma and, therefore, revealing the significance of their trauma may seem meaningless to them, but has great value to their caretakers.

For the adult patient, however, unearthing the trauma and clarifying the trauma may not always be a positive experience. The time period following the completion of the Trauma Assessment is often a critical time where many patients suffer depression, outrage or general upheaval. It may be during this time period when patients leave treatment, refusing to return. The satisfaction of discovering the nature of trauma may be reserved for the clinician as the patient may experience a period of rejection or sadness.

The coping skills and footprints that kept the pain deadened or under control have been pulled out from under the victim. Outrage toward the perpetrator, anger toward the significance of the trauma, or, most importantly, frustration regarding the loss of childhood may occur during this time of crisis. The response may be a desperate effort to rekindle footprints, to refocus frustration, or simply to discontinue the process by rebelling from the therapeutic intervention. Previous pain for the victim has been in small doses, step-by-step, leaking out in less profound, but nonetheless consistent, trauma. Through the Trauma Assessment, a focus has been made to examine, clarify and unearth trauma that has been superficially under control. The ugly head of trauma has now emerged and responses from patients may be as ugly.

Ownership

It is important that the patient *owns* the Trauma Assessment. The Trauma Assessment must be accepted by the victim and brought under the victim's control. Perhaps for the first time in the patient's life, something pertaining to the sexual abuse is potentially controllable. Because of the victim's frustration in divulging the trauma, the task of accepting ownership of the trauma becomes more difficult.

Enough Is Enough

A revisitation of Trauma Assessment closure begins the process of ownership and prepares both the patient and the therapist for *The Mourning After*. As finalization of the Trauma Assessment process reaches closure, ownership can be encouraged if the patient is allowed to make the decision when *enough is enough*. This is especially important for those patients who have foggy memories or less than clear perspectives of sexual abuse. A survival skill may be to postpone resolution and clarification because an absolutely clear picture does not emerge.

But, I want a video, the victim replies. This may be a resistance to stopping the Trauma Assessment process since memory of the sexual abuse or dynamics of the family are not as clear as the evening news. Preparing the victim for these frustrations and allowing the victim to choose when enough information has been gathered starts the process of ownership and prevents resistance from continuing.

I want to keep working on remembering. It is very important for me to get it right. Each time I practice the Memory Recapturing Exercises, I get another piece. I have also had flashbacks or feelbacks that provide even more information. Why should I stop now? If I have made this kind of investment of time and money, why not make it right?

Darlene is an obsessive-compulsive perfectionist. Revealed in her Trauma Assessment is a tendency towards compensating through her accomplishments. It is very difficult for Darlene to do anything that is not perfect. The Trauma Assessment is no exception. It is very important to Darlene that the process continue. Unfortunately, continuing the process leaves her in limbo, constantly hopeful that if she ever becomes perfect, the race can begin again, and perhaps she will be accepted by the perpetrator.

Red Light

It is important to build up to a crescendo in closing the Trauma Assessment process. If the Trauma Assessment is done haphazardly, quickly, or under total direction of the clinician or the referring person, it seems less powerful to the patient. It is important for the patient to have a sense of control and it is important to build up intensity and *grandness* for the Trauma Assessment completion. The clinician hopes that the victim has learned that the Trauma Assessment is a document that will provide a vehicle for rehabilitation. Without this preparation, a situation similar to Darlene's may emerge.

As intensity is encouraged for the grand day of completion, the victim should be able to hoist the *red flag*, signaling when *enough is enough*. A date should be set or activities should be organized signaling a closure of the Trauma Assessment process. The red flag can be hoisted either chronologically, through ac-

tivities, or through other means. The most important issue is that the victim chooses the closure process in advance. The subtle significance implies success and control — something that has been absent in much of the victim's life.

When the red light or stopping period occurs, the Trauma Assessment Data Collection process has stopped. A mini celebration should take place providing the victim with congratulatory remarks or activities. These positive responses should be followed up by a telephone call or personal contact approximately 24 to 48 hours after the victim has *closed the door* on more data collection. This is an important therapeutic technique since previous to the door slamming shut, footprints were in action, resisting, fighting, rationalizing. By the time the Trauma Assessment has been completed, many of the coping skills should have lessened in power. The subtleties of resistance, however, are often still at work.

When the victim is allowed to make the decision to stop the data collection process and when the victim is finally allowed to breathe, relax, and enjoy the congratulatory remarks, memories often resurface. The resistance to memory may be resting and relaxing. It is not uncommon for victims who have closed the door to have a tremendous amount of reoccurring memories within a very short period after the red light closed the door. If memories have not been rekindled, but the victim is asked about reoccurring memories or continued involvement with the Data Collection process, power is again returned to the victim. For a final time, the patient may need to remind the therapist that *enough is enough*.

The Presentation Process

When the Trauma Assessment has been completed, an appointment should be scheduled for the patient or patient's caretaker. The Trauma Assessment must be understood as a vehicle for recovery, but, in addition as an exhibit of pain or terror. Trauma Assessments are not easy to read for individuals who have empathy toward victims or for victims who have suffered. For parents or caretakers, the Trauma Assessment may be the first opportunity to truly examine what has happened to someone who is treasured. Whether the patient is an adult or a small child, the first exposure to the Trauma Assessment will, in most cases, cause trauma to the reader.

Handle With Care

If the Trauma Assessment is mailed or simply submitted to a parent or caseworker, the effect of the Trauma Assessment may be lost. The action suggests insensitivity for the pain suffered by a victim. A *grand* presentation needs to be made for the first time the Trauma Assessment will be perused.

In some instances, the Trauma Assessment may be submitted to attorneys, therapists, or other professionals. Sensitivity must be directed toward nonprofessionals as defined by the caretakers of victims or the victims themselves. In most cases, however, the Trauma Assessment should be presented under the control of the clinician.

The Trauma Assessment may be extremely important for parents or caretakers who are in denial or who may have survived the abuse of their children by discounting trauma. When the Trauma Assessment is read by those individuals in a controlled, therapeutic atmosphere with grand ceremony, then efforts to deny trauma will be more difficult and efforts to understand the trauma will be enhanced.

For the adult patient who has never truly examined the pain, therapeutic support is essential. Often, there is tremendous anxiety, repression, pain, and fear as the Trauma Assessment externalizes something previously uncontrollable and unmentionable. The victim may be absolutely devastated by this process and all effort must be made to provide therapeutic support. Often, contingency plans need to be established for the patient following the official presentation of the Trauma Assessment.

The Big Day

An appointment should be scheduled for either the patient or the caretakers of the patient approximately two hours before actual contact with the therapist. Those reading the Trauma Assessment should be sequestered in a room far away from distraction, noise, or interruptions. Pad and paper should be provided, as well as refreshments. It is important to spend at least two hours alone with the evaluation.

The Trauma Assessment is presented with instructions that the document should be read several times and then reread so that the discussion following the reading session will resolve superficial or immediate questions and concerns. It may also be helpful to caution victims about denial systems or footprints that may emerge as this exercise is taking place.

Darlene, you have in your hands the result of at least two months of painful therapeutic work. You are going to be reading, in black and white, an assessment of your pain. This is a very important process. I hope you will take the task seriously. Let me tell you of my concern.

*One of my worries is that you will read the evaluation very, very quickly in order to complete the **task**. Remember how we talked about your tendency to be perfect and to constantly cleanse yourself from the pain you suffered. One of my fears is that you will go through the evaluation quickly and work toward completing the assignment without letting any of the awareness or any of the value of the Trauma Assessment become real. I want you to be successful and you would not be here today if those old roads or footprints were comfortable. Try to*

avoid them, try not to hurry, try not to be perfect. Try to feel what is contained in these pages.

This is the first day in taking a look at the damage that has been caused to you. Don't go quickly. You are much too important for that. Read each word and try to take each word into your mind. I know there will be words that are confusing to you and I know there will be times when you will have many feelings. You may write on the evaluation, you may circle things that you want to discuss. Don't hurry, don't be perfect.

This assignment is something for you and it has been done with care. You are worth every step. You have put so much effort into going this far. Don't hurry with the second step. The evaluation belongs to you, no one else. We do not have another copy in the entire world. The next step in treatment will be for us to decide what to do with the evaluation, but the first step is for you to meet your pain.

Clearly, victims will have a much greater opportunity to avoid falling into old patterns of footprints if they are warned in advance. Without this warning or assistance, the patient will have greater tendencies to resort to old patterns and failure will surface.

Basking in the Pain

When victims are finally approached, many coping skills are used. It is not uncommon, as an example, for victims to have difficulty holding the Trauma Assessment in their hands. Victims have been observed on one side of the room under a comforter while their Trauma Assessment sits powerfully on the other side of the room. It is as though their privacy has been invaded once again. The victim may be outraged toward the *invasion*. The victim's outrage may be superficial and directed toward a typo or a misspelled word, or an improper name. *I didn't attend school at Greenwood Elementary until the fifth grade. It's listed here as the fourth grade.* There is some sense of power for the victim in pointing out details.

Good Grief

Another typical response seems to be grief and sadness. Although grief is certainly painful, it may signify progress for the victim. Other coping skills such as manipulation, resistance, or outrage suggest that the victim is not able to focus on the grief and that task must occur before there can be progress. Grief may be a healthy indicator.

Depending upon the victim's response, intervention must occur, giving complete power back to the victim in a never ending process. Permission should be requested to make a copy of the evaluation. If technical objections to the Trauma Assessment surface, those changes should be made. An effort should be made to focus on the victim's wishes.

Move Closer

The next task goes beyond reading the Trauma Assessment. Victims may acknowledge reading the evaluation several times, but incorporation of the Trauma Assessment from a psychological perspective may not have occurred. Being able to assess the assessment is the second step, which will allow the victim an opportunity to come even closer to the pain.

Some patients may not be able to take the second step of assessing the assessment. Some patients may need more time to read the Trauma Assessment or to recuperate from the process of reading the Trauma Assessment.

I took the Trauma Assessment out of the office under the advice of my therapist. It seemed simple to me and I didn't understand the purpose. Even though I had spent the last four hours sobbing while I read the evaluation, the task of taking it home seemed simple. I was asked to have the Trauma Assessment in my possession until the next appointment. It seemed easy. I am such a competent person. Thirty minutes after I left the office, I became hysterical in the shopping mall. I couldn't tell what was wrong with me. I was in total panic over a complicated task of buying socks for my son. I couldn't seem to breathe. I felt four years old. It was the Trauma Assessment in the car! I couldn't stand it. Within 45 minutes, I returned the Trauma Assessment to the clinic, feeling much better and in control. I was not aware that it would take me approximately four months to actually incorporate the Trauma Assessment and its information into my life (or my purse).

Assessing the Assessment

Possession of the Trauma Assessment is an extremely important step in recovery. The Trauma Assessment must be carefully incorporated into the victim's repertoire of understanding and feeling. The victim has spewed forth the information regarding the abuse and the pain is now in black and white on a ten page document. Assessing the assessment allows the patient to get closer to the externalized pain, hopefully under a more protective situation.

In the past, the trauma of sexual abuse has been internal, in an out of control way. The victim has stumbled because of vulnerability. Through the Trauma Assessment process, the pain has been externalized and now belongs on paper. The goal is to have the trauma under the control of the paper, externalizing and controlling the pain even more. Now, the victim must move toward the pain in an external framework.

The patient should be provided with a variety of options in assessing the assessment. The competency of the victim will dictate a variety of choices. The patient's current functioning level may also dictate the modalities presented. As an example, being able to rewrite the Trauma Assessment from the perspective of *little Suzie* may be too painful for the victim at this time. The victim may need to choose another more comfortable modality. A variety of choices should be presented with the victim's competency and current functioning level in mind.

The Red Pen — Mrs. Barktrop, Where Are You?

Perhaps, one of the safest modalities to suggest in evaluating the assessment is the one similar to a grade school teacher with the dreaded *red pen*. The victim may choose to correct errors in the Trauma Assessment. Hopefully, professional errors will be at a minimum, but other errors in details, etc., may be a very safe method of evaluation for the patient. If there are no errors, the patient may wish to take on the task of simply indicating an affirmation of the facts, paragraph by paragraph. This very safe process allows the patient to be completing an assignment with success and will force the patient to peruse the evaluation, word by word, through another modality.

Secretary, Please

Another option allows the victim to rewrite the Trauma Assessment in his or her own words. This modality requires the patient to be a secretary and simply rephrase the evaluation in more familiar words. This technique is somewhat within the cognitive realm since the victim will need to use a dictionary for many words that are beyond the victim's comprehension. This modality is *task oriented* and allows an intellectual framework to operate, perhaps protecting the affective process.

Future Plans

Consideration may also be made for the option of sharing the evaluation with another person in the victim's life. The patient may take on the task of perusing the Trauma Assessment in order to either remove or change information for presentation to another person. If the victim, as an example, intends to exhibit the Trauma Assessment to a husband or to a parent who does not have knowledge of psychological terms, the victim may choose to rewrite the Trauma Assessment for the purpose of *helping others*. Again, this is a secretarial task, but it may be quite helpful to the victim.

> *I can't bear to have my wife know the part about my homosexuality. She wants to be involved in my therapy and support me, but I fear she will leave if she finds out I have had affairs with men.*

Jacob chooses to omit the section in his Trauma Assessment regarding his homosexual tendencies. Control and choice must be given to Jacob. That portion of the Trauma Assessment is omitted. A year later in treatment Jacob

is reminded of his omission. Through introspection, Jacob can see more clearly the progress he has made. Jacob needed the opportunity to control his evaluation, yet the removal of that component became a therapeutic issue with successful results months later.

Let the Child Do It

An extremely effective modality for assessing the assessment occurs when the abandoned child within the victim responds to each paragraph from an affective perspective. This requires the victim to look inside the child and write the child's responses to the evaluation. This may be painful for the victim, but also very important.

> *This paragraph makes Julie Jo feel really angry. How could they do that to her, how could they tell her she was ugly and skinny and that no one liked her, while, on the other hand, they said her boobs were making him molest her? How could they do that to her?*

Critical Critique

Another modality for assessing the assessment requires the adult part of the patient to respond, but from an affective framework. With the adult in operation, attempts are made to respond to each paragraph in the Trauma Assessment, but from an affective modality. The adult (cognitive) describes the feelings (affective).

This part really makes me angry. I became so upset when I read this part about how I have become like my mother. The last thing I wanted to do was continue the cycle. I am so disgusted with myself, but even more disgusted with her.

It is important that the victim has assessed or readjusted the Trauma Assessment to the point of perfection. Treatment is likely to be more difficult unless this process is completed. Without an acceptance of the trauma, without ownership, repairing the damage will be difficult, if not impossible.

For smaller children who cannot possibly proceed through this process, accepting or affirming the evaluation is very important for parents or caretakers. The caretakers of children, as indicated previously, also have denial systems and resistance patterns. Some form of accepting the evaluation must occur for these caretakers in order for this child's rehabilitation to be possible.

Sharing the Assessment — People Power

After the evaluation has been confirmed, accepted, or *owned*, the next step in using the assessment as a treatment tool occurs as the victim shares the evaluation with a significant person. Primarily, this step pertains to an adult or an adolescent victim who seems to be in a traumatic bond with other individuals. The first step in sharing the assessment requires carefully choosing the *helper*.

The purpose of sharing the assessment is to align support, not to resolve or clarify. In fact, those issues related to specific individuals involved in trauma bonding should be avoided. If, as an example, the Trauma Assessment reveals that the victim is particularly damaged by a father's lack of support, father would be a highly improper person to be involved in sharing the assessment. Certainly, treatment recommendations would diagnose the father as an important component to rehabilitation, but not in the important process of sharing the assessment.

The most attractive choices are individuals involved in the victim's life post trauma. A likely example would be the partner of a victim who did not appear to be significant in the relationship triangle. A sibling who lived in the same family and who is already supportive and empathic may be an excellent choice. The *helper* could be a distant relative, friend, or a group member. This is not a time of resolution, but a time of desensitization, of sharing the trauma with another helpful individual.

Outlining Goals

It is important to outline goals for the process of sharing the assessment. Sexual abuse is something that has been out of control for the victim. Each therapeutic step is designed to place the victim in control. This step requires the victim to outline goals, to ponder goals, and to redefine goals so that success can be assured.

If, as an example, the victim's goal is to have the chosen person receiving the Trauma Assessment *feel the depth of pain*, the process is doomed for failure. Through therapeutic intervention, the victim must design goals that are more attainable. Limitations should be set and caution should be raised against setting goals that are impossible. Generally, experiencing the depth of someone's pain is an unattainable goal. More reasonable and attainable goals need consideration. The following are a list of more attainable goals that have a likelihood of success:

I just wanted you to know what happened to me as a child. I simply want your acknowledgement.

I want to stop bleeding all over you. I want my pain to be assigned to my offender and not leaking over you and our family.

I want you to read my Trauma Assessment and understand that my pain is not related to you.

I just want someone in my family to know what happened. Just knowing and believing will be okay.

Preparing the Victim

Since this is an important step, the victim needs to be properly prepared for responses from the person receiving the Trauma Assessment. Even though goals may be carefully outlined, the patient needs to be prepared for responses from

the other person in order to assure the greatest opportunity for success. Without preparation, it is likely that the victim will be disappointed in the response from the person receiving the Trauma Assessment.

Even the most empathic and sensitive *helpers* tend to respond inappropriately. Without guidance, victims become vulnerable to these painful responses even though the insensitive actions are unintentional. The victim needs to proceed through a process of outlining the painful responses that could occur so that desensitization takes place.

What would be the most painful thing John could say to you when he reads the Trauma Assessment? From this question, the victim may outline all possible avenues of trauma. 3 x 5 cards could be used for the victim's recording of the most painful responses possible.

Why didn't you stop it?

Why didn't you tell someone?

Why didn't you come to me for help?

Is that all that happened?

Why are you bringing this up now?

And perhaps one of the most important responses reflected one 3 x 5 card is *nothing*. A *nothing* response can be extremely painful for victims and sadly tends to be a typical response even from a caring, concerned partner.

Through this process, the victim is contemplating what could occur from an extremely negative perspective. If these responses occur as the patient presents the Trauma Assessment to another individual, the patient has already been desensitized and control is available. The world outside the therapeutic office is also cold and insensitive for victims. This entire exercise teaches the patient that survival is possible when potential trauma is met in a controlled manner.

> I wanted so much for my mother to acknowledge my abuse. I knew that the chance of her treating me the way I wanted was very slim. I nonetheless practiced her responses that were, more than likely going to happen. After presenting the Trauma Assessment to her, my heart was in my throat hoping she would finally protect me like I had always wanted. She read the evaluation, looked at me with that critical eye and explained, *you never seem to be satisfied with things the way they are. You are always wanting to blame someone for your problems.* My first response was to cry, but my second response was to say, *hold it a minute, Mom, I have that card right here. I knew you were going to say that.*

Even though the *helper's(?)* responses were disappointing, the patient had a sense of control in predicting her mother's action. The pain was desensitized and, although not alleviated,

the victim learned an important lesson in controlling trauma from others.

Help the Helper

In some cases, assistance may be given to the person receiving the Trauma Assessment. Using 3 x 5 cards previous to the presentation may provide the *helper* with skills to be more empathic and sensitive. In many instances, family members do not know the proper responses or how to alleviate the pain for the victim.

> My husband was pained by my abuse and felt victimized himself. He was supportive of my therapy and put forth effort to understand. I knew, however, that he copes with my pain by being silent. I feared his silence more than any other response. I prepared three cards for him. One card said, *I want you to read this so you will know none of this is your fault.* The next one said, *I don't want you to be miserable or take on my pain. I just want you to know what happened to me.* The third card said, *Your silence will kill me. If you don't know what to say, ask questions. If you can't ask questions, hold me.*

In this case, Phylis is giving her partner suggestions and covering nearly every potential trauma that could occur. Phylis is outlining options for her partner and taking the step to *help her helper.*

Time is of the Essence

Finally, guidance must be given in choosing an appropriate time and place for the presentation of the Trauma Assessment. Obviously, during the middle of the Super Bowl would be an inappropriate time to share the Trauma Assessment with an avid football fan (partner). In the bathroom while Jacob's wife is getting ready for work and had just discovered a run in her pantyhose would not be an appropriate time for Jacob to discuss his homosexual tendencies or present his Trauma Assessment. A therapeutic session may be the most appropriate time and place for sharing of the assessment.

The Mourning After

Following the presentation of the assessment, assessing the assessment, and sharing the assessment, a mourning period, may occur again. Grief and sadness may overtake the victim who initially experienced grief but became enthusiastic with the tasks presented. As the victim settles into another acknowledgement of trauma, the grief response may again surface.

> *I just felt empty, as though something had been taken away from me. I knew the reason, but it didn't seem to stop the grief. I had given away my pain and now it was on paper. I had shared it with someone else and I received support. Now, I feel like a piece of me is missing. I feel lonely.*

The purpose of the Trauma Assessment was to clarify and pinpoint areas of pain. The patient may feel a sense of emptiness once that process has taken place. To relieve the grief, the patient must then look toward the next step of outlining a treatment plan and organizing even more painful, yet successful, steps toward recovery.

THE ROAD MAP HOME

What are the tools of treatment? Is treatment traditional or typical? What is the method or the map leading to recovery?

There are basic treatment modalities and treatment goals whether victims are two or ninety-two. Recognizing that the Trauma Assessment itself is treatment, it is inappropriate to suggest that the therapeutic process begins after the Trauma Assessment. The process of the Trauma Assessment, owning, evaluating and sharing the Trauma Assessment has already started the therapeutic process. Following those steps, goals should be considered for continued therapeutic success.

The Trauma Assessment lends itself to specific issues, unique for each patient just as trauma is unique. Each therapeutic goal within a treatment plan, however, is found in general goals and objectives pertinent to most victims.

Specific methodologies to accomplish goals will always remain unique for each patient. As the treatment plan is organized, general modalities and goals can become part of the foundation for treatment planning.

Treatment Modalities — Thou Shalt Not Be Traditional

The way in which treatment goals are met within the therapeutic environment is not traditional. Just as the Big Four needed abandonment in assessing trauma, relieving trauma also needs readjustment. Traditional methods of treatment may not be effective with sexual victim patients. This is a time for reflection and examination of new ideas. What a tragedy to conduct a Trauma Assessment with innovative techniques and establish an archaic and traditional treatment plan to relieve the trauma.

There are six treatment modalities or methodologies that tend to be effective with sexual victims. In appreciation of distorted cognitions, footprints, damage to developmental systems, relationship trauma, confusion about the offender/victim identity, etc., these modalities have been designed.

Modality 1 — Doing

No Deep Dish Therapy Allowed

Traditional methods of one-to-one clinical interviews regarding *feelings* can be found in a traditional psychoanalytical model or humorously described as *deep dish therapy*. Asking victims how they *feel* or requiring victims to introspect on a surface level may be asking an impossible task. Internal pain should be externalized, which is a process within itself. However, the traditional method of inquiring about internal feelings and expecting appropriate responses may need to be discarded.

Rather than requiring the victim to externally project confused and distorted internal feelings, the methodology of *doing* allows the process to occur in nonverbal terms. There is an inherent process of *possession* in activities that require the patient to *do*. The methodology of *doing* smacks of capability, of ownership, and eventually becomes a much more effective way of learning. Externalization is the ultimate in the process toward rehabilitation. *Doing* is a very important process for allowing the internal pain to become externalized.

Inside Out Control

Because of the trauma suffered, sexual victims tend to feel out of control, incapable and vulnerable. Any activities or exercises that allow the patient to bring the pain outside, but under control, is an effective modality. *Doing* fits into this process.

Artwork, letter writing, journal preparation, body exercises, role playing, flash cards, list preparation are all specific examples of assignments, skills and techniques that allow the patient to have some sense of capability in the process of healing. If therapists are only to rely on discussions through the clinical interview, this process may not occur. In appreciation of *footprints* which have forced the patient to distort, to confuse and entangle, the process of completing small increments of activities divided by the process of *doing* has a much greater chance for success within a therapeutic environment.

As the patient sees accomplishments, as the patient touches and feels success, as the patient is able to focus on external activities, rehabilitation can begin.

Modality 2 — Trusting, Unfolding, and Releasing

A raging conflict over the therapeutic relationship with sexually abused patients exists. Some advocate that only those therapists who have been sexually victimized themselves should be providing services to sexual victim patients, suggesting that empathy is impossible unless trauma is directly experienced. On the other end of the spectrum are those who suggest that professional objectivity is only with therapists who were not sexually abused as children. As the debate rages, common sense dictates the most appropriate therapist/patient relationship.

The ideal relationship should be one in which the patient finds the therapeutic environment a sanctuary. Trust is extremely important. The sanctuary occurs when all feelings, attitudes, responses and ideations are acceptable and safe. The patient should be free of any obligation to the therapist, other than financial. The patient should be able to express feelings and most importantly change feelings as the road to recovery is taken. When an intimate relationship occurs between the patient and a therapist, the sanctuary is lost, therapy may be retarded, but, most importantly, trust cannot exist.

The Three R's

The destructive result of an intimate or subjective patient/therapist relationship comes in three packages, with the first dealing with the issue of reciprocity. Even though a therapist may not issue a demand of reciprocity, a subtle or underlying obligation to return personal feelings is clear. The *I care for you* has a subtle demand for *Do you care too?*

Reciprocity

Sexual victims have traditionally been responsible for many things in the family as a result of sexual abuse. The demand of reciprocity in the patient/therapist relationship seems unfair. If the patient has a sanctuary within the therapeutic environment and if the patient is to rehabilitate, the patient's work should be directed toward recovery, not toward reciprocal demands.

Children who have been sexually abused have often been obligated to care for the perpetrator, to keep the family together or to fulfill the sexual needs of the perpetrator. The victim may have been responsible for keeping the perpetrator out of jail or for keeping the perpetrator employed. Whether the patient is three or thirty-three, obligations should discontinue. The sanctuary of the therapist/patient relationship should have no demands for reciprocity.

Ouch!

This suggestion may be painful for therapists who believe that caring, on a personal level is good for the patient. In reality, *the therapist benefits from a personal relationship since successes in recovery are shared.* Although the overall intention may be for the patient, the ego of the therapist is nurtured in the sharing of successes and conversely the therapist feels *stung* if success is not shared.

Running

A second potential of difficulty in an improper therapist/patient relationship is the deadly result from attempts to become personal with an individual who has been traumatized by intimacy in the past. If a therapist reaches out on a personal level to a patient who has been offended and traumatized by personal relationships, the result may be that the victim copes by running. The *I care for you* may be interpreted by the patient as another opportunity to be exploited. As the therapist reaches for the patient, the victim may reach for the door.

Running from intimacy or from those who seem to care is a common pattern for many sexual victims. Patients have spent much of their childhood associating tenderness, intimacy and caring with exploitation and abuse. Again, good intentions may exist, but the major reaction is one from childhood. Intimacy or personal relationships sets up the victim to be exploited if the only option for the victim is to run.

Release!

The ultimate objective in the patient/therapist relationship should be one in which the patient can be rehabilitated and released into a world where survival will continue. The patient must be freed into a world where day-to-day coping occurs without the therapist. If an intimate relationship is established, it may be difficult for a patient to be released.

For some patients who choose not to run from the personal relationship, feelings of nurturing and tenderness are comfortable. Intimacy in the patient/therapist relationship allows the victim to feel protected, needed and perhaps loved. The destructive result of this combination may be resistance to rehabilitation.

The victim may need to *stay sick* in order to keep the relationship. It may be impossible for the patient to be released from the therapist because of the personal feedback. Leaving, (getting better) may seem lonely and cold. Remaining traumatized may seem more comfortable.

What Tadoo

In revisiting the debate over whether therapists must disclose information about childhood sexual abuse, one clear fact emerges. Regardless of what answer is given to the patient, a *no win* situation occurs. If the therapist is a victim and that information is disclosed, the underlying message suggests the issue is important. Initially, the patient may feel protected, understood, and contented with knowledge of the therapist's childhood abuse. By answering the question, the therapist has acknowledged the importance of the issue and has closed the door to the victim feeling an opportunity to be understood, nurtured, and protected by anyone who is not a sexual victim. Vulnerability for victims is consequently heightened. The answer suggests that the releasing process requires the victim to venture into a world of critical disbelieving, antagonistic *nonvictims*.

If the therapist denies sexual abuse as a child, the message to the victim again is one that suggests the issue is important. It is as though the therapist is saying, *I have limitations.* The victim who may be looking for reasons to avoid pain may either leave the therapeutic environment or may stay in therapy with the denial system heavily entrenched, *I will stay with this therapist who will never understand anyway.*

The most deadly issue in answering these questions is the suggestion that *it matters.* Ultimate therapeutic success allows sanctuary and safety of feelings in an environment where survivorship will take place. Power and control over the victim's destiny must be internal. If the issue of abuse or non-abuse for the therapist is important, the victim is rendered out of control in the process toward survivorship. The message from the therapist, to the victim is:

You must choose carefully, only those people who allow you to survive.

Survivorship should depend on the victim not on others.

My victimization or lack of victimization as a child does not matter. I am going to help you help yourself to heal. You have the power to heal, and I am going to guide you through that process. When you are finished, you will be able to look back and say, I did it regardless of my therapist's childhood, my husband's childhood, or anyone else's childhood. There will always be people who will help you and there will always be people who

will not. Your success or failure does not depend on people outside of you, it depends on you. Let us not look outside for where we should go, but look inside and find the road map to recovery.

Modality 3 — Processing . . . And Product

Because of victim's distorted thinking, compartmentalized tendencies, confusion, and disastrous coping skills, *processing* must occur in order to establish a successful treatment plan. Victims who are established in open ended, non-specific treatment often remain confused, disconnected, and distorted. For some victims, even the smallest of tasks seem overwhelming. Small increments or steps to success, lead the patient toward the product. Each one of those steps is as important as the product itself.

Cassandra is a frustrated twelve-year-old in the beginning stages of becoming the *uncomfortable* victim. Cassie has been brutally abused by both her grandfather and stepfather. By the time disclosure was made, Cassie was age 10. Her perpetrator was sent to prison, but her grandfather was ruled incompetent to stand trial and, therefore, was placed on probation with the Psychiatric Security Review Board.

Cassie entered into victim's treatment for prepubescent girls. After eighteen months, Cassie is outraged, resistive, and disinterested. Also, after eighteen months of therapy, Cassie's symptoms are not only present, but seem to be worsening. Cassie is involved in what appears to be self-abusive behaviors, such as consuming alcohol, shoplifting, and failing in school. Her therapists seem to be baffled because her treatment appears successful.

Cassie is such a good group member. We can always count on her to tell her story. She never hesitates or seems to be embarrassed. The only problem we have is her disgust and verbal attacks on other group members who seem to be unable to talk with the same competency. We don't know why Cassie isn't getting any better.

The problem in Cassie's treatment is related to a lack of product. She has no sense of accomplishment since her treatment is open ended and without goals. Yes, she is able to *tell her story* competently and certainly, in the first few months of therapy, she benefited from knowing she was not alone and that a crime had been committed. Certainly, the positive peer relationships in group assisted Cassie in the early stages of her disclosure.

Treatment goals for Cassie should have taken approximately three to four months to accomplish. Unfortunately, her treatment has continued without a process toward a specific product. Upon interview, Cassie feels as though she has been *sentenced to treatment*. While her grandfather continues to work in his garden, and her stepfather continues to write her mother love letters, Cassie feels imprisoned in treatment. Cassie stated, at one point, *at least my stepdad knows when he is finished.*

Cassie later entered into a treatment program that set specific goals with a specific product at the end of treatment. This is not to suggest that rehabilitation for victims involves simply creating a product and accomplishing six goals listed on a violet piece of construction paper. There is value, however, in setting specific goals and products. More importantly, Cassie needs to be involved in the process of recognizing those goals and working toward a sense of satisfaction. In Cassie's new treatment program, the Trauma Assessment reveals specific issues regarding her needs. Cassie was involved in directing and understanding the steps toward treatment success, which eventually outlined the *product*. Directionless treatment for victims seems to be another way to echo the robbery from the past. In sexual abuse, victims have no control, no sense of power, and no direction. Helplessness is a common feeling. Directionless treatment may be somewhat similar to the victim's past abuse.

Past, Present, Future

Not only does a therapeutic program need to be directed toward the future, but reminders of the past can make the future even more successful. The road to recovery always contains a past and a future. Each successful step toward recovery can be enhanced through therapeutic reminders of the past. Showing the victim each step of success directs more hope toward the future. Etiology of past successes enhances future successes.

Before we close tonight's group, I want to remind you of your successes. Pause for a moment and think about your first night in therapy. Remember your anxieties, your fears, and your hope that the couch would swallow you, so you wouldn't have to be noticed. Look at the beautiful people in this room and think about the past. Always remember from where you have walked and the road ahead will be much sweeter.

Modality 4 — Education

An important modality for sexual victim treatment is to educate, educate, educate. Often, the very simple approach of education is overlooked in the victim's treatment. Education certainly is not the only treatment methodology

or sexual victims could find successful therapy in libraries. Education is important within the treatment environment, especially in consideration of distorted cognitions and damage to normal development.

The P Word

Prevention of sexual abuse is an important issue for victims of all ages. Victims of sexual abuse tend to be at a higher risk for additional abuse in the future. Abusive individuals may be attracted to abusable people and, therefore, sexual victims have a greater potential to be revictimized.

The educational model of prevention is extremely important for these children. Educational efforts should go beyond preventing sexual abuse, however, and should be more profound than *just say no*. Effective prevention is a process of internalizing a reason for protection, which results in a much more comprehensive educational program.

For the older patient, breaking the cycle of sexual abuse is an important treatment goal and can be accomplished through an educational modality regarding prevention. Mothers who were sexually abused in childhood are at greater risk to have their children sexually abused. Breaking the cycle of abuse can be impacted through the modality of teaching prevention.

The Stud Horse Theory — Revisited

Another important component of the education modality is teaching how human beings are different than animals. Although sexual arousal may not be controllable, sexual activities are more under control for adults than for stud horses grazing in the field of frisky mares. As described in Chapter Eight, society will teach victims that it is possible to cause perpetrators to offend or that somehow offenders were driven out of control by what the victim wore or by the body language of the victim. Teaching the difference between animals and human beings is important in stopping this guilt ridden learning.

Orgasms are Orgasms are Orgasms

An additional component of the educational treatment modality is human sexuality. There are many capacities in which sexual education becomes a treatment issue. Teaching the patient to have successful sexual relationships is absolutely necessary for adults. Teaching adult patients to become sex educators of their children is another example. Teaching about the human sexual response is an important modality for repairing the damage to victims.

As an example, as outlined in trauma research, *orgasms* tend to be particularly painful to victims. Sexual stimulation can be extremely traumatizing. Additionally, victims may be confused or feel guilty about causing sexual arousal in the perpetrator. A *clinicalization* of orgasms in order to undo this entanglement of guilt for the victim may be important. Teaching the demystification of orgasms or of human sexual responses may assist the victim in accomplishing important goals. A simple definition may be helpful.

An orgasm is an explosive discharge of accumulated neuro-muscular tensions.

The orgasm must be demystified, chopped up, *clinicalized*, understood, calculated, graphed, charted, and observed. The educational model will be extremely important since the therapeutic model may be more emotional and, therefore, more difficult. Victims may have spent years filled with degradation and repulsion about body responses that seemed to be out of control. Through an educational modality, the insignificance of orgasmic responses can be a very valuable lesson for the victim.

Becoming the Perpetrator

Another example of an educational treatment modality requires teaching victims about perpetrators. It may seem absurd to teach individuals who have spent their lives with perpetrators to better understand these individuals. Victims can benefit, however, from hearing about profiles, characteristics and thinking patterns of sexual offenders.

A common trait or symptom for some victims is the potential to become very much like the perpetrator. Teaching victims how to avoid taking on those characteristics is important and can be accomplished much more comfortably within the educational model.

Additionally, educating victims to become helpers, to be sensitive, or involved in such activities as peer counseling is another important treatment modality. Teaching group members to provide constructive criticism, to be thoughtful, to listen effectively, is a more subtle method of preventing victims from becoming perpetrators and makes a direct contribution to breaking the cycle of sexual abuse. Again, the direct approach may be uncomfortable, but an indirect, educational approach, has tremendous potential for success.

Teach Bicycle Robberies

The ultimate in sexual abuse prevention as mentioned previously is to internalize a reason or a desire to protect. Teaching children that their genitalia and sexuality is as important as their bicycles, begins this process. A treatment modality, under the educational model, must teach the beauty of sexuality and the beauty of sexual consent. We cannot expect children who have had consent violated to automatically know what is expected of them. It must be taught.

A large nationally known residential treatment center for adolescents inquires of the consultant, *we have so many problems with these boys and girls acting out sexually. We bring them here and we give them everything. They have nice homes, excellent healthcare, psychological counseling, and perhaps better conditions than they dreamed imaginable. Why do they continue to act out sexually with attempted rape, sexual manipulation,* *promiscuity, or at times, prostitution. What are we doing wrong?*

The answer to the dilemma is not concerned with what the staff is doing inappropriately, but what is lacking in the model of treatment. At the same residential program, behaviors such as lying, stealing, or failing in school are carefully monitored. Adolescents see the goal for which they are working and understand the behavioral steps toward reaching the goal. The behavior which will determine success is clearly outlined and behaviors which determine failure are also within a clear format of understanding. The map is in place. For positive sexuality, the question can be raised *where is the map?*

Where have these young men and women been taught the beauty of sexual contact? Their genitalia gives them a clear message of pleasure. Their society has clearly taught that sexual power and sexual control is important. Where is the education for the beauty of consent? If the behavior needs to be changed, why isn't the goal toward being sexually successful carefully mapped and computerized as the goal of being honest?

Where do these adolescents learn about the beauty of establishing a relationship with someone, becoming intellectually intimate, and then physically intimate? Where is the continuum of sexual involvement beginning with kissing, holding, caressing, and perhaps working toward intercourse?

Is it common to present adolescents with *exciting* plans concerning sexual consent? Are children expected to avoid the exciting messages and know how to be enthused about consent? In order to combat society's messages, education needs to be active, exciting and intense. Obviously, it is not a popular contention at the local PTA meeting to suggest *we need to get kids excited about sex!*

Vulnerable children need to learn about their bodies and they need to learn that their bodies and genitalia feel different to touch than other parts of their body. They must be encouraged to feel positive and excited about sexuality. Too often, treatment plans focus on the damage and fail to recognize what lies ahead for a victim who continues to cultivate these ideas. Bicycle robberies are an excellent example to begin this process.

The reason children protect their bicycles is because their bicycles are wonderful. Children become excited about their bicycles long before their legs can reach the pedals. The reason they protect their bicycles lies in the positive ideations about bicycles. There is very little opportunity to protect something that is smelly, dirty, awful, nasty, and certainly unmentionable.

Modality 5 — Touching

Touching of patients is a tremendous source of controversy among professionals. Some ideations suggest that victims should never be touched since touching has been a source of trauma. Others advocate that touching should occur and be forced upon patients. The *middle*

of the road group would suggest that children should be touched if they give consent.

Nonsexual Touching

All sexual victims have been abused through sexual touching. Although some behaviors are of a *non-touching* modality, touching is the primary issue in sexual abuse. It is an important treatment modality to incorporate nonsexual touching in order to continue the *sanctuary* environment. Touching is a wonderful action between human beings and certainly there is a professional obligation to provide safe, nonsexual touching with absolutely no commitments. Learning to touch in the safety of the therapeutic environment may be one of the most important therapeutic activities.

Desensitization

It is rare that sexual abuse between a child and a perpetrator only involves genital touching. In many instances, entire bodies of children are involved. Hugging, holding, caressing, kissing are all examples of extraneous touching that occurs during sexual abuse. There is tremendous potential for the victim to incorporate reactions toward these normally wonderful human interactions as a response to sexual abuse.

Judy explains, *If we just didn't have to hug or kiss or anything like that. I don't mind intercourse once he gets into it. I hate all that other stuff. Intercourse is the one thing that **didn't** happen to me* *in my abuse. All the other stuff makes me want to throw up.*

Certainly, Judy would have benefited as a very small child from being able to return to many nonsexual kinds of touching. The desensitization of those behaviors would have been very helpful to her in a therapeutic environment. Judy was a victim of constant fondling and *dry humping* by many male members of her family. She is totally *touching phobic*, being unable to endure any kind of affection. Genital touching which did not actually occur is pleasurable, provided no other touching takes place. What a shame for Judy to have missed the opportunity to become *detraumatized* to one of the most pleasurable human activities.

Skin Memories

Skin memories are some of the loudest memories in adulthood as far as connections to childhood abuse. Many times the cognitive awareness is unavailable, but the tactile, as well as affective responses remain. Approaching those skin memories and undoing the potential for phobic reactions is extremely important in therapy. These techniques go far beyond providing noncommittal affection and attention to the patient. These activities are not limited to hugs and hand holding, but actually require the therapist and the patient to design activities concerning *body work*. Often, memories will be rekindled through touching areas of the body that hold secrets. Without the modality of touching, skin memories remain powerful.

Patient/Therapist Guidelines

In accepting the commitment to touch patients in teaching noncommittal and affectionate touching, several guidelines and recommendations exist. *Talking and touching* is an important issue for therapists. First, a statement should be made that touching will occur and, when touching does take place, it should be extremely non-secretive. Hugs in the waiting room next to the secretary's desk or in a session with other family members are examples of non-secretive touching. Talking and touching is very important. *It feels so good to have good touching. How about if you give this hug that I am giving to you, to your cat when you get home?* When words trail from the therapist's mouth explaining that first touching will occur and then talking about the touching while it does occur, secretiveness subsides. Talking about touching and desensitizing touching is extremely important.

No Thank You, Please

And what about the resistive patient? If the statement is made, *We need some good touching out here in the waiting room next to your mom,* it may be common for the victim to resist or to refuse. A comeback statement may be, *Well, how about if we start with giving some good touching to the cats. Would that be all right for this time and then maybe next time we can give big hugs to each other?* Allowing children choices, such as *Do you think you mom should get some good touching,* or, *Do you think I should get some,* or, *Do you think we should give our hugs to the cats?* is another important way to establish touching consent. If extreme resistance occurs, the final technique would be to inquire of the patient, *when do you think you will be ready for some good touching?*

Modality 6 — Externalization

An important treatment modality concerns the externalization of issues surrounding sexual abuse. Sadly, this modality is often viewed as *talking about the abuse.* It is not uncommon for victim groups to be focused on discussion of feelings or describing stories. Certainly, if all patients were able to externalize their feelings, therapy would be much easier. The problem remains that in the internalization or stifling of feelings, victims fail at externalizing, or they externalize other issues.

This important treatment modality requires therapy to be focused around a process of externalization. Returning to the abusive scene is far different than relating elements of the abuse to a group of preteen girls.

> Robin was sexually abused by her adolescent brother for approximately three years. An important treatment component for Robin was to return to the scene and externalize. Robin's mother made lemonade and cookies and the van drove Robin's preteen group to her country home. Therapy involved teaching Robin how to not only return to the scene and desensitize, but also by sharing this process with group members Robin was even more successful.

> As part of her therapy, Robin cut out footprints the size of her brother's feet and taped these to the carpet. With grand *pomp and circumstance*, Robin took all group members down the hallway from her brother's room into her own room, with each group member stepping, stepping, stepping on the bright green footprints. Robin then portrayed her brother and explained exactly what had happened to her, but not necessarily in sexual terms. Robin demonstrated where her brother had stood, waiting quietly, before he abused her. Robin pointed out the bedspread and the wallpaper she could see while the abuse was taking place. Robin even displayed her nightgown which she wore during the last year of her abuse.

Nothing changed and nothing profound occurred as far as the sexual abuse itself. What is taking place is an externalization process while Robin shares with other group members the physical attributes of her abuse. The potential for phobic reactions is melting away. The memory of her friends being in the same bedroom can be planted beside the memories of her abuse.

Clarification/Resolution

Clarification and resolution of sexual abuse is an extremely important component or modality under the externalization process. The resolution scrapbook will be described later as will the clarification process between the perpetrator and the victim. Without these two processes, externalization is difficult.

As indicated in Chapter Five, one factor that seemed to provide opportunity for little or no trauma to victims was continued access to the information separating sexual abuse from normal sexual development. This is a classic indicator of the need for the externalization process. For children who internalized their abuse and build upon those perceptions through sexual development, there was obviously more trauma. For children who are allowed to externalize abuse, feelings and attitudes, rehabilitation was imminent. Through the resolution scrapbook or through offender/victim clarification, the abuse is dissected, externalized, and desensitized. Unless some form of these processes occur, the victim is likely to feed upon and cultivate trauma.

Not Front, Back, But Beside

What is the ultimate modality in victim rehabilitation? The answer lies in how the victim responds to sexual abuse in the future. In order to understand the answer to this question, all options must be explored.

Common coping responses suggest *I have put it in back of me, I have forgiven, it is behind me, I have gone on.* Sadly, the victim is suggesting vulnerability with this response. With trauma in back, the victim is vulnerable to trauma at an unsuspecting time. With the sexual abuse *in back*, there is tremendous potential for the affective responses returning to the vulnerable victim and *biting in the butt* when they least expect it. When sexual abuse is *behind* or when the perpetrator has been forgiven, the victim is vulnerable to the pain of abuse for sporadic times in the future. Rehabilitation is momentary through forgiveness, and the victim remains vulnerable and out of control.

On the opposite end of the option spectrum, victims may choose to place their sexual abuse and trauma in front of them. This activity computes to *becoming an eternal victim,* living the life of a victim and stumbling over the sexual abuse each day. This is not rehabilitation, but an eternal victimization, always vulnerable, always needing to be victimized in order to have consistency. Placing sexual abuse *in front* is as deadly as victims throwing sexual abuse *in back* through forgiveness.

The solution involves the externalization process. The sexual abuse belongs beside the victim under control, clear, crisp and recognizable. Through this analogy, the victim needs to recognize that sexual abuse does not need to drive the victim's life forever, nor does sexual abuse need to be pouncing upon the victim at any time of vulnerability. The externalization modality teaches victims how to control. It teaches the victim how to see the abuse in the proper perspective and in some cases benefit from understanding sexual abuse.

Examples within these modalities should not suggest an end to the list of possibilities.

Creativity is as important as uniqueness in treatment planning. As basic treatment goals are explained, the modalities for which these goals can be met, should be understood.

Remember

The Trauma Assessment outlines specific and unique levels and areas of trauma. Treatment modalities provide general methods of approaching those unique areas of pain. The following six treatment goals are general and basic, but also extremely important for implementation of treatment modalities.

Goal 1 — Identify the Victim and the Perpetrator

The identification of the perpetrator and the victim is the most important component in the Trauma Assessment Relationship Perspective. Victims who view themselves clearly as innocent and not responsible, and as being the victim of a robbery, obviously rehabilitate faster. Confusion about the offender/victim identity indicates potential for continued trauma. Certainly, levels of acceptance of the offender/victim role will emerge. Additionally, the status of the victim and the offender may change over time. Within the Trauma Assessment, accomplishments or failures in this goal can be understood and more specific treatment goals can be established.

And what would indicate success? How would a victim demonstrate this goal had been met? Does the identification of the perpetrator and victim require the victim to hate the perpetrator, to avoid the perpetrator or to have only negative feelings toward the perpetrator? The answer is *NO*. Separating the perpetrator from the perpetrator's acts may be important in some cases in order for victims to accomplish this goal. Positive attributes of the perpetrator may prevent the offender identification. Separation of those positive attributes from the crime of sexual abuse may need to occur before rehabilitation can be successful. The Relationship Perspective of the Trauma Assessment examined a culmination of the issues in order to determine how the victim viewed the identity of the guilty and innocent. For the sake of resolution the cumulative effect will be disastrous. Separation and acceptance of some perpetrator qualities may need to occur in order for the perpetrator identification to be successful.

Changing Times

The status of victim identity also needs understanding and preparation. As an example, at seven, the victim may learn in therapy that he was innocent and the acts committed upon him were unacceptable. He may appear to have accomplished this goal. However, the Trauma Assessment may predict a change in attitude for this young man due to homophobic responses in society. Care must be taken to recognize the potential for change as this young man becomes more aware of the homosexual stigma. The young man's erectile responses during the sexual abuse may predict a need for ongoing identification of the victim. Protecting this young man from later attempts to reorganize his status as victim is an important treatment activity.

Survivorship

And what about survivorship? The first goal in identification of the victim and the perpetrator is carefully related to the sixth goal which is to become a survivor. Some victim programs are offended by the word *victim* and choose to adapt the semantic term of survivor. There is a pervading sense of accomplishment and control in the word *survivor* and comfort may be gained from this process, if becoming a survivor is logistically managed.

Band Aids

Being a *victim* requires recognition of the innocence and the victim's status. Survivorship, if completed initially, becomes a *band-aid approach*. Survivorship often takes on a tangible or externalized process, such as returning to graduate school, protecting children from being abused, obtaining a college degree, or having a late model sedan in the garage. Unfortunately, unless the internal process of identification of oneself as truly a victim, an innocent child, survivorship is superficial. Survivorship may abandon the small child *within* who needs to be identified as a victim.

On the other hand, if sexual victims remain in the identification process this would be the same as placing sexual abuse *in front* and stumbling over it throughout the victim's future. Survivorship is a process to work toward in therapy. It is not something automatic and if given automatic, without accomplishing the first goal of victim/offender identity, rehabilitation may be retarded.

Victim Voices

And what is the sound of the victim who has accomplished this first and important goal in the identification of the perpetrator and the victim? What are the sounds of success in attempting to balance perpetrator attributes and liabilities, and victim assets and liabilities.

> I am/was a child. I did not have the option to say *no* to adults. My cooperation in a sexual act only indicates I was manipulated into cooperation in order to survive. I reported the crime.

> I am not responsible for family upheaval, for lack of money, for the breaking of family ties, for no contact with children, for expensive treatment, alcohol problems, or family embarrassment. In order to have sexual abuse happen in a family, many systems must break down. I did not cause this to happen. These problems are residual effects of the abuse for which I was a victim.

> I reported a crime — I did not let anyone down or *rat* on anyone.

I accepted an obligation to secure treatment for my family. I am only responsible for stopping a sexual crime.

A sexual decision is important in this society. I was robbed of my right to make my own sexual decision.

We are not animals driven by instinct. Adults do have control over their sexual activities.

Children are protected by the law and a crime was committed against me, a precious child.

Perhaps the most important word in these voices from victims is the word c-r-i-m-e. One of the most empowering words in accomplishing this first goal is allowing victims to recognize that a crime was committed upon them. In the physical and emotional sense, our system can assist in accomplishing this goal by charging the perpetrator with the crime. However, if the system cannot respond, or if sexual abuse occurred decades previously, making the system *not applicable*, the issue of crime still needs to be considered in accomplishing this goal. Understanding the elements of the crime, understanding the punishment that could have been given to the perpetrator, understanding the basis for protection of children under the law may be extremely important in working on this goal. *I reported a crime* may be the first step in accomplishing this treatment goal.

Goal 2 — Create Sexual Self-Esteem

So much has been stated about improving self-esteem and relieving guilt, that this goal may appear to be repetitious or so obvious it is impotent. Improving sexual self-esteem however goes far beyond reliving guilt or identifying the victim as a victim. Certainly if the first goal is accomplished and the victim status was clear, a prerequisite to accomplishing that goal would have established a sense of innocence or lack of responsibility. The second goal of improving sexual self-esteem goes far beyond the first goal. As indicated in Chapter 5, severely traumatized patients were children who already struggled with self-esteem previous to sexual abuse. Children who have healthy self concepts and self-esteem have greater chance for minimal trauma. Certainly sex offenders are capable of choosing children who are struggling, so that secrecy will be more of an option. Even though intellectually, the victim status may be clear, tremendous effort on the part of the offender may continue to invade the victim's self-esteem. Being intellectually innocent is not the same as believing in an innocent body image.

The second goal of improving sexual self-esteem is much more internal and affective. As the first goal accomplishes an intellectual and cognitive process of recognizing the child's innocence, the second goal travels much further, strengthening attitudes about the victim in many aspects. This second goal nurtures the first and expands the victim identity to a body image perspective.

This second goal requires such issues as body image, self-esteem, and positive personal impressions to be created. Issues such as contamination, devaluation and poor body image will emerge from the Sexual Victim Trauma Assessment especially in the developmental perspective area. This goal needs to specifically address those elements of trauma.

Victim Voices

And what would be the voices from victims suggesting this goal had been accomplished? If the first goal identifies the perpetrator the second goal hears *victim voices* far more internal, taking into consideration the whole child.

> I am/was a precious beautiful child. I have a beautiful sexual body that has been misused not used. Since as a child I could not consent, that means my future sexual decisions will be wonderful, private and special. My sexuality is something of value.

The *victim voice* or affirmation suggests a renewal, a rebirth of positive attitudes. This goal travels far beyond the crime itself and points the victim towards a future of positive interpersonal ideations toward the sexual *self* of the victim.

Why, Oh Why

As an example, if a resolution and clarification occurs between the perpetrator and the victim, an important obligation of the perpetrator is to explain WHY the abuse occurred. There are four major components to the WHY EXPLANATION. As the perpetrator travels through the explanation, the second goal of treatment is cultivated and finalized.

First the perpetrator must indicate that at the basic core of why the crime was committed is the fact that sexual touching feels good and the offender wanted to *feel good*. Rather than a mystical presentation, the issue was one of robbery. Robbery, like sexual abuse, is a crime of selfishness. In a robbery someone steals something that is wanted. Therefore the first part of the WHY EXPLANATION is *I was selfish and I wanted to do this.*

A stumbling block in logic occurs, however, since children are often confused why someone would want something that was degrading, humiliating, painful or uncomfortable. One child explained after hearing that the perpetrator was selfish and wanted to commit the crime, *Why would he want to do that yucky stuff?*

The second portion of the WHY explains why sexuality is something robbed or something desired. This must occur in order for the child to make sense of what the perpetrator is saying. If the perpetrator, as an example, described taking the child's birthday cake because of selfishness, a clear understanding would occur. There are very few purposes for birthday cake. In the second part of the WHY the perpetrator must explain the value of sexuality in order to make sense of the robbery. The perpetrator will be required to describe the beauty of sexuality and why that touching feels different than touching elbows or ears. The dissertation on sexual consent must occur in childlike terms and be extremely positive.

The third portion of the WHY requires a discussion of the *character disorder* of the offender. In other words, the perpetrator has broken the rules and discounted the child's rights. The reason for that disregard explains the selfishness of the perpetrator again but with more understanding.

The final portion of the WHY returns to the issue of the second treatment goal. Decontamination must occur. The victim must walk away from the clarification process recognizing they have been misused not *used up.* Their sexual decisions in the future should be viewed as wonderful and their sexual body and their right to sexually consent must be portrayed as still intact. Without consent, the sexual activity was nullified. As one little girl explained, *Oh, I get it. I haven't picked yet!*

The final statement in the clarification process points towards the child's future sexual decisions as being important. The child is not *damaged goods.*

Truck Accidents

What is the barometer of success for Goal #2? If sexual self-esteem has been restored, how would the victim proceed through adulthood? What would the voice of rehabilitation say?

I want you to feel the same as you would if you had been run over by a truck rather than sexually abused. And how would that be? How would you feel if you had been standing on the sidewalk looking in a shoe store and a truck ran over you? Would you be filled with guilt, remorse, and sadness over your responsibility? Would you feel as though you had caused this to happen or that you were guilty or damaged goods? By standing on the sidewalk and being involved in an accident, it was quite clear you were innocent. You would feel this internally and you would always understand your innocence concerning the truck accident.

And how would truck accidents be taken into the future? The male victim as an example, would be able to describe the casts on his legs and the four months of missed work. Additionally, he could describe frustration and outrage toward the truck driver. The victim may also describe continued involvement in the community to alleviate drunk driving. The victim may be able to discuss his accident at a cocktail party if *truck accidents* was the topic of conversation.

Certainly, the truck accident will always be traumatic for the victim. Anger and frustration can be called forth, but the victim will not be overwhelmed and preoccupied by the truck accident, the same as is common to observe in sexual victims. Truck accidents can be discussed, but generally they do not control the entire life of a victim. This second goal of improving sexual self-esteem points toward the future and the truck example is evidence of successful completion. Being able to teach victims to respond much the same as they would if they had reported an accident is testimony of this goal accomplished.

Goal 3 — Breaking the Trauma Bond

As Chapter Six described, *trauma bonding* is prevalent in the residual effects of sexual abuse. Goal #3 attempts to break the trauma bond or release the victim from the power of the offender, or from the power of any trauma bonding. Caution should be exerted in understanding that the power of a specific offender may be less than the power in the relationship between the mother, family members, or *collateral clamps and cramps.*

The Relationship Perspective of the Trauma Assessment will generally pinpoint trauma bonding through relationships. Extraneous events that cause trauma bonding will be found in other sections of the Trauma Assessment. The goal of breaking the power of the trauma bond requires careful identification of the trauma bond.

Spectrum Syndrome

As indicated in Chapter Six, sexual victims remain in trauma bonds vacillating in a spectrum of childhood. On one end of the spectrum is the outraged child stomping, screaming, indignant, *why did you do this to me?* The outraged child is out of control and often abusive. If the outraged child takes action against the perpetrator, the outraged child often *becomes the perpetrator* causing even more trauma than previously existed.

On the other end of the spectrum is the disheveled, beaten, bewildered, depressed child begging for acceptance and love. The pleading child is often a result of aftermath from the outraged child. The outraged child acts inappropriately and then retreats to feelings of guilt and remorse.

Outrage to Pleading

Trauma bonds exist because the victim, as an adult, remains a child either outraged or pleading. Accomplishing this third goal for the adult breaks the trauma bond and, for the small child, prevents the trauma bond from occurring. Being released from the power of the offender, as an example, is breaking the trauma bond and being released from perpetual bondage in the deadly spectrum.

> Bonnie is a 41-year-old female who was sexually abused by her father. Her father is a minister and remains heavily involved in the church. Bonnie's sexual abuse took place for nine and one-half years with her father using a great deal of religiosity concerning needs to fulfill the desires of not only Heavenly Father, but *father of the household.* During Bonnie's abuse, she spent most

of her life trying to please her father in hopes that she would be successful and loved. Obviously, her father used Bonnie's desperateness to keep her as his sexual partner and keep her distracted from the reality of the abuse.

For Bonnie, she is clearly under a traumatic bond with her father who, in adulthood, continues to write her letters of a religious and sexual nature. *My God has forgiven me for all of my transgressions, even those concerning the flesh of the body. When are you going to ask for forgiveness, too?* These statements devastate Bonnie, making daily life nearly unsurmountable whenever she has contact with her family.

The traumatic bond does not stop with Bonnie's perpetrator and is enmeshed in Bonnie's relationship with other family members. Bonnie's family is extremely important to her, especially her siblings and the matriarchal power of Bonnie's mother. It is nearly impossible for Bonnie to conceive of living a life without her family, yet each contact with her family results in victimization.

Bonnie attempts suicide for the fourth time. Intake interviews reveal she has been sexually abused and Bonnie enters into a MAC Group for *molested as children*. In the weeks ahead, Bonnie writes a scathing letter to her father. The outraged child is in control.

Bonnie's 22-page letter diagrams her pain over the last twenty-four years. She lashes out and although she receives a great deal of support from group members, careful attention to this treatment goal and to Bonnie's trauma bonding allows the therapist to withhold sending the letter. In a short period of time, Bonnie is devastated. She is now the pleading, guilty child hoping her family will forgive her. The contemplated loss of her family is devastating and the outraged child has departed, leaving the pleading, begging child in control. Since the letter was not sent, the next few months allow Bonnie to regroup and eventually send a final three sentence letter releasing her from the power of the perpetrator. Certainly, the letter Bonnie writes is not as powerful as her first letter, nor does it have the ability to reduce Bonnie to a pleading, begging child.

Mom and Dad,

I want to tell you that I am finally getting therapy for the sexual abuse you did to me for nine and one-half years. I also want to tell you that I am volunteering in a Little Girls Group Therapy Program so that I can help other little girls avoid the pain I have suffered. I just wanted to share my happiness with you.

In this letter, Bonnie is saying *you did it, it hurt, and, most importantly, you are not kicking me out of the family.* The power of the offender has been broken. Bonnie is neither the pleading child, nor is she outraged, out of control. Bonnie has made a decision according to what she wanted and the power of the offender has been broken.

But, Wait?!

Perhaps, like no other goal in the treatment plan for sexual victims, this goal provides a struggle for therapists. It is easy to take on feelings of outrage toward someone like Bonnie's father. As Bonnie revealed in treatment, one of her father's techniques to control her was to be critical of the fact she could not take his full penis into her mouth. Rather than identifying her father as a flaming sex offender, Bonnie worked diligently for years to accomplish the task her father requested. This is the test for therapists. It may be much easier to be pleased with Bonnie's first letter. Certainly, the perpetrator deserves the 22-page scathing letter, rather than Bonnie's three sentences. The potential for Bonnie to remain under the power of the perpetrator, however, is prevalent in the first letter. The task for the professional is to clearly understand trauma bonding and be able to have the victim's goals appreciated.

Victim Voices

I have a right to feel *any* or *many* feelings about the person who abused me. I am not obligated to forgive. If I choose, I can reevaluate the person who abused me.

I have the right to change my feelings about the person who abused me.

People who should have protected me, let me down. That doesn't mean I wasn't worth protecting

I have the right to withhold my feelings about the person who abused me.

I have a right to separate my feelings for the offender and for the criminal.

I have a right to walk about in the world without being zapped by my abuse.

The perfect world of families does not exist. I must say good-bye to the one I never had.

People have betrayed me, but the betrayal is over.

Although it is typical to concentrate on the power of the offender, breaking the trauma bond may require concentrating on the trauma bonding through collateral clamps and cramps, as well as through trauma bonding with family members. Breaking the trauma bond will be specifically discussed in Chapter 18. Breaking the trauma bond, as characterized by phobic reactions and other *clamps* will be processed through externalization and desensitization processes as previously outlined.

Goal 4 — Setting Goals

It may seem absurd to designate a goal of *setting goals*. It would appear that the therapist has taken a vacation and the victim is left being in charge of the treatment plan. Quite the contrary is true. As in the case of Bonnie, success came only through carefully setting attainable goals. The goals Bonnie set were carefully directed toward her treatment plan and her ability to succeed. In order to accomplish breaking the power of the offender, the victim must be able to set realistic goals on one hand and be able to see ways to measure success or failure. Without victim input and without teaching victims how to set attainable goals, treatment may be directionless and less effective.

Not only is trauma specific and unique to each sexual victim, but rehabilitation and treatment planning is also unique. The therapist must guide patients toward specific rehabilitating directions, but accomplishing the goal of being able to set goals within that unique framework is extremely important.

A Victim Is A Victim Is A Victim

The final goal in the treatment of victims is to *become a survivor*. Becoming a survivor does not mean a college education or a new carpet in the family room. Becoming a survivor may be dependent upon the victim setting goals that are appropriate. Just as the victim was forbidden consent and choice during sexual abuse, the victim will benefit from consenting to treatment goals.

This is obviously not appropriate for young children since issues of consent and developmental limitations make consent to treatment decisions inappropriate. Children's caretakers involved in the process of setting goals, however, will also be important.

Bonnie is a classic example of appropriate goal setting. Had Bonnie been able to dictate her treatment plan without going through the process of understanding all potential options, her 22-page scathing letter would have been sent and Bonnie may have been eventually successful in her suicide attempts. The pained and pleading child of Bonnie would have taken over for the outraged child and the perpetrator would have remained in control.

Taking Bonnie through the process of recognizing her potentials, her possibilities, and then setting goals allowed her to understand what could happen and what may not happen. Most importantly, Bonnie did not want to lose her family. She ran the risk of being expelled from the family due to her father's power. Bonnie also needed to go through the process of recognizing that *changing her father* was an inappropriate goal. Changing her family was also futile. As her options were sorted, Bonnie made the decision to:

A. Let him know he didn't get away with it.

B. Let him know it hurt and he is responsible for the pain.

C. Let him know that he is not kicking me out of the family.

And what does the epilogue reveal in Bonnie's case? A Utopian world for Bonnie would have allowed her father to throw himself at her feet begging for forgiveness. Mother would have been compassionate as would Bonnie's siblings. Bonnie would have been elevated to a hero status and the next Thanksgiving dinner would begin with a toast to Bonnie's courage.

Unfortunately, Bonnie does not live in a Utopian world. She lives in a real world where her entire family are products of a dysfunctional incest family. Nonetheless, it is Bonnie's family and she wants a piece of that family. Setting goals allowed Bonnie to have the best of all worlds *possible*, not the best of all possible worlds.

Voices from Victims

I have the power over my own destiny. I have the ability to set my own goals and accomplish my goals. I do not need to be under the control of others either through outrage or shame. My victimization was out of my control. My future is in my control.

Goal 5 — Breaking the Cycle

Breaking the cycle of sexual abuse has two very important components, both extremely valuable. First, there is an inherent need for the cycle of sexual abuse to stop. Most importantly, the continual victimization of children from one generation to another is devastating. A commitment should be made to rehabilitate victims so that the cycle does not continue.

Second, on a more personal level to the patient breaking the cycle is a sign of rehabilitation. Victims tend to be abusable and tend to attract abusive people. It would be appropriate to stop the cycle of abuse for potential victims, but more personally, stopping the cycle of abusability for the current victim is also extremely important. Victims tend to continue their abusive cycles, perpetuating victimization.

Tammy is treated in a therapeutic environment for a short period of time. Tammy's mother has been sexually abused as a child by five offenders and she has also been rudely ignored by the system. When Tammy was involved in treatment, she acknowledged her third offender. Tammy's mother became interested in relocating in the midwest and eventually moved with her children without completing any treatment goals.

Six months later, requests for information are received since Tammy has been *gang raped* at a junior high football game. The sexually abusive scenario is described by the therapist now working with Tammy as one of chilling affirmation of the cycle of sexual abuse.

Police report that two 18-year-olds, a 23-year-old, and a 20-year-old male attended a football game under the influence of alcohol. The young men reported to police they were *looking for butt*. During the entire athletic event, these young men perused the stands and eventually chose their victim, Tammy. Their comments suggested they had carefully made their decision based on which female looked as though she was *easy*. Their comments also suggested a commonly examined theme that sexual victims appear abusable and they are attractive to abusive individuals. Caution should be exerted in believing that Tammy's abusability was manifested in her seductiveness. Tammy was a rather large child who was uncomfortable with her size. She held her head low and attempted to cover her body with baggy clothing. Tammy did not appear *easy* to these young men from a sexual perception. She appeared easy to abuse, nothing more, nothing less.

Tammy's plight is dreadful, suggesting that she will continue in the cycle of sexual abuse being vulnerable and being abusable to individuals who are abusive.

The Ultimate Trauma

Treatment for sexual victims must go beyond the cycle they themselves perpetuate. Certainly, future victims are important, but the ultimate goal in stopping the deadly cycle is preventing victims from continuing to be victimized.

Another Deadly Spectrum

Another deadly spectrum emerges as victims attempt to put forth effort in stopping the cycle of abuse. On one end of the spectrum is the distrustful, hateful, angry victim who chooses to break the cycle of abuse through outrage and rejection.

> *All men are the same. They can't be trusted. They are all perverts. The only way I am going to be safe or my kids are going to be safe is to avoid men.*

In this response, Alice is admitting her vulnerability and suggesting she has absolutely no control over her safety or the safety of her children. Her response is an avoidance of men. The only way Alice can survive is to avoid men and, therefore, men have won the battle. There is no empowerment to this approach. Alice has continued to be victimized.

On the other end of the spectrum is the vulnerable victim who takes on the *Pollyanna* attitude of trust. There is a pervading sense for *Ms. Polly* of, *Isn't it all wonderful?* For Polly, being distrustful will bring about a reason to distrust. Polly emerges from therapy believing that there is a solution by thinking positive. Polly develops an unrealistic attitude of positive thinking. She believes she can carefully diagnose offenders and pick out a deviant in the grocery store.

In reality, Polly has externalized the process. Just the same as Alice believes that all men are *perverts* and should be avoided, Polly decides that she has become so adept at diagnosing *perverts* that she will be safe. Both Polly and Alice have returned power to the perpetrators. Breaking the cycle of abuse requires victims to internalize protection and to have faith in themselves at the closure of treatment rather than externalizing the ability to find sex offenders in K-Mart.

People who avoid situations where children are vulnerable, do so with tools and techniques within themselves. There is not a sweeping generalization as in the case of Alice nor is there a nice tidy profiling package as in Polly's situation. True rehabilitation and accomplishment of this goal allows the victim to step forward into life, on a *case by case* basis to examine and to continue to examine. Pollyanna believed that one evaluation of a sex offender or potential offender is sufficient while Alice has totally avoided any opportunity for the cycle to continue. Neither of these approaches have been internalized for the patient and neither will provide safety.

If goal #2, improving sexual self-esteem, was truly accomplished, the overriding issue of self-protection would be the matrix or the continuing evaluation modality for this goal. If the victims truly felt valuable, worth protection and worth the very best treatment from others, breaking the cycle of sexual abuse would be easy. This goal should not be treated lightly but certainly the victim's sense of self-worth, self-esteem, lack of guilt, etc., will be an overriding issue in the accomplishment of this goal.

Voices From Victims

I was abused but I will not be abusable. I can trust but mostly in myself. I have learned from this experience.

I am handicapped to be a protective parent if I continue to feel victimized and guilty. I need to be positive and *alert*.

I know clues and *red flags* that tell me things are ok or not ok.

I deserve and will demand honesty and respect in future relationships. I can also give this in return.

I have the capability to survive on my own. Failure will be tempting to me so I must be aware.

Goal 6 — Become A Survivor

Is survivorship that deadly prospect of saying *it's over, I've made it?* The common cry given by those individuals who have survived too quickly is, *But wait a minute, I'm still hurting.* What is the definition of survivorship and what does it mean?

If survivorship means no more pain, no more tears, no more alerts, no more vulnerability, no more suffering, and no more need to remember, then the therapeutic treatment plan is doomed for failure. A very important component in setting goals for the victim is to define survivorship as outlined in goal #4. Survivorship will be outlined and survivorship will occur according to the goals set in the therapeutic process. What is survivorship, then, if the first five goals have been accomplished?

Would not survivorship be inherent in the first goal, i.e. identification of the perpetrator and the victim? Additionally, if the second goal was accomplished, i.e. that of improving sexual self-esteem, relieving guilt, would not survivorship be successful? Thirdly, being released from the trauma bond suggests that survivorship is imminent if the offender or those involved in the trauma bond are no longer in control. If goals are set appropriately, as described in goal #4, and the cycle is broken, as described in goal #5, then has the ultimate in rehabilitation occurred — survivorship?

Maintenance, Maintenance, Maintenance

Becoming a survivor has to do with the maintenance of the first five goals. Treatment for the sexual victim requires the ongoing development of coping mechanisms to maintain success created in accomplishing the first five goals.

Becoming a survivor is consistently using the tools gained from the first five goals in treatment. It is not the process of *now it's over* but a process of maintenance, of continuing to control, of continuing to combat against vulnerabilities. Just the same as the victim who has been run over by a truck needs to respond to perhaps some injuries (such as arthritis or a shortened leg) in the future, the sexual victim needs to learn a plan of maintenance. If survivorship comes at an appropriate time, following completion of the first five goals, the tools of maintenance should be in place. If survivorship comes too quickly the victim is left with pervading feelings of guilt, hopelessness, vulnerability, outrage and anger.

Voices of Victims

I will remember, but only to be aware and safe.

I am capable. I do not need to be afraid and distrustful.

I do not need to live my life as a victim. My victimization is out of my control. My future is in my control.

If I choose, I can set the abuse in a proper perspective and *accept* that person who abused me back into my life. I do not need to forgive the behavior in order to accept.

I understand the majority of adults do not molest children. I also understand that sexual abuse can happen. I do not need to live in total fear, nor total abandonment.

Maintenance for children requires revisiting the scrapbook or participating in therapeutic *tune-ups* as the victim proceeds through different stages of development. Maintenance for the changing child requires changing the focus of the first five goals.

For the older patient, survivorship also may require refocusing from time to time. As an example, body image may be seen as positive at one time but may also need further nurturing. The identity of the offender may be clear until the offender dies. Re-examination of the innocent child may need to occur in order for the patient to safely attend the funeral. Survivorship must never be assumed as constant. Survivorship is a *toolbox* of skills to maintain therapeutic accomplishments.

Summary

These goals are basic, somewhat generic, but have a process and purpose. Much the same as sexual victim treatment, these goals need to be specifically adjusted and redirected in appreciation of the information gleaned from the Trauma Assessment. Although there is a certain generic quality about these goals, they should provide a road map or guideline to that place of recovery.

BREAKING THE TRAUMA BOND

What are the chains of love, hate, confusion, repulsion, and how can they be broken? How can the victim, trapped in a trauma bond, undo the power of the offender?

Regardless of where the trauma bond originates, the offender, the mother, family members or collateral clamps and cramps, the trauma bond must be broken. And what *is* breaking the trauma bond? It is directing the mad, the sad, the hate, the pain; it is sorting, dissecting, resolving, returning, undoing, and freeing the child within. The child of sexual abuse must return and break the bonds. The process for breaking the trauma bond is divided into four components:

- Identification of the Bond
- Setting Goals for Attacking the Bond
- Carrying the Child Out
- Rebirth

Caution, Caution, Caution

It is important to recognize that breaking the trauma bond is a process, not necessarily a product. Often, time is a healer. Simply setting goals sometimes heals. Allowing hurts to be held, diagnosed, dissected and resolved is important. The power between the victim and the offender must be equalized. Time tends to be a healer and an important component for working toward the process. Quick intervention may not have the same power.

An additional caution recognizes that the process is as important as the product. When choices are made and goals are set, the value will be enhanced if many, many options were

375

available at the time of choosing. Choices, choices, choices tend to enhance working toward the product.

Another area of concern is the professional's subjectivity. It is not the goals of the professional or the feelings of the professional that are of primary importance. This is particularly difficult for a professional who has personal feelings about either the victim or the perpetrator. Disgust for the crime may become a barrier to outlining an effective treatment process. *Rip his liver out* may be the affective reaction, but certainly an inappropriate one toward someone who holds the victim in a trauma bond. This is a time to calculate, organize, repair, strategize for the victim. It is not time for subjectivity.

Step One

The first step in breaking the trauma bond is to conduct a Trauma Assessment. The nature of the trauma bond will not emerge unless a Trauma Assessment has been administered either formally or informally. Victims live most of their lives in a lack of control over their trauma. The Trauma Assessment is absolutely necessary in being able to examine the trauma and plan for breaking the bond.

But, What If?

For the adult or the resistive patient, memory may be a barrier to conducting the Trauma Assessment. Memory recapturing exercises may be necessary before the Trauma Assessment can be completed. A caution should be exerted, however, with the definition of memory and what patients feel is required in order to complete the Trauma Assessment.

> *There is no way I can finish this Trauma Assessment since I can't remember what happened to me. You tell me I can't go forward in therapy until I have had a Trauma Assessment, but I certainly can't assess something that I don't remember. I am doomed to this deadness. I see no hope.*

Since victims have cognitive distortions and denial systems they may be subconsciously resistive to finishing the Trauma Assessment. On one hand, the patient may be extremely motivated. On the other hand, the patient may be resistive due to lack of memory. Fear of memory may be the subtle and underlying issue. A certain amount of memory recapturing exercises should be conducted and will be outlined in this chapter. However, memory recapturing exercises may not be effective for those patients who have adopted a footprint of refusing to remember.

Videos

Memory recapturing exercises can be extremely helpful, provided that appropriate goals are set between the victim and therapist. There will never be a video presentation. Just the same as with other childhood memories, videos do not generally occur. Proceeding through memory recapturing exercises will succeed or fail depending upon the goals set by the patient.

The patient who believes that a certain amount of effort must be exerted toward memory recapturing, but that success or failure in rehabilitation does not depend on the *video*, will obviously rehabilitate with greater ease. The therapist's obligation is to set appropriate goals and to allow the patient to feel success. For patients who set difficult goals, failure may be on the horizon.

Memory Recapturing Exercises — Plan A

One option in recapturing memories requires the victim to collect extraneous items or elements involved in the sexual abuse to try to understand or see what has happened with the base of sensory involvement from these extraneous objects or items. Activation of the senses toward these objects may encourage memory.

Just as valuable as memory, may be the affective responses associated to extraneous objects. Being in contact with, as an example, a childhood toy may elicit feelings of shame or guilt of an unknown origin. Although the patient may not have recaptured an explicit memory, if goals were properly planned, the affective responses may be as valuable as the memory.

Please remember you may not have a video, but you may have feelings.

Sexual abuse of children is not something you want to create. It is not something we want to have had happen to us. It is something we have experienced or we have not experienced. I want you to return to the scene where your abuse may have occurred. I want you to activate as many senses as possible. If you have a partner, I want you to activate sexual experiences during this return to your childhood sensory world. If you experience feelings, try to record them, try to remember them, but do not diagnose. Don't second guess yourself. Allow yourself to re-experience within the same environment as much as you can by activating your senses.

If you believe you were sexually abused in your family home, try to return and try to activate every sense possible. If it is possible for you to be sexually involved in your family home, this may activate the ultimate response and help us understand or retrieve the rest of your memories. Do this with caution and do not worry about understanding. I will help you diagnose. I will help you sort it out. Simply return to the experiences and take baseline data. Together, our computers will evaluate what happened.

Lies, Lies, Lies

At the forefront of confusion about sexual abuse is the issue of whether children lie about being sexually abused. When memory recapturing exercises are provided to the patient, the entire issue of fabrication, falsification, and lying needs discussion. Traditionally, the patient who doubts, who does not have a clear memory, will question and may be fearful that others will question. It is important, as memory recapturing exercises begin, that the issue of fabrication of sexual abuse is discussed. If the sexual victim proceeds through memory recapturing exercises and memory is recalled, a counter-productive issue may surface as the victim feels tremendous guilt, doubt, and blame for *lying*. As important as the instructions for memory recapturing is the protection of the victim regarding the issue of fabrication or *lying*. Not only will memories be recaptured, but many affective responses (such as *you're a liar*) will occur. Those affective responses may reveal a guilt-ridden child who was not *supposed to tell*. The doubts of the child and the insecurities may surface along with the memories resulting in a deadly combination of remembering the abuse and feeling like a fourth grade liar.

The Big Question

Do children lie? Of course they do! They lie about such things as trucks and cookies. Children lie to get out of things or to get into things. Rarely, do these motivations fit for sexual abuse.

It is obvious that adults become crimson-faced at any mention of sexuality or genitalia. The three-year-old who has discovered the delights of his penis in the Safeway shopping cart learns very quickly how his mother, his grandmother, and the rest of the customers in the checkout line feel about him touching his erect penis. This negative learning teaches an important message.

Secondly, sex offenders put forth effort to make children feel like *partners*. If children learn that touching anything between their belly button and their knees is bad and then sex offenders teach them that they are partners, it does not take a Rhodes Scholar to recognize that children feel *bad* about sexual abuse.

Since children lie about trucks and cookies in order to get something or to get out of something, the question is asked *Is there a motivation for children telling lies about sexual abuse?* If children feel bad, a more important question can be raised, *how often do our children tell us they have been bad and it turns out to be a lie?*

And another question is, *Why would a child make up these complaints if unfounded?* Children appear to gain nothing telling about sexual abuse, whether they are four or a forty-four year-old attempting to understand what happened to his *four-year-old*. What will the child gain from making these statements except feelings of badness?

The victim attempting memory recapturing exercises has nothing to gain by making false claims. Typically, victims are hopeful their fears are unfounded. What would the victim gain from recapturing memories where the victim emerges as a partner in deviant acts? Children, even *44-year-old children,* gain nothing from remembering sexual abuse except feelings of discomfort and humiliation.

Perhaps, Sometimes, Occasionally

There may be some situations where victims develop a purposeful intent for making claims of sexual abuse. These cases will be rare and will most often not be instigated by children. If false claims are made for the purpose of vindictiveness, certainly struggling with memories would be absurd. Clear, crisp memories would be the tools of a vindictive patient. When patients complete memory recapturing exercises and doubt themselves, comfort should be given regarding these issues.

Read the Map — Plan B

Sexual victims may need to examine *baseline data* or those peripheral events that already seem to rekindle memories. Different than the first activity in memory recapturing exercises, this assignments asks the victim not to return to the physical place of sexual abuse, but to examine extraneous events that seem to return the victim to the abuse. These events occur in sexual encounters, on the job, or in a variety of activities in which the victim participates. These memory *zaps* may not be understood by the victim until exercises are conducted.

The most obvious vehicle in returning the victim to memories is found in sexual activities. There are two road maps or processes which may be helpful, provided the appropriate goal is in mind. These processes can be detrimental if careful planning is not implemented.

If memory recapturing exercises are to be implemented during sexual activity, the partner of the victim must be aware of the implications and responsibilities. Allowing sensory stimulation to occur during sexual activities is very helpful in recapturing memory. However, once memory begins, careful attention toward proper direction must occur.

Pee Pees or P.P.s

When sensory stimulation occurs in the form of sexual activity, the memory begins. Also beginning is the *P.P.* that has been altered in the past. In other words, the victim has been involved with the practice principle (P.P.) of pushing memories away. When sexual stimulation occurs, memory attempts to invade and the *P.P.* pushes it away.

The helpful partner must recognize that memory can only be visited under a veil of safety. As sexual stimulation occurs for the victim and the victim begins to feel the affective responses, the partner must become a *traveler* with the patient and encourage the patient to take the partner to the memories. Whispering quietly in the victim's ear encouraging the victim to stay with the memory will allow the process to occur.

Don't be afraid. Tell me what you are seeing, tell me what you are feeling. I am going to keep touching you, but you will be thinking about remembering something else. Tell me what you see, tell me what you feel, tell me what you hear. I will be with you. Don't worry, go with the memory.

In this response, the patient is taking someone safe, someone protective, into the memory and may be able, while sexual stimulation occurs, to describe the memory. This is very effective, but obviously requires a protective and helpful partner.

Conversely, these discussions during sexual behaviors would be extremely detrimental in the last part of treatment when the victim is attempting to readjust sexual experiences and *become a survivor.* Having the victim discuss sexual feelings, attitudes, and memories during sexual experiences would be destructive to re-establishing a new sexual repertoire. During later scenarios, the partner needs to keep the victim in the present. Talking about his/her arousal, providing pleasurable sensations in the ear and touching sensuously, keep the victim experiencing the present.

Stay with me. I like it so much for you to touch me there. I like touching you here. Think about where I am touching you. This feels good. I like your hands all over me. Listen to my words. Stay here with me. It's only you and I.

Sensory Deprivation — Plan C

Sensory deprivation appears to be the opposite of stimulating the senses in order to rekindle memories. Both techniques can be effective and have the same purpose, but with a different modality. Sensory activation exercises use the senses to stimulate cognitive memory. Sensory deprivation exercises attempt to shutdown all senses so that the cognitive process can be heard. Many patients describe *static* in regard to memories. The obvious solution may be to alleviate the static so cognitive memory can occur. It is also important to recognize that if cognitive memory takes place, many of the affective responses will be present.

Andrea presents herself for symptoms of a chronically locking jaw. On occasion, Andrea is devastated by physiological responses out of her control, which result in being unable to move her jaws. After eighteen months of therapy, there appears to be no medical reason for Andrea's difficulties. Approximately three years ago Andrea began to have jaw pain and was believed to have had dentistry problems. With a great amount of dental attention the problem was diagnosed as being related to neck strain. Continued involvement with chiropractors revealed no substantial etiology and eventually Andrea was admitted to a psychiatric hospital for depression.

Andrea, an interior decorator, found herself being unable to complete transactions or be successful in business interactions. Eventually, through hospitalization, Andrea lost the use of her jaws and was eventually placed on intravenous feeding.

During the intake interview, Andrea seems to become emotionally distressed when asked about the possibility of sexual abuse. Andrea has no clear memory, but an obvious affective response to these questions. After several months of therapy, memory recapturing exercises were implemented. Andrea participated in sensory deprivation of all her senses, attempting to activate cognitive awareness.

I spent two days collecting pieces of my childhood. I called my mother and talked to her for thirty minutes, not about anything specific, just general chit chat. I got my childhood treasure box from the attic and looked at my dolls. I also examined my childhood pictures and other paraphernalia from early years. Finally, my friend accompanied me to a secluded home where she was house-sitting. Contingency plans were implemented for any crisis that might emerge. I placed beside the bed, an easel with fat crayons (not big people writing material). I also had a tape recorder that could last several hours. I then attempted to deprive myself of all other sensory interactions so that only my thoughts would emerge.

Later, in therapy, I couldn't believe I had drawn the pictures. They looked so little, so incompetent, but yet so much like a four-year-old. The choking of my grandfather's penis in my throat emerged as loud and clear as my alarm clock on Monday morning. I couldn't believe the fatigue level I had after this experience. My jaws felt as though they were bleeding. I could feel his hands grasp around my jaws and the gagging reflex was the same as it was when I was four. If I had not drawn the pictures, if I had not listened to my terror on the tape recorder later, I know I would have denied this happened. It must have been some other little girl. By shutting everything down, the horrible but very real nightmare was allowed to emerge.

The first tragedy is that Andrea was orally raped by her grandfather. The second tragedy is that she has been severely traumatized by affective responses, culminating in tremendous medical problems with her jaws. Andrea's jaws have remembered the incident, but *another little girl had to take over for Andrea's thoughts.*

The most significant tragedy is that much of Andrea's pain could have been salvaged. Months later in therapy, Andrea chooses to share her Trauma Assessment with her mother. Andrea's mother is not necessarily impressed. *Of course, this happened to you. We all knew it. You were in the hospital. We just thought you would outgrow it.* What could have been saved for Andrea? What damage has occurred without the cognitive awareness? What power would the cognitive memory have had in alleviating her suffering?

Guided Imagery — Plan D

Often, the fear of remembering is extremely powerful for victims in preventing memory recapturing. On the other hand, the sensory bombardment of the clinician's office prevents adequate memory recapturing. There are times when relaxation tapes or guided imagery tapes can be provided to the victim in order to assist in establishing a more appropriate environment to rekindle the memories. Cassette tapes can easily be made by the clinician for a victim to use in a more secluded and protective environment. Cassette tapes encourage focusing on one aspect of childhood and then expanding to a complete discussion, examination, and investigation of those items. It is often through this guidance from one image to a larger picture that the victim will be able to recapture memories.

I want you to think about that fourth grade classroom when you threw your lunch pail through the window. I want you to think about the room, I want you to think about your teacher, and I want you to think very hard about your lunch pail. Think about the handle, the color, and the shape. Bring it to your eyes. Try to look at only the lunch pail and get rid of anything in your adult life that may be interfering. Take yourself back to the fourth grade and to your lunch pail. Try to think about your hand on the lunch pail and see, feel, think, and smell your arm on the lunch pail. Look at your hand on the lunch pail, try to get in touch with the feelings of your hand on the lunch pail. Move your hand up to the elbow and your arm and think, feel and see, smell. If the room in the fourth grade is in your mind, close it out and think about your lunch pail, your hand, and the handle. Concentrate carefully. Think about what you are feeling and what you are sensing with your hand on the lunch pail. Travel from your elbow into your arm and try to take a tender step toward your neck. Don't lose sight of the lunch pail. Keep thinking, keep feeling, keep seeing, keep smelling. Keep the lunch pail, your hand, the handle, your arm, your elbow, and finally your shoulder in mind. Tiptoe carefully with those thoughts in your mind from your shoulder into your neck. Once you have reached your neck, regroup and grab backwards down to your lunch pail. Make sure you keep your lunch pail in your mind again. Try to recapture what is happening with your arm, your fingers, the handle, your lunch pail, and your neck. Now, take a very careful step back up to your head. Try to think about you and what you were thinking. Try to imagine throwing the lunch pail out of the window, but don't do it. Get the picture in your mind of what it will be like when it happens and then take baby steps backwards. What were you thinking? What do you remember? What is happening? Go backwards, go backwards, go backwards.

There are times when guided imagery will allow the victim to return to the sexual abuse scenario with safety. Again, contingency plans and safety mechanisms should always be implemented. Although victims' fear about remembering are usually greater than necessary, it is important to protect patients and have support systems available during these exercises.

Laboratory Conditions — Plan E

Use of the physiological laboratory has traditionally been reserved for sexual offenders in order to predict arousal and diagnose success or failure in treatment. It is often neglected as a source of use for victims. The laboratory for physiological testing of sex offenders provides tremendous opportunity for assisting victims in memory recapturing exercises.

Most laboratories contain a two-way communication system, a natural deprivation of sensory bombardment, as well as a means to measure arousal for both males and females. The plethysmograph has the capabilities of measuring male arousal through a variety of gauges placed upon the penis. Some physiological testing occurs for female arousal as well. Most importantly, the laboratory provides a natural environment for memory recapturing.

Sensory deprivation or guided imagery through the use of two-way communication is extremely valuable. The laboratory provides even more ease with which these activities can be completed. Guided imagery is more possible through the one-way communication system with the clinician being able to guide the patient through these difficult exercises, rather than relying on an audio tape. Additionally, contingency plans and control issues are much more possible in the laboratory than with the victim who may need to do these exercises away from the therapeutic environment.

Additionally, and perhaps most importantly, is the component measurement of arousal. As indicated previously, sexual victims may be aroused to their abusive scenario and this is a neglected component of treatment. Careful notations of arousal for victims through such issues as guided imagery may provide a physiological feedback system, which will assist the victim with *bio-feedback*, thus giving a physiological sanction for returning to those dreaded memories.

Finally, if a patient does not have a partner with whom to participate in stimulation exercises to recapture memory, the patient can become involved in self-stimulation in the laboratory and perhaps accomplish the same goals. Memories may be rekindled as physiological sexual responses occur through masturbatory activities. Encouragement through the communication system from the therapist can provide some of the same feedback as a partner.

Revisiting Childhood — Plan F

A final technique for rekindling memories may involve the patient's efforts to rekindle experiences or activities with children. Two of the *potholes* occur when sexual victims either have their own children or when children turn the age of the adult victim at the time of the abuse. Both of these issues should shed light on the fact that children often rekindle feelings of abuse and may have the potential to rekindle memories. Being in contact with children, especially if the victim suspects a certain age of onset, may be very effective for recapturing memory. Such activity as visiting children's therapy groups, schools, churches, or any other places where children may be, has the potential to recapture memories. Visiting the library and reading children's books or looking through pictures of children at the age the victim fears abuse took place, may also be helpful.

Engaging in activities commonly set aside for children also has memory-rekindling potential. Playing children's games, interacting with therapy dolls (especially anatomically correct dolls), singing children's songs (especially those familiar to the *child within*), as well as playing sexual games that were typical of the victim in childhood may also recapture memories.

Finally, memory recapturing exercises should always occur in a creative way, carefully recognizing that memory becomes confused due to coping skills or bombardment of new stimulus material. In adulthood, information becomes overwhelming. Any activities that stop the bombardment of adulthood stimuli will enhance the victim's focus on childhood feelings, attitudes, thoughts, and ultimately, memories.

Step Two — Presentation Process

If memory recapturing exercises are reasonably successful and the Trauma Assessment has been completed, presentation of the Trauma Assessment must occur under controled circumstances. As outlined in Chapter 16, the Trauma Assessment must be presented, evaluated, shared, resolved, and, most importantly, *owned* before being able to proceed to the next step.

Step Three — Setting Goals

In order to break the trauma bond, specific information must be understood about the dynamics of the trauma bond. The trauma bond has emerged from the Trauma Assessment and goals must be set for breaking the bond not according to the nature of the bond, but what is possible for the victim.

A careful balance must occur between the therapist's knowledge, victim's vulnerability, and reality. Goals that are too harsh may result in the victim becoming the perpetrator. Goals that lack assertiveness may encourage the victim's cycle to continue.

Identify the Bond

It is also important to assure that the proper bond has been identified. Traditionally, the offender seems to be the main focus and often errors are made in assuming that the offender is the source of the trauma bond. Trauma bonding can come in the form of family members, memory, lack of memory, out of control hatred, phobias, fears, etc. Breaking the trauma bond may not always involve the perpetrator. The trauma bond may also have many different faces.

> Okay, I know I was abused and I know who did it. My father is dead and I don't seem to hate my mother. I can't seem to get rid of my fear for women, however. Every time my father abused me he told me **this is what women will do to you.** *I know he is a bastard and I know that's not true about women. When I'm with women I can't help but have the same feelings I had when my father was jerking things in and out of my rectum. It is so stupid. I am competent in many areas. I can't get rid of his voice. I want to be married, I want to be involved with a woman, I want to have children. The* **rip off** *is that I keep hearing his words about women. I know in my head, they are not true. With every piece of my body, I know he is right.*

In this situation, Michael's trauma bond is not with the perpetrator, with any other incestuous family member, not with recapturing of memory, but with elements that emerge in the situational portion of the Trauma Assessment. The voices and the scenario continue to plague Michael. The sexually abusive scene has the answers to understanding Michael's trauma bond.

Step Four — Setting a Plan

The plan must be set, goals must be established, and it is important to bask in the plan. Process, process, process is important. The patient must be given a variety of choices, choices, choices. When a decision has been made about what will happen, and many options have been presented, the choice becomes even more powerful, especially when success occurs.

> Let's pretend like we have your entire family sitting in my office and I present your entire Trauma Assessment. First, tell me what you think they would say and, second, tell me how you felt when I suggested that option.

> How about tomorrow morning, all of the members of your family receive a copy of the Trauma Assessment? Delivered at the breakfast table of your mother and your aunt who abused you will be your Trauma Assessment with a white ribbon around it. Strategically planned after their first cup of coffee, I will contact them, inviting them for an appointment in my office. How do you feel about that option and, most

importantly, when I gave you that option, what happened?

What about the option of writing a letter to your perpetrator indicating that she is facing civil litigation if she does not attend an appointment with me next Thursday? How do you feel about that option in your head and how did the rest of you feel when I suggested that option?

Many of these choices may be inappropriate and not a realistic option for the patient. The purpose of this step is to have the patient consider many different options, making the final option even more potentially successful. The patient cannot make a decision alone without many options, and the final decision is always more important in direct proportion to the number of options available when the choice was made.

And Always . . .

An important option to always present to patients is one of *no action*. Each victim should be aware that rehabilitation may, in fact, occur without involvement of the perpetrator or members of the family. Trauma bonding can be broken without involvement with the person to which the bond is connected. Self preservation, self restoration can often imply healing. *No action* in some cases is the best action. Assuming that breaking the trauma bond always requires the perpetrator to be involved would

be erroneous and may cheat the victim out of an opportunity for rehabilitation.

But What If?

When the victim's decision has already been made concerning what steps will be taken to break the trauma bond, effort must be put forth to caution the victim regarding all options and responses. Not only do goals need to be set adequately, but responses to victim's actions must include a wide variety of options.

Of course, I would have liked my family to have supported me and admitted their knowledge of my sexual abuse. I clearly recognize this was a **hope** *and I had only reasonable chances of success. My ultimate goal was to have them acknowledge my abuse even though I knew they would never be able to talk about it and never be sympathetic. My secondary goal was simply wanting them to know I was abused and I wanted them to be forced to live with that idea for the rest of their lives. I carefully examined my family and I knew that to continue my involvement with them under the present circumstances would cause my death or mental breakdown. To live the rest of my life without secrets was carefully examined as the best option. Even though it would have been nice for them to treat me the way I had hoped, still having them know, and for me to know, that they know, gave me* *success. If I had believed that the Fairy Godmother would somehow zap them into loving me and giving me the childhood I lost, my second goal would have been impossible.*

The victim needs to contemplate all actions. What if? What if? What if? Contemplation of responses to the victim's actions will prepare the victim, should such actions take place, but will also allow the victim to appreciate success even more.

And what if your perpetrator or someone in your family commits suicide?

And what if your perpetrator or someone in your family dies due to the stress?

And what if you are disinherited due to your actions?

And what if your family disowns you because you contact them?

And what if your family labels you a liar?

And what if your family accuses you of causing trouble and, in fact, destroying the family?

And what if you find out that someone else in the family was also abused, perhaps more severely?

And what if you learn that your mother knew about the abuse and has always known?

And what if you are labeled as being responsible for the abuse?

And what if ... nothing happens? What if the family's responses is *So what, who cares?* And after all this work, it just doesn't matter to them.

The Options

The Correspondence Option

Breaking the trauma bond may require or designate the victim simply to respond to the perpetrator through correspondence. There are several options which may occur for the victim by using this modality. Some choices may include informing the perpetrator that the victim remembered the abuse and that the abuse did not go unnoticed. At a very minimum, this response is qualified as simply a notification to the perpetrator from the victim. There can be tremendous satisfaction for the victim in this response and there is little risk involved. The purpose of this response is simple. The victim simply wants the perpetrator to be advised that the abuse was not unnoticed. The patient demands nothing and, in fact, cautions the perpetrator about making any response. The satisfaction of the victim is simply recognizing that the perpetrator was not allowed to continue the secrecy.

Choices will be given for the victim in this situation. The victim must choose whether there will be a request or desire of a response from the perpetrator and, if so, what is that request? Asking for a response can be precarious, but also more rewarding, if successful. The victim must be careful to close doors from unwanted responses and open only the doors where the victim has control. Vulnerability must be avoided.

Dear Vince,

The purpose of this letter is to inform you that you did not get away with sexually abusing me as a child. I want you to know that I remember what you did and that I have struggled with that abuse for most of my adult life. I don't expect you to feel anything since you are a sexual offender. In fact, I expect nothing from you nor do I want anything from you. If you respond in any manner, by discussing this letter with anyone, by contacting me or anyone close to me, I will return with a response that I am sure will make you uncomfortable. The purpose of this letter was to simply live the rest of my life knowing your eyes had to pass over these words.

In this case, the victim sends the letter registered mail so that information can be provided back to the victim that the letter was received. Failure to do this may provide an even more agonizing situation as the victim wonders, wonders, and wonders.

Some options for the correspondence clarification include a request from either family members or the perpetrator. Often, the patient wants a response from the family or from the person who committed the crimes. This is always more risky, but, if successful, has a greater opportunity for success. Victims who ask for responses must carefully encase boundaries and guidelines so that further traumatization will not occur, and so that all responses from the family can be under the control of the victim. Choices must be made whether the victim will write the letter or whether the therapist will write the letter.

Dear Mr. and Mrs. Ryan:

Enclosed you will find the Sexual Victim Trauma Assessment of your son. He has been my patient for approximately the last nine months. He has carefully contemplated all options available to him and has chosen to have you read his Trauma Assessment. He is hopeful you will want to participate in his recovery. He is also very well aware that this may be impossible for you.

Your son desires to be protected and excluded from contact with you because he is a victim. Any correspondence with your son should come directly through me and I will do what

*I can to assist you if your are interested in rehabilitation of the family. Any attempt to contact him directly will be viewed as noncooperation and as a direct indicator you are not interested in his recovery. If you wish to work with me for resolution, please contact my office within the next two weeks and we will hopefully set about a plan for you and your son. If, by October 30, we have had no response from you, we will assume you have chosen the option of **no action**. If you do contact my office, you can trust I will do everything possible to orchestrate a resolution regarding your son's childhood sexual abuse.*

Installation of Insulation

In most situations, the victim needs to be insulated from contact with a family member or with a perpetrator. By virtue of sexual abuse, inequality abounds even if the victim is an adult. Traditional family therapy where all family members attempt to communicate on an equal basis will not be appropriate in the early stages of family resolution. If the victim makes an attempt to contact the perpetrator or makes notification of abuse to the family without insulation, disaster will be imminent.

Traditionally, the family or the perpetrator will be outraged with the lack of opportunity to have contact with the victim. There will be tremendous effort to re-establish old patterns of dysfunctional family dynamics where power was inequitable and the victim was, in fact, a victim.

The family or the perpetrator will desire contact with the victim and will want to re-establish patterns that have proven so effective in the past. Efforts to insulate the victim will be viewed as sabotage by the family and there may be a cry for traditional family therapy.

Insulating the victim and attempting to communicate through a third party is not effective therapy in resolving family issues under a traditional family systems model. Family therapy, however, is not appropriate when one family member is a criminal and one is a victim. Care must be taken to teach the family why insulation of the victim is important.

Whenever possible, antagonism should be avoided. Every effort should be made to assist the family in understanding why insulation is important and that, through cooperation, family goals may also be met. Even in situations where the victim desperately wants a resolution in the family, the inequities in the family dynamics must be rearranged in order for success to occur. The result of separating the victim from a desperate family is often an attack on the professional, since the family would like to return to old patterns.

How can we possibly do anything about resolving this when you won't let us talk to Sarah? You are a stranger. We don't know you, and we certainly are not going to discuss personal family things with someone like you. Don't you know how upsetting it has been for us to receive your letter?

You have hurt us all and we can't trust you. You're the one who is responsible for ruining the family.

Perhaps like no other therapeutic requirement, insulating the victim is painful for the professional. Setting up a scenario of equality for the incestuous family would certainly be a more popular approach, but would revictimize the victim. If the outrage from family can be directed toward the professional rather than toward the victim, then the process of resolution and rehabilitation may occur. Popularity contests for clinicians are not important. Acceptance from the family may never occur. The professional must take the criticism from the family until trust can be gained and until the issue of resolution can become the most important goal.

The most important approach for the family is one of passivity. The family should be allowed, in spite of their insensitivity to the victim, to vent their anger, to attack, and to attempt manipulation. Accepting this behavior from the family will insulate the victim and may eventually work toward resolution. It should be recognized that if the family behaved in this manner toward therapists, the victim would have received these attacks. More appropriately, the family's response should be directed to an objective individual until steps toward resolution can occur.

The Untreated Offender

Many victims desire to have contact within the therapeutic environment with an untreated sexual offender. Although the treated sex offender can provide tremendous opportunity for rehabilitation in breaking the trauma bond, the untreated offender provides tremendous risk.

The first step in attempting to resolve issues with an untreated sex offender is for the victim to set goals that are attainable.

I just want him to listen to me.

I just want him to hear and listen to the family talk about what he did.

I want you to work with her and I want to have a message from her on the video.

I don't ever want to see her again in person, but I want to see if she will prepare a video with you.

I want to see his whole denial in uncensored form.

I want to make a video and I want to see his reaction when he is watching my video.

I want to watch him with my family evaluating my Trauma Assessment.

Preparation Plus . . .

If the untreated sex offender is to be involved, great preparation must occur. In fact, it is the preparation that provides the victim with the most valuable component of treatment. The victim needs to be educated about sex offenders, their denial systems, their rationale, their etiology, and their thinking processes. It may be appropriate for the victim to visit sex offender group therapy sessions or visit with other offenders within the treatment program. Understanding the way sex offenders think, feel, and act, before the encounter with an untreated offender is absolutely essential.

Again, if the victim is hopeful for things that are beyond an untreated offender's capability, failure is imminent. If the victim predicts the behavior from the sex offender, even though the behavior may not necessarily be molded in Fairy Godmother form, success will nonetheless occur.

Preparing 3 x 5 cards for the victim who is meeting with the untreated offender can be helpful. Records must be made with the cards indicating the most painful response or destructive behaviors that could occur on the part of the offender.

I didn't do it.

So What?

That's nothing. You can't believe what I did to your sister.

You wanted me to do it.

What happened to you is nothing compared to what happened to me as a child.

The offender will cry.

It is likely that some of these behaviors will occur if the victim is meeting with an untreated sex offender. In respect for offenders who have spent most of their life rationalizing and denying their abuse, it is generally impossible to be responsive in an appropriate way. Breaking the trauma bond occurs if the victim is properly prepared and if the results of the session are consistent with the victim's preparation. When the offender behaves in a way that was predicted by the victim, control occurs. If the victim is expecting the perpetrator to be suddenly remorseful, sorry, and repentant, failure is on the horizon.

From the Voice of Pauline

I was so ready for anything he had to say. Looking at him, I began to feel guilty, then I quickly ran through my cards and found *pitypot*. It reminded me that he had sexually abused me, both my sisters, and several children in Sunday School for probably two decades. As I continued talking with him, I anticipated his next response. When he finally opened his mouth and said, *Well, I remember doing this to lots of kids, but I can't quite remember you.* I said, *Hold it a minute, Dad, I have that on a card.*

The pain was so much less knowing what he was going to say. Part of me wanted to scream, *How dare you forget me. How dare you think I was so insignificant you can't even remember abusing me.* The other part of me said, *Wait, I have control here. It's on a card. I knew you were going to say that.*

As we proceeded, I could see his discomfort with my control. Finally, he asked if he could speak and said, *You know, Pauline, there is something you should understand. Your mother, God rest her soul, couldn't stand sex and she believed this was a better way to handle my needs.* Outrage filled every vein in my body, but with practice I was prepared. I said, *Hold it, Dad, I don't have that on my card. Let me make one.* My hand shook as I wrote it out, but I would not give up that control.

Video Advantage

Some scenarios with an untreated offender allow the victim to simply present information to the offender while some situations require the offender to participate. Again, separation is the key to success. Some scenarios for breaking the trauma bond can occur through the use of video. The video can provide a desensitization process and a great deal more control than face to face contact.

Katherine is so devastated by the trauma bond between herself and her father, she is nearly agoraphobic. With a motivated offender, sessions take place between the perpetrator and the therapist without Katherine. Katherine is unable to have any contact with her father, but desires some resolution. Katherine prepares a list of questions and her father answers while his responses are videotaped. Obviously, therapeutic intervention was given to the perpetrator in adjusting his answers.

In the next session, Katherine watches the video and toward the end of the session agrees to have her responses to her father's answers videotaped. At the next session with the perpetrator, a videotape is made of the perpetrator watching Katherine on video. In the subsequent session with Katherine, while Katherine is watching her father watching her on video, she explains, *He is getting so very little.* The slow process of desensitization eventually culminated in breaking the trauma bond. Katherine is free to move about the community, although she has not made contact with her father. Whether Katherine is ever able to be with her father or establish a relationship may or may not be in the future. What is important is that the trauma bond was so powerful that Katherine's life was under his control. Through this kind of intervention, the control diminished.

Proxy Clarification

There are times when a substitute for the perpetrator can provide the victim with an opportunity to break the trauma bond. Proxy offenders can be a group member, another sex offender involved in a treatment program, or a family member connected to the victim. Often, the trauma bond is with other family members and not necessarily with the perpetrator, rendering the family's participation or other individual's participation extremely important. Role playing, gestalt activities or psycho drama may be important components to include in the process of breaking the trauma bond. The relationship portion of the Trauma Assessment may indicate that the perpetrator's relationship with others has been extremely significant and the victim will not rehabilitate until some resolution regarding that relationship occurs.

> Daniel is an attractive, talented teacher who is involved in a traumatic bond with his family who adores Daniel's perpetrator. Although the offender is incapacitated in a nursing home, the family worships Daniel's grandfather in every respect. Daniel's dysfunction becomes more pronounced until he is admitted to a psychiatric hospital. Daniel's failed marriages, his homosexual tendencies are indicators of damage. Daniel set goals to have his sister and his mother and father become aware of the traumatic abuse and to be exposed to his trauma assessment. The family receives a letter of invitation requesting an opportunity to meet in a therapeutic situation. The family's first response is outrage at Daniel's insulation and his actions. Although Daniel is protected, the family is extremely vindictive, angry and thoughtless in their responses. Daniel is not only protected from the family, but protected from being aware of his family's insensitivity.

> The family eventually agrees to meet within the therapeutic environment. A great deal of effort is put forth to convince the family that both the therapist and Daniel have the same goals., i.e., family resolution. As the family agrees to continue the involvement, they are made aware that Daniel's perpetrator is his grandfather. The family is given this information before they read Daniel's Trauma Assessment for fear that as the family searches for the name of the perpetrator, the issues of trauma will be overlooked.

> Daniel's family is then allowed an opportunity to be sequestered with a copy of his Trauma Assessment. Each family member is given a pad, pencil, and an opportunity to spend at least one hour with Daniel's Trauma Assessment. On returning as a family unit, again a great deal of insensitivity occurs. In defense of incestuous families, inappropriate responses are not always intentional. It

is not uncommon for family members who are extremely supportive of victims to make such statements as,

Why in the hell didn't he tell us?

Why did she let it go on for such a long time?

I just can't believe it.

These responses are typical for family members learning of sexual abuse. Unless time is spent insulating the victim from these early remarks, revictimization will occur. The following hours of intensive therapy desensitizes the family. Eventually, the family is provided with guidance on how to respond to their brother/son. By the time Daniel joins the family session, the family has had time to learn appropriate responses for a family member they love.

Although it seems impossible for the family to provide victims with complete understanding of the trauma, these processes as outlined can give victims an opportunity to come very close to resolution.

Breaking the Trauma Bond through correspondence, through proxy, through resolution, through desensitization, or through work with unresolved family members can be extremely helpful for the sexual victim patient struggling under the trauma bond. The ultimate in breaking the trauma bond involves direct contact with the perpetrator who has been involved in a treatment process focusing on repairing the damage to the *victim*. The ultimate in breaking the bond is when the offender uses a *restitution* philosophy, putting forth effort to repair the damage to the victim.

RESTITUTION THERAPY

But what about breaking the trauma bond with the treated offender? Can the person who has committed the crime repair the damage? Is identification of the victim and the perpetrator constant, never changing? Is there hope in rearranging the identity if the perpetrator contributes to treatment?

The Raging Debate

Not only has sexual abuse of children been recognized in epidemic proportions during the last decade, but a variety of models have emerged, often in conflict. Tremendous debate arises, as professionals put forth effort to design appropriate treatment modalities and methods. Confusion and conflicts abound. Recidivism rates are staggering; the *system* designed to protect children is often viewed as causing more trauma. Some suggest *decriminalizing* sexual abuse of children, while others request *creative castration.*

As the horrors of sexual abuse are realized, the response toward sex offenders is often outrage or a scream for stiffer penalties. *More prisons* is sometimes a proposed solution. Communities live in fear. At the forefront of debate, the conflict between the *victim advocacy* and the *family systems approach* emerges. *Pure* victim advocacy professionals suggest more emphasis on the crime that has been committed. Efforts to punish, incarcerate and restrict the perpetrator are encouraged. The victim advocacy approach suggests the most appropriate treatment may be separation of the victim from the perpetrator.

On the other end of the spectrum, the *family systems* professionals defend a nonprosecutorial position by citing the trauma to families through involvement in the criminal justice system. In typical cases, such as father/daughter incest, family system advocates argue that in punishing the perpetrator, the victim becomes responsible for family separation and this may be more traumatizing than the sexual abuse itself. Additional support for the family systems model is found in the resistance of mental health professionals to be involved in the criminal justice system. It seems difficult for those in the *helping profession* to focus on criminal issues within a therapeutic environment.

Answers to the Dilemma

The *Restitution Treatment and Training Program* (RTAT) has attempted to find a middle ground or reasonable answer to these opposing forces. This model attempts to *marry* the victim advocacy model with the family systems model. In order to balance controversies, the Restitution Model does not necessarily delineate or reject either approach. Rather, the restitution program purports a logistical organization of *when* different modalities are most effective.

RTAT first recognizes that the *criminal* aspects of child sexual abuse should always be of paramount focus in organizing and implementing a treatment program. This philosophy recognizes that a crime has been committed and should be prosecuted to the fullest extent of the law. At the same time, Restitution Therapy recognizes that criminal court may be adversarial for children and all efforts must be made to offer the sex offender an opportunity

for treatment in order to avoid further traumatizing a child through the criminal court process. This model believes that prosecution, as well as protection of the child from *system damage* can coordinate.

Second, the restitution model recognizes that *change* or rehabilitation for sex offenders is divided into two stages. First, the offender must be motivated in order for the second step of change to occur. Following the motivation phase, therapy involves learning, unlearning, and relearning. The restitution model believes that without effective motivation (provided by the system with a *criminal spirit*), learning, unlearning, and relearning will be ineffective and may actually encourage recidivism on the part of the offender.

In addition, the restitution model focuses on the importance of families and recognizes that children are generally psychologically attached to their families forever. The restitution model appreciates trauma bonding. This program has been founded on the belief that the family unit, especially the offender, can often be used to repair damage to victims. Program philosophy suggests there will come a time when traditional family therapy will be appropriate for sex offenders, but RTAT also dictates that the treatment within that model is a privilege not *automatic*. Finally, this model purports that the *criminal* aspects of the offender's behavior must never be forgotten and must always provide the motivation for the offender's continued change and avoidance of recidivism.

Program Philosophy — A Trauma Bond Focus

The restitution model is founded on the philosophy that the sexual offender must pay emotional, psychological, and financial restitution to all four levels of *victims*. The restitution model attempts to coordinate conflicting and controversial attitudes concerning treatment of the incestuous family. RTAT protocol is founded in the thought that a very serious crime has been committed and that treatment should not be automatic. Philosophy dictates that the perpetrator should have received the stiffest penalty possible *except* that consideration for the victim and trauma bonding needs to be made.

If offenders are offered the opportunity to pay emotional, psychological, and financial restitution through a community based program, the most important solution may have emerged. The restitution model believes that treatment for offenders should be initially difficult, confrontive, and with a criminal spirit, but also provide the offender with the best opportunity to repair the damage caused to not only the victim, but to the family, the community, and society. The most important issue then, is repairing the damage to the victim.

Phase I

The Restitution Model is divided into four phases of treatment, with the first phase beginning with intervention and ending with acceptance of offender into the program. The "spirit" of Phase I is that probation is a *privilege* and the offender must work toward being accepted into the program. The intervention must be swift, coordinated, and governed by the Sexual Abuse Treatment Protocol. Emotional protection of victims is a primary concern during Phase I.

Phase I: Complaint To Program Admission

1. Complaint Received

2. Interviews — Victim — Non-Offending Parent(s) — Alleged Offender

3. Peer Counseling Arranged for all Participants

4. Arrest/Indictment Through Grand Jury

5. Condition of Release from Incarceration

    A. No Contact with any Minor Child (Close Door)

    B. Stipulate right to Investigate Program Without Consequence (Open Door)

6. Intake/Orientation with Offender, Non-Offending Parent(s), Victim (separately)

7. Treatment Begins for Non-Offending Parent(s) and Victims

8. Offender May *Visit* Program

9. If Offender Agrees to Evaluation, He/She Must:

   A. Enter A Plea of Guilty

   B. Sign Treatment Contract

10. If Evaluation Conducted, Considerations Are:

    A. *Why Not?* (Risk Assessment)

    B. *Why?* (Offender's Value in Paying Emotional, Psychological, and Financial Restitution)

11. Offender Evaluation Submitted to Pre-Sentence Writer

12. Offender Continues to *Visit* in Anticipation of Sentencing

13. Offender Sentenced by the Court— Rejected or Accepted into Program

Phase II

Phase II occurs after the offender is sentenced into the treatment program and allowed to begin Phase II. In the interim period between sentencing and *official* admission into the program, the offender may receive a period of county incarceration, community work service, electronic surveillance or other forms of consequence. This decision is based upon outpatient risk factors and the offender's attitude or history. Some offenders begin treatment immediately following sentencing without a consequence from the court.

Phase II places victims of all ages in *preclarification* groups or individual therapy. An intake session occurs with non-offending parent(s) and non-abused siblings for understanding or for awareness of program rules and requirements. Play therapy is provided through the local mental health center for young children. Preteen and adolescent groups are also held for older children in the *preclarification phase*. Non-offending spouse groups are also conducted until the offender is ready for clarification. The *flavor* of Phase II for the victim, non-abused siblings, and non-offending spouse is one of strengthening dynamics within the family to compensate for past inequitable power and control from the offender. All family members are involved in therapy and are awaiting the offender's progress toward clarification.

While in treatment the offender is restricted from any contact with minors. The *no contact* order is explained to victims as a result **and** consequence of the crime the offender committed. The *no contact* restriction is compared to incarceration. It is clear that *the system* is responsible for the *no contact order*, not necessarily the therapists or the victim who reported the crime. The *no contact* order becomes the motivation for the offender to change. The *No Contact Order* must not be viewed by the family as a punishment for the children.

Limited and pre-arranged contact may occur between the non-offending parent and the offender upon request, provided the emotional needs of the victim and family children are of primary consideration. It should also be noted that victims and the non-abused siblings have one-way contact with the offender through the offender's therapists. This process allows cards, letters, gifts, etc., to be given from the children to the offender without reciprocity being allowed from the offender. This *one-way* communication demonstrates the offender has lost the privilege of contact with children.

For the offender, Phase II begins with rearranging distorted cognitions and recognizing the reality of the crimes that have been committed. Phase II is primarily designed to change the thinking of the offender, to reach compliance with the Offender Contract, and establish an open and honest therapeutic relationship through successful completion of a polygraph examination of the offender's sexual history. For the family, Phase II involves restrengthening and restructuring family dynamics and conducting Trauma Assessments for all victims.

Phase II
Change Distorted Thinking
Rearrange Power Dynamics
In Family

1. Court Consequence (Electronic Surveillance, House Arrest, Community Service, Incarceration)

2. Non-Offending Parent(s)/Victim Intake with Offender Therapist

3. Family Counsel Taught to Non-Offending Parent and Children. One-Way Communication Established for Victims to Offender if Needed.

4. New Group Member Packet Presented to Offender

   A. Group Rules

   B. Contract Assignment

      1. Rewrite Contract

      2. Complete Contract Quiz

   C. Thinking Error Awareness

   D. Thinking Error Log Instructions

   E. No Contact Report Instructions

   F. Prepares Sexual History Generic

   G. Prepares Sexual History *Victim Specific*

5. Trauma Assessment of Victim Begins

6. Offender Presents Sexual History to Group (Approve/Disapprove)

7. Sexual History Preparation for Polygraph

8. Polygraph Administered (Fail/Success)

9. If Pass/All Victims on Offenders Sexual History, Reported to Child Sexual Abuse Team

10. If Fail/Offender Returns to the Beginning of Phase II

11. If Fail/Court Consequence Contemplated by Sexual Abuse Team

12. Trauma Assessment of Victim Completed

Phase III

Phase III involves the process whereby the offender works toward repairing the damage to the victim through the clarification process. It is hoped that Phase II forces the offender to change distorted thinking and allows the offender to focus on the needs of the victim. The offender earns the *privilege* of receiving instructions for preparing the clarification. If violations occur or if lack of cooperation is observed, the offender loses the privilege to work toward the clarification goal.

The clarification process has evolved over a long period of time within the *Restitution* philosophy. The clarification process is not an apology nor a letter of responsibility. The clarification is a carefully designed process to clarify, resolve, and rehabilitate the victim. The clarification process gives the offender the ultimate opportunity to change distorted thinking and move toward a future of sensitivity and empathy. The process toward preparing the clarification therefore, is an extremely important component for the offender. Anticipating the offender's completion of the clarification (placing all burden on the offender) is also a rehabilitative process for the victim and the family.

The offender verbally prepares the clarification components for the acceptance and critique of group members and therapists. Additionally, the offender uses video productions to not only prepare, but to become internally sensitive by watching personal video preparations. Finally, the offender prepares the clarification in written form to be contained in the victim's *resolution scrapbook*.

All choices and decisions regarding clarification are given to the victim with support and encouragement from a team of therapists. The victim has learned the value of clarification and is anxious to participate regardless of the victim's attitude toward the offender. During Phase I, II, and III, victims learn that the clarification is *for* their benefit and part of the offender's obligation of restitution.

When the clarification is prepared, the offender first must gain permission to meet with the victim through presenting the entire clarification to the custodial parent(s). The clarification may or may not be accepted by the victim's guardians. All choices, arrangements, and procedures concerning clarification are chosen by the victim and the family.

The last step in completion of Phase III is the presentation of the clarification scrapbook. In appreciation of developmental changes that occur as the victim proceeds through sexual development, a written document of not only the clarification, but of *system* documentation and support for the victim must be provided. Trauma Assessment data and research indicates that those children who were able to separate the sexual abuse from normal sexual development have the greatest opportunity for rehabilitation. The scrapbook provides this vehicle.

Phase III
Preparing For Repairing
Damage To Victim

1. Offender Demonstrates Successful Polygraph/Evidence of Change in Thinking

2. Offender Receives Clarification Components Package

3. Offender Proceeds Through Clarification Preparation

   A. Round Robin

   B. Video Privilege

   C. Written Form for Scrapbook

   D. Letters of Permission

4. Offender Clarifies to Non-Offending Parent

5. Non-Offending Parent Accepts/Rejects Clarification

6. Victim Given Choice of Clarification Process

7. Clarification Proceeds with Victim

8. Clarification Proceeds with all Family Members

9. Clarification Scrapbook is Presented

10. Offender Status is Changed to *Contact with Children Under Adult Supervision*

11. Family Visit Issue Contemplated

12. If Visitation is to Occur — ACT II Begins with Visitation

13. Family Transferred to ACT II Program

Phase IV

Phase IV of the treatment program will continue for the offender and the family throughout the duration of the offender's probation. Generally, offenders in the RTAT Program receive five years probation and spend twelve to eighteen months proceeding through Phase I, II, and III. Offenders and their families will remain in ACT II for the remainder of the probation period and will always be encouraged to remain in the program as a supportive therapy component, years following probation.

Phase IV or the ACT II Program (Aftercare Treatment) is similar to traditional therapy within the family systems model. Protection and safety of the family, as well as continuing to repair the dynamics of the family is a primary concern. This phase of treatment should be extremely positive for all family members as they proceed through regaining skills in preventing turmoil.

For offenders and other family members where reunification is not desired or possible, future family plans are the focus of treatment. The spirit of the ACT II Program is one of support and encouragement. Program philosophy dictates, however, that if this positive treatment modality occurs for the sexual offender previous to repairing damage to the victims, this suportive phase of treatment will be counter-productive to the offender's rehabilitation.

It should also be noted that the ACT II phase of treatment is less expensive for the perpetrator and may result in family reunification, which will also be financially helpful for the family. Offenders who work toward reunification will have the financial burden of supporting two households lightened. With reasonable fees for treatment, all family members will become involved in the treatment program and will continue with ACT II's positive support system throughout the child's developing years.

Offenders will participate in many supportive therapeutic involvements including a Sexual Arousal Control Group. Offenders will continue being monitored through polygraphs and physiological assessments (plethysmography) as they proceed through Phase IV. Should difficulties occur or should there be a change in attitude of the offender, placement may be made back to an earlier phase of treatment. Although the ACT II Program is positive and supportive, the offender must recognize requirements for monitoring, in respect for the privilege of remaining in the community. The offender must also recognize that in spite of the positive aspects of ACT II, treatment remains an obligation and progress must continue.

The following is a list of components that the offender, victim, or non-offending parent may experience while involved in the ACT II or Phase IV of treatment:

Phase IV
Motivate Offender/Family Members To Maintain Progress Level

1. Family Therapy

2. Reunification Decision Making

3. Communication Skills

4. Human Sexuality

5. Couple Counseling

6. P.E.T. (Parent Effectiveness Training)

7. Positive Citizenship

8. Offender Support Group

9. MAC (Molested As Children) Group

10. Non-Offending Spouse Support

11. Sexual Abuse Prevention

12. Sexual Arousal Control (SAC) Group

13. Peer Counseling Development

14. Polygraph Examinations

15. Physiological Monitoring Assessments

Repairing the Damage

How does an offender pay emotional and psychological restitution to a victim who has been robbed of childhood? How can that debt be paid? In consideration of trauma bonding and the Trauma Assessment, what is the contribution from the criminal who has committed this most serious crime?

Resolution and Clarification

For The Victim

The resolution or clarification with the victim requires careful preparation on the part of the perpetrator. Evidence from the Trauma Assessment points to how the perpetrator can make an important contribution. Information gleaned in the Trauma Assessment regarding relationship difficulties, developmental problems, and destructive coping skills can be undone and resolved by the perpetrator in many situations.

The purpose of the clarification is to resolve, to clarify, to explain, and to empower. The clarification is not an apology, it is not an attack on the perpetrator, nor is it a process of forgiveness. The clarification requires the perpetrator to put the sexual abuse in perspective, so that trauma as a result of confusion, can be avoided.

For The Perpetrator

For the sexual offender, repairing the clarifica-

tion is an extremely important component of offender treatment. Sexual offenders have, in essence, *masturbated in vaginas*. This is a figurative statement (not limited to females) to describe the depersonalization of children by those who offend. The *objectification* of children is a process that offenders have learned. As indicated in previous chapters, offenders are able to maintain erections and have sexual pleasure, while children are in emotional or physical pain. *Masturbating in a vagina* is a very selfish, self-eroticizing activity similar to the molestation of children. The task of discovering trauma and repairing damage from that trauma may give sex offenders the most appropriate opportunity to change the thinking that allowed *masturbation in vaginas*. In other words, one of the reasons offenders are able to have pleasure while someone is being hurt is that they have objectified their victim. Repairing the damage to victims requires the opposite of *objectification*. Most adults do not offend children because they have some sense of the damage caused through sexual abuse. Offenders think differently and the process of repairing the damage may give sex offenders the best opportunity to change their distorted thinking.

The Goals

Kid's Talk

There are four basic rules for the clarification process, with the first relating to language and the power of words. The clarification must be written and presented in words or examples providing the victim with control and clarity. If the victim is age nine and the sexual abuse began when the victim was five, the clarification must be presented in language consistent with a five-year-old. Language or rationale beyond the victim's capability will empower the perpetrator and revictimize the child.

Uniqueness

The clarification must be unique and must fit a specific child. Those clarifications which could be published in the *New England Journal of Medicine* are not unique and they may be inappropriate. Generic clarifications may further traumatize children. As an example, such generic terms as *betrayal of trust* could pertain to nearly every victim who has been offended. The clarification requires specific terms, conversations, incidents that would pertain only to the unique child offended. Victims must feel that the clarification process could belong to no other child in the world.

Recapture Childhood

The clarification process must return the victim to childhood and recapture the robbed childhood. This goal will be accomplished primarily with the uniqueness of examples, incidents and scenarios. Childhood will be revisited and experienced in a clarification that is successful.

Victim Power

The clarification must be under the control of the victim or the victim's parents. The clarification should never be forced upon a victim or viewed as a requirement. The offender will have many answers that will help the victim. Participation is for the victim's rehabilitation and can occur regardless of how the victim feels about the offender. All decisions regarding the clarification should be made by the victim through the process of empowerment. Certainly, guidance from professionals will occur, but the clarification should provide a vehicle with which the child is empowered but not obligated.

Clarification Components

The GREETING

The *Greeting* is the first portion of the clarification presented to a victim in the clarification session. Because of difficulty, the *Greeting* is usually the last component prepared by the perpetrator. It is difficult to prepare this portion of the clarification because of the clarification rules. *Greeting* rules dictate that the offender cannot ask a child a question since *victims* are innocent and do not **need** to participate. The victim should be protected from answering any questions. Because the offender is unable to ask questions during the first part of clarification, particular problems arise. Most adults tend to visit with children by asking questions and interrogating. *Hi, how are you? How is school?*

The offender must design a different approach in order to protect the status of the victim.

Without being able to ask questions, the offender will sometimes resort to discussing nonsensical or unimportant things, such as the child's appearance or what the child may be doing. *I heard you are in 4-H.* These are inappropriate responses since discussing current activities of the child may appear intrusive. The child may feel as though the perpetrator has been *spying on the victim*. If the perpetrator decides to discuss nonsensical things, such as the child's 4-H project or the third grade Christmas play, the message suggests the clarification is unimportant. If the perpetrator discusses the child's physical appearance, the child may feel objectified. The perpetrator must work toward developing a *Greeting* that defers all power to the victim. The victim should feel a choice whether the clarification will continue. Much the same as a competent dentist explains what may happen in the appointment, the perpetrator needs to take on the same stance in the greeting. The *Greeting* must explain what will happen *should the victim choose to continue* and provide the victim with complete understanding of the victim's power.

Hello, Joseph, it has been a very long time since I have seen you. This is the first day I have even been allowed to be in the same room with kids. I made a big mistake with the secret touching that I did to you and I haven't been able to be around kids. I lost that privilege. I am very, very lucky to be sitting in this chair.

Joseph, I have always been the boss in the family. I have been the biggest and I have been the dad. I have always told you and everyone else what to do. Today, is different and that's the first thing I want to tell you.

Today, you are the boss. Even though you are not as big as I am, you are the most important person in this room. You get to decide everything. Because of the secret touching that I did, I don't get to decide anything. When people do those things, they lose all of their privileges.

If you decide to stay and listen to what I have to say, I will be talking about lots of different things. First, I am going to be telling you about all the special things that I remember about you. I am going to talk about things you used to do that were wonderful. I am going to talk about how you are special and like no other kid, if you decide to listen to me.

The next thing I am going to talk about, if you decide to stay, is how I think I might have hurt you by doing the secret touching. I know that you are the smartest person about that, since it happened to you. I am going to be talking about something called a *Trauma Assessment*. In the Trauma

Assessment, I am going to be explaining some of the ways that I think I might have hurt you. Nobody knows for sure how you have been hurt except you, but I am going to try to talk about some of the ways.

If, after hearing that, you still think it might be a good idea to keep listening, I will be talking about what I did to you. That may seem kind of silly since you already know what I did to you. This part is important so there are no more secrets. Secrets are what I did to you because I was selfish. There aren't any more secrets now and I will be telling you about what I did so that you will know there aren't any more secrets. You're a lot smarter about what happened, but I will tell it just like I remember it and you can know if I am telling the truth. I am going to be telling you lots and lots of times, if you decide to listen to me, that none of the touching was your fault. If I say *IT* wasn't your fault, I want you to make sure that you know I told the whole truth about *IT*.

The last two parts of the clarification are called the How and the Why. I would like to tell you how I was able to trick everybody in the family. I would like to tell how I was able to keep the secret. And the last thing I would like to tell you is why I did this. Most kids wonder why anybody would want to do these kinds of things to kids, especially great kids. If you decide to listen to me, I have a lot of things to tell you about why this happened.

Joseph, I know that I don't have any right to ask you to stay and listen to me. When people do things that are not okay, they lose lots of their rights. I remember on your birthday you were such a good kid, we decided to give you the *right* to stay up until 8:30. When people do what they are supposed to do, they get to have lots of privileges. When people do what they are not supposed to do, they lose their privileges and that's what happened to me. You don't have to stay and listen because you didn't do anything wrong. If you do decide to listen, I think I have some things that will help you understand.

It is important to note that all power is being returned to Joseph in the decision to stay and listen to what his father has to say. It is also important to recognize that the wording of the greeting and all other parts of the Clarification are not grammatically correct or smooth, but expressed in the words and language of the child.

The DESCRIPTION

The second part of the resolution/clarification session is called the *Description*. The *Description* of the victim is very important for a variety of reasons. First, it is important to return the victim to childhood, providing a vehicle for the child to recapture the precious, unique aspects of being a child. A more complicated issue, however, is provided in a coordination with another part of the clarification.

Historically, sex offenders were asked to explain to their victim *nothing about you caused me to do this*. Certainly, it is important for victims to understand that they were not responsible for the sexual abuse. Unfortunately, the generic *nothing about you caused me to do this* provided no reason for the sexual offense. Victims walked away from clarification sessions in the past being totally vulnerable. Innocence is important, but innocence is different than total vulnerability. Without any tangible reasons for the abuse, feelings of vulnerability were enhanced.

It also became clear to those professionals involved in the restitution program that certain characteristics of sexual victims tended to be the reasons offenders molested specific children. Commonly, an obnoxious brat seemed difficult to sexually abuse at least more than one time. A pattern emerged. Victims tended to be more abusable by their positive qualities. It appeared that sex offenders chose children who had positive, but nonetheless vulnerable qualities. The attributes of the child that would normally be treasured possessions, seemed to be the tools of sex offenders in abuse.

With these two issues in mind (returning the victim to childhood and providing victims with awareness of certain characteristics within themselves), the *Description* was developed. The sex offender is required to describe specific attributes about each child, which were precious, unique, but also related to another component of the clarification describing *How* the offender was able to abuse. The *Description* should lay the foundation for revisiting childhood, seeing specific, unique, and precious qualities emerge. Each quality described by the offender must contain a *story or example*, unique to the childhood of the victim.

> Suzie, one of the special things about you is that you are the kind of little girl who always had a good attitude and who always smiles. I remember at Christmas time, at Grandma Ida's house when everyone had opened their presents, you wanted to keep everybody happy. You would run around the living room and wrap the presents back up so that your brother, Brandon, and sister, Missy, could open them all over again. You even wrapped one for Old Uncle Bert! You weren't interested in playing with your own toys or being selfish, you wanted everyone to be happy and for everyone to have the same smiles Suzie had. You would wrap all the presents back up so that we could all have the fun of opening them again.

> I also remember another time when you had an especially good attitude. I remember when we were taking Franko, the cat, to Dr. Applegate be-

cause he was sick. Franko was sitting on your lap and you had on your yellow dress with the green buttons. Franko wasn't feeling very well and he threw up all over your pretty dress. Even though it was yucky and awful, you kept smiling and petting Franko. You just kept giving Franko Good Touching and he appreciated you, even though he kept burping. That's one of the very special things about you, Suzie. No matter how yucky things are, no matter if everyone else is sad, you always smile and have a good attitude.

This special quality in Suzie is precious but also clearly a tool used by the perpetrator in his abuse. Now the clarification must coordinate components to help Suzie appreciate that quality but also understand how she was abused.

Parallel Components for the HOW Portion of the Clarification

Suzie, one of the ways I was able to do secret touching to you and keep it a big secret in our family was that I knew you tried so hard to have a good attitude. When I did secret touching, it was yukky for you. I made you do things that you didn't want to do. I tricked you. It was very yukky. One of the ways I was able to do this was that I knew Suzie would always be smiling and always tried to have a good attitude even if things were yukky. Other kids are sometimes brats and don't care about happy things or keeping everyone else in the family happy like you do. Some little girls think only about themselves. I knew you were the kind of little girl who wanted things to be happy in the family. I knew you were someone who had a good attitude even if things were yukky. That's one of the ways that I could do secret touching to you was I knew that I could do yukky things and Suzie would keep her good attitude and not tell.

Suzie, I want you always to know that being a happy kid and having a good attitude is wonderful. You should be proud of yourself and keep that good part forever and ever. There is nothing wrong with having a good attitude when things are yucky, there is only something wrong with people like me who trick little girls who have good attitudes.

TRAUMA ASSESSMENT

The cry from many sexual victims is, *No one cares, no one understands the pain.* On the other hand one of the most insensitive things for offenders to say is, *I understand how you have been hurt.* No matter how empathetic or competent a therapist, a parent, or a family member may be, no one truly understands or feels the pain, the same as the victim.

The *Trauma Assessment* presented by the sexual offender in the clarification attempts to categorize traumatic responses to sexual abuse. Recognizing that pain is unique and recognizing that offenders desensitize the trauma *(masturbating in vaginas)*, this is a difficult task. Avoidance of feelings allows the perpetrator to be sexually competent. This is a time for that competence to be lost.

Traditionally in the Restitution Treatment and Training Program, a *Trauma Assessment* is conducted for the sexual victim during Phase II. As the offender is proceeding through the treatment and clarification preparation, professionals have become aware of the intricacies of damage to the victim. The job of the perpetrator is to *match* the offender's *Trauma Assessment* with the professional's. Certainly, matching as far as professional terms or *psycho babble* is not a requirement, but the major areas of damage within the Relationship Perspective, the Developmental Perspective, and the Situational Perspective must be resolved in the offender's clarification — even for a five-year-old.

Excerpt From Trauma Assessment

Suzie, one of the ways I hurt you is that I robbed you of your mom. Little girls should grow up in families being safe and happy and, most important, being able to trust and talk with their moms. Little girls should be able to take their baths and put on pink, Strawberry Shortcake pajamas if they want. They should be able to have their moms help them get dressed and when they need a good night kiss, have their moms carry them into their bedrooms with blue umbrellas on their yellow wallpaper. Just before going to bed, little girls should be able to talk with their moms about anything they want. They should be able to trust their moms and ask their moms questions or tell their moms about anything that is bothering them. I remember once when you were little in the Red Roof Market by our house, you asked your mom, *How do the store men get the stems in the apples?* Everyone laughed, but it was a really good question. You wondered about the apple stems and like little girls are supposed to do, you asked your mom.

But, then, Suzie, I started tricking you and doing secret touching to you. I told you that your mom wouldn't like you any more if you told her what we were doing. I made it seem like you shouldn't talk to your mom or ask your mom any questions. I made you afraid to trust your mom. This was just like robbing a little girl of her mom. This was not fair for me to do because little girls have a right to trust their moms with lots of things. Even though your mom was really wanting to help you, wanting to talk to you, and wanting to answer your questions, I hurt you by making you think you couldn't ask her. I robbed you of your mom by not letting you think you could talk to her about secret touching or apple stems.

WHAT HAPPENED

The fourth component of the clarification is a description of *what* actually took place during sexual abuse. The *Trauma Assessment* will reveal distorted cognitions and the potential for continued distortions of reality. A record, a clear understanding of what actually took place, will have lasting value for the sexual victim. This portion of the clarification unfortunately tends to be the easiest for the perpetrator since fantasies about *What Happened* may pervade and occupy the offender's thoughts. Caution should be raised, however, that this portion of the clarification should not revictimize the child for the pleasure of the perpetrator. Offenders may wish to be extremely graphic in this part of the clarification for their own gratification.

On the other hand, some offenders may wish to minimize or describe vague terms, such as *I molested you* or *I did the secret touching*. Although those phrases may be appropriate in other parts of the clarification, those terms are vague and suggest a lack of importance. The perpetrator is generally protecting uncomfortable feelings by describing the sexual abuse in vague terms.

On the other end of the spectrum, offenders may choose the *Penthouse* approach. The *Penthouse* approach allows perpetrators to describe the sexual abuse in terms that are arousing and that present the sexual abuse in rather adultlike terms. If this portion of the clarification could be published in *Penthouse*, then certainly the status of the perpetrator as a deviant offender is lessened.

This part of the clarification requires a mechanical but very specific description of the sexual abuse that occurred. For abuse that has happened over many years, the offender may need to categorize certain sexual behaviors that were committed or a chronological categorization may be used.

> Every time you came into Sunday School class, I would get you to sit on my lap. You were a good little boy and you would always do what I wanted. I made sure that I could put my hands between your legs and touch you on your penis with my hands. I pretended like I was reading a book or doing something else. My hands would be rubbing the front of you and touching your penis. Sometimes when we were standing up singing, I would make sure that the back of your head touched me between my legs. I did this lots of times when you came into Sunday School.

For children who have a tendency to misperceive, to re-evaluate and to distort, this portion of the clarification may be extremely valuable. Understanding exactly what happened and hearing what happened from the perpetrator can provide reality conditioning, but most important is a desensitization process. Adult victims, during this portion of the clarification, also receive a validation not possible in other treatment modalities.

HOW

The fifth portion of the clarification process requires the perpetrator to describe manipulation, bribery, and coercion. The offender must *revisit* the *Description* of the clarification and coordinate each special characteristic of the child with a specific manipulation used to maintain secrecy. It was a requirement of the *Description* component to discuss only those issues pertaining to the child that were used for manipulation. Each portion of the *Description* and the *How* must pertain directly to those personal qualities of the child that were the focus of manipulation.

> I remember talking to you earlier about what a great kid you were. I remember telling you how you were the one at the Easter Egg hunt who always looked out for everyone else. I remember when your little sister, Shannon, was sad because she couldn't run very fast and find any Easter Eggs. While all of the other kids were running as fast as they could, you saw Shannon. All the grown-ups saw <u>you</u> sneaking in back of Shannon and putting Easter Eggs in her basket. When the Easter Egg hunt was over, Shannon had lots of eggs and was happy. That was a great thing about you because you thought of your sister's feelings and took care of her.

> I was your sister, too, and I wanted to do secret touching. Most important I wanted to make you do secret touching to me. I knew that you took care of Shannon and you always tried to make your sisters feel great. When I told you that I wanted you to do secret touching, I knew you were a good sister. I tricked you because I knew you liked your sisters and always wanted to do things to make them happy. That's one of the ways I was able to trick you. I knew you were a good sister.

> There is nothing wrong with being a good sister, Marci, you are a great sister and that's what is great about you. Don't ever change. There is only something wrong with people like me who have good sisters and trick them.

It's important for the victim to conclude this portion of the clarification by recognizing that each special characteristic was misused by the offender. The qualities that the offender misused need to be continued. The victim needs to feel a sense of *rebirth* concerning the special qualities. Blame for the manipulation needs to be placed upon the perpetrator and the victim needs to feel extremely proud of these special, unique qualities.

The WHY

As explained in Chapter 17, *WHY* the sex offender committed the crime requires a four-part presentation. The first section begins with the statement of selfishness and the second portion explains the value or commodity of sexuality. This seems to be hard for offenders to understand and is a very difficult portion of the clarification process.

When kids are little, they have special parts of their bodies just like grownups. Special parts of their bodies are on their chest and between their legs. Kids have a right to keep those parts of their body really, really special. They don't show them to people at the supermarket and they don't share them with people in school or on the school bus. They keep these parts really private and special and like no other part of their body because something wonderful happens when they grow up.

When kids work really hard to keep those parts of their body private, that means when they grow up something terrific happens. When kids grow up, it is really terrific when they choose to share their body with someone. They think about all the other grownups in the world. They think and they look and they meet lots and lots of people. They wonder and they wait. Finally, when they meet the most special person of all, they decide that they want to share their body with that person. The reason sharing those parts is so wonderful is that kids keep those parts of their body really private and special when they were kids and they don't share them with anybody else. Since this is the most special person they choose, sharing of those parts of the body for grown ups is really wonderful.

When kids are kids, they are too busy picking out which puppy they want or which kind of ice cream they want or which television show they want to watch. Kids shouldn't have to pick someone to share their bodies with until they are grown up. That's too big of a decision even for great kids.

What this means is that the touching of those parts of our bodies feels different from touching any other part. If we touch those parts of our bodies every day in lots of different ways, then the touching wouldn't feel as good as it does. When grownups share those parts of their body, it's a great feeling. The grownups should only be sharing those parts of their bodies with other grownups who are old enough to pick someone. Secret touching between grownups is a wonderful thing because both of the grownups are old enough to *pick*.

I didn't want to follow the rules and I didn't want to pay attention. I knew that you needed time to pick out somebody all on your own when you grew up. You had a right to do that. I knew that touching those parts felt good and I wanted to have my way. I liked the feeling and I wanted more and more and more of that feeling. I broke the rules and that wasn't okay for me to do.

It is important in this part of the clarification that the child feels a sense of *robbery*. The positive nature of sexuality must be imparted in order for the child to feel like a victim. Sexuality must be presented as something positive, unique and special. Saying *I did it because I was selfish* is not enough. The second portion of the *Why* needs to explain the value of the commodity that was taken.

The third part of the *Why* requires the sex offender to discuss the *character disorder* within. A history of the offender could be presented, as well as restating the sense of selfishness. The final portion of the *Why* explains the issue of consent and, it is hoped, returns the victim to the feeling of choice or consent. The child should walk away from the clarification recognizing that since consent did not occur, contamination is not a factor. The sex offender has explained why sexual consent as a child was impossible, (even if the child cooperated, initiated the sexual contact, or may have been sexually responsive). Sexual consent of children must be explained as impossible since saying *yes* means nothing if *no* was not a choice. The victim should leave the last portion of the clarification with a sense of, *I haven't picked yet.*

Clarification Procedure

The clarification procedure is indeed delicate. As the offender becomes prepared, approximately nine to twelve months transpires. The offender and the child have not been in contact and often the first meeting occurs in a clarification session. The words of the clarification both verbal and in written form have been carefully prepared. In actuality, however, the process may be as important as the actual content of the clarification.

Letters of Permission

The first part of the process requires the offender to write letters of permission requesting the *honor* of being in contact with the non-offending or custodial parent, as well as the victim. Letters are perused by the guardian and a decision is made regarding meeting with the perpetrator. If permission is granted, clarification occurs between the perpetrator and the protective parent(s). The clarification must be exactly the same as what will transpire between the perpetrator and the victim, if permission is granted. The offender uses the same words prepared for the victim. The custodial parent hears the clarification and makes decisions to grant permission for the clarification between the offender and the victim to occur. Permission can also be denied.

This may be the first opportunity for custodial parents to hear what the offender has prepared. This may be the first time parents hear details of the abuse, the nature of coercion and the offender's viewpoint of the damage that has been caused. This can be an extremely emotional session and must be handled carefully. Due to the potentially painful nature of the session, effort needs to be put forth to explain the purpose so that cooperation will occur.

I don't know why I have to listen to this stuff. I hate him for what he did and I don't want to give him the time of day, let alone listen to him. I don't want to hear what my child went through. I am so filled with anger and hate I can't imagine even being in the same room with him.

Silent Screams

Explanation for parents needs to include an understanding of how pain and trauma continues to fester through the years without some resolution and clarification. *Not knowing* tends to keep memories alive. By knowing each detail, by having clarity concerning what has taken place, the desensitization process occurs. Without clarification, parents will ponder, wonder and continue to cultivate trauma from sexual abuse.

It is also important to point out that the clarification is not **for** the *perpetrator,* the clarification is **for** the *victim* and the parents of the victim. Providing parents with a variety of choices, opportunity and these explanations, assists in understanding their power in the clarification process.

Power to the Parents

A tremendous sense of empowerment should occur as parents are given the opportunity to listen to offenders. If clarification is properly orchestrated, parents feel in control and able to benefit from the session rather than having the clarification session seem to be for the perpetrator. By the very nature of parents being in control and being able to choose whether the clarification will occur, tremendous power is returned.

Victim Power

Clarification with the victim also occurs after many, many choices have been given. If the victim is resistive, many options are presented concerning ways in which the clarification might be comfortable. The child may be able to choose a specific office, furniture arrangement or time of day. The child may choose the presence of individuals or the exclusion of people. Orchestration of the choices, both for the child and the parents, is as important as the clarification itself.

As an example, a nationally known treatment program demonstrated a clarification process on public television. As the camera comes into focus, the sex offender is sitting comfortably in a large chair next to his therapist. Both men are chatting and smiling. The door opens and the victim walks into the room holding hands with her mother. The first thing the sex offender says is, *Hello, Jennifer, how are you?*

Before clarification has begun in this situation, all power is given to the perpetrator and failure is imminent. The offender, comfortably sitting in the room, chatting with his therapist, sets the tone of power and control for the perpetrator. The victim walks conspicuously into the room, obviously powerless. The final blow occurs as the offender asks the child a question.

More appropriate clarification sessions allow the child to make choices about everything, even the physical arrangement of the room. The victim should be comfortably nestled in an office using any kind of *prop* the child chooses. The offender should walk obtrusively into the room, not the victim. It is the offender who must talk and work, unless the victim chooses to intervene and inquire.

Speech Time

The first process of the clarification occurs with the therapist presenting a *speech* to both the perpetrator and the victim. Under the restitution concept, it is explained, repairing the damage to the victim is the most important issue. Victims are given the opportunity to interrupt, to ask questions, or to leave. This *speech* should take at least three to four minutes while anxiety and apprehension in the victim subsides. The offender is then allowed to present the *Greeting*, finishing in approximately five to ten minutes. As the offender leaves the room, the victim and therapist regroup. Options are discussed, decisions are made regarding the choice to continue.

Now More

The sex offender then proceeds through each component of the clarification process. Ideally, several appointments will be made allowing the child to digest information and rekindle a sense

of empowerment. The sex offender is also allowed to regain composure during these intermittent periods.

The Answer, Please

Generally, as clarifications begin, the victim is apprehensive, anxious and emotionally distraught. As the process continues on a step-by-step basis, victims generally, but not always, seem to become more comfortable. As the clarification comes to a close, many questions arise. Victims should be able to ask questions and receive answers. Hopefully, the offender is no longer entrenched in a denial system and will answer questions appropriately, without using *thinking errors* or minimizations. The question and answer period can be the most dangerous portion of the clarification if offender thinking has not changed. By the time question and answer periods have concluded, the victim usually has regained a tremendous sense of empowerment, clarification and resolution. Growth and comfort hopefully are a response.

> *I hated him so much I didn't even want to be in the same room with him. I did want to hear what he had to say, but I couldn't stand the sight of him. I would only agree if he was already in the room facing the corner and I could enter without him looking at me. I wanted to sit on the couch, but I did not want him to see me. I listened to the first part of what he had to say. I*

knew he couldn't hurt me because he couldn't even look at me.

The second session I wanted to see what he looked like from the front to see if he was any different. I still couldn't stand to have him look at me. I asked that he be blindfolded and he agreed. It was easier for me to listen to what he had to say by seeing his face. In the other session, I didn't know if he was laughing or smiling or crying, so I wanted to see him, but I didn't feel comfortable with him looking at me.

By the third session, I didn't want him blind folded. I thought that was stupid because he couldn't hurt me anyway. I wanted him to do some of the parts of the clarification, but I didn't want him to look at me. I wanted him to look at my therapist. As he talked to my therapist, I could watch his whole body and I knew what he was thinking.

By the time we came to the last session, he seemed so little. I couldn't wait to ask him questions. I couldn't believe what he had to say about how little I was and how I had been tricked and used. It was amazing how much better I felt listening to him and being able to be in the same room with him.

By the time the clarification was over, all of my questions had been answered. I had more things to say

that I had ever imagined. I really was a kid and I really wasn't responsible. He said he didn't mind being blind folded if it helped, and it did. He got littler and littler and littler.

All in the Family

In cases of family incest, there may be an opportunity or obligation for additional clarifications within the family. The victim may dictate which components of the clarification would be appropriate for other family members to hear. With cooperation from the perpetrator, the process may include the entire family working toward making decisions about visitation and eventually reunification in some cases. Families that make decisions to reunite or begin visitation need to have control over sexual abuse. Sexual abuse needs to be placed in a package where it can be discussed, but not where sexual abuse becomes the focus of the family.

The following is a list of goals or *directions* that the sexually abusive family may adopt following clarification processes.

1. TO REMEMBER in a positive manner that reinforces and promotes progress. Remembering old arguments and past disagreements will serve to be a negative factor in a family that is attempting to resolve new issues. Remembering positive issues from the past helps to enhance growth and progress in families.

2. TO COMMUNICATE, because secrets al-

lowed the sexual abuse to flourish, therefore, families that talk and communicate regarding both positive and negative issues cannot have secrets. Families should be encouraged to understand the effect of communication and the effect of noncommunication.

3. TO TOUCH, TALK, TOUCH, TALK, TOUCH, TALK, because touching must be re-established in families where sexual abuse has occurred. Touching should not happen, however, unless there is a great deal of discussion about touching. Families need to learn to *talk and touch* to avoid secrets regarding touching.

4. TO DEVELOP EQUITABLE SYSTEMS OF DISCIPLINE, because families need to become consistent and predictable regarding discipline. Rules need to be set before misbehavior occurs. Consequences for misbehavior need to follow on a regular basis. Sexual abuse breeds inequitable systems and, therefore, consistency needs to occur.

5. TO ESTABLISH PRIVACY RIGHTS, since families need to have a sense of pride and privacy in their family system. Children need to feel as though they have as much right to their privacy as adults. The right to privacy even in a very large family is an important part of rehabilitation.

6. TO HAVE OUTSIDE ACTIVITIES, because sexually abusive families tend to be isolated or tend to be totally disconnected. The family must make a commitment to not only operate as a family unit, but to have activities independent, outside the family, for each family member.

7. TO DISAGREE AND RESOLVE, because it is an important part of the family system to learn how to solve problems. Families who set goals for themselves in *always agreeing* will establish a dishonest system. Disagreements and conflicts can be healthy, provided the family has adequate problem solving techniques.

8. TO HAVE OPEN AND HONEST SEX EDUCATION, because sexual abuse usually occurs with negative or non-existent sexual education within the family. When sexual abuse has occurred, overt efforts must be made to unlearn the negative and relearn positive education.

9. TO AVOID SEXIST TRAINING OF BOYS AND GIRLS, because cultural and societal sexual role training that is sexually exploitive is extremely dangerous for incestuous families. Both males and females need to learn positive role training.

10. TO TRUST AND TALK, because family secrecy and parallel relationships will undermine attempts to harmonize. Parallel relationships within the family should be avoided. Each family member should refrain from alliances and establish relationships as a whole or a family unit.

11. TO RECOGNIZE THE VICTIM'S IDENTITY BUT AVOID AN ONGOING VICTIM STATUS. It is important to resolve issues

between the offender and the victim through clarification. It is also important to prevent the victim's status from overlapping into areas within the family system. The offender/victim identity should never be forgotten, nor should the sexual victimization become the cornerstone of conflict and resolution within the family. The purpose of clarification is to provide an opportunity to resolve the sexual abuse. Traditional family system therapy is inappropriate until that resolution has taken place. When sexual abuse has been clarified within another therapeutic setting, family system therapy, on a more equitable basis should be employed. If issues regarding sexual abuse resurface, those issues should be handled within the therapeutic confines connected to the resolution and clarification process.

12. TO AVOID FORGIVENESS, but concentrate on resolution. The word *forgiveness* implies deadly connotations on some levels. Re-establishment and understanding of the proper term is very important for the incestuous family.

Forgiveness — Process or Product?

January, 1983

Dear Victim:

If you are like most victims who have been sexually abused, you are asking many questions of yourself. We have all heard the old favorites from sex offenders, family members, ministers, and clergy, *Forgive and forget, let bygones be bygones, let's bury the hatchet and start over.* These statements seem to encourage victims to feel as though it is their responsibility to take action regarding resolution and forgiveness. This seems strange, since victims are innocent and not responsible for what has occurred. The question is then raised, *Who is responsible for resolving sexual abuse?* If the offender can ask for forgiveness, then the victim is responsible for *yes or no,* refusal or acceptance. The *I'm sorry* subtly demands the victim give something back. This traditional meaning sounds as though forgiveness demands reciprocity from the victim. Just like the sexual abuse you endured, the offender is again asking you to carry the burden.

In this letter, I will share with you my answers to this dilemma. When I asked myself, as a Christian, *Should the <u>victim</u>, the innocent one, take on responsibility for forgiveness?,* I knew I had to find the answer. The questions shot right at the heart of my Christian faith. At first,

I was confused, but as I studied, it all began to make sense. I hope these questions and answers help you as they have helped me.

In order to solve this very special problem of forgiveness between the victim and offender, I looked up the Greek words for forgiveness, repentance, and confession. Looking up the Greek words is a good way to find answers, because in translating, a lot of words get changed. A very special minister taught me that.

The Greek word for forgiveness is APHIEMI. This word primarily means to send forth, send away or remit. It has two conditions with no other limits, just like Christ's forgiveness. The conditions are repentance and confession, as shown in Matthew 18:15-17 and Luke 17:1-13. The noun form of the word forgive is APHESIS. It denotes a dismissal or release. Notice, in neither definition is the word *forget* used. *Forgetting* is not a part of forgiveness. For forgiveness to occur then, two things must happen, first, repentance and second, confession. Without these two components, there is no forgiveness. Also, please take care to note that neither of these two conditions are the burden of the victim. If the process belongs to the offender, then what is the offender's job or responsibility? Let's look at those two demands.

The first part is *repentance*. The Greek word is METANOEO. This word means to *perceive, afterwards*. Then, METEA means *after,* which implies a change. NOEO, is to perceive; and NOUS is the mind; seat of moral reflection. So, if you put all of that together, you have repentance equals recognizing in your mind what you have done. Now, hang on to that thought and we will put all of this together soon.

The second part of forgiveness is the component of *confession*. The Greek word for confession is HOMOLOGEO. This word means to speak the same thing, to admit, to declare openly by way of speaking out freely.

Now, if you put repentance and confession together, you have: *To speak out openly and freely of what one has recognized in your mind that you have done,* and that is the essence of forgiveness. This means that if someone truly wants forgiveness, they must speak of what they recognize in their own mind they have done. This takes work on the part of the person asking for forgiveness, it does not mean work needs to be done on the part of the victim.

Apply that to your own life and to the relationship between you and your offender. If the offender wants forgiveness, the requirement is to speak openly and freely of what has been recognized in the mind, especially regarding what has been done to you, the victim. The *forgiveness* the offender may receive from Christ, can happen in a matter of moments, but I am convinced that it takes a long time for offenders to recognize wholly what they have done to their victim. Let's face it, it took years for them to get to the point of becoming an offender. It will take many months for them to sort out all of the information in their minds in order to truly repent and confess.

This means that the burden is on the sexual offender to go through a *process*. Offenders typically would rather have the *product* of forgiveness. They would rather have the act completed quickly of *I'm sorry. Now you forgive.* If we understand the true meaning of forgiveness, it is the sexual offender who must move through a process and work toward the final product.

Hopefully, one day your offender will go through a therapeutic process to sort out and understand what damage has done by the offender's selfish actions. If this process occurs, then the offender may be given the opportunity to talk with you in a *clarification* session. It will then be your choice to examine and evaluate whether you believe *the process* has, in fact, taken place. It will be your judgment of the offender's repentance and confession that will give you the information needed to help you know whether or not you choose to accept the *process* completed by the offender. This is certainly not something that can be done in the beginning. It is something that needs to take place with careful contemplation on your part examining the offender's efforts at *the process*.

As you contemplate choosing whether or not to forgive, be sure and remember what we learned about forgiveness. Part of the definition of forgiveness is to release. I like that. You have the opportunity to be released from the power and the control the offender has had over you, not only in the sexual abuse, but in your quandary about whether or not forgiveness should occur. The choice will be yours and because it is your choice, you have been given back your own power, you have been released.

If your offender does not want forgiveness this will happen. Resistance in understanding the damage and trauma will occur. Speaking about the *crimes*, the pain, and the resulting suffering will be avoided. Therapy and change will be battlegrounds of conflict. Attack may be made with religion as a weapon; *God has forgiven me, why don't you?* This kind of statement only indicates the offender's unwillingness to understand the true meaning of forgiveness and work toward the process. If the offender has truly repented, an eagerness to change will replace minimization and rationalization.

You see, the center of sin is capital *I*. That inner self and selfish self that molested a child must change and this will take time. When people molest children, they are thinking of themselves and quickly, upon discovery, they want to be forgiven so that they will feel better. Offenders have practiced being selfish for many years and it will often take years to change. Therapy is a process of unlearning, relearning, and learning. This takes time, effort, and often pain on the part of the offender. This process, this pain, this effort, is, in fact, the true process toward repentance.

Remember, all of the people in this program care most about the victim. That's why this program is called *Restitution* therapy. We believe you as a victim are innocent and we demand restitution be paid to you in some form. You will learn that your rehabilitation is our goal. You are not responsible for the sexual abuse and you are not responsible for forgiveness. Your sexual offender is responsible for both of these things. The program is going to give your sexual offender an opportunity to go through this process. The choice will be up to the offender and whatever the offender chooses will not be your responsibility. You are a victim who was robbed of something precious and special. You need to be cuddled, nurtured, and protected, and we want to guarantee that happens. It is the offender who must do the work.

I hope this letter has answered some questions for you. It was fun to write and share this with you. There are some very special ministers who have helped me write this and have helped me put this letter in your hands. Your therapist can tell you about some of them if you want to talk with them further. Your therapists appreciate these ministers and appreciate the job they do. Hopefully, we can all work together in the months ahead.

Have a great day; you deserve one.

ONE WHO WALKS WITH GOD

Restitution Philosophy

Obviously, the restitution philosophy of treatment for offenders and victims provides the best opportunity to fulfill the goals as outlined in the letter of forgiveness. Clearly, the obligation belongs to the perpetrator and clearly the restitution program provides that vehicle. Trauma Bonding regarding foregiveness is only resolved through these modalities.

To the Offender

The greatest gift we can give you in this Restitution Program is to have two memories. First, you must always remember that you committed a horrible crime against an innocent, precious child. The second memory should stand beside the first and echo, *and I did everything humanly possible to repair the damage.* Under this therapeutic process, you have paid emotional, psychological, and financial restitution to your victims. If you keep both memories, you may have the best opportunity for success in the future. If you remember only repairing the damage, the first memory regarding your crime will fade and you may become grandiose and likely to reoffend. If you remember only being a criminal, you may become so depressed and guilty, you will have nothing to offer yourself or your family. The balance of both memories will provide you with the greatest chance of success in your the future.

FOR THE RECORD

Is time a healer or a culprit? Will clarification for the five-year-old be lost in time distortions? How does the 34-year-old maintain the innocence of childhood? How can the resolution be saved for the future and how can resolution be rescued from the past?

And, from the research, *those victims who had ongoing access to information separating sexual abuse from normal sexual development had the greatest opportunity for rehabilitation.* A record, a permanent record is the solution.

Where is my childhood . . . is any piece of me remaining that was innocent, precious, or good?

I have such confusion and *smearing.* I don't know what really happened or what have I dreamed.

Why didn't I do something about it? Why didn't I stop him? How could I have been so stupid?

I feel so creepy. There is nothing upon which to focus. I just feel dirty. If only I could find it and wash it.

Where were my mother and father when this happened? Did they allow it? Did they care?

Permanent Planning

The voices of victims scream for a need of permanency, something recorded, something tangible, and eventually something controllable. Research for this publication clearly demonstrated that children who had some

423

mechanism adjusting their sexual development were less traumatized. Without some form of mechanism, adults feel confusion, distortions, and wondering. A lack of resolution seems to keep the abuse alive. Something permanent is needed.

The resolution scrapbook becomes the mechanism or a permanent record taking victims through their upcoming developmental years, with care. For adults or older patients, the clarification scrapbook allows a return to childhood for recapturing. Distorted cognitions, phobic reactions, unresolved relationships can be desensitized through the scrapbook.

Creation Theory

Each resolution scrapbook must have a certain amount of creativity and uniqueness. As children are not traumatized in the same manner, scrapbooks and resolutions are dissimilar. Creativity must occur.

The greatest contribution for the younger patient through the scrapbook is prevention. If the Relationship Perspective of the Trauma Assessment reveals confusion regarding the offender/victim identity, documentation in the scrapbook can readjust that identification process. If predictions through the Developmental Perspective of the Trauma Assessment suggests damage to sexual development, many problem areas can be avoided or diverted through the scrapbook. The potential for dis-

torted cognitions and phobic reactions, as discovered in the situational perspective of the Trauma Assessment can be desensitized and rearranged through the resolution scrapbook. The scrapbook becomes the vehicle, taking the younger patient to the future with proper readjustments and perspectives.

For the older patient who has lost childhood, the scrapbook can reaffirm, return to childhood, and rescue the abandoned *child within*.

> The 54-year-old male patient (attorney, father, minister) may intellectually identify the perpetrator. A picture of himself without front teeth, a letter from his sister or a police report from the investigation two decades ago may provide the affirmation needed for his recovery. Nothing has really changed through the collection of the picture, his sister's letter and the police report. These items have always existed. The scrapbook simply allows for focus to emerge — a focus of clarity and resolution.

The Trauma Assessment

The Sexual Victim Trauma Assessment clarified the pain of current suffering or predicted future difficulties. Although the Trauma Assessment is typically written in psychological terms respectful of the DSM III *Bible*, it nonetheless provides the guideline or the framework for the resolution scrapbook. Since the *child within* needs rebirth and since the Trauma Assessment is a blue print for not only the problem but solution, adjustment is needed.

The resolution scrapbook must mirror the Trauma Assessment. The age of onset of abuse provides the standard of criteria for words, explanations and difficulty. Regardless of the patient's age at the time of Trauma Assessment, the scrapbook is for the *child within*, not for the DSM III enthusiasts. Even though written for, as an example, a seven-year-old, the Trauma Assessment must mirror the psychological intricacies of the Sexual Victim Trauma Assessment.

Hello, Hannah

For the purpose of example, a Sexual Victim Trauma Assessment is presented. Form and presentation is much the same as presented to the parents of Hannah. For the purpose of demonstration, Hannah's Trauma Assessment is presented and components of the resolution scrapbook will follow:

SEXUAL VICTIM TRAUMA ASSESSMENT

ASSESSMENT SUBJECT:

Hannah Helvicia Leigh
DOB: 06/10/83
Chronological Age: 6

ASSESSMENT DATES:

08/02/89
08/09/89
08/18/89
08/25/89

ASSESSMENT REFERRAL:

Hannah Leigh is a six-year-old, white female who was referred for a Sexual Victim Trauma Assessment by her mother and father. Recently, Hannah was sexually abused by an adolescent stepbrother and his friends. Upon reporting the abuse, Hannah was processed through the legal system which recommended some kind of therapeutic intervention. Both of Hannah's parents requested the Sexual Victim Trauma Assessment for the purpose of appropriate treatment planning.

EXAMINATION ENVIRONMENT

Contained in the informational packet submitted by Hannah's parents was a Psychological Evaluation, administered by Dr. Joseph T. Chombic, 1989; Bay City Police Report, from Office H. Milbray; Adolescent Sex Offender Evaluation, submitted by Dr. Martin B. Biggs, 1987; Progress Notes, submitted from the file of Hannah Leigh, submitted by school counselor, Carol VandenPlee; as well as Children's Services Division Case Report, submitted by caseworker, Marcus Ripley. It should be noted that none of this information was perused by this examiner until completion of the involvement with Hannah Leigh.

The Sexual Victim Trauma Assessment of Hannah Leigh was conducted through a one hour referral from caseworker Marcus Ripley, a one and one-half hour intake interview with Hannah's parents, as well as four hours of interaction with Hannah on two separate occasions.

In total, the Sexual Victim Trauma Assessment comprises approximately seven hours of interaction with the patient or collateral contacts.

Initially, Hannah presented herself in a somewhat resistive, but nonetheless cooperative demeanor. Hannah appears to be a very bright child who establishes comfortable relationships rapidly. Although some apprehension was noted during the first stages of interaction, Hannah was cooperative during the second session and not only completed tasks assigned to her, but contributed to a congenial testing atmosphere.

BACKGROUND INFORMATION

Hannah Leigh was the first and only child born to Mary Lou and Jim Leigh. This was the first marriage for Mr. Leigh, but the second marriage for Hannah's mother. Neither parent report having any other children except Hannah. The couple courted for approximately two years previous to marriage. Upon making a matrimonial commitment, Hannah's mother worked as a school counselor while her father was employed as a stock broker. The couple was married for approximately four years previous to Hannah's birth. By the time Hannah was born, serious conflicts emerged between the couple regarding household duties, responsibilities, and child rearing issues. By the time Hannah reached her first birthday, the couple was in severe conflict. When Hannah was age three, the couple agreed to separate and subsequently divorced.

Custody arrangements are described by the couple as being for Hannah's benefit. Both parents reiterated the desire to remain in contact with their daughter and continue reasonable harmony as far as Hannah was concerned. Mr. and Mrs. Leigh reported that *lifestyle* conflicts were the main reason for the couple's separation. Mr. Leigh reports frustration with Hannah receiving care outside the home. Mrs. Leigh reports reluctance to forego her career in order to provide babysitting arrangements requested by Mr. Leigh. This appeared an unusual conflict since Mrs. Leigh indicates she was primarily the instigator of the commitment to have children while Mr. Leigh was resistant, only acquiescing because of pressure exerted by his wife. Once Hannah was born, however, Mr. Leigh reports becoming over-protective and insistent upon specific daycare arrangements.

During the first two years of Hannah's life, she experienced an environment of constant conflict. On one hand, both parents were totally dedicated to her while in constant conflict over her care. Hannah seemed to be a child who was loved, but a child who was also a source a source of conflict. Hannah's care alternated between her mother and father as did her affection and attention. Hannah seemed to be showered with positive strokes from both parents, while, at the same time, showered with conflict from both parents.

By the time Hannah was three, the couple had agreed to divorce. Ironically, the divorce was less acrimonious than the marriage. Joint custody was awarded to both parents without any resistance. The arrangement required Hannah to spend 50% of her time with each parent. The first 18 months of the separation seemed harmonious.

Approximately six months ago, Hannah's father established a relationship with a woman twelve years his junior. *Sandra* has three children ranging from age eight to sixteen. Initially, Hannah seemed somewhat depressed and anxious regarding visits with her *new family*. Eventually, Hannah reported to her mother a wish to discontinue contact with her father. Hannah's mother contacted Jim Leigh regarding Hannah's wishes and the couple determined Hannah was *jealous* of her new siblings. Neither parent seemed alarmed about Hannah's complaints. Approximately two weeks after Mr. and Mrs. Leigh conferred, Hannah reported to her teacher she was being sexually offended by Sandra's 16-year-old son and his friends. Hannah was placed in fostercare due to demonstrated fear of vindictiveness from her parents. Both Mr. and Mrs. Leigh were shocked at their daughter's fears and within 24 hours authorities determined Hannah's fears were unfounded. Hannah was eventually returned to the custody of her mother and both parents initiated the Sexual Victim Trauma Assessment.

SYMPTOMATOLOGY PERSPECTIVE

The Symptomatology Perspective of the Sexual Victim Trauma Assessment evaluates symptoms from a relationship perspective, psychological area, as well as within the living skill arena. It should be noted that children of Hannah's age tend to be asymptomatic and, therefore, a lack of symptoms should not be considered as an indicator of diminished trauma. Contrarily, for children Hannah's age, predicting symptomology *potential* may be the most important aspect of the Trauma Assessment.

Within the Relationship Dysfunction area, Hannah appears to be well adjusted, especially in relationships with her parents. Hannah does not have siblings, therefore, it is somewhat difficult to assess Hannah's ability to establish relationships with other *family children*. Upon inquiry, Hannah reports her resistance to visiting her father was not due to jealousy toward the other children in the home, but due to her sexual abuse. It is also reported that Hannah seems able to establish positive relationships within the academic realm, which may indicate very few peer relationship difficulties.

Most importantly, Hannah seems to have established a positive relationship with her parents. In spite of conflicts in the early years of marriage, Hannah views both parents in a positive light and views herself as being supported by both parents. There appears to be no evidence of symbiosis, superficiality, or abnormal attachments in her relationships with Mr. and Mrs. Leigh.

From a Psychological Perspective, Hannah seems asymptomatic at this time. The abuse Hannah has suffered, however, suggests a potential for psychological problems in the future. Since Hannah's abuse was reported in a reasonable amount of time, it may be apparent that Hannah currently views herself as *innocent*, which suggests excellent prognosis for avoiding psychological dysfunction.

Within the living skill dysfunction arena, Hannah appears to be a child with competency in the academic realm. Hannah seems to have a positive self-image, no self-abusive behaviors are noted, nor does Hannah seem to be plagued with sleep disorders. Except for the sexual abuse, Hannah's life seems to be productive and harmonious.

RELATIONSHIP PERSPECTIVE

The Relationship Perspective of the Sexual Victim Trauma Assessment evaluates the relationship between the victim and the offender, the offender and others who are important to the victim, as well as the relationship between the victim and others who are important to the offender. Positive and negative relationships within this triangular approach provide information regarding the victim/offender identity. Those patients who perceive themselves as innocent and who perceive the perpetrator as guilty, have a much greater opportunity for rehabilitation. Those patients who are confused about the offender/victim status tend to be more traumatized.

Evaluating the relationship between Hannah and her perpetrators, Hannah seems to have little regard for Greg Powell or his friends who also participated in Hannah's abuse. Hannah did not have an opportunity to establish a relationship with this young man and there is an absence of bonding. Obviously, Greg's friends who participated on the periphery of the abuse were even less important to Hannah. Those children who have superficial or unimportant relationships with the perpetrator tend to devalue the relationship and subsequently seem to be less traumatized through issues of betrayal. In Hannah's case, the relationship between herself and the perpetrator are insignificant.

Concerning the relationship between Hannah and others who are significant to the perpetrator, Hannah also appears to manifest positive potential. In the eyes of Hannah's parents, she is clearly the victim. Upon discovery, Hannah was immediately *rescued* by her parents who seemingly never doubted her abuse nor the identity of the *victim and offender*. Hannah also appears to be a bright, intelligent child who had pre-existing positive self-esteem. The rejection of *significant others* who may doubt her status as the victim would appear to be less important due to Hannah's strong support system from her parents. Regardless of potential rejection of Hannah's victim status from the category of *significant others*, Hannah continues to view herself as an innocent child, wronged by a perpetrator.

Concerning the relationship between the sexual offender(s) and others who are significant, Hannah also appears to be in the process of rehabilitation. Hannah's mother clearly views Greg as the perpetrator, as does her father. Greg's mother, Sandra, reports having a difficult time raising her son, Greg. In Hannah's mind, Greg has been in conflict with his mother as much as he has been in harmony. Hannah views Sandra as being supportive in the identification of Greg as the perpetrator. Although Hannah has had no contact with Sandra since disclosure, she nonetheless seems to believe that Sandra will be supportive of her in identifying Greg as the perpetrator.

In summary, there appears to be little traumatization for Hannah in the relationship portion of the triangle. Hannah is a child who seems to have a strong sense of self and views her support system as profound. Currently, Hannah does not seem to have any reason to be confused about the offender/victim identity.

DEVELOPMENTAL PERSPECTIVE

The Developmental Perspective of the Sexual Victim Trauma Assessment examines how the child perceives what has happened according to their stage of sexual development at the onset of abuse. Additionally, information available to the child at the time of the abuse is also computed. It is often the child's perceptions of sexual contact that provide information which result in trauma at a later time. Additionally, it should be examined *what has been lost in normal sexual development* (or what will be lost in normal development) due to the sexual abuse that has been committed.

Hannah Leigh was sexually abused in, during what this examiner determines as, the *unaware* stage of sexual development. Children who are *unaware* often do not understand the significance of the sexual contact. It is not uncommon for children in this stage of development to endure sexual abuse over a long period of time without reporting. The child's lack of awareness prevents children in the unaware stage from understanding the abuse. Unfortunately, with an advanced stage of development and better understanding of the sexual abuse,, trauma often emerges.

Hannah's sexual stage of development cannot be accurately evaluated without consideration of her informational perspective regarding sexuality. How Hannah perceives information about her abuse depends not only on her stage of development, but upon sexual information available.

Hannah has lived in a household where she has been the center of attention. Mr. and Mrs. Leigh have actively educated their child not only within the academic realm, but in the personal safety arena. Hannah seems cognizant of personal safety issues, positive body image exercises, and rights to privacy. Hannah's morality training has not necessarily been religious, but within a strict code of assertiveness. Male and female role training has been equitable, as Hannah's father has taken an active part in child rearing. Although conflict has occurred between the couple, strict male/female sexual roles have not been part of the conflict or clearly defined.

Even though Hannah was sexually abused in, during what this examiner determines as, the *unaware* stage of sexual development, Hannah seems to have had a sense of awareness regarding the inappropriateness of the sexual contact. Hannah's sexual abuse occurred for approximately 21 days during a prolonged summer visit with her father. Specific circumstances prevented Hannah from reporting. Developmentally, Hannah seemed to be far beyond her age in recognizing that the sexual abuse was inappropriate. *I knew it was nasty, but I didn't want to talk about it to my mom on the telephone. I didn't want Sandra and Greg to have a big fight.*

Currently, a loss in Hannah's *normal* sexual development is not evident. Actually, Hannah is developmentally competent beyond her development stage. Hannah is aware of the proper names for genitalia and she appears to be sexually assertive beyond her age. Hannah has a sense of privacy and an apparent comfort level for discussing sexual issues with her parents.

The nature of Hannah's sexual abuse, however, has tremendous potential for trauma in the future unless her sexual abuse is separated from normal development. Although Hannah is competent beyond her developmental stage, she also has very little understanding of such things as coprophilia and coprophagia, sado-masochistic activities, or sexual humiliation. Unless eradicated, Hannah has a tremendous potential to be traumatized in the future regarding these issues.

SITUATIONAL PERSPECTIVE

The situational portion of the Sexual Victim Trauma Assessment examines three components concerning the actual sexual abuse. Sensory input, as well as extraneous elements in the sexually abusive *scene* must be examined to determine the potential for phobic reactions in the future. Additionally, the child's *environment* provides information regarding how the child will cope with sexual abuse in the future. Cognitive distortions are common for sexual victims due to what occurs before, during and after sexual abuse. Victims use information from sensory input, from elements in the sexually abusive scene, and finally from the environment in order to establish *footprints* or coping skills for the future.

Specific information regarding the sexual abuse reveals that the first incident occurred in June while Hannah was spending the weekend with her father. Hannah reports that Greg Powell was baby sitting and had invited several friends to join him. Hannah reports that Greg and his friends came into her room smelling of gasoline. These young men forced Hannah to disrobe and, in an extremely humiliating and degrading manner, Hannah was forced to submit to digital penetration. Each one of the boys placed their fingers inside Hannah's vagina during this process. Hannah reports her offenders to be *acting weird*, giggling, swearing, and being extremely loud. In all likelihood, these adolescents were intoxicated from sniffing gas.

Several incidents of abuse by Greg followed over the next few days. Some activities included fondling, but the behavior escalated to attempted intercourse and finally forced fellatio. The final incident occurred when Greg and two of his friends abused Hannah in an extremely humiliating experience.

As far as sensory activation is concerned, Hannah describes smells of ejaculation and gasoline. From a tactile perspective, Hannah seems to be particularly uncomfortable about touching Greg's penis and being vulnerable while she was in the darkened bedroom. Hannah's visual perceptions during several of her abuse incidents focused on her perpetrators and their activities.

As far as cognitive connections are concerned, many issues are revealed in this portion of the assessment. Much of Hannah's abuse took place with her father close by. Hannah's desire to scream was stifled as she anticipated family upheaval should she report. Hannah seems to feel extremely vulnerable to Greg and obviously quite helpless.

Hannah also reports being terrified during the abuse especially when it became clear to her that she would be left alone with Greg again. Anticipation of the abuse was extremely painful. When Greg was sexually abusing Hannah, he told her that he would kill her father if she reported. Since Hannah only visited her father and because of developmental limitations, Hannah believed the threats against her father. In Hannah's mind, it appears that both Hannah and her father were helpless as far as Greg was concerned.

Another issue that seems to be significant in the sexually abusive scene pertains to conversations that occurred during the abuse. This seems to be one of the most profound areas of trauma for Hannah. When Hannah was being abused by Greg and his friends in the first occasion, there was a great deal of laughter, humiliation, and ridicule. Since the room was dark when Greg abused Hannah in the interim period, her only auditory stimulation was listening to Greg *pant* and make threats against her father. During the last incident when Hannah was abused, she was forced to not only listen to sexual conversations, but she was forced to, as Hannah describes, *talk dirty*. Hannah was required to talk about her desires to suck on Greg's penis, she was forced to indicate that the touching felt good, she was forced to beg Greg and his friends to touch her, and she was forced to use a variety of vulgar phrases. It is difficult for Hannah to view herself as noncooperative in light of the sexual conversations forced upon her.

Descriptions of Hannah's abuse indicate that the first incident occurred while Greg and his friends seemed to be intoxicated. Hannah estimates at least ten incidents occurring with Greg coming into her bedroom or abusing her. A final incident culminated in extremely abusive behaviors with Greg and his friends. The last incident seems to be particularly painful for Hannah as she was forced to disrobe and not only submit to a variety of sexual experiences, but she was forced to perform fellatio and object penetration on Greg and his friends.

During the last incident, Hannah was brought into the living room and after she disrobed, she was forced to expose her rectum to Greg's friends. A variety of objects were placed in Hannah's rectum, including a pool stick. Hannah was then forced to commit the same acts against each one of Greg's friends. In the bathroom, Hannah was forced to urinate and drink her own urine. Defecation also occurred and attempts were made to engage Hannah in eating her own feces. Although Hannah refused, she was nonetheless forced to smear her feces on several objects and on the boys' buttocks. Hannah's head was emersed in the toilet, filled with urine, and the toilet was flushed several times. It should be noted that medical examination of Hannah reveals physical trauma to her introitus and tearing of her rectum. Hannah is also being monitored for potential medical contamination from activities involving urination and defecation.

As far as phobic reactions are concerned, obviously Hannah is asymptomatic at this time. Hannah's demeanor during the Trauma Assessment demonstrates very little understanding of the significance of the behaviors in which she has participated. The potential for Hannah to have phobic reactions toward urination, defecation, toward penetration, or to any kind of male group activities is significant. Many of Hannah's senses were activated, such as the sense of smell, and visual sensations. Although Hannah is asymptomatic at this time, she has tremendous potential to be phobic toward many other comparable sexual activities taking place during the sexually abusive scene.

Finally, in examining Hannah's *situation*, it seems that Hannah is generally involved in a supportive or potentially supportive environment. As indicated previously, Hannah's parents have put forth a great deal of effort to educate her, and Sandra, the perpetrator's mother, seems to augment that process. Unfortunately, Hannah will be moving into a world where peer acceptance is extremely important.

Currently, Hannah is attached to her parents and peer involvement is less significant. As Hannah moves into the prepubescent or early developing years, peer support will become even more important. Hannah was sexually abused by a group of adolescents and she has a potential for feeling degraded and humiliated by these individuals, and therefore, unaccepted by her future group of peers. She also has a tendency to discount her sense of self-worth because of the sexual humiliation. While most of Hannah's friends will be discussing kissing, Hannah will be approaching a world or a situation where she has already participated in a variety of extremely deviant behaviors.

Post-disclosure issues at this time appear to have tremendous potential for rehabilitation, but also tremendous potential for the opposite effect. Currently, as indicated in the relationship perspective, Hannah is supported in her victim status. Unfortunately, state services may be reluctant to charge Greg and his friends with the crime, which may have an opposite effect. Hannah is extremely fearful of visiting her father if Greg is present. Without the system's support, Hannah will be vulnerable and her vulnerability may damage her relationship with her father (from resistance to visits) or may result in Hannah's continued helplessness.

In Hannah's situation, her footprints or cognitive distortions have not yet been fully formed. The potential exists for Hannah, to develop either a helpless attitude or an extremely aggressive attitude. Hannah's potential for developing the footprint of helplessness is created due to her own helplessness in the abusive situation. It is important to recognize that Hannah had a great deal of support and self-esteem development from her family, which certainly assisted her in making a report of sexual abuse. Unfortunately, it is also clear that a great deal of contemplation needed to occur before Hannah could take that final step. This resistance, in spite of her assertiveness suggests a potential for Hannah to discount the teachings of her parents concerning self-esteem and assertiveness and adapt a role of helplessness.

On the other end of the spectrum, it is possible for Hannah to take on an extremely aggressive stance in outrage against her helplessness. This is especially true if Hannah develops phobic reactions and fantasies (sexual arousal) to these abusive scenarios. Hannah is unable to describe at this point sexual stimulation, but the potential always exists for either extreme phobic reactions or for *fixation* to these activities. As Hannah develops, she may become outraged with her sexual responsiveness and may adapt an aggressive or terrorizing stance similar to her perpetrators.

SUMMARY AND RECOMMENDATION:

In summary, Hannah Leigh is a female child who seems to identify the offender and the victim accurately within the Relationship Perspective. The *system*, in making a decision regarding prosecution, may change this status if prosecution does not occur.

From a Developmental Perspective, Hannah is asymptomatic. She does not understand the significance of what has happened to her. She has a repertoire of self-protective ideations, which allowed her to make the report within a reasonable length of time. Hannah's sexual development at this time appears to be intact. However, tremendous potential for phobic reactions and for arousal to humiliating and degrading sexual activities exists.

From a Situational Perspective, Hannah appears to be more traumatized. She participated in extremely repulsive, humiliating and degrading sexual activities. Group activities always seem to create tremendous potential for shame. Although Hannah does not appear to have dissociated or adopted other *splitting* coping mechanisms, she demonstrates a potential to relive her sexually abusive scene in the future. There are many extraneous events that may trigger Hannah in the future. Elimination is an example of the kind of problems Hannah may have as she attempts to move toward her future.

It is strongly recommended that those planning for Hannah recognize the importance of the system's action against the perpetrators, especially Greg Powell. Hannah needs to be protected and she needs to have a relationship with her father in a *safe* situation. Brief family resolution and clarification should occur between Hannah and her *three* parents. Hannah is in need of knowing that her parents acknowledge her right to report and that the relationship between Hannah and Sandra will not be destroyed due to Hannah's report.

Hannah is in desperate need of desensitizing the potential for phobic reactions. She needs to participate in the process of completing a resolution scrapbook as a culmination of therapeutic endeavors to prevent phobic reactions from developing. While Hannah is *ripe* for treatment, she should participate in exercises that prevent symptomology regarding repulsion to sexuality or to trauma bonding. The trauma to Hannah does not appear to be significant within the relationship area. Her victim status seems clear, however, her sexual development appears vulnerable.

Finally, it may be appropriate to have Hannah involved in a resolution and clarification process with the perpetrator. Although Greg Powell is not important to Hannah, he nonetheless has the potential to provide some contribution to her rehabilitation through coordinated therapy. It is important that Hannah develop role models separate from her perpetrators and that she not take on a stance to cope with her fears by adapting an abnormal attachment to Greg Powell. Hannah has the potential to develop this attachment and through coordinated efforts within a therapeutic environment, this potential may be thwarted.

Hannah is an attractive, bright child who is supported by her family and who has the potential to be supported by the system. She has endured horrible sexual abuse that is particularly degrading and repulsive. Because of her support system, because of Hannah's early reporting and because of present asymptomatic situation, Hannah has every opportunity for rehabilitation.

Portrait of Treatment

What does Hannah need in treatment? How can Hannah's potential for phobic reactions be stopped and how can the deadly patterns that lie in Hannah's future be resolved? In consideration of general treatment goals, in consideration of trauma bonding and in consideration of the components of restitution therapy, Hannah's needs seem to emerge clear. The following treatment plan/organization should be implemented for Hannah:

Sanctuary

First, Hannah's therapy should occur in an environment where expression of her feelings toward the perpetrator has the opportunity to vacillate. She must be safe in her attitude. The potential for Hannah adopting a symbiotic trauma bond with the perpetrator is tremendous. Therefore, Hannah needs an opportunity to express both positive and negative attitudes toward this individual.

A Blueprint

Hannah needs to see a plan, a product, or a goal. Involvement in therapy should point Hannah toward completion of her scrapbook, a graduation ceremony, and possibly a resolution with her family. Treatment should not be ongoing without a direction. Hannah should also be involved in a therapeutic process that encourages her to believe treatment is a prized opportunity not a *mandated sentence.*

Primary Patient

Hannah's parents should be involved in treatment, but Hannah should be the primary patient. Parental therapeutic involvement should never occur following Hannah's sessions with the therapist. Consultation should occur by telephone or before Hannah's sessions. Hannah needs to feel as though she is the primary patient and that her parents do not *undo or redo* what she has accomplished. in each session.

Seasonal Doing

It will be helpful for Hannah to participate in a wide variety of *doing* activities. Her therapeutic plan should coordinate with the holidays, since other activities in Hannah's life will do the same. Hannah should be able to discuss the issue of secrecy during Thanksgiving, during Halloween, and during Christmas. Hannah should be able to have a methodical process in her therapeutic involvement, much the same as she would participate in a process within the academic realm. Hannah's world beyond therapy will continue. She needs to experience each season, each of life's events, with control.

Caretakers Care

Hannah's parents should be taught to be her *therapists in the future.* Goals, objectives, and activities should always be explained to Hannah's parents so that follow-up can continue within the home. Therapy needs to begin healing but healing needs to be augmented by others.

Recapture, Control, Memories

Desensitization from the memory must occur. Hannah may need to take her therapist to the home where the abuse occurred. Hannah may need to draw pictures of her father's house for inclusion in her scrapbook. Photographs of where the abuse occurred may also be needed. Hannah needs to be able to explain each detail of her abuse to her parents and she may be able to have each detail explained to *her* by the perpetrator in a resolution process. In order to prevent phobic reactions, the memory must be desensitized and at the same time, Hannah's sense of victim status must be fortified in these memories. Hannah must not be a slave to her memories. She must remember two things. First, remembering what happened is important, but second, Hannah must remember, *I was innocent.*

Body Image

A great deal of body image work needs to occur with Hannah. The use of videos, drawings, photographs may help accomplish this goal. Because of the humiliation and degradation that occurred, Hannah has a potential to have a distorted body image. She has a potential to feel shameful about her sexuality. While Hannah is receptive to intervention, a tremendous amount of body image work needs to occur.

Resources such as *A Very Touching Book* or other positive body image books need to be used. Activities need to be arranged to include desensitization of potential skin memories such as with *whole body movement* exercises. Hannah needs to understand the reasons for sadomasochistic activities or for the other sexually humiliating behaviors. Hannah needs those activities separated from normal sexual activity. She needs to recognize that her body was *misused not used* and that those behaviors occurred without any physical consent from her own body.

Mental Health Insurance

Hannah needs to have a positive attitude created about mental health for *insurance* regarding future problems. Currently, Hannah has a strong support system and she has a tremendous potential for rehabilitation. She also has a potential to have sexual abuse trauma resurface in her future. If Hannah is *sentenced* to treatment, if she has a feeling that she was forced into therapy and that her perpetrator *escaped*, Hannah may not believe that mental health intervention can be helpful to her in the future. A positive attitude about mental health intervention needs to occur. If the potential for trauma exists in the future, Hannah must also be given the opportunity for assistance in the future.

A Cruel World

Desensitization exercises must occur for Hannah concerning her sexual world. In the prepubescent or adolescent years, Hannah will be examining the sexual world that will provide her with conflicting messages. Hannah's *unaware* stage of development prevents her from understanding about such issues as male/female role trauma. Examining women's magazines, discussing rock music, being sensitive to other media input, opens the door for prevention of trauma. At a very minimum, Hannah's parents should be taught about this potential and placed in a position to organize contingency plans in Hannah's future development.

Footprints — Helpless to Help Yourself

Hannah has a potential to become either helpless or extremely aggressive. Teaching Hannah within a group process to be a *helper* of others is important considering her potential footprint of aggressiveness. Teaching Hannah appropriate methods of expressing anger and involving Hannah in exercises that enhance her sense of empowerment (possibly martial arts training, gymnastics, or any other activity that not only enhances body image but enhances sense of body strength) would also provide opportunities to prevent trauma through these potential coping skills.

For The Record

Most important, Hannah is in need of a scrapbook, of a permanent record to take her through development. As indicated previously, Hannah is generally asymptomatic. She has reasonably positive ideas about her sense of self and about her victimization. Hannah has the potential to continue these ideations provided some kind of permanent record is made.

The Scrapbook

Step 1 — Special Book

The first item in the resolution scrapbook is a statement separating the scrapbook from Dr. Seuss or Peter Pan. For the victim and for anyone in contact with the victim, it is important to explain the importance of the scrapbook and to protect trauma from occurring because of this document. Hannah's scrapbook, being passed around at her first slumber party would obviously be less than appropriate. If Hannah is developmentally unable to understand her abuse, she is developmentally unable to understand the importance of confidentiality regarding her scrapbook. Clarification needs to protect Hannah.

Dear Hannah,

This book belongs to you. Lots of people wrote in this book so you would be able to remember what happened to you in a very special way. As you learned in the treatment program, SECRETS HURT! All of the people who have written in this book wanted *No More Secrets* for you because they care. These people wanted you to remember not only what happened, but most important, they wanted you to remember how important you were.

Everyone also wanted you to remember the good things that happened.

This is a very special book — not like the other books you may have in your room or at school. This is a special book and it should be kept in a special place. It is for you, but you should always make sure that you read it with someone who can help you understand. It is best to read this book with one of the people who helped write it. If you read this book one time or 101 times, always remember, Hannah, how many people cared for you and how many people were proud of you for giving up your secret.

Hannah was this big when she got rid of the secret!

Step 2 — Rekindling and Revisiting Childhood

The scrapbook should now contain those elements of Hannah's six year old life that will constantly remind her she was an innocent child, helpless, not because of incompetencies, but because of her childhood status. A variety of items should recapture and revisit childhood. Photographs of Hannah are examples of this process. Hannah drawing a picture of her house where she lived *when the touching trouble happened* or drawing a picture of the house where her perpetrator resided and where the abuse took place, will also accomplish the goal of rekindling childhood.

Another example of returning to the scene and recapturing Hannah's innocence may include pictures of her dog, her school, her report card, or some facsimile representing the town in which she lives. Most adult victims have a sense of outrage at their inability to protect themselves or respond appropriately. The more childlike, the more innocent, the more *incapable* the victim can be portrayed in this section of the scrapbook, the more successful *rescuing the child* can be.

Hanna A

Fido, Hannah's Cat
He didn't like Secret Touching

Step 3 — Self Esteem

The third step in the resolution scrapbook should resolve the potential for poor self-esteem and lack of confidence. Hannah is already a competent child with a support system. She has the potential to lose that assertiveness through ongoing development. The scrapbook now must contain a variety of elements bolstering Hannah's status as a competent child. This may seem to be in conflict with Step 2, which encouraged Hannah to view herself as innocent, childlike and incapable of preventing abuse. Actually, these steps are not in conflict.

Creating a positive atmosphere about not only mental health intervention, but Hannah's accomplishments in mental health intervention will give her a sense of empowerment and strength to solve problems in the future. A collection of Hannah's accomplishments in treatment should be included in this portion of the scrapbook.

Treatment modalities and goals as outlined in Chapter 17 indicate a need for an educational modality. The products of that educational modality should now be included in Hannah's scrapbook.

Learning When is it Okay or Not Okay to Talk About Secret Touching

Thanksgiving is an Okay Time for Secrets — (It is not Okay to have a Secret about Putting Gravy on the Jello)

Christmas is a Good Time to have Secrets about Presents Because Presents are Opened and the Secret is Over. There Should Never be a Secret about Touching.

The list is endless. These are the titles of a few suggestions that could be included in Hannah's scrapbook. If Hannah spends approximately six to nine months in therapy, most of her accomplishments should be *collected*. Perusing these accomplishments (profoundly important at age six) will, at ages twelve, twenty, thirty and forty years, have a different impact, but a positive impact nonetheless. Hannah must feel that the therapeutic intervention was positive, that she accomplished a great deal, *as a child*.

Step 4 — People Power

The fourth step of the resolution scrapbook should pertain to the Relationship Perspective of the Sexual Victim Trauma Assessment. Ideally, the Trauma Assessment revealed potential problem areas within the triangular approach. Seeking responses from individuals within that scenario will elicit excellent contributions to Hannah's scrapbook.

In Hannah's situation, she has less trauma within the relationship area. She is supported by many individuals and this step in her scrapbook would be easily resolved. Many children, however, do not have that support system and, in fact, are extremely traumatized within the Relationship Perspective. If that occurs, tremendous effort must be made to elicit support.

Hold Hannah

If Hannah is put on pause for a moment, another case scenario should indicate the importance of this portion of the scrapbook.

Hello, Martin

Martin is sexually abused by his father. Martin's father is an important community member, a powerful person, and the obvious head of the household. Martin reports sexual abuse and causes tremendous upheaval within the family. Due to mother's lack of emotional support, Martin spends 12 days in foster care. Agency intervention results in Martin eventually being returned to the home and his mother recognizing his tremendous need for familial support.

Martin's father is eventually evaluated and placed in the Restitution Treatment Program. Slowly, the status of Martin as a victim is cultivated within the family over the next nine months. Finally, the resolution and clarification sessions occur. Martin's father takes responsibility for sexual abuse and assists the family in understanding Martin's status as the victim.

However, it is recognized that the pain of the early rejection by Martin's mother will be remembered. Resolution of Martin's rejection needs to occur in his scrapbook. The offender resolved the issue, but Martin is in need of resolution from a variety of individuals emerging in the relationship triangle. Martin's mother is a primary example of the need for resolution.

> Dear Martin
>
> Once upon a time a little boy was born, you that's who. Your mom, me, was so happy. You were so soft and happy. We just hugged and kissed you all day. Even your sisters were happy with their new baby brother. Bruno the dog gave you lots of puppy kisses.
>
> Then there was some touching trouble. I know that made you sad. It made me sad too, but first I was so angry that it happened. I know it seemed like I was mad at you but I was mad that it happened. No matter how mad it seemed we were, we never stopped loving you.
>
> Thank you for telling
> Love
> Your Mom

Martin's grandparents were also pivotal in the triangle of trauma. The parents of the perpetrator initially rejected Martin due to allegations against their son. Even after Martin's father confessed, the grandparents continued to blame Martin and eventually reached a point where they *only minimized* Martin's abuse. Martin's grandparents were never involved in therapy and continued a rejection of the therapeutic intervention. Martin's father *clarified* for his parents and encouraged them to acknowledge Martin's status as a victim. *We'll write the letter, but we never want that stuff discussed in our house again,* was their response. Psychologically, they may have resisted, but were willing to cooperate on some level. The letter in Martin's scrapbook is a tremendous contribution to his rehabilitation, even though there may be some question about the sincerity of Martin's grandparents.

> Dear Martin
>
> You are a special grandson. Any grandma or grandpa would be proud to have you for a grandson.
>
> When we found out what happened to you it was sad. We were mad that it happened. We were not mad at you. We love you.
>
> Love
> Grandma
>
> P.S. Grandpa loves you too but he doesn't write very good.

An important issue needs to be raised regarding the scrapbook. Ideally, the main focus of the scrapbook will be the offender's contribution. Components of the offender's clarification should be included and occupy two-thirds of the scrapbook. What the offender writes is a realistic examination of a horrible and traumatizing crime against an innocent child. Letters, certificates, pictures, assignments *included* in the scrapbook suggest an *inclusion* that may not actually be present, but may be therapeutic. As an example, Martin's grandparents write a letter of affirmation of his victim status. Psychologically, they may be reluctant, but the inclusion of that letter in the same scrapbook where Martin's sexual abuse is discussed by the perpetrator suggests a powerful message to Martin and makes an important contribution to his rehabilitation.

Uncle Bert was an extremely important individual to Martin, as well. Even though Uncle Bert is an extended family member, certain post-disclosure issues reveal trauma. Uncle Bert was a favorite uncle who consistently took all the children fishing. When the sexual abuse was reported, Uncle Bert not only refused to take the children fishing, but he refused to attend the traditional Christmas dinner. The *environment* of the situational portion of Martin's Trauma Assessment revealed tremendous upheaval in the family by disruptions in attending Christmas dinner at grandma and grandpa's house. The tradition of Christmas dinner and of Uncle Bert taking the children fishing had been broken. Although insignificant to others and perhaps unintentional, Uncle Bert's rejection of Martin had a profound effect.

Eventually, Uncle Bert agreed to write a letter for Martin's scrapbook. Like Martin's grandparents, Uncle Bert was not interested in discussions of sexual abuse nor was he receptive

of any therapeutic intervention. *I don't want to talk about that stuff and, if anyone does, I'm history.*

Uncle Bert, however, did care about Martin and agreed to write a letter for Martin's scrapbook. The therapeutic intervention with Uncle Bert failed in every respect except the scrapbook letter. Uncle Bert refused to participate in clarification and refused to discuss the sexual abuse with his brother. His letter, however, by including extensive information about the sexual abuse, made a tremendous contribution to Martin's rehabilitation.

There are a variety of people within the Relationship Perspective who can make contributions to children. Siblings are especially important, especially if either the Relationship Perspective or the post-disclosure issues in the Trauma Assessment reveal areas of difficulty. Aunts, uncles, church members are also likely candidates for making a contribution to the resolution scrapbook.

The person who received the report (Martin's teacher) as an example can reinstate Martin's victim status and make an important contribution to his scrapbook.

> *Being able to write a letter in Martin's scrapbook was one of the most rewarding things I have done. It is so difficult to continue reporting abuse to insensitive cops and caseworkers. We report sexual abuse and we hear nothing. We never know if the child got any better, we never know if our report made it worse or better. Being able to write the letter in Martin's scrapbook was probably as helpful to me as to Martin.*

> *Mrs. Rainey*

All aspects of the Relationship Perspective in the Trauma Assessment should be examined except perhaps responses from the *system*. One of the most important steps in constructing a scrapbook is to assist the child in understanding the term, C.R.I.M.E. System contributions to the scrapbook will make a valuable contribution in this area. Although this step in compiling the scrapbook deals primarily with the Relationship Perspective, those issues surrounding the system should be postponed until a later step in the scrapbook.

Step 5 — Intimate Images

Issues concerning trauma to the sexual development of the child will be resolved throughout many portions of the scrapbook. Certainly, recapturing childhood is a developmental issue. Much of what the sexual offender writes, as an example, also makes contributions to re-establishing sexual development. This step requires consideration of any developmental trauma that has not already been examined or resolved in the scrapbook.

Holy Mother Hospital
Pediatrics Division
1108 S.E. 10th
Elliottsville, CT 03201

Dear Hannah:

My name is Dr. John Randolph, and I am the doctor who examined you after you had your touching trouble. I don't know if I will ever get to see you again, so I wanted to write this letter. I know you didn't feel too good when you came into see me because touching trouble is not fun. I do want you to know that I checked your body and you are just fine. There is nothing wrong with you. You looked just beautiful. If you ever have any questions, come see me.

Sincerely,

John Randolph, M.D.

Contamination in sexual development will occur unless this portion of the scrapbook is enhanced. Body image work, pictures of the child, descriptions of the child's body image are all examples of items that could be contained in the scrapbook. If medical examinations of children are conducted, documentation should occur.

If Hannah, as an example, has participated in gymnastics, in martial arts, or in any kind of physical activities, documentation of those *body accomplishments* should occur during this portion of the resolution scrapbook.

Step 6 — Clarification Please

This step of the resolution scrapbook is a contribution from the sexual offender. As described in Chapter Nineteen, the sexual offender must prepare many clarification components to be presented verbally and to be presented in the scrapbook. If Hannah's perpetrator is not included in the treatment program, therapists must create the clarification components with reasonable representation. The ultimate power to offenders occurs if the victim's treatment is not successful without the perpetrator. If the perpetrator is not available, those adults working with the victim must create those components. The *description*, the child's *Trauma Assessment* (in the victim's words), an explanation of *what happened, how it happened*, and *why*; all must be presented. Ideally, the offender will make these contributions. If not, the potential for trauma bonding

must be prevented by clinical preparation of these clarification components as outlined in Chapter Nineteen.

Step 7 — Victims and Survivors

A final portion of the scrapbook should combine the first and the last goals of treatment (as outlined in Chapter Seventeen) using the Trauma Assessment as a guideline. The identification of the child as a victim *of a crime* must occur. However, a tremendous sense of survivorship must close the scrapbook. Not only is the final portion of the scrapbook important for victims who need to feel like victims, but this portion needs to have the sense of survivorship coordinating treatment goals one through six.

And For The Professional

Some professionals such as Law Enforcement, corrections officers or attorneys rarely have the opportunity to make contributions to victim rehabilitation. At this point, interagency coordination, as outlined in Chapter Three, can be enhanced. The sexual victim needs to recognize that a crime was committed. The sexual victim also needs to have a sense of survivorship from those people who acknowledged the crime. Bringing all professionals together in the final portion of the scrapbook helps both the victim and interagency cooperation.

The investigating officer may write a congratulatory letter to the victim upon graduation. The probation officer who supervised the perpetrator may also make an important contribution. Any professional directly or indirectly involved in the case can make a written contribution and affirmation of the victim's status.

The following letters are not grammatically perfect or proper. They are in the language of children. These letters also may be insignificant as far as time, cost, and fiscal budgets. These letters, however, have a priceless contribution to the victim's rehabilitation.

Central Counseling Clinic
1432 Washington St.
Vale, CT 08332

Dear Hannah:

I wanted to write this letter to you and tell you what a good job you have done in treatment. A long time from now you might forget about me and I wanted you to remember what a good time we had when you came to visit. Usually, on Tuesday, your mom would bring you in and we would visit and talk about lots of things. Sometimes we talked about your touching trouble. You were so brave and you did such a good job of giving up the secret. One day you even helped me fill up the candy jar with Valentine candy so that the other kids would have a treat. If I remember, you and I slipped a couple of pieces in our pockets for ourselves and for our office kittens, Clyde and Claude.

Thanks for your help, and thanks for bringing some sunshine into our office. You did such a good job and we will always remember your smile.

Tracy Martin
Primary Therapist

Lane Treatment Center
1125 Elm Lane
Elmhurst, CT 04211

Dear Hannah:

My name is Douglas Elliott, and I am the man that usually gave you a big smile when you came in to visit Jan Hindman. If you remember, we had a big dog named, *Alex*, who usually sat in my office. Every now and then when you were finished with Jan, you would come into my office and give Alex a big hug. Sometimes she gave you a slurpy kiss. One day Alex even gave you a ride out to your car. She is really big!

Someday you will be big and you might have a hard time remembering all of the good things that happened to you here. I hope this letter will help you think of us and think about how important you were. You had touching trouble, but you also did a great job. Everyone will remember you.

Cordially,

Douglas Elliott

Restitution Treatment and
Training Program
987 Island Road
Treasure Land, CT 06897

Dear Hannah:

My name is Mary Stewart and I am the person who got to see you when you came into the office on Mondays for your treatment group. You did such a good job. You talked just a little at first about the touching trouble, but then after a while you seemed to feel really great and told us all about it. You learned lots and lots of good things about touching and pretty soon you got to help other little girls and boys. Some kids had a hard time talking about what happened and you made them feel much better. Your favorite story to tell new kids was the one about eating mud pies with your babysitter. That story always made everyone laugh.

You did a great job in treatment. It was not okay what happened to you, but it was great what you did to fix it.

Yours truly,
Mary Stewart
Bookkeeper

P.S. Don't eat too many mud pies.

Child Sexual Abuse Interagency Team
9999 Edison Hwy
Maple Grove, CT 01223

Dear Hannah:

We have never had a chance to meet you, but we wanted you to know that we are the people on the Sexual Abuse Team who thought about you and hoped you were doing great in treatment. You may not have known it, but many people were thinking about you and wishing you well. We wanted to sign this letter so you would always know how many people knew what happened to you was not okay, but also thought about you each Tuesday at our meetings. Wherever you go and whatever you do, remember there are people on the Treatment Team that were on your Team, too!

Good Luck.

Elliott Ellsworth, Managing Caseworker, Children's Services Division
Frank Fawnworth, Sheriff's Department
Glenda Johnson, County Mental Health Clinic
Belinda Myers, District Attorney's Office
Julie Edmark, Juvenile Department
Mike Little, Police Department
Edward Hoffman, Probation and Parole

Nicholas Center for Rehabilitation
911 S.W. Telly St.
Cambridge, CT 06140

Dear Hannah:

My name is Jana and I am the secretary at Jan's office. You always came in to see her, but first you would ask about Clyde and Claude, our two office cats. You and I would find the kittens while you waited for Jan. What I remember most is that when you were done talking to Jan, you always got a piece of candy from the jar on my desk. Once, you even got a piece for Clyde and Claude.

The secret touching that happened to you was not okay, but you are okay. Clyde and Claude think so, too.

Yours truly, Jana

Mental Health and Counseling Center
432 Owyhee St.
Brendon, CT 02349

Dear Hannah:

I am the director of the treatment program where you visited for many months. I never really got to know you or talk to you, but I kept track of you. Lots of people in my office talked to your mom and tried to help fix the touching trouble in your family.

I am glad to hear you graduated. I was also glad to hear you did such a good job in treatment. Lots of people who work for me told me how great you were.

This program is for kids — we decided a long time ago that kids were the most important people. I am glad you were here to help us remember that.

Sincerely,
Verne Cantrell, Director

Department of Human Resources
Corrections Division
45678 Ventura Park
DrapeVille, CT 08765

Dear Hannah:

My name is Russell Barnes. I am the probation officer that has supervised Greg Powell. He has been on probation and I have been keeping track of him.

It makes me happy to hear what a good job you have done in treatment. You should be proud of yourself. I never got to see you, but I was thinking about you. I wish you the best in the future.

Yours truly,
Russell Barnes

Rockwell Treatment Center
1100 Rockwell Road
Rockwell, CT 66798

Dear Hannah:

My name is Sandy and I am the therapist who talked to your mom and dad on Wednesday nights. They told me that those were your favorite nights because you got to eat at McDonald's instead of at home. They came to their groups to learn how to help you with your touching trouble. They also told me how great you were at McDonald's with good manners. I hope I can meet you someday and maybe you can tell me all that you know about the cats, Clyde and Claude.

Yours truly, Sandy

Newton A. Smith
District Attorney for Elliottsville County
Elliottsville County Courthouse
Kingtree, CT 09845

Dear Hannah:

I don't know if you remember me, but you came to talk to me in my office about the touching trouble. You didn't like what happened to you, but you did a very good job of telling me. What Greg did to you was a CRIME and that's a very important word for you to remember. It is not okay to do secret touching to kids. You told me about it and we even talked in the courthouse. Like a very brave six-year-old, you told the judge what happened. Everybody believed you.

I want you to know that it took a lot of courage to tell about the secret touching and to go to court with me. You did a great job. Don't ever forget two things. First, don't forget that what happened to you was not okay, but, secondly, don't forget what a great job you did.

Sincerely,
Newton A. Smith

Millwood Police Department
1200 Lilac
Millwood, CT 04390

Dear Hannah:

I wanted to thank you for helping me with my job. I have to talk to kids who have trouble with touching. You came into my office in August and told me what had happened to you. We were thirsty and bought two Cokes. We kind of spilled one on my pants, but it was okay. You were doing such a good job that I had a hard time writing everything down without being sloppy.

I hope you will always remember what a good job you did and that what happened to you was not okay. If you ever want to come by my office, we might have another Coke and I might not be so sloppy.

Yours truly,

Officer Bracht

Monroe County Prosecutor's Office
8745 Grand Ave.
Monroe, ID 87543

Dear Robert:

I want you to know that I am the lady you talked to and I am the lady who took you to court. You were very brave to sit on the witness stand and tell what happened to you. Lots and lots of people believed you. You told the truth, but lots of other people lied.

I want you to know that you did just great for a five-year-old. There was nothing wrong with what you said. Lots of people believed you, especially me. Wherever you go and whatever you do, always remember that you did just fine for a five-year-old and that lots of people thought that what happened to you was not okay. You're a great kid. I hope I get to see you again some day, but maybe not in court.

Yours truly,

Ann Austin, District Attorney

Dear Hannah:

We are the two kittens in Jan's office that got to sit on your lap whenever you came to see her. When you first started coming in, we were two little puffs of fur, but by the time you had your clarification, we were teenage cats. We got to sit on your lap while you listened to Greg Powell talk about what happened. It made you feel better to hear what he had to say, and made us feel better to be with you.

Don't forget us. We will probably be sitting on kids' laps for a long time, but we will never forget a single kid.

Love,

Clyde and Claude

(our paw prints)

Throwing The Baby Out With The Bath

Hannah's scenario has tremendous potential for success. In those cases where success is not obvious, contributions from professionals are even more important. As an example, the prosecutor may make a tremendous contribution to a child even in the case of an acquittal.

Throwing the baby out with the bath often occurs without a conviction of the perpetrator. The system is designed for adults, not children and failure is very possible. Failure does not need to occur in the resolution scrapbook, however. Success can be documented even if ultimate goals and wishes concerning conviction of the perpetrator did not occur.

Finally . . .

The resolution and clarification scrapbook becomes a tangible item encouraging clarity, resolution, and most important, control. For adult patients, the scrapbook signifies an end or a successful completion. It is a *doing* exercise. The scrapbook resolves and works toward a product. All generic modalities and treatment goals described in Chapter 17 are enhanced through this process. Like no other technique, this may be the victim's vehicle for traveling toward survivorship.

Using the analogy of *front, back and beside*, resolution of sexual abuse occurs through the scrapbook. Sexual abuse that has been forgiven, or thrown in back, results in vulnerability or *bites on the butt* when the victim least desires. Sexual abuse *in front* of the victim encourages eternal victimization and abusability. The scrapbook can be opened and closed under the control of the victim. The scrapbook becomes the way in which the victim has the abuse *beside*, clear, crisp and controllable.

Resolution scrapbooks may remain in the therapist's office forever and may be examined by the victim upon request. Some families place the scrapbook in a safety deposit box, while other families have the scrapbooks carefully secured at home. Some victims have chosen to destroy their scrapbooks as a token of control. The scrapbook places the sexual abuse in something tangible and returns control to the victim and the victim's family.

My daughter's scrapbook was completed when she was approximately three and one-half. She had been brutally abused by her grandfather and uncle who were never prosecuted due to her age. We felt so outraged. We completed the scrapbook, however, and I cannot describe the results. When she was 10, my husband and I were sadly divorced. We agreed cooperatively on joint custody. The biggest disagreement occurred regarding custody of the scrapbook. My daughter's perceptions of the sexual abuse have changed over the years. If the scrapbook had not been available, I cannot imagine how distorted her views would be. When difficult times have arisen in the family regarding contact with the perpetrators, such as at Thanksgiving dinner or a death in the family, the scrapbook allowed us to reorganize and refocus. Both my husband and I wanted custody of the scrapbook and eventually agreed to joint custody of not only our beautiful daughter, Brandi, but of the scrapbook, as well.

DEER THERAPIST

With a closer look, trauma is more accurately revealed, recovery more carefully planned, and patients more often healed. But what about the toll on those who take a closer look? What is the pain for those who care about victims' pain?

The field of sexual abuse has a significant rate of *burnout* compared to all other social service specialties. Caring about children seems to be a prerequisite for those involved in sexual abuse therapy. Yet caring for children can have a traumatic effect on those who care. Perhaps different than physical or emotional child abuse, sexual abuse contains a particular element that creates more discomfort or trauma for those who have empathy and sympathy for children.

Sexual abuse, different from other areas of child abuse, takes place for the purpose of *pleasure*. It may be more understandable to beat a child or strike at a child in frustration. Neglect may

be understood as a product of environmental responses. Emotional abuse may be a response to the abuser's emotional neglect. But sexual abuse of children is different. *Sex feels good.* People who abuse children have *pleasure*. Regardless of psychological interpretations regarding pedophiles, etiology, arousal cycles, profiles, etc., the basic reason people sexually offend children pertains to *pleasure*. While children's lives are being destroyed, perpetrators are experiencing *pleasure*.

The *pleasure principal* seems to be most traumatizing for those professionals who care about children. Other kinds of abuse may be more understandable and more comfortable. In this field of human services, it is the *pleasure* issue that inflicts professionals with frustration and traumatization.

For those who take a closer look at the pain of victims, personal and professional traumatization occurs. For those dedicated to the eradication of sexual abuse and to a more productive look at trauma, more discomfort lies ahead. Traditional ways of examining trauma may be easier for the professional. This publication asks that an innovative examination of trauma emerge. What is the good news? With a better understanding of trauma, victims will rehabilitate and prevention of sexual abuse will be possible. The bad news reports a devastating toll on professionals.

Some therapists will leave the field exhausted, and pained. Others will remain but prefer old, less painful ways. Some will have the courage to stay. Armed with *new reflections* in assessing trauma and planning treatment, the dedicated professional enters the battle. The following story may provide encouragement and solace for the pains and strains of *battle*.

My father would take us hunting. Three beautiful, little girls delighted with following their father through the mountains of Eastern Oregon. We thought it was wonderful! For us, hunting meant an exciting day with daddy and candy bars. Although not a psychologist, our father had the brilliance to recognize that if our mouths were busy, we might not talk. Chattering and jabbering deer hunters are rarely successful. Our father kept us supplied with Hersheys to keep us from sending deer into other counties.

Many seasons were filled with excitement of hunting, being with our father, and consuming an endless supply of sugar. One special day, to our amazement, the gun was fired. Our father said, *Yea!*, and with a mouthful of Snickers, we said, *Yea!*

Our father ran to the bottom of the ravine and we followed, having no idea what awaited us. There was a deer dying, bleeding from its eyes, ears, nose, and mouth. The scene was horrible. We turned quickly and tried to run away while he grabbed us by the seat of our pants, pulling us back. *You stay right here and watch. I want you to feel very bad. On the way home, we will feel good that we are the kind of people who feel bad.*

Later, driving home in a darkened pick-up, our lips continued to quiver. Not even a fresh supply of Baby Ruths provided consolation. He was right, we did feel bad.

It's good that we feel bad about this, he said. *We are the good people because we feel bad. Jannie, some people don't even feel bad.*

Our father's purpose was to teach us that to be sensitive was a virtue and to be pained was good. He wanted us to appreciate our sensitivity even though it hurt. Unfortunately, what he did was raise three *flaming environmentalists*! He is actually quite perplexed and wonders if perhaps he failed.

This story has a powerful message to those professionals in the field of sexual abuse. Understanding the trauma of victims *feels bad*. Burnout occurs when there is very little appreciation for feeling the pain. Unless therapists follow my father's advice and *feel good because they feel bad*, involvement in the field of sexual abuse will be short. No one who cares about children can survive learning more about the tragedy without some resolution regarding ongoing pain. My father's words are filled with wisdom. *Feeling good because we feel bad* may be the only way we can survive this closer look at the traumatization of sexual abuse.

From past, present, and future victims (and from my father), thank you for your courage.

BIBLIOGRAPHY

Abel, Gene G., Judith V. Becker, Jerry Cunningham-Rathner, Mary Mittelman, and Joanne L. Rouleau. *Multiple Paraphilic Diagnoses Among Sex Offenders.* A research paper supported by the National Institute of Mental Health, *The Evaluation of Child Molesters.*

American Psychiatric Association. *Diagnostic and Statistical Manual of Mental Disorders,* (third edition — revised). Washington, D.C.: American Psychiatric Association, 1987.

Armstrong, Louise. *Kiss Daddy Goodnight.* Pocket Books, 1978.

Barbach, Lonnie Garfield. *For Yourself: The Fulfillment of Female Sexuality.* Garden City, NY: Anchor Press, 1976.

Bass, Ellen and Laura Davis. *The Courage to Heal: A Guide for Women Survivors of Sexual Abuse.* New York, NY: Harper & Row, Publishers, 1988.

Bear, Euan. *Adults Molested as Children: A Survivor's Manual for Women & Men.* Orwell, VT: Safer Society Press, 1988.

Butler, Sandra. *Conspiracy of Silence: The Trauma of Incest.* Volcano, CA: Volcano Press, Inc., 1978.

Cameron, Catherine. *Study in Amnesia and Sexual Victim Patients.* University of LaVerne, Irvine, CA. Upcoming Publication, 1990.

Crewdson, John. *By Silence Betrayed: Sexual Abuse of Children in America*. Boston, Mass.: Little, Brown and Company, 1988.

Fillmore, Ann. *Research Regarding Trauma Bonding and Stockholm Syndrome*. University of Aberdeen, Scotland.

Finkelhor, David. *A Sourcebook on Child Sexual Abuse.* Beverly Hills, CA: Sage Publications, 1986.

Finkelhor, David. *Child Sexual Abuse: New Theory and Research*. New York, NY: The Free Press, 1984.

Finkelhor, David. *Stopping Family Violence: Research Priorities for the Coming Decade*. Newbury Park, CA: Sage Publications, 1988.

Fleischhauer-Hardt, Helga. *Show Me*. New York, NY: St. Martin's Press, 1975.

Forward, Susan and Craig Buck. *Betrayal of Innocence: Incest and It's Devastation*. New York, NY: Pequin Books, 1978.

Foucault, Michael. *The History of Sexuality, Volume I: An Introduction*. U.S.A.: Vintage Books Edition, 1980.

Foucault, Michael. *The Use of Pleasure: The History of Sexuality, Volume II*. U.S.A.: First Vintage Books Edition, 1986.

Freeman-Longo, Robert E. *The Adolescent Sexual Offender: Background and Research Perspectives*. In *Adolescent Sex Offenders: Issues in Research and Treatment* (Otey, Emeline M. and Gail D. Ryan, editors), Rockville, MD: U.S. Department of Health and Human Services, 1985.

Freund, Kurt. *Does Sexual Abuse in Childhood Cause Pedophilia?* A Paper presented at The First International Conference on the Treatment of Sex Offenders. Minneapolis, Minn., 1989.

Gil, Eliana. *Outgrowing the Pain: A Book For and About Adults Abused as Children*. New York, NY: Dell Publishing, 1983.

Goldstein, Seth L. *The Sexual Exploitation of Children: A Practical Guide to Assessment, Investigation, and Intervention*. New York, NY: Elsevier Science Publishing Company, 1987.

Haeberle, Erwin J. *Sex Atlas: A New Illustrated Guide*. New York, NY: Seabury Press, 1978.

Hagans, Kathryn B. and Joyce Case. *When Your Child Has Been Molested: A Parents Guide to Healing and Recovery*. Lexington, Mass: Lexington Books, 1988.

Hechler, David. *The Battle and the Backlash: The Child Sexual Abuse War.* Lexington, Mass: Lexington Books, 1988.

Herton, Anne L. and Judith A. Williamson, eds. *Abuse and Religion: When Praying Isn't Enough*. Lexington, Mass: Lexington Books, 1988.

Hillman, Donald and Janice Solek-Tefft. *Help for Parents and Teachers Of Sexually Abused Children.* Lexington, Mass: Lexington Books, 1988.

Hindman, Jan. *Abuses to Sexual Abuse Prevention Programs, Or, Ways We Abuse Our Children As We Attempt to Prevent Abuse.* Ontario, OR: AlexAndria Associates, 1986.

Hindman, Jan. *A Very Touching Book: For Little People and Big People.* Durkee, OR: AlexAndria Associates, 1983.

Hindman, Jan. *Impact: Sexual Exploitation Interventions for the Medical Professional.* Community Health Clinics, Nampa, ID and AlexAndria Associates, 1985.

Hindman, Jan. *National District Attorney Association Bulletin. Research Disputes Assumptions About Child Molesters.* Volume 7, Number 4. July/August, 1988.

Hindman, Jan. *Step By Step: Sixteen Steps Toward Legally Sound Sexual Abuse Investigations.* Boise, ID: Northwest Printing, 1987.

Hutchens, Lucy. *Restitution Therapy — Coordinating Victim/Offender Treatment.* Upcoming Publication, Safer Society Press, 1990.

Kelley, Kathryn ed. *Females, Males, and Sexuality: Theories and Research.* Albany, NY: State University of New York Press, 1987.

Kempe, Ruth S. and C. Henry. *The Common Secret: Sexual abuse of Children and Adolescents,* 1984.

Langfeldt, Thore. *Developmental and Social Aspects of Sexual Violence.* A paper presented at The First International Conference on the Treatment of Sex Offenders. Minneapolis, Minn., 1989.

Lew, Mike. *Victims No Longer: Men Recovering From Incest and Other Sexual Child Abuse.* New York, NY: Nevraumont Publishing, 1988.

Maltz, Wendy. *Partners in Healing: Couples Overcoming the Sexual Repercussions of Incest.* Eugene, OR: Independent Video Series, 1988.

Maltz, Wendy and Beverly Holman. *Incest and Sexuality: A Guide to Understanding and Healing.* Lexington, Mass: Lexington Books, 1987.

Mandell, Joan Golden and Linda Damon. *Group Treatment for Sexually Abused Children.* New York, NY: The Guilford Press, 1989.

McCarthy, Barry W. *Treatment of Sexually-Abused and Traumatized Clients.* A paper presented at a workshop sponsored by the American Healthcare Institute. Silver Spring, 1988.

McQuirk, Betty. Presentation at Restitution Treatment and Training Program, *The Adolescent Sexual Offender.* Ontario, Oregon, 1984.

Porter, Eugene. *Treating the Young Male Victim of Sexual Assault: Issues and Intervention Strategies.* Syracuse, NY: Safer Society Press, 1986.

Russell, Diana E. H. *Sexual Exploitation: Rape, Child Sexual Abuse and Workplace Harassment.* Beverly Hills, CA: Sage Publications, 1984.

Samenow, Stanton. *Inside the Criminal Mind.* New York, NY: Times Books, 1984.

Salter, Anna C. *Treating Child Sex Offenders and Victims: A Practical Guide.* Newbury Park, CA: Sage Publications, 1988.

Sgroi, Suzanne M. *Handbook of Clinical Intervention in Child Sexual Abuse.* Lexington, Mass: Lexington Books, 1982.

Sgroi, Suzanne M. *Vulnerable Populations: Evaluation and Treatment of Sexually Abused Children and Adult Survivors.* Lexington, Mass: Lexington Books, 1988.

Tharinger, Deborah. *The Sexual Development of Children.* Paper presented in Albuquerque, New Mexico, *The System as Perpetrator.* 1988.

Wyatt, Gail Elizabeth and Gloria Johnson Powell, eds. *Lasting Effects of Child Sexual Abuse.* Newbury Park, CA: Sage Publications, 1988.

Zilbergeld, Bernie. *Male Sexuality.* Toronto: Bantam Books, 1978.